Agricultural Policy in Western Europe and the United States

Agricultural Policy in Western Europe and the United States

Ken A. Ingersent

Senior Research Fellow, Centre for Research in Economic Development and International Trade, University of Nottingham, UK

A.J. Rayner

Professor of Agricultural Economics, University of Nottingham, UK

Edward Elgar
Cheltenham, UK • Northampton, MA, USA

Published by
Edward Elgar Publishing Limited
Glensanda House
Montpellier Parade
Cheltenham
Glos GL50 1UA
UK

Edward Elgar Publishing, Inc.
136 West Street
Suite 202
Northampton
Massachusetts 01060
USA

A catalogue record for this book
is available from the British Library

Library of Congress Cataloguing in Publication Data

Ingersent, K. A.
    Agricultural policy in Western Europe and the United States / K.A.
    Ingersent, A.J. Rayner.
        1. Agriculture and state—Europe, Western.   2. Agriculture and state—
    United States.   I. Rayner, A. J.   II. Title.
    HD1918.153   1999
    338.1'84—dc21   98–56514
                                                                          CIP

ISBN 1 85278 020 7

Printed and bound in Great Britain by Biddles Ltd, Guildford and King's Lynn

Contents

v

Figures

Tables

Preface

Much of this book is written both in a historical sequence and in a historical context. This is deliberate as we are firmly of the opinion that present day policies can be fully understood only within the context of their historical evolution. Following an introductory chapter, most of those which follow are broadly divided into two sections, dealing with policy developments in Western Europe (that is, the EC/EU after 1958) and the United States respectively. The later chapters also encompass developments in international relations, especially the Uruguay Round of GATT negotiations, which have increasingly obliged nation states to open their domestic agricultural policies to international scrutiny. The EU and the US were the two largest players in the agricultural negotiations in the Uruguay Round.

Although substantial differences in agricultural policy between the EU and the US remain, these differences appear recently to have been on the wane, due partly perhaps to a fundamental similarity of the forces pushing for reform and partly to the harmonising effects of international negotiations. However, we refrain from predicting whether EU and US policies will continue to converge or speculating on the possibilities for future divergence.

We both acknowledge intellectual debts to professional colleagues, who are too numerous to mention by name, on both sides of the Atlantic. K.A. Ingersent also gratefully acknowledges the financial support of the Leverhulme Foundation in granting him a Leverhulme Emeritus Fellowship, 1987–90, used mainly to travel and study in the United States.

Abbreviations

AAA	Agricultural Adjustment Act
AMS	Aggregate Measurement of Support
AMTA	Agricultural Market Transition Act
AP	Area Payment
ARP	Acreage Reduction Programme
AUA	Agricultural Unit of Account
BHA	Blair House Agreement
BSE	Bovine Spongiform Encephalopathy
CAP	Common Agricultural Policy
CBO	Congressional Budget Office
CCC	Commodity Credit Corporation
CEECs	Central and Eastern European Countries
CG	Cairns Group
CP	Compensation Payment
CRP	Conservation Reserve Programme
CSE	Consumer Subsidy Equivalent
DDA	Dunkel Draft Agreement
DP	Deficiency Payment
EAGFF	European Agricultural Guidance and Guarantee Fund
ECU	European Currency Unit
EEC	European Economic Community
EEP	Export Enhancement Programme
EFTA	European Free Trade Association
EMS	European Monetary System
EMU	European Monetary Union
ESA	Environmentally Sensitive Area
EU	European Union
EUA	European Unit of Account
FACTA	Food, Agriculture, Conservation and Trade Act
FAIR	Federal Agricultural Improvement and Reform Act
FEOGA	European Agricultural Guidance and Guarantee Fund
FERP	Fixed External Reference Price
FFA	Freedom to Farm Act
FOR	Farmer Owned Reserve

GATT   General Agreement on Tariffs and Trade
GDP   Gross Domestic Product
GNP   Gross National Product
LFA   Less Favoured Area
ITO   International Trade Organisation
MCA   Monetary Compensatory Amount
MFN   Most Favoured Nation
MGQ   Maximum Guaranteed Quantity
MIP   Minimum Import Price
MTN   Multinational Trade Negotiations
NRP   Nominal Rate of Protection
NTB   Non-Tariff Barrier
OECD   Organisation for European Cooperation and Development
PEG   Producer Entitlement Guarantee
PERTs   Political Economic Resource Transfers
PESTs   Political Economic Seeking Transfers
PIK   Payment in Kind
PSE   Producer Subsidy Equivalent
QRs   Quantitative Restraints
SMU   Support Measurement Unit
SPS   Sanitary and Phytosanitary Measures
SSP   Special Safeguard Provision
TAB   Total Acreage Base
TEA   Targeted Export Assistance
TP   Target Price
UA   Unit of Account
UR   Uruguay Round
UR–AA   Uruguay Round Agricultural Agreement
USDA   United States Department of Agriculture
VER   Voluntary Export Restraint
VES   Variable Export Subsidy
VIL   Variable Import Levy
WTO   World Trade Organisation

1. Background to agricultural policy

INTRODUCTION

Agricultural policy has a long historical pedigree in that the performance of the food and agricultural sector(s) has been a primary concern
of governments from the ancient world onwards. In the face of the
primary need of the populace for food, ensuring the adequacy of its
supply has traditionally been of importance in securing the legitimacy
of the established political authority. Food security is still an objective of
agricultural policy in the modern industrial society where an ample
provision of food is taken for granted.[1] However, other concerns such
as agricultural resource allocation and income distribution are now
more dominant objectives.

The implementation of government policy goals does not necessarily
imply that the state will use instruments to intervene into agricultural
markets. Thus *laissez-faire* or a reliance on market forces may legitimately be described as a national policy toward a particular industry.[2]
Nevertheless, in the long history of agricultural policy, *laissez-faire* is
the exception rather than the rule. Two types of intervention policy that
stand out from the past have been practised at length in the more recent
policy period discussed in this book. These are, first, stabilisation policies
attempting to equalise grain prices between years and, second, pro-
vision/protection policies attempting to lower/raise (grain) prices below/
above open market levels.[3]

Stabilisation policies in ancient times were concerned to mitigate the
effects of bad harvests and secure food supplies. The Egyptians (2000
BC–1700 BC) had granaries for interyear grain storage as recorded in the
biblical story of Joseph (c. 1700 BC). China between 1100–300 BC had
an active grain (rice) stabilisation policy based on the principle of the
'constantly normal granary'[4] whereby the state bought grain in years of
abundant harvests to release in years of poor harvests thereby reducing
price instability. The literature of the time will be seen to be relevant
to modern agricultural policy:

There are two sets of interests: those of producers and those of consumers.

1

> But nothing more markedly affects the interests of both sides at once than prices. Therefore price is the great problem for society as a whole – the government should level prices by the adjustment of demand and supply in order to guarantee the cost of the producer and satisfy the wants of the consumer. It is the task of the superior man to adjust demand and supply to keep prices on a level.[5]

However, it was recognised that the major problem with implementing the constantly normal granary lay in difficulties of administration: 'it is not easy for commercial functions to be undertaken along with political duties'.[6]

A provision policy may be described as making 'cheap' grain freely available to the domestic market, being implemented by trade devices which encourage imports and discourage exports. Conversely a protection policy restricts supplies to the domestic market making grain 'dear' by discouraging imports and encouraging exports. Whilst Lacy (1923) records the existence of provision policies in, for example, Athens (400 BC) and Rome (300 BC), the use of trade tariffs and subsidies in Medieval Europe has more relevance for this work. Most noteworthy were the English Corn Laws operating between 1463 and 1846. Import tariffs and export subsidies (bounties) were on a sliding scale varying inversely with the domestic price. Whilst over the whole period there were elements of both provision and protection, the dominant theme in the later years was that of strict protectionism.[7] The main implication of provision/protection intervention is that it redistributes income in favour of consumers/farmers.

THE SCOPE OF AGRICULTURAL POLICY INTERVENTION IN THE LAST 200 YEARS

The scope and prevalence of agricultural policy in the last two centuries in the Western world can be viewed as a reflection of the current orthodoxy regarding the limits of the government intervention. By the end of the nineteenth century there was a fair measure of agreement amongst 'liberal' economists (but excluding Marx and other socialists) that, in a world of Pareto optimum equilibrium, the obvious economic functions of the State would be confined to:

1. maintaining industrial competition (or curbing monopoly),
2. redistributing income somewhere in the range between minimum social security for the most needy and full egalitarianism, according to the degree of equity sought by the government.

In the present century welfare economists have challenged the restrictiveness of the nineteenth century liberal view of the limits to government economic intervention on three main grounds, namely:

1. the existence of externalities and the need for public policy to control their effects,
2. the need to satisfy the demand for public goods (as foreseen earlier by Adam Smith, see, for example, Cannan, 1937),
3. the tendency for private entrepreneurs to make short-sighted decisions, not in the best long-term interests of society as a whole, including private investors' tendency to over-discount longer-term investment, including the conservation of natural resources (for example, Stigler, 1975, ch. 7).

There has been a parallel widening and deepening of agricultural policy. Thus in late eighteenth century Britain, for example, government intervention in agriculture was largely confined to price control (mainly of grains) by the regulation of external trade (through the enactment and implementation of the 'corn laws') and the authorisation of changes in agricultural property rights (through the so-called 'parliamentary enclosures'). In the USA also the regulation of external trade emerged as an issue to be dealt with by the federal government after the end of the colonial period culminating in the War of Independence. However, in the early post-independence years tariff protection was only nominal, possibly reflecting, in part, the sectional interests of those farmers, particularly in the South, intent on expanding exports of commodities like tobacco, rice and cotton rather than seeking protection from competitive imports. The second major issue of US policy in the immediate post-independence period was the disposal to farmers by the federal government of the very large area of land it had acquired in the public domain. Much of this consisted of what had formerly been Crown land, in the colonial period, but also including land acquired from other colonising powers like France and Spain. Although different from the parliamentary enclosures in Britain, early US land policy was also concerned with property rights allocation.

In the present day, the extent and complexity of agricultural policy, both in the EU and the USA, reflect two interrelated developments. First, vast changes have occurred in the norms of government intervention as perceived both by the politicians who frame policy and by the people who elect them. In virtually all developed countries, despite differing degrees of emphasis by the ruling parties on the tenets of capitalism and socialism, the acceptance of the ideals of the welfare state has resulted in a degree of government involvement in the affairs of private individuals and firms which would have been unimaginable in the nineteenth century. This is still the case despite the rolling back of the frontiers of state intervention in recent years. Thus, in the case of agriculture, the forces of public opinion and pressure group politics are such that no government can afford to disregard entirely the welfare of any of the major market participants. Policy must somehow combine equitable treatment of farmers (as reflected by the level and stability of their incomes) with due regard for the welfare of consumers (as reflected by the level and stability of food prices and their effects on the cost of living). Although, for the reasons just discussed, the broad objectives of agricultural policy in different countries tend to be similar, the choice of policy instruments for achieving those objectives is more diverse.

The second interrelated development helping to explain the growth of government in agriculture is the growth of bureaucracy.[8] Employment statistics of the British civil service reveal that in 1902 the Board of Agriculture had only 136 full-time employees. By 1923, following the First World War and the establishment of the Ministry of Agriculture, the payroll had increased to 2160. By 1950, following the Second World War, the size of the British agricultural bureaucracy peaked at over 17 000 before declining again to just over 11 000 in 1986. By comparison, in America in 1910 the United States Department of Agriculture employed under 10 000 people. By 1923, the number had more than doubled to over 20 000 and by 1950 it had quadrupled again to over 80 000. Employment by the USDA peaked at just under 130 000 in 1980, since when there has been a slight decline to about 119 000 in 1986. The US figures understate the size of the American agricultural bureaucracy to a substantial degree, since they relate only to federal government employment and exclude considerable numbers of agricultural bureaucrats employed by the 50 state governments.

The 'administrative revolution'[9] has permitted an increase in the scope and complexity of government intervention, but the relationship between the size of the agricultural bureaucracy and the extent of government intervention into agriculture is bi-directional. In the long term, the degree of government involvement in agricultural markets depends on an adequate size of bureaucracy to administer policy instruments but enlargement of the administrative infrastructure tends to follow the enactment of new policy measures. There is plenty of empirical evidence to link the growth of bureaucracy with the growth of taxation and public expenditure which is, in turn, linked with national crises like the outbreak of wars (see, for example, Browne and Jackson,

1982, ch. 5). Certainly there is evidence that the agricultural bureaucracies in both Britain and the USA grew substantially in the wake of the First and Second World Wars.

In the contemporary world, the nub of the prima facie case for government intervention in agriculture is that without intervention, agricultural producers, consumers and society at large would be adversely affected by market failures of various kinds. In this context, 'market failure' includes not only the more traditional market imperfections such as price distortions and unequal bargaining power amongst market participants, but also a wide array of externalities such as pollution of the environment by agricultural chemicals. Agriculture is associated with markets which are either absent or incomplete in four main areas, namely, agricultural R&D, pollution, information and instability.

First, due to the peculiarities of agricultural technology, particularly in the realm of biology, it is almost inevitable that a proportion of agricultural R&D will be organised and conducted in the public sector rather than by private enterprise. Thus not only is the agricultural sector characterised by small firms but also the homogeneity of products and the nature of technological change makes it difficult for the farm firm or private innovator to capture the benefits from research.[10] Amongst the most important technological changes in agriculture are plant variety changes which can be easily reproduced for open pollinated varieties. The skill and size requirements for efficient research organisation and the difficulty of appropriating returns imply that farm firms will carry out little research of a biological nature. Furthermore the free rider problem is a barrier to research financed by voluntary cooperation by farmers. The difficulty in appropriating returns also constitutes a barrier to research by specialist seed firms.[11] Farms are also too small relative to the size of the market to carry out mechanical and chemical R&D where there are substantial economies of size in the production and marketing of these innovations. However, R&D is undertaken by 'large' firms in the industrial sector who can appropriate returns by patenting innovations. Consequently, if R&D was left entirely to the private sector, the portfolio of research projects would tend to be biased in favour of technology types from which discoverers might expect to capture a substantial share of the gains from their adoption by producers (for example by the registration and enforcement of patent rights). In addition, there might also be a tendency to concentrate upon short-term, early maturing, 'applied' projects, to the neglect of longer term, more basic projects with a less certain outcome. There is also the danger in highly concentrated input industries that potential lines of research will be suppressed if they favour rival products or firms.

The second area of market failure concerns pollution and the case for government action to moderate its effects. Although the well-known compensation principle of welfare economics visualises the possibility of polluters compensating affected parties for the damaging effects of pollution within a market system,[12] it is well recognised that, for practical reasons such as ambiguities concerning the ownership of property rights, properly articulated markets in pollution 'products' scarcely ever exist. Consequently, public control becomes necessary to safeguard the interests of the victims of pollution. Public control has the effect, to some degree, of 'internalising the externality', that is compelling the polluter to be confronted with at least a proportion of the social costs of pollution. Control may take the form either of prohibition of the polluting practice, or of regulation to limit the amount of pollution, or of taxes or charges levied according to the level of pollution. In agriculture, prohibition has been applied, for example, to the use of especially noxious chemicals such as the insecticide DDT. Regulations are applied to limit the amount of drainage effluent which farmers are permitted to discharge into public sewers or water courses with treatment charges sometimes also being applied. In Britain, under a recent scheme, farmers in so-called 'environmentally sensitive areas' who voluntarily agree to limit their farming activities and practices according to a 'conservationist code' are eligible to receive a conservation subsidy.

The third area of market failure concerns gaps in market information and government action to remedy these. Knowledge imperfections affecting both producers and consumers are characteristic of virtually all markets, though to different degrees. Lack of knowledge extends to the availability of production technologies and product quality assessment as well as product and input prices. Pricing efficiency is affected by market structure. As a broad generalisation agricultural markets are reasonably competitive, due, in part, to the large numbers of sellers and buyers involved. However, large producers tend to be better informed than small ones and similarly with large and small buyers. Producers tend to be better informed about prices than final consumers, and market intermediaries, such as wholesalers and large retailers, best informed of all. Although private markets exist for the provision and purchase of impartial market intelligence, particularly for commodities which are important in international trade, most governments provide a public service disseminating information not only about current market prices, but also supply prospects (including imports if permitted by government policy) and anticipated changes in demand (including exports). It is also common for governments to intervene in disseminating technical information, particularly the fruits of R&D, to farmers through what is termed the 'agricultural extension' service. The case for public provision of agricultural extension is based mainly on the argument that advice given to producers needs to be impartial. A secondary argument relates to 'economies of size' in the dissemination of information. If the giving of advice was left entirely to the private sector, and particularly to firms supplying farmers with production requisites, the advice might tend to be biased in favour of purchasing the supplying firms' own products. Also, with many firms giving similar advice, competition can be wasteful (as in advertising). Government intervention in the provision of information also extends to consumers, for example advice on nutrition.

The fourth and final area of market failure is concerned with welfare losses due to the instability of prices, incomes and market supplies. Although price flexibility is needed to clear markets and to signal shifts in demand from consumers to producers, the uncertainty generated by excessive price instability is apt to result in inefficient resource allocation by producers (unless they are risk neutral). Moreover, to the extent that unstable prices cause unstable producer incomes, producers may suffer a welfare loss. Consumer welfare may also be adversely affected by excessive instability of prices. In view of the results of recent work on the theory of commodity stabilisation, it is impossible to be dogmatic about the effects of unstable prices on the welfare of either producers or consumers. Almost any statement on this subject must be hedged by limiting conditions and assumptions. There are likely to be losers as well as gainers from any act of stabilisation, even though a net benefit may remain after the gainers have over-compensated the losers (see, for example, Newbery and Stiglitz, 1981, ch. 2). The instruments of stabilisation are various and extend from the ever normal granary through price guarantees and price controls, to direct income payments to farmers and consumer food subsidies and, in some countries, free or low-cost crop insurance for farmers. State intervention to protect producers from the risks and uncertainties of being in business on their own account inevitably gives rise to the problem of 'moral hazard', that is producers are encouraged to undertake hazardous enterprises which, for reasons of financial prudence, they would not undertake without the risk being underwritten by the government and taxpayers. Although this would probably be socially acceptable during times of national emergency, such as war-time, it is much harder to rationalise over-protection of farmers under normal peacetime conditions, particularly if there are structural surpluses of grains and other agricultural products. Thus, in finding the most appropriate level of government intervention at which to stabilise agricultural prices and incomes, a fine judgement has to be made between 'acceptable' and 'unacceptable' levels of uncertainty for farmers.

The largely static market failure arguments, as presented so far, give some *ex ante* validity to various forms of interventionist policy toward agriculture. However, being without a historical context these cannot fully explain the scope, prevalence and persistence of policy measures enacted over the past century or more. As will be seen in later chapters, the introduction of new and substantial policies tended to occur in times of 'crises' for the agricultural sector in the countries under review. Furthermore new policy measures tended to be sustained as governments attempted to cope with a perceived agricultural adjustment problem in the context of economic growth. Finally, the persistence of policy measures that have long lost their original justification requires that some attention be paid to government failure. As a backcloth to these issues we turn next to the transformation of the agricultural sector in the context of the sustained economic growth experienced in the Western world over the last 150 years or so.

ECONOMIC GROWTH AND THE AGRICULTURAL TRANSFORMATION PROCESS

The USA and the developed market economies of Western Europe have experienced modern economic growth – a substantial and sustained rise in per capita income at a rate far higher than in previous centuries – since around the middle of the last century.[13] The 'driving force' has been modern science or 'a high rate of accumulation of useful knowledge and of technological innovations derived from it' (Kuznets, 1980, p. 410). The role of institutional change in encouraging, channelling and accommodating technical change has also been important in realising the potential payoff from scientific discovery. Associated with modern economic growth have been shifts in the production structures of the relevant economies as reflected in the shares of different sectors in GDP, labour and capital. Of importance here is the continuing decline in the relative importance of agriculture in economic output and the labour force in a growing economy. This is called the agricultural transformation process. Table 1.1 illustrates the growth in national income per capita and the declining relative importance of agriculture over a long time scale for some of the major countries examined in this book. Two other important characteristics of the transformation process are,

Table 1.1 Economic growth and agriculture's share of national output in Western Europe and the US, 1800s–1986

Economic growth rates

	UK		US		France		Germany		Denmark	
	g	p	g	p	g	p	g	p	g	p
	1.2	1801/11 to 1851/71	1.5	1800 to 1879/88	2.0	1831/40 to 1861/70				
	1.1	1855/64 to 1920/29	1.5	1880/89 to 1910/14	1.3	1861/70 to 1891/00	1.5	1850/59 to 1910/13	1.9	1865/6 to 1963/67
	1.6	1920/29 to 1963/67	1.7	1910/14 to 1963/67	1.7	1896 to 1963/66	1.9	1910/13 to 1963/67		
	1.7	1965 to 1986	1.6	1965 to 1986	2.8	1965 to 1986	2.5	1965 to 1986	1.9	1965 to 1986

Agriculture's share of national output

	UK		US		France		Germany		Denmark	
	a.s.	y	a.s.	y	a.s.	y	a.s.	y	a.s.	y
	34	1801/11								
	20	1851/61	43	1839			41	1850/59	45	1870/79
	4	1924	11	1919/24	25	1896	14	1935/38	20	1950/51
	3	1965	3	1965	8	1965	4	1965	8	1965
	2	1986	2	1986	4	1986	2	1986	6	1986

Notes
p: period; g: average annual compound growth rate (%) in real national income per capita; y: year; a.s.: agriculture's share of national product.

Sources: Derived or abstracted from Kuznets (1971) chs. I and IV. 1965 and 1986 figures are World Bank data reported in Stern (1989).

first, agricultural growth in terms of productivity as well as output, and, second, after a turning point, a declining agricultural labour force. Table 1.2 illustrates these facets for a number of countries.

Table 1.2   Indices of agricultural output, agricultural labour force and agricultural productivity in Western Europe and the US, 1880–1980

	1880	1910	1930	1960	1980
AO					
US	29	48	60	100	146
UK	54	56	60	100	149
France	43	53	62	100	167
Denmark	24	41	66	100	128
AW					
US	200 (55)	260 (36)	236 (26)	100 (9)	43 (3)
UK	151 (16)	143 (12)	134 (10)	100 (6)	57 (3)
France	193 (49)	190 (40)	157 (33)	100 (21)	51 (10)
Denmark	107 (54)	114 (45)	131 (38)	100 (27)	40 (9)
AO per W					
US	15	19	25	100	324
UK	36	39	45	100	265
France	22	28	40	100	325
Denmark	22	36	51	100	319
AO per L					
US	64	64	69	100	151
UK	57	57	61	100	157
France	43	50	60	100	182
Denmark	26	44	64	100	138

Notes
Figures in parentheses are percentage of labour force in agriculture.
AO: agricultural output.
AW: number of male workers in agriculture (percentage of male workers in agriculture).
AO per W: Agriculture output per male worker.
AO per L: Agriculture output per ha agriculture land.

Source: Hayami and Ruttan (1985, Appendix B).

Rapid agricultural growth appears to be a necessary condition for general growth in the developmental stage in most economies. Also of importance is the stimulation of agricultural productivity by private sector, and arguably more important, public sector R&D.[14] As an economy matures with growth, the institutionalisation of agricultural technical change still has a high social pay off.[15] However, rising agricultural productivity in conjunction with shifts in relative demand away from food in a growing economy (Engels' Law)[16] gives rise to the possibility of a structural disequilibrium known as the agricultural adjustment problem. This problem is typified by an income gap between the urban and farm sectors: as is discussed later, in the context of policy analysis in different countries, there have been arguments as to whether the income gap is temporary or persistent and whether or not the gap is 'large' or 'small'.[17]

The core elements of the agricultural transformation process in the developed economy are encapsulated by two sector growth models. Here we briefly highlight these elements within the context of an assumed closed economy with two sectors, agriculture (A) and manufacturing (X).[18] Assume that the economy has undergone sustained growth for a sufficient period of time such that the agricultural labour force is declining in absolute terms: that is the turning point in the agricultural labour force, associated with around 30–40 per cent of the labour force in agriculture, has been passed. However, assume that agriculture is still the predominant sector of the economy in that say between 20 to 30 per cent of the labour force is directly engaged in agriculture. Let there be roughly equal productivity growth in A and X generating economic growth, but let the income elasticity of demand for A's products be substantially less than unity with the income elasticity of demand for X's products necessarily being more than unity. The income-led changing demand pattern implies that the gross value of A's sales rise less rapidly than GDP so that agriculture has a declining share of national income.[19] Moreover, the assumption of equal productivity growth in the two sectors implies that in the market economy the equilibrium internal terms of trade move continuously against agriculture; that is, real agricultural prices tend to fall over time. As a result there is continuing pressure for resources (particularly labour) to move out of agriculture into the more rapidly growing sectors of the economy. As explained by Schultz (1945, p. 82) there is a tendency for a 'chronic disequilibrium adverse to agriculture', and 'agriculture is burdened constantly with an excess supply of labour even when business is expanding and there are brisk job opportunities in non-agricultural industries ... what is constantly required is a constant redistribution of the labour force with relatively fewer workers engaged in agriculture ... as the economy develops slowly but always belatedly this happens'. However, out-migration from the farm sector is slow because of barriers to mobility and depends more upon the availability of jobs in the non-farm sector than upon farm prices and incomes. The presence of imperfect mobility implies that resources can earn persistently more in the X sector than in the A sector with continuous economic growth.[20]

The conclusion that agriculture declines in relative terms in a growing economy is not invalidated by examining an open economy with a comparative advantage in agriculture.[21] (Agriculture's relative share is higher (lower) in the agricultural exporting (importing) country than in a comparable closed economy at the same level of per capita GDP.) In an open economy with a comparative disadvantage in agriculture, the adjustment problem may be exacerbated by growing imports of farm products particularly if transport innovations or rapid technological change in competitor countries lead to large and rapid falls in real prices.

Several other facets of structural change in the economy are also relevant to agricultural policy analysis. First, agriculture's declining share of GDP is exacerbated by a rise in marketing services attached to food products with economic growth: the farmer's share of retail food expenditures declines.[22] Second, technical change in agriculture involves a shift from a natural resource-based activity reliant on farm-produced inputs and labour to a science-based technology using inputs purchased from the non-farm sector. The ratio of value added to gross output in the farm sector tends to fall continuously as does labour's share of gross inputs. Third, during the transformation process in the developed economy, agriculture becomes integrated into the rest of the economy as labour and credit markets link the urban and rural economies. Transportation and information innovations also reduce barriers between the farm and the city. These forces imply that over time the barriers to resource mobility fall. The effects of the macro economy on agriculture also change. On the one hand, the falling income elasticity of demand for food means that agriculture becomes less and less affected by business cycle influences; on the other hand, the integration of agriculture into the economy and the increasing reliance of farm technology on purchased inputs means that it becomes more and more vulnerable to the impacts of changes in inflation and the cost of credit affecting the costs of non-farm inputs and the ability to service the purchase of these inputs. Finally, world economic growth leads to a larger interaction of national economies via trade and agriculture becomes more vulnerable to shocks emanating from changes in trade balances and exchange rates.

In short there is a quite substantial period of time in the course of the economic growth of a developed economy when there may be a 'chronic disequilibrium adverse to agriculture'. Although many farm households may be sharing the fruits of economic growth via high incomes derived from new farm technologies or through migrating to well-paid off-farm jobs, there may be a persistent income gap between farm and non-farm sectors because of barriers to labour mobility. Given the 'largeness' of the agricultural labour force at this stage of economic growth, governments may decide rightly or wrongly, under pressure from the farm sector, that there is a farm income problem. Thus there is a fear, particularly in the agricultural importing or even largely closed economy, that the social and political fabric of society cannot withstand the burdens imposed by *laissez-faire* market forces. Government action may then be taken under political pressure from the farm sector to moderate the disruptive impact of economic growth on the farm sector and to slow down the transformation process.[23] With farmers regarding technology and input prices as given parameters, it is natural for farm groups to demand intervention on farm product prices to effect income transfers. Such intervention, if carried out, then alters the partitioning of income streams resulting from technological change in agriculture in favour of farmers in comparison to *laissez-faire*.[24] This then is the nub of the prevalence of price intervention agricultural policy in a dynamic setting as discussed within specific institutional contexts in later chapters.[25]

FARM POLICY IN THE HIGH INCOME MODERN INDUSTRIALISED ECONOMY

The continuing agricultural transformation process as supported by growth in agricultural productivity and general incomes eventually leads to agriculture becoming just another industry; important but no larger than many others in the economy. Thus agriculture's share of GDP and the labour force in the high income countries has dropped to 5 per cent or less and the share of food expenditure in urban budgets has dropped to 20 per cent or less. Barriers to labour mobility are small;[26] it becomes less easy to identify an adjustment problem specific to agriculture. From this point of view, it is difficult to justify large-scale agricultural interventionist policy although resource adjustment problems exist if urban unemployment is endemic. However, agricultural policy retains a high profile for two different sets of reasons. First, if commodity price supports introduced in earlier years in the face of the farm income problem have been retained then these induce high budgetary costs and severe resource misallocation. Further, insofar as agricultural policies are linked through trade, then the resource distortions become international and budgetary costs in one country may be magnified by policy action in a second country.[27] Second, the high technology, science-based agriculture in the modern industrial economy gives rise to environmental and food quality concerns with pressures for government action. Several environmental concerns are prominent: (1) the management of the disposal of residuals from agriculture (such as pollutants in river courses and ground water supplies); (2) the impact of modern farm technology on the conservation of the natural resources used in production (for example erosion of land); (3) the effect of modern farming on perceived environmental amenity – a product supplied jointly with the production of agricultural commodities (with the growth in incomes there is a tendency for the demand for environmental services – direct consumption of amenity and freedom from pollution and congestion – to rise more rapidly than the demand for food);[28] (4) the extent to which the size of the farm population is important in maintaining the fabric of rural areas; (5) the transmission of residuals in the food chain, food quality standards and the embodiment of 'artificial' substances in processed foodstuffs. As noted earlier, the concepts of externality and public goods provide guidelines for the framing of environmental policies with the existence of unpriced goods (or bads) providing the justification for intervention.

The pervasiveness of continuing agricultural commodity price support intervention in high income countries cannot be fully explained on the grounds of either market failure or the dynamics of the agricultural transformation process. Economists have sought to 'explain' inappropriate state policies under the umbrella of government failures. These are ascribed to the success of the rent-seeking activities of special interest groups. In the case of agricultural policy, it might be closer to the truth to regard the activities of farmers, landowners, food manufacturers and traders as 'rent preserving',[29] that is, they attempt to retain the benefits from policies set in train in earlier times.

The concept of government failure allows a distinction to be made between (a) political economic resource transactions of government (or PERTs) which attempt to correct for market failures, and (b) political economic seeking transfers (or PESTs) or rents resulting from the political lobbying activities and other pressures on government for favourable treatment exerted by numerous interest groups (see Rausser, 1982). The PERT approach to policy analysis assumes that government intervention has a positive sum or, at worst, constant sum result. In contrast, the PEST approach points to negative sum results because the costs of PEST activities (lobbying costs, and so on) represents social waste. Although lobbying or PEST activities are undeniably bad in a first-best world, in a second-best world they may be either bad or good (ibid., p. 823).

The public interest theory of government regulation, which posits that government intervention in any part of the economy is simply a response to public demand for the correction of obvious imperfections in the operation of the free market and other market failures, is clearly open to criticism. First, government intervention and regulation are by no means confined to highly concentrated industries with an inherent tendency to practice monopoly. Agriculture, for example, tends to be atomistic but is also highly regulated. Second, there is no clear systematic relationship between the degree to which an industry is regulated and the extent of the externalities associated with it. Thus, although the use of public transport services contributes less to traffic congestion than the use of private cars, public transport tends to be more highly regulated than the car manufacturing industry. Although the chemical industry is almost certainly responsible for more pollution than agriculture, its markets are much less highly regulated by the government.

The main alternatives to the public interest theory of government regulation are (a) the capture (or interest group) theory, and (b) the economic theory of regulation (see Posner, 1974). Capture theories take various forms, spanning the ideological divide between free market economists and Marxists, but share the belief that economic regulation results from private groups seeking to promote their own interests through government. Different versions argue both that capitalists capture the government to further their own interests and that the government captures the market to promote the interests of its political allies. A major weakness of all theories emphasising either the conspiracy of big business against the government or the alliance of big business and the government against the rest of society, is the commonplace observation that much government regulation serves the interests of small-scale business (as in agriculture) as well as non-business (such as trade unions).

The second alternative theory, the economic theory of regulation, posits that from the point of view of private industry, government regulation is an alternative to cartelization. Cartel theory lays down that 'successful' cartel formation depends upon the number of sellers (the smaller the number the better) and the homogeneity of their interests (the greater the homogeneity the better). The larger the number of sellers and the greater the heterogeneity of their interests, the more individual firms are likely to be tempted to try to reap the benefits of membership without joining the cartel, that is, to 'free ride'. The principal costs of forming and maintaining a cartel are (a) the costs of finding a mutually agreeable cartel price, and (b) the costs of enforcement. It follows that for industries which lack the characteristics favouring cartelisation – high concentration, small numbers and homogeneity of interests – campaigning for government regulation may be an attractive alternative, particularly if the costs are lower than those of forming and maintaining a cartel. However, unlike forming the cartel, persuading the government to regulate the market requires political intervention and, in particular, the lobbying of both politicians and public officials by representatives of the affected industry. Moreover, lobbying is apt to be costly. The economic theory of regulation postulates that in the political market-place the supply of legislation favourable to a particular industry responds to the voting strength of the affected interest group or industry. By comparison, the strongest demand for such legislation is exerted by industries composed of large numbers of firms and an asymmetry of interests, both of which discourage cartelisation. The voting strength offered to the governing party as an inducement to enact favourable legislation can be increased through the formation of coalitions in which different interest groups agree to support each other in campaigning for a common programme of protective legislation.

Thus the economic theory of regulation is useful in explaining why protective legislation in widely diverse areas like agriculture, trade unions and professional organisations, where cartelisation would be difficult, is so widely observed in practice (Posner, 1974, p. 347). The theory is particularly convincing in explaining the prevalence of protective measures enacted in favour of agriculture and other atomistic industries, particularly in developed countries.

Within the agricultural sector, broadly defined, the principal rent-seeking groups are landowners, farmers and the manufacturers and suppliers of agricultural inputs. Although there are divergencies of interest, between landowners and tenant farmers for example, these groups tend to form a coalition in pressing for the installation and maintenance of a high level of protection for domestic agriculture. Because land is the least elastic resource, much of the economic rent embodied in 'high' agricultural support prices, resulting from the regulation and restriction of trade, eventually accrues to landowners in the form of higher land values. The owners of more elastic, complementary agricultural resources – labour, capital and entrepreneurship – obtain less permanent benefit from agricultural support. As land values go up, so tenant farmers are obliged to pay higher rents for the use of the land. On the other hand, the owners of non-land resources would suffer severe short-term income losses if protection was summarily withdrawn, whereas the major consequence for landowners would be a severe decline in the capital value of their land.

Food manufacturers and traders generally remain outside the agricultural rent-seeking lobby. The protection of agricultural products inflates the costs of food manufacturers' raw materials, as well as depressing the demand for the final products they sell. For food exporters, high raw material prices are a handicap when competing in third country markets. The position of food consumers is similar.

In sum, the attainment of government objectives for agriculture (based on PERT-related policies) tends to be subverted by rent-seeking (or PEST) activities of private interest groups and coalitions.[30] However, if government failures become increasingly visible, public pressure can set in motion corrective forces. In the case of agricultural policy, large commodity surpluses, high budgetary costs and disruptive international trade effects have set in train a reform of policy in both the US and the EU.[31]

Heightening 'green' concerns have led to a coalescing of the two issues of reining in agricultural support and accounting for the environmental impacts of modern farming methods. Thus, edging to the forefront of policy making is the recognition that externality issues are linked with the reform of commodity policy. But policy makers have to decide who should bear the cost of environmental protection: should externalities be internalised via the taxation of agricultural inputs and the regulation of farm production processes, or should the farm community be rewarded from the public purse for the provision of amenity benefits and the use of environmental-friendly practices?

Government intervention justified on the basis of environmental protection and related concerns such as food quality/safety and animal welfare, is also likely to raise difficult policy questions in relation to agricultural trade liberalisation. On the one hand, domestic environmental, safety and welfare regulations can represent incidental or deliberate 'green' barriers to trade. On the other hand, multilateral trade liberalisation may pose a threat to environmental protection as well as food quality and human health.

The linkages between emerging environmental and related concerns, and the current high-profile topics of the desubsidisation of domestic farm policies and the liberalisation of agricultural trade, are identified in the final section of this book as the new agenda for agricultural policy.

APPENDIX: AGRICULTURE DECLINES WITH ECONOMIC GROWTH: A TWO SECTOR MODEL[32]

It is empirically observed that the agricultural sector declines relative to other sectors in an economy undergoing sustained economic growth. Two important factors help to explain this phenomenon: a slower rise in the demand for food as compared to other goods and services (Engels' law); and technological change in agriculture expanding food supplies per hectare and per worker.

The way in which these forces lead to a declining agricultural sector can be illustrated via a basic two-sector growth model of the closed

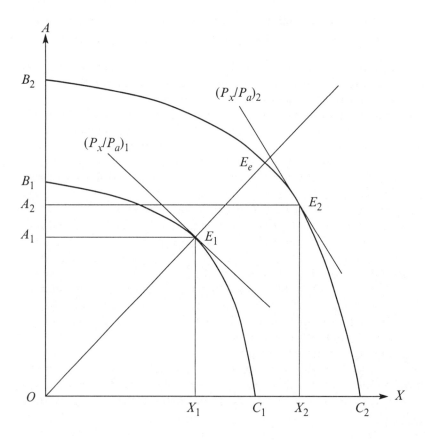

Figure 1.1   Economic growth in the closed economy

economy. Let the two sectors be defined as agriculture (A) and an aggregate of other sectors (X). Factors of production are categorised into labour (L) and an aggregate of non-labour inputs called capital (K). Technological change increases the productivity of resources over time in both sectors. However, for simplicity, population is assumed to be constant.

The analysis proceeds by analysing equilibrium in the economy in two periods. In the first period, aggregate technology defined in terms of A, X, L and K gives a production possibility frontier (PPF) represented by B_1C_1 in Figure 1.1. Point E_1 on the PPF represents equilibrium where supply is equal to demand for the goods produced by the two sectors. The equilibrium price ratio $(P_x/P_a)_1$ is given by the tangent to the PPF at E_1 with A_1 and X_1 being produced and real income being $Y_1 = P_{a_1}A_1 + P_{x_1}X_1$.

Technological change shifts the PPF outwards. Suppose that productivity growth is output neutral so that the PPF shifts equiproportionately and becomes $B_2 C_2$ in period 2. Real income has increased but because the income elasticity of demand for food is less than unity, the new equilibrium point, E_2, will be on the new PPF to the right of the ray passing through OE_1 – that is, to the south-east of point E_e.[33] The new price ratio $(P_x/P_a)_2$ is higher than that previously observed $(P_x/P_a)_1$, and the internal terms of trade have turned against agriculture. The movement from point E_1 to point E_2 corresponds to an increase in the production of both A and X goods, but the rising relative price of P_x compared to P_a induces an increase in X production relative to A production. New real income is $Y_2 = P_{a_2} A_2 + P_{x_2} X_2$. Consequently, in this simple model (with no intermediate inputs) agriculture's share of national production declines.

The more rapid growth of X production compared to A production is brought about by a transfer of resources from the A sector to the X sector given fixed stocks of L and K. The demand by the X sector for resources increases more quickly than the demand by the A sector for resources. This initially sets up a factor market disequilibrium where the wage of labour and the rental of capital services increase in X relative to A. Resources are induced to transfer from A into X. In equilibrium, resource returns are increased in both sectors but X uses proportionately more resources than A in period 2 compared to period 1.

Resource transfer in the factor markets is illustrated in Figure 1.2 with reference to the stock of labour. Technological change in each sector is assumed to be factor neutral: at given factor prices, the use of resources changes proportionately. In period 1, employment in the A

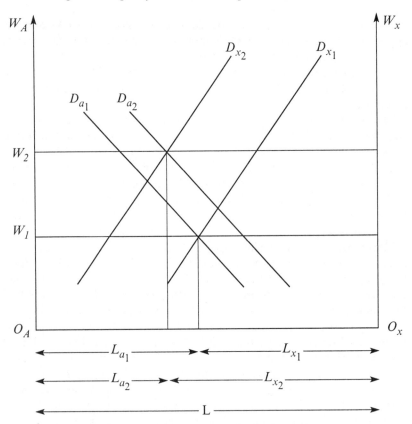

Figure 1.2   Economic growth and the labour market

sector is L_{a_1} and in the X sector is L_{x_1} with the wage in both sectors being W_1. With technological change, labour demand increases in the X sector more than in the A sector. The equilibrium in period 2 is represented by labour employment of L_{a_2} and L_{x_2} and at a higher real wage W_2. Employment in the A sector declines both relatively and absolutely with economic growth within the confines of the model.

This simple model can be modified in various ways to take account of capital investment (including the embodiment of technological change in capital inputs), population growth and the opportunities for trade in an open economy. Capital investment represents the deferment of current consumption in order to obtain more consumption in the future. In the model, A and X consumption can be defined as production net of investment and the shift in the PPF represents the combined affects of technological change and capital investment. Population growth can alter demand patterns within the model: a high population growth rate encourages the demand for food relative to the demand for other goods and services and tends to offset the income effect. However, population growth rates in the developed economies are 'low' and consideration of the factor does not invalidate the foregoing analysis. Finally, at least three considerations are relevant to the open economy case. First, for a food importing (exporting) country, the external terms of trade are biased more towards the $X(A)$ sector than the autarkic internal terms of trade so that the economy produces less (more) food than under autarky. Second, if agriculture's external terms of trade decline over time because of growth in the world economy, then agriculture's share of national production will decline. Historically, the real international prices of agricultural products have tended to fall secularly (see Anderson, 1987). Third, in considering the open economy case, it is necessary to consider explicitly the production and consumption of non-tradeable items (largely services).[34] With economic growth, the share of non-tradeables in national production tends to increase and the share of tradeable goods and services to decline along with agriculture's share of tradeables.

NOTES

1. However, the exigencies of the Second World War led to food security being a dominant aspect of government policy in Western Europe in quite recent times; see Chapter 4.
2. *Laissez-faire* across the whole spectrum of economic activity nevertheless assumes the existence of minimalist actions by the state of (a) maintaining public order and providing for external defence and (b) enforcing contracts.
3. For a review of active interventionist policies into agriculture over 20 centuries of history up to the twentieth century, see Lacy (1923).
4. The concept of the 'ever normal granary' was a central feature of US agricultural policy between 1938 and 1996, and was implemented via the activities of the Commodity Credit Corporation.
5. H.C. Chen (1911), *The Economic Principles of Confucius and His School*, Longmans, NY quoted in Lacy (1923) p. 625.
6. Ibid., p. 627.
7. The 'traditional' Common Agricultural Policy of the EU might be described as the Corn Laws 'writ large' except that the import tariffs and export subsidies vary inversely with the world price: see Chapters 4 and 5.
8. The ever broadening scope of public policy in recent times, both in Western Europe and Northern America, mirrors the growth of the state. In the British case a major reform of the civil service in the 1850s eventually resulted in the replacement of entry by patronage with entry by open competitive examination. The first agricultural census (administered by the Board of Trade) was taken in 1866. But there was no government department specifically responsible for all agricultural matters until the Board of Agriculture was established in 1889. Even then, the Board remained a minor department of government until 1919 when it was upgraded to Ministry status

with its minister in the cabinet. Whereas in Britain the nineteenth century reform of the civil service was intended to destroy class patronage, the parallel reform in the USA (immediately following the end of the Civil War) was brought in to put an end to nepotism by career politicians (the 'spoils system'). The United States Department of Agriculture was established (by Abraham Lincoln) in 1862, though the commissioner of the USDA was not promoted to Secretary of Agriculture with cabinet status until 1889.

9. A term coined by Hicks (1969).
10. Whilst farmers perform little R&D, they nevertheless contribute to technical progress via screening new techniques, learning by doing, improving management skills, assessing the optimal time for the application of crop inputs and readjusting input combinations. In short, farmers carry out informal 'research' and produce farm level innovations.
11. Such barriers are reduced by hybridisation and by plant variety protection legislation.
12. According to another welfare economics principle concerning property rights and efficiency (Coase theorem), it is immaterial to society whether the polluter compensates the victim or the victim bribes the polluter to desist.
13. Approximate dates vary between countries. For some countries in the EU (15), for example Spain, Greece and Portugal, modern economic growth is a more recent phenomenon.
14. See the arguments in the preceding section for public sector involvement in biological R&D.
15. See, for example, the rates of return collated by Ruttan (1982, ch. 10).
16. Engels' law: the general tendency for the share of the consumer's budget spent on food to decline as per capita income rises or equivalently, the observation that the income elasticity of demand for food is less than unity and declines as per capita income rises.
17. See Chapter 4.
18. See Appendix 1 for a brief formal treatment. Anderson (1987) and Antle (1988) provide concise modern treatments. Students should also read the classic text by Schultz (1945).
19. This assumes a constant population. Considerations of demand side-effects resulting from a slowly growing population, as typical of a developed economy, modify but do not invalidate the general conclusions.
20. Barriers to mobility include physical isolation of the farm community, uneven geographical dispersion of employment opportunities, urban unemployment and inappropriate skills and inadequate education of the farm population.
21. The explanation for an open economy involves extending the analysis to include non-tradeable goods and services as well as tradeables, the former being assumed to have a relatively high income elasticity of demand (see Anderson, 1987).
22. This is partly explained by the urbanisation of society, with a concomitant rise in transport and storage services attached to food transfer from farms to consumers. In addition, there is a higher income elasticity of demand for other value added activities associated with food processing, grading and so on than for food on its own.
23. In this context politics (and policy) is viewed to have a 'coping' rather than a 'solving' role with respect to perceived social problems and the pressures of conflicting interests within society (see Gordon, 1980, p. 13).
24. In a partial equilibrium setting, the agricultural adjustment problem may be regarded in terms of the supply curve of farm products shifting to the right (under the influence of technological advance) at a faster rate than the demand curve (under the influence of domestic population and income growth and any net foreign trade influences). Farm product prices are tending to fall; this rate of decline may be moderated by government intervention with an increased share of the gains from technical progress accruing to farmers rather than domestic consumers. Note that Heady (1966) and Schultz (1961) regarded it as acceptable to pay compensation to

the suppliers of agricultural labour for the costs imposed by economic growth and rising farm productivity. However, these authors regarded agricultural price intervention as an inappropriate form of compensation (see Chapter 4 for further discussion).

25. See Chapters 4 and 5.
26. Although slow structural adjustment within agriculture may be seen as a 'problem' arising out of restrictions on the reaping of economics of size at the farm level.
27. See Chapter 6. See also D. Gale Johnson (1973b, 1991).
28. For a fuller discussion of the environmental problem in an agricultural context see Ruttan (1971).
29. We owe this term to our colleague, Robert Hine.
30. Phasing out agricultural support seems to be difficult: first, because the amenity value of the countryside is linked in the eyes of policy makers with the economic survival of farming; second, because governments are unwilling to allow unrestricted markets to determine the degree of self-sufficiency; and third because the resultant fall in asset values would be unacceptable to the farm sector.
31. See Chapters 6 and 7.
32. For a fuller exposition of the material contained in this Appendix see Anderson (1987) and Antle (1988).
33. That is E_e would represent the new point of equilibrium if demand expanded from E_1 in proportion to the expansion of production in both sectors: this would occur if both goods had unit income elasticities of demand.
34. See Anderson (1987).

2. History to 1930: development policy and trade intervention

INTRODUCTION AND OVERVIEW

This chapter reviews agricultural policy in some of the major economies of Western Europe[1] and in the USA over the period from the nineteenth century to around 1930. This period witnessed the onset of modern economic growth in these economies and the concomitant evolution of the early stages of the agricultural transformation process. Thus, the phenomenon of a high and sustained rise in national per capita income can be dated at around the mid 1700s for Britain, around 1800 for France, and the early to mid-1800s for Germany, Denmark, Holland and the US (see Kuznets, 1970 and Reynolds, 1985). In the subsequent years to around 1920–30, the growth rate in real national income per capita was over 1 per cent per annum in these economies (see Table 1.1 in Chapter 1). Population growth rates for most of the countries were around 1–2 per cent per annum. Structural change accompanied economic growth and agriculture declined in relation to other sectors although agricultural output increased significantly in absolute terms (see Table 1.2 in Chapter 1).

The period 1850–1914 witnessed rapid growth in world production and trade. Kuznets (1966) estimates the median growth rate of national product in Europe and North America at 3 per cent per annum and 2 per cent per annum in per capita terms. There were improvements in and cheapening of transport, specifically in rail and shipping. 'Ocean freight rates in 1913 were some 30 per cent of their 1870 level; overland transport costs fell even more spectacularly' (Reynolds, 1985, p. 33). Falling transport costs coupled with economic growth stimulated international trade which rose as a proportion of world production to some 33 per cent in 1913. Trade volume grew by some 50 per cent per decade from 1850 to 1880 and some 40 per cent per decade from 1881 to 1913 (ibid.). Trade was dominated (75 per cent) by Europe and North America with third world countries exporting primary (tropical) products to the growth centres. For this study, an important feature of the development of trade was rising agricultural exports from the 'New World' to Europe.

Growth rates in Europe and North America fell after the First World War and declined significantly from 1929 to 1938. The growth in national product was just over 2.5 per cent per annum from 1913–1929 and 1.3 per cent per annum from 1929 to 1938 (ibid.). Trade grew only slowly and was seriously interrupted by the Great Depression of 1929–33.

Agricultural policy in the nineteenth and early twentieth century was largely but not entirely confined to actions promoting economic development. More specifically it sought to initiate institutional and technological change increasing the productivity of agriculture. Policy toward (a) property rights and farm structure and (b) agricultural research and development were of particular significance. The period also saw the growth of government bureaucracy, initially with limited functions, but later on with enabling powers to control and regulate the agricultural sector. The exigencies of the First World War, in particular, brought about a sizable rise in the agricultural bureaucracy. There was a parallel rise in farmer representative organisations who increasingly sought to 'capture' government policy in their own interests. In addition, farmer cooperative movements sprang up to further the interests of farmers by economic and political means.

Prior to the establishment of a sizable government bureaucracy and the introduction of capital equipment into its administration, intervention into agricultural markets was perforce limited to tariff policy. There had been a long tradition of using import taxes and export bounties to regulate the grain trade in Western Europe but policy attitudes varied from the late nineteenth century until the onset of the First World War, after a period of free trade in the mid 1800s. Specifically, France and Germany adopted protectionist grain policies whilst the UK, Denmark and Holland maintained a *laissez-faire* stance during a period of severe international competition in agriculture between North America and Europe. Importantly, from the 1870s onwards, the agricultural economies of the two continents became increasingly intertwined.

During the First World War, there was extensive government regulation of agriculture in Western Europe whilst American agriculture benefited from a boom. After the war, countries in Europe re-adopted traditional stances on trade; however agricultural prices collapsed worldwide with the onset of the Great Depression in 1929 and extensive government intervention in agricultural markets became the norm in the 1930s in both Europe and America.

POLICY IN WESTERN EUROPE TO 1930

Introduction

By the middle of the nineteenth century, feudalism had been abolished over most of Western Europe and freehold ownership and private land use rights had been established in agriculture. However, tenure systems and farm size structures varied considerably, a diversity which was to remain for the most of the next 100 years. Briefly, the UK had a predominantly landlord–tenant system, particularly in England, but with a growing proportion over time of owner-occupied farms, and relatively large farm units. Denmark and Holland had mainly owner-occupied farms, although smaller in scale than those in the UK, whilst small-scale peasant units predominated in France and much of Germany.

There was diversity too in the extent to which the population of the various countries derived a living from agriculture. By 1880, the UK was already an industrialised and food importing country, with only around 15 per cent of the work force in agriculture and a declining rural labour force. In contrast, in the other countries – France, Germany, Denmark and Holland – some 40–50 per cent of the labour force was still employed in agriculture. However, Germany was industrialising rapidly and the agricultural labour force had peaked by 1880. Over the next 50 years, the proportion of the labour force in all countries declined, although the absolute size of agricultural employment did not peak in Denmark and Holland – the agricultural exporting nations – until around the mid-1920s. Some salient data indicating the nature of the agricultural transformation process with respect to agricultural employment in this period is presented in Table 2.1.

Agricultural policy varied across Western Europe during the period 1850–1930. The UK, Denmark and Holland enacted structural legislation but not France or Germany. Government participation in and public funding of agricultural research and education became a significant feature of policy in all countries except France. Trade intervention existed in France and Germany, but not in the other countries. However, stemming from a collapse of agricultural prices around 1929, active and extensive government intervention into agricultural markets became the norm in all countries. Agricultural policy in the 1930s and following decades was to be dominated by various forms of price support and market management.

Table 2.1   Agricultural employment in Western Europe, 1880–1930

Year	UK		France		Germany		Denmark		Holland	
	L	S	L	S	L	S	L	S	L	S
1880	100	16	100	49	100	50	100	54	100	41
1910	95	12	99	40	101	35	108	45	113	25
1930	89	10	81	33	80	17*	123	38	116	21

Notes
*1933
L: index of employment in agriculture (male labour for UK, France, Germany and
     Denmark, and all employment for Holland).
S: percentage of workforce in agriculture.

Sources: Ruttan et al, (1978), Hayami and Ruttan (1985), van de Meer and Yamada
(1986), Tracy (1982), Clark (1960).

Property Rights and Farm Structure[2]

In medieval (feudal) Europe, the manorial system of agriculture prevailed in most of the arable areas. The nobles held their estates as a
fee or benefit from their king and granted tenures of land to peasants.[3]
Cultivation of land was based on open-field farming: the arable land
attached to an estate was arranged into two or three large fields subdiv-
ided into strips. Peasants had strips in each field allocated by lot and
there was a common rotation in each field. Peasants paid for the use
of land in kind and by working on the lord's own land. In addition, the
peasant had common or communal grazing rights on pastures.

Non-attenuated private property rights did not exist under the manorial system since there were neither exclusive nor transferable land-
use rights. The system was incompatible with self advancement or the
pursuit of individual self interest. Whilst the system persisted for centuries, it eventually broke down as 'enclosure' of the open fields and
commons was introduced by evolution or revolution or reform in different countries. By the mid-nineteenth century, freehold ownership
and private land-use rights had been established in agriculture, although
the farm structure and tenure arrangements varied considerably from
country to country. The incentive for change was market expansion in
Europe for foodstuffs.

In England the enclosure movement evolved over centuries, but had
particular force in the eighteenth century. It began in Tudor times due
to a labour shortage following the Black Death (mid-fourteenth
century) and received added impetus from the dissolution of the monas-

teries in the sixteenth century by Henry VIII. The lords of the manor became landlords turning the open fields into estates with the peasants becoming tenant farmers, landless labourers or vagrants. Enclosure involved either forcible eviction of peasants, particularly where arable land was converted to sheep pasture, a process stimulated by the profitability of wool production, or by private agreement between open field farmers and the lord. By the beginning of the eighteenth century probably half of the arable land was enclosed. From the mid-eighteenth century further enclosure took place through private Acts of Parliament. The procedure for government-regulated enclosure included the appointment of a commissioner to survey the area and form 'squarish' fields from five to sixty acres in size. Hedges were planted around the fields and the landscape began to take on 'its characteristically English appearance' (Tracy, 1982, p. 40). Between 1760 and 1815 more than 1800 private enclosure Acts of Parliament were passed and by the mid-nineteenth century the process of enclosure was virtually complete. The property rights system that had evolved was for landlords to own land and their tenants to cash rent farms. Importantly, for the productivity of agriculture, the farm units were large enough to reap economies of scale. Furthermore, although there was no statutory control over leases, close social ties between landlord and tenant often ensured reasonable security of tenure.

In France, the main impetus to enclosure was given by the Revolution of 1789, which abolished the feudal system.[4] Before the Revolution, enclosure was slow, although occurring in parts of northern France. Under the Revolution, the land of nobles and the church was sold off to augment state revenue. However, it has been suggested that the peasants obtained and retained ownership of less than a third of the land redistributed by the Revolution (Clapham, 1968, p. 20). Some land passed into the hands of the new bourgeois landlord class and a further proportion was recovered by the original owners following the restoration of the monarchy in 1815. The redistribution of land also had little effect on farm structures dominated by very small and over-fragmented holdings. Furthermore, fragmentation was encouraged by the practice of division among heirs. In contrast to Britain, peasant farms in France in the mid-nineteenth century were inefficiently small and overfragmented.

In Germany, the vestiges of feudalism survived at least until the middle of the nineteenth century. But taking the united German state which emerged from the Franco-Prussian war in 1870 as the unit of observation, the pattern of development differed between the eastern and western regions. To the west of the river Elbe a peasant type of agriculture prevailed with many absentee landlords. To the east of the

Elbe (that is, Prussia) a different system had evolved under which large agricultural estates were managed directly by their owners (known as the 'Junkers'). A measure of land reform under which the peasants gained possession of their holdings started in territories annexed by Napoleon near to the Rhine and spread eastwards but was not completed until the Revolution of 1848. But land reform had little effect on farm structure. Peasant holdings were small and fragmented. Fragmentation was aggravated by the code of equal division of property amongst heirs. In Prussia, the large estates managed to survive defeat in the war with Napoleon. Consequently, there were quite divergent farm structures in Germany by the end of the nineteenth century: relatively large farms in Prussia and small fragmented peasant holdings in the west.

Denmark was a leading country in the abolition of feudalism, the reform process being virtually complete by about 1800. Following the abolition of serfdom, most landowners chose to sell land to their former tenants. The enclosure of open fields was complete by about 1810. A favourable farm structure resulted based on a predominance of owner-occupiers with compact adequate sized farms (Tracy, 1982, p. 115). Indeed, Danish farms became so large that before the end of the nineteenth century there was considerable political pressure on the government to purchase and partition estates to create smallholdings. This pressure culminated in the Lands Act of 1919 which created a new class of smallholder tenant farmer with the state acting as landlord. This smallholder legislation attracted internal criticism on both economic and social grounds.

In the northern region of the low countries, an area now constituting part of the state of Holland, the suppression of the feudal system occurred in the sixteenth century. Land reforms took place giving rise to the creation of a new class of wealthy middle-class farmers adopting modern methods of farm management. In addition, considerable capital was invested in building dams and dykes to reclaim land from the sea (Tracy, 1982, pp. 8–9).

In short, the enclosure movement and the establishment of private property rights over land occurred at different speeds and took different forms over much of Western Europe. A diversity of farm structures and tenure systems existed by the mid-nineteenth century. In Great Britain, relatively large farm units were established, with a landlord tenant system predominating in England. Danish farms, although small in comparison to farms in Britain, were large relative to those in other countries and free of fragmentation. They were typically owner-occupied. In Holland small family farms dominated, with farms in the coastal regions being larger than further inland. In France and Germany much land was farmed by small-scale peasant owners with considerable fragmentation of units, although in Prussia large estates were consolidated.

Whilst the freehold farm structures were established by the mid-nineteenth century, these were amended by subsequent policy reforms in the various countries. In England, the main emphasis was on the conditions of land tenure and the taxation of agricultural landlords. Until 1875, agricultural tenancy agreements were unregulated by law, apart from the normal legal requirements of abiding by the terms of a contract. From 1875 through to 1923 a succession of Agricultural Holding Acts were passed advancing tenant rights with respect to improvements and compensation for eviction. In parallel with the granting of tenant rights were changes in the taxation of landlords. In 1894, estate duty was levied for the first time on agricultural land. This was a contributory factor to the break up of the large estates with a changeover from the predominance of tenant farmers to a predominance of owner-occupiers which was to become a marked feature of British agriculture in the twentieth century.[5]

Statistics on the tenure structure of British agriculture reveal the strength of the trend away from tenancy and in favour of owner-occupation during the present century (Table 2.2). Thus, between 1914 and 1987 the proportion of agricultural holdings in England and Wales which were rented or mainly rented fell from nearly 90 per cent to less than 30 per cent. A similar downward trend occurred in the relative proportions of owner-occupied and rented land.

In France, in contrast to Britain, tenancy reform and legislation to encourage farm consolidation were both neglected. Likewise in Germany no significant structural legislation was enacted. However, in Denmark, a series of Land Acts led to the partitioning of estates to create smallholdings (especially the Land Act of 1919). In contrast, in Holland, legislation was introduced in the 1920s to encourage farm rationalisation and consolidation (Land Reparcelling Act, first introduced in 1924) although farmers showed little interest in this until after the Second World War.

Historical comparisons of farm size in the countries now comprising the European Community are hard to come by. However, rough comparisons are shown in Table 2.3 which indicates national trends from the late nineteenth century until after the Second World War. The most notable features brought out by the table are firstly, the relatively large farm size structure of England and Wales and, secondly, the lack of any convincing upward trend in farm size over the period shown. In fact,

Table 2.2 Tenure structure of British agriculture, 1914–87

A: Number of holdings by tenure, England and Wales

Year	Rented or mainly rented		Owned or mainly owned		Total holdings	
	No. (000s)	%	No. (000s)	%	No. (000s)	%
1914	386	89	49	11	435	100
1960	144	43	189	57	333	100
1970	93	40	141	60	234	100
1980	60	33	125	67	185	100
1987	49	26	137	74	186	100

B: Holding areas by tenure, England and Wales

Year	Area rented		Area owned		Area of total holdings*	
	million acres	%	million acres	%	million acres	%
1914	24.1	89	3.0	11	27.1	100
1950	17.6	62	10.8	38	28.4	100
1960	14.5	51	14.0	49	28.5	100
1970	12.8	47	14.5	53	27.3	100
1980	11.3	42	15.7	58	27.0	100
1987	10.1	37	16.9	63	27.0	100

Note: Comprises area of crops and grass only in 1914, crops and grass plus rough grazing in 1950, and total holding area in subsequent years.

Sources: MAFF (1968), *A Century of Agricultural Statistics: Agricultural Statistics*, UK, various issues.

the Danish data are suggestive of a downward trend in that country, apparently reflecting Danish government policy of creating substantial numbers of new small holdings during the early part of this century. Inter-country comparisons of farm size are in any case imprecise due to differences in statistical practice and the basis of land enumeration.

Agriculture's Official Status in Government

In the period under review, there was an increase in the scope and complexity of policy intervention. Associated with this was the establish-

Table 2.3   Farm structure in Western Europe, 1900–1950

Country	Year	Median farm size (ha)*	Basis of land classification
England and Wales	1875	70	Crops and grass area
	1924	63	"
	1949	65	"
Denmark	1901	40	Agricultural area
	1951	24	"
Netherlands	1910	20	"
	1950	15	"
France	1892	30	Total farm area
	1929	26	"
	1942	28	"
West Germany	1901	13	Agricultural area
	1939	14	"
	1949	13	"

Note: *Median values derived from census data on the distribution of national farm areas by size-classes.

Source: Dovring (1956, Table 14).

ment in each country of a government department responsible for agricultural matters. The size and status of such departments increased during the First World War when emergency powers were enacted for food production and distribution.

In the UK a so-called Board of Agriculture was established as early as 1793 to collect and publish agricultural information. This Board, consisting mainly of prominent landowners of the day, possessed no executive responsibilities or powers and was dissolved in the 1820s after its annual Treasury grant had been discontinued. After that British agriculture was left without a definite focal point in government until near the end of the century. Agricultural problems and issues of national concern, such as the outbreak of cattle plague (rinderpest) in 1865, and the decision in 1866 to collect agricultural statistics on a regular basis, were dealt with in an ad hoc fashion. In 1889 a new Board of Agriculture was created by Act of Parliament to combine the functions of collecting agricultural statistics, supervising veterinary work on livestock diseases and dealing with land administration. In 1903 the Board of Agriculture became the Board of Agriculture and Fisheries. In 1911 a separate

Board of Agriculture for Scotland was created and the following year a Welsh regional office was created in Aberystwyth.

The Board of Agriculture and Fisheries was not a fully-developed government department in the modern sense. Although from 1909 the Board had a Parliamentary Secretary, its political influence was limited by not having a minister of cabinet status.[6] Agriculture's political status was enhanced by the food emergency which developed during the 1914–18 war. In 1917 a separate Food Production Department was created within the Board of Agriculture and Fisheries. The Board was also given considerable powers to control cropping and stocking which it exercised through local wartime agricultural executive committees. As an incentive to increase agricultural production, the Corn Production Act of 1917 took the unprecedented step of providing farmers with guaranteed minimum prices for wheat and oats and, as a corollary, farm workers were granted minimum wage guarantees and agricultural rents were frozen. The Board of Agriculture and Fisheries thus emerged from the First World War with many additional responsibilities and a much larger staff than before. Moreover, it was now responsible for the difficult process of postwar agricultural re-adjustment. In these circumstances it was considered appropriate that the status of the Board should be raised to reflect these increased responsibilities, and in 1919 an Act was passed under which, from 1st January 1920, the Board became the Ministry of Agriculture and Fisheries under a Minister with full cabinet status.

In nineteenth-century France, agricultural policy was dominated by protection of domestic agriculture against the effects of external trade and the administration of agriculture was in the province of a department dealing with trade. However, a separate Ministry of Agriculture was created in 1881, largely for political reasons. Intense rivalry had developed between right- and left-wing political factions for the allegiance of the peasants who still represented a large proportion of the electorate. The right-wing Société des Agriculteurs de France, founded in the 1860s, encouraged the formation of peasant farmer syndicates. Although the goals of the syndicates were economic – like the formation of requisite and marketing cooperatives – rather than political, the socialists were suspicious of their political neutrality. Consequently, when the Republicans formed a new government in 1881 they not only laid the foundations of their own separate system of agricultural marketing and credit cooperatives, but also created a Ministry of Agriculture to promote and administer them. But this change did not result in any major shift in policy away from protectionism towards a more positive policy for the development and modernization of French agriculture. The Ministry of Agriculture's powers of intervention were limited by very small agricultural budgets, not only in the period leading up to the First World War but also during the 1920s and 1930s. In the aftermath of the 1914–18 war bills were adopted not only for financing the re-equipment of farms in areas devastated by war, but also for structural reform to reduce fragmentation and measures to improve and systematise agricultural education. But apart from rehabilitation of the battle areas these measures lacked teeth or adequate financing. However, some progress was made during the inter-war period with rural electrification and the improvement of water supplies, though the improvement of rural housing standards remained neglected.

A further factor mitigating against the evolution and implementation of a long-term agricultural policy in France during the period of the Third Republic was the inherent instability of the political system. Between 1881 and 1914 there were more than 40 changes of government and 19 different Ministers of Agriculture (Tracy, 1982, p. 81); the instability remained during the inter-war period.

The civil administration of the central government of Germany did not include a Ministry of Agriculture until after the First World War. Up to 1914 the administration of the federal government's agricultural policy, such as it was, remained purely with the governments of the individual states forming the Reich. During the 1914–18 war the central government set up a War Food Office to regulate food rationing. After the war this institution became the nucleus of a federal Ministry of Agriculture set up by the Weimar Republic in the 1920s. But, even after the creation of the new Ministry, the states retained their autonomy with respect to some aspects of policy such as farm consolidation and agricultural research and development. Thus, during the Weimar Republic, the Ministry of Agriculture had problems in asserting authority over the states.

By contrast, in Denmark agriculture has enjoyed a high status in government for a considerable period of time. An Agricultural Commission was set up in 1767, during the reign of Christian VII to promote peasant liberation. In 1768, the Commission became an Agricultural Department charged with the functions of collecting information and making proposals for dealing with rural problems (Skrubbeltrang, 1953, p. 30). The modern Danish Ministry of Agriculture dates from 1888.

Holland did not have a central department for the administration of agricultural affairs until 1905.[7] Rather, the government relied on ad hoc commissions for the formulation of agricultural policy. However, during the First World War extensive emergency intervention was used to regulate virtually all aspects of agriculture.

Farmer Representative Organisations and Farmer Cooperative Movements

The rise of the pluralistic state saw the growth of farmers' representative organisations and farmers' cooperative movements. These had the objectives of furthering the interests of their members by political and economic means.

Up to the end of the nineteenth century the collective voice of British agriculture was almost exclusively that of large landowners who were generously represented in both Houses of Parliament, but particularly in the House of Lords. By comparison, the views of tenant farmers and, even more so, those of hired farm workers, were not heard due to a lack of representative organisations. But the dominant position of the landowners was gradually undermined by the legislation on agricultural land tenure enacted from 1875 onwards, which greatly strengthened tenants' legal rights with respect not only to compensation for improvements and unreasonable disturbance, but also freedom of cropping. Thus, over a period of less than 80 years culminating in the Agricultural Holdings Act of 1948, landlords lost virtually all their traditional powers of controlling the farming activities of their tenants and were reduced to the status of being mere receivers of rent. In the changed situation the time was ripe for a farmers' trade union to emerge.

The first overt farmers' representative organisation to be formed was the Lincolnshire Farmers' Union established in 1908 on the initiative of a migrant Scottish farmer, Colin Campbell. Membership was restricted to tenant farmers and owner-occupiers. This association rapidly developed into the National Farmers' Union (NFU) with a branch in every county and with Campbell as its first President. The NFU grew rapidly in membership and quickly became the sole representative body speaking on behalf of British farmers. (A parallel body, the Central Landowners' Association was started at about the same time as the NFU to represent the landowning interest.) The NFU gained prominence during the 1914–18 war as the only farmers' representative organisation to which the government could turn in planning and executing its emergency food production campaign. After the war the Union was able to retain its position as the one body representative of farmers which governments could consult. No legislation affecting agriculture was passed or even drafted without first consulting the NFU (Orwin, 1949, p. 120).[8]

Britain in the nineteenth century was the home of some of the earliest examples of agricultural cooperation.[9] The first agricultural cooperative was formed in 1867,[10] but development of the cooperative movement was slow over the next 30 years: one explanation was resistance to the movement on the part of landlords. However, the agricultural depression at the end of the nineteenth century reduced tenant loyalty and created an atmosphere more favourable to cooperation (Sargent, 1982). A society (the Agricultural Organisation Society) was formed in 1900 to promote cooperation. It subsequently received subventions from government. The movement expanded rapidly between 1900 and 1920, when nearly one third of farmers in England belonged to a cooperative. But the movement declined in the 1920s, when depression in agriculture put many cooperative societies into financial difficulties. Moreover, although government exhorted the benefits of cooperation, the NFU was not disposed to promote voluntary cooperation amongst its members. Rather, farmers' leaders sought direct intervention by government on agriculture's dismal terms of trade.[11] The size and influence of the cooperative movement declined further in the 1930s when governments introduced legislation permitting the formation of Agricultural Marketing Boards.

There is a long historical tradition of regarding French agriculture as being dominated by peasant farmers. However, the peasants dominated only in the sense that they outnumbered large-scale commercial farmers and landowners; they did not dominate in an economic sense (for example in terms of production for the market), nor did they exert much political pressure, at least until the 1930s economic depression.

The first agricultural representative organisation in France was the Société des Agriculteurs de France (SAF) founded in 1868. This body was not representative of all French agriculture, including the peasantry, but rather of prominent landowners, old nobility and bourgeois estate owners. The Société had a vested interest in wheat and played a leading role in campaigning for increased agricultural protection in the 1880s and 1890s. Another ingredient of its political strategy appears to have been that of preserving the image of a single, unified peasant class whilst simultaneously discouraging the peasants from organising themselves into an effective political force. In 1884 the Republican government which had come to power a few years earlier legalised the formation of trade unions and this led to the formation of peasant farmer syndicates with the active encouragement of the SAF. But the syndicates concentrated on economic goals – like the formation of agricultural cooperatives – rather than politics. A central organisation of the farmer syndicates was founded in Paris in 1886 under the patronage of the SAF. Because Republican leaders of the centre and left suspected the political motives of the SAF in encouraging the peasants to form syndicates, they proceeded to organise their own agricultural syndicates to rival those organised by the right. Since the Republicans were in power they were able to enact, in 1890, legislation providing government subsidies for newly organised agricultural credit and mutual insurance societies.

After the First World War an umbrella organisation called the Confédération Nationale des Associations Agricoles (CNAA) was created to coordinate the activities of local agricultural syndicates and cooperatives. But this body remained weak due to professional jealousies and political rivalries. During the 1920s and 1930s the role of political lobbying for agricultural interests was assumed not by the CNAA but by special associations representing producers of particular commodities, such as wheat, wine and beet sugar. A convincing interpretation of this development is given by Wright (1964, p. 36):

> By 1930 it was clear that the specialised association was the most effective formula yet devised for attracting peasant support and lobbying in parliament. Its advantage over the syndicates was obvious: its principle of action was based on common material interest. Each association knew exactly what it wanted and could devote its full effect to formulating a precise set of demands.

The commodity associations were controlled not by the peasants but by large producers with the time, resources and training needed to organise and administer them efficiently. Large producers also stood to gain more than the peasants from favourable government concessions, such as higher protection from external competition, for the simple reason that they produced more. But to the extent that the producer associations could be successful in enlisting the support of peasant members, this was to the advantage of the large producers in representing to the government that they spoke on behalf of producers as a whole and were defending the welfare of small producers as well as their own (Wright, 1964, p. 37).

Also after the First World War new measures were adopted on the government side both to strengthen existing farm organisations and to create new ones. The major initiatives were the establishment in each department of two kinds of state agency. These were:

1. 'Offices agricoles' to promote farm trials and demonstrations. However, these were abolished in 1935 as an economy measure.
2. 'Chambres d'Agriculture', elected by the peasants to act as their official representative organs. The Chambres were empowered to discuss how agriculture might be improved and to transmit their

views to the government. They were public bodies financed by means of a supplementary land tax (Wright, 1964, p. 33).

In general, the growth of producer organisations in France especially after the First World War, enabled farmers to promote their interests through political means. However, there was little progress in economic cooperation, particularly in the field of marketing cooperation (Tracy, 1982, p. 187).

The original agricultural pressure group in Germany was the Bund der Landwirte (Farmers' League) founded by Prussian landlords in 1893. At the time of its foundation the main purpose of the Bund was to exert pressure on the government for higher agricultural protection, particularly for grain producers. Though founded by the Junkers, the Bund succeeded in enlisting the support of smaller farmers and landowners in western Germany and in becoming the main representative organisation of agriculture. The Bund acted mainly through the Conservative party by supporting candidates willing to represent its views. The Bund also inspired the formation of an economic group within the Reichstag which subsequently played a major role in the debates on commercial treaties. Non-parliamentary demonstrations and other forms of propaganda were also organised. After the First World War, the Bund amalgamated with a second farm organisation, the Deutscher Landbund, to form a new body, the Reichslandbund. This new body was, in turn, later absorbed by the Nazi-dominated 'Green Front'.

Cooperation was prominent in Germany. During the nineteenth century cooperative banks (Raiffeisen) also acted as cooperative requisite purchasers. Marketing cooperatives, particularly in dairying, were also set up. The credit cooperatives ran into difficulties during the inflationary period of the 1920s; the other cooperatives made progress.

In Denmark, there is a long history of farmer cooperation. Agricultural cooperatives formed an important channel of communication between farmers and government from the time of their establishment during the late nineteenth century. But numerous agricultural societies – mainly representatives of larger-scale farmers – and smallholder societies were also politically active. The Royal Agricultural Society (first established in 1769) was also influential in forming and expressing opinions on questions of agricultural policy.

These somewhat diverse sources of agricultural opinion were formally brought together in 1919 with the establishment of an Agricultural Council. It was intended that this body should consist of representatives from all four of the major agricultural organisations, namely the Royal Agricultural Society, the agricultural societies, the smallholder societies and the cooperative societies. However, the smallholders declined to accept their seats in the Council, preferring to exert their influence separately through their own national organisation. The Council's terms of reference included putting itself at the disposal of the government for consultation and proposing reforms. The crisis conditions of the early 1930s induced the smallholders to join forces with the Agricultural Council in advising the government on economic planning measures to meet the crisis (Skrubbeltrang, 1953, p. 242). Some new right-wing agrarian organisations emerged during the depression years but failed to survive the partial economic recovery of the late 1930s and, later, the German occupation (ibid., pp. 284, 290–1).

The cooperative movement in Denmark was also important in organising and rationalising the processing of livestock and dairy products in the late nineteenth century. The numbers of such cooperatives were large by the turn of the century, and later they were to assume a particularly important role in developing export markets for butter and bacon.

Agricultural cooperation was also important in the development of Dutch agriculture. From about 1880, agricultural and horticultural cooperatives developed autonomously without government financial support apart from tax concessions. The main developments were in cooperative credit, marketing and services. Farmers' organisations also developed from the mid to late nineteenth century. Three main organisations were established: the KNLC (Royal Dutch Agricultural Committee) founded in 1888 and non-denominational; the KNBTB (Dutch Catholic Farmers' and Growers' Union) founded in 1896, and the CBTB (Dutch Christian Farmers' and Growers' Union) founded in 1918 and Protestant. These organisations worked together particularly during the 1920s and 1930s in representing producer interests (Robinson, 1961).

Agricultural Research, Education and Technological Change

From the eighteenth century onwards, technological advance accompanied the commercialisation of agriculture which had been facilitated by the enclosure movement. Initially, both mechanical and biological/chemical innovations were developed by the industrial sector and private individuals. However, government participation in and public funding of agricultural research and education became a significant feature of agricultural policy from the late nineteenth century and early twentieth century onwards in all the countries under review except France. This investment policy laid the groundwork for significant technical progress in agriculture in later years.

Britain

There was a technological transformation (a so-called 'agricultural revolution') of British agriculture in the eighteenth and nineteenth centuries. In the early stage, individual landowners such as Jethro Tull (1674–1740), Viscount Townshend (1674–1738) and Robert Bakewell (1725–95) achieved prominence for introducing or popularising innovations in the design and use of farm machinery, in crop rotation and in livestock breeding respectively. Later on the more progressive landowners founded agricultural societies to exchange experiences and try out new methods. The Royal Agricultural Society of England was founded in 1839 and set up the Royal Agricultural College at Cirencester in 1845 to provide systematic instruction in the principles of agricultural science, as then understood, and a centre for research by the teaching staff. At about the same time a Hertfordshire landowner, John Bennet Lawes, who had trained as a chemist at University College, London, started experiments with crops and mineral fertilisers (recently invented in Germany by von Liebig) on his estate at Rothamsted. During the remainder of the nineteenth century Lawes and his colleague J.H. Gilbert, who had been a fellow student in London, established Rothamsted as a leading centre for agricultural research, not only in Britain but throughout the world. But Rothamsted received no financial support from the state during Lawes' lifetime (he died in 1900).

The technical basis for the initial transformation of agriculture in the eighteenth century was the 'Norfolk' four course rotation of turnips, barley, clover, wheat – which integrated crop and livestock production. The rotation alleviated the need to keep land idle in fallow and the turnip (a new crop) provided a winter feed which revolutionised the keeping of livestock. The main impact of the Norfolk system was to raise output per land unit whilst maintaining soil fertility. A further transformation occurred during the mid-nineteenth century (the period of 'high' farming). This was based on mechanisation of arable tasks and the use of guano (seabird manure imported from Peru) and artificial fertilisers on crops. The mechanical innovations embracing new ploughs, reaping and binding machines were a product of the industrial revolution in early Victorian England and the US and reduced labour requirements in farming.[12] Other innovations that were introduced included tile drainage and the use of the steam engine, first as a stationary and then as a mobile source of power, although a million or more working horses provided the main mobile power source for draught purposes. Progress in livestock farming occurred via selection for characteristics to produce improved breeds for meat and dairy production. The dissemination of new techniques was aided by machinery demonstrations and livestock classes at agricultural shows.

The period of high farming which came to an end around 1870 in a changing economic climate had witnessed rising output and productivity. In the eastern parts of Britain, cereal production expanded; in other areas meat and milk production rose rapidly. Productivity growth rates were higher in the period 1815–1880 than in the subsequent period 1880–1930 (Thompson, 1968).

The mechanisation of British agriculture continued after the high farming era, aided by the growth of machinery manufacturing firms in the main industrial centres. By the First World War these firms manufactured a wide range of agricultural equipment with up to 75 per cent of output going for export. However, tractors were not manufactured in Britain until the 1930s, even though the internal combustion-engined tractor was developed in the US in the 1890s. Some agricultural tractors were imported from the US into Britain after the First World War and from the mid 1920s onwards the number of horses on farms began to decline. An embryo fertiliser manufacturing industry producing phosphate fertiliser was initiated in the late nineteenth century, but nitrogen and potash fertilisers were imported. It was not until the early 1920s that the manufacture of artificial nitrogenous fertiliser began.

Whilst the private sector was an early source of agricultural innovations, it was not until the early twentieth century, that agricultural research and education was institutionalised. Britain's strong *laissez-faire* tradition meant that the state eschewed public funding of technical training and scientific research. However the Reay Committee's report of 1908 was fundamental in initiating publicly funded agricultural education. This Committee recommended a two-tier system of university teaching and research and vocational courses run by county councils. The recommendations were implemented in 1910. In the following two years a fully integrated system of agricultural education and research was inaugurated. Grants were made available for teaching, capital investment and research embracing the county councils and the universities. Research specialisation was also encouraged by setting up ten research institutes (including Rothamsted), each specialising in a particular sub-discipline of agricultural science. This structure remained substantially unchanged for many years and much of its underlying philosophy remained intact at least until the neo-liberal 'revolution' starting in the 1980s. Two further developments occurred after the First World War. First, increased funding for research was introduced in 1921 as compensation for the withdrawal of government guaranteed prices for cereals (Corn Production Acts (Repeal) Act 1921). Second, a decentralised agricultural advisory service, initiated as part of the vocational training remit of county councils, was strengthened and linked to university agricultural centres.

However, technological progress in agriculture was slow-moving between 1880 and 1931, in part because of the late establishment of public sector research and education. (See Table 2.6 for estimates of annual average rates of change in output, output per hectare and output per worker.)[13] Whilst productivity growth was slow, British agriculture was becoming slowly mechanised as machine power substituted for labour effort. The number of male workers engaged in farming fell by around 10 per cent between 1880 and 1930 and the cropland (arable plus permanent grass) area handled per worker rose at an annual average rate of around 0.29 per cent (Ruttan et al., 1978, p. 49).

France

The French experience shows some similarities with the history of technological progress in Britain. Thus Kindleberger (1964) has argued that during the eighteenth and nineteenth centuries France experienced two agricultural revolutions. The first was the product of land enclosures which made it feasible and profitable to suppress fallow and grow 'new' crops like potatoes and corn (originally imported from North America) as well as sugar beet, clover and other forage crops. This change in agricultural techniques lasted until the mid-nineteenth century. The second innovation involved the introduction and widespread adoption of mineral fertilisers, extensive land drainage and limited mechanisation. Between 1850 and 1880 wheat yields increased by some 50 per cent (Kindleberger, 1964, p. 212). Further advances took place between 1900 and 1914 relating to sugarbeet, wine, fruit, vegetables and dairy products. However, despite more favourable natural resources, output per hectare was little different from that in Britain in 1881 (see data in Ruttan et al., 1978, pp. 85–6). Moreover, given the fragmented small scale production units, the use of machines was limited in France compared to Britain: cropland area per worker and output per worker in France was about half that in Britain at this time.

There was little state intervention in France to foster agricultural education and research.[14] Moreover, relatively slow economic growth in the early twentieth century limited the growth of demand for agricultural products and rural–urban migration was slow (Ruttan et al., 1978). Between 1880 and 1930, French agriculture was largely static. (See Table 2.6 for estimates of annual average rates of change in output, output per hectare and output per worker.) By 1930, output per hectare was some 30 per cent higher but output per worker some 30 per cent lower in France compared to Britain. In short, to judge by available partial factor productivity measures, France, like Britain, experienced a slow, if somewhat higher, rate of technological progress in the period 1880–1930.

Germany

During the nineteenth century there was significant technical progress in some sections of German agriculture, particularly on the large Prussian estates. Improved crop rotation followed the gradual abandonment of the open field system. A German chemist, J. von Leibig, pioneered the development of artificial fertilisers which were widely adopted. However, the most significant innovation was the founding of the first publicly endowed agricultural research institution in the world at Mockem, Saxony in 1852. The Saxon farmers drafted a charter for the station, which the Saxon government legalised by statute, and secured an annual appropriation from the government to finance its operation (Hayami and Ruttan, 1985, p. 207). This action was a response to Leibig's initial work in 1840 on fertilisers and provided a model for 'the application of science to agriculture'. Further specialist institutions were subsequently set up leading to an expansion of research in other directions. The development of a publicly funded agricultural research system was in keeping with the social and political climate of the time: science and technology were regarded as instruments of economic growth and the funding of science was regarded as the responsibility of government. Subsequently, of course, this became conventional wisdom across the western world.

During the second half of the nineteenth century considerable development of agricultural education occurred at different levels extending from universities to full time agricultural schools and part-time 'winter schools'. These schools also undertook farm advisory work. The adoption of new technology was also facilitated by the producer cooperatives formed during the nineteenth century.

In 1880 output per hectare in Germany was slightly above that in Britain and France, output per worker and land per worker similar to that in France and near to half that in Britain. However, over the next 50 years there was substantial land augmenting technical change in Germany in contrast to France and Britain (see Table 2.6 for estimates of annual average rates of change in output, output per hectare and output per worker). However, land area per worker hardly changed, implying limited mechanisation. Thus Germany experienced reasonable biological technical progress over the period resulting in part from the institutionalisation of agricultural research inaugurated in the mid-nineteenth century.

Denmark

In Denmark there was substantial government encouragement of agricultural education and research in the nineteenth century. Farmer support for and interest in research was first channelled through the Royal Agricultural Society established in 1769. From its foundation the Society sought to promote the economic and technical development of agriculture by awarding prizes for both theoretical and practical work. It was also active in promoting improvements in peasants' economic and social welfare. From 1857 the Society organised laboratory work of interest to farmers and later embarked upon providing an agricultural advisory service: it also encouraged the formation of local agricultural associations. The Society played a leading role in persuading the state to establish in 1858 the Royal Veterinary and Agricultural College (under an enabling law passed in 1856) to provide university level teaching and research in all fields of agriculture.

Denmark adopted compulsory education for children between the ages of 6 to 14 years from as early as 1814. The Folk High Schools, providing further education for students of 18 and over with emphasis on technical subjects, were started during the 1840s. The courses were not free but government grants were provided to subsidise attendance by poor students. The Folk High Schools and agricultural colleges increased rapidly both in number and in terms of student enrolment.

During the latter part of the nineteenth century and the first quarter of this century, Danish agriculture shifted its product mix from cereals to livestock products, particularly butter and bacon. A number of technological advances facilitated the transformation of Danish agriculture. These included tile drainage, increases in the application of fertiliser and lime, and improvements in seed and livestock varieties. The innovations that were most crucial to the agricultural transformation were the invention and diffusion of the cream separator and the cooperative creamery system (Hayami and Ruttan, 1985, p. 431). The cream separator was developed under patents in the late 1870s. The potential of the separator was exploited by the cooperative creamery. The skim by-product from separation provided a cheap feed for pigs and the basis for the Danish bacon export industry.

In 1880, agricultural output per worker and per hectare of land was comparable with that of France and Germany. However, over the next 50 years Denmark enjoyed much higher rates of growth in output and land and labour productivity (see Table 2.6 for estimates of annual average rates of change in output, output per hectare and output per worker). Land area per worker declined slightly, reflecting the shift in the product mix with livestock production being much more labour intensive than cereals production. In contrast to Britain, France and Germany, the farm labour force rose over the period rather than declining.

As Hayami and Ruttan (1985, p. 432) comment: 'the Danish experience demonstrates the critical role of technical and institutional innovations for agricultural transformation'.

Holland

Publicly funded agricultural research and education were major elements of Dutch agricultural policy dating from the 1870s. The first state agricultural school was established at Wageningen in 1876 to promote agricultural education, extension and research. In 1906 the school was upgraded and expanded to encompass horticulture and forestry, and in 1918 it was granted university status. The school also included an experimental station. By the end of the nineteenth century a further five experimental stations had been set up. Thereafter the scope and specialisation of agricultural research widened considerably. A state extension service was developed alongside agricultural education.

A data series on output growth and partial productivity indices for Holland comparable to that in Ruttan et al. (1978) for the other countries is not available. However, estimates based upon data in van der Meer and Yamada (1986) suggest that for the period 1880–1929, annual average rates of growth for output (measured as Gross Value Added), for output per hectare and for output per worker were relatively high (as shown in Table 2.6). Land area per worker showed no discernible change over the period. The labour force in agriculture rose over the period.

Summary on technological change and productivity growth[15]

Following the enclosure movement and the switch to commercialised farming, land productivity increased in Western Europe as the open field system, which included fallow in rotation, was replaced by more labour-intensive techniques with the fallow replaced by legumes, potatoes and root crops. The increased fertility of the soil resulting from nitrogen fixed by legumes and manure from integrated crop–livestock farm systems led to increases in productivity. From around 1750 to about 1870–80, agriculture in the five countries displayed this pattern of agricultural growth.

By 1870, the countries were still predominantly agricultural; only in

Britain and Holland was less than 50 per cent of the workforce employed outside agriculture. The efficiency of agricultural production was highest in Britain, Denmark and Holland with Britain and Denmark excelling in labour productivity and Holland (and Belgium) in land productivity (van Zanden, 1985, pp. 9–10). French and German agriculture was less efficient. Livestock farming was more important in Holland (64 per cent of gross output) and Denmark (48 per cent of gross output) than in the other countries (for example, livestock production was only 30 per cent of gross output in France).

New inputs were being gradually introduced into agriculture in the nineteenth century. British (and Belgian) farmers had begun to adopt fertilisers; Dutch and British farmers were importing maize and oilseed cakes for feeding to livestock and British farmers were beginning to use machinery. However, after 1870–80, there was an acceleration in the use of new inputs, particularly those that saved land. 'Foremost was the spread of the use of chemical fertilisers, which resulted from a massive increase in the supply of these fertilisers . . . fertiliser prices fell dramatically in the years after 1880' (van Zanden, 1988, p. 21).[16] Fertiliser use was also facilitated by the development and adoption of new seeds, responsive to fertiliser application, particularly in Germany and Holland (see Table 2.4).

Table 2.4   Application of fertiliser in Western Europe, 1880–1930 (kg/ ha agricultural land)

Year	Fertiliser type	UK	France	Germany	Denmark	Holland
1880	Unspecified	7	2	4	1	1
1910	N + P205 + K20	11	11	29	11	36
1930	N + P205 + K20	12	22	50*	38	55*

Note: *Estimate derived from fertiliser data in International Yearbook of Agricultural Statistics (1930–31) and land area in Ruttan et al. (1978) and van der Meer and Yamada (1986).

Sources: Van Zanden (1988, Tables 4 and 8); Wade (1973, Appendices); *International Yearbook of Agricultural Statistics* (1930–31).

The second important land saving input was concentrated feed for livestock. Maize was imported from the US and oilseed cakes were based on imports of tropical oilseed. The prices of maize and oilseeds fell sharply after 1880. Livestock farming based on these inputs became more land intensive as they were used as substitutes for fodder. New cattle breeds were also developed; livestock productivity increased in Denmark and Holland in particular.

An indication of the impact of biological technological change is given in Table 2.5 which summarises data on wheat and dairy cow yields.

Table 2.5   Wheat and milk yields in Western Europe, 1880–1930

	UK	France	Germany	Denmark	Holland
Wheat yields[a] (tonnes per ha)					
1880	1.8	1.1	1.4	2.4	1.8
1910	2.2	1.1	2.3	3.0	2.4
1930	2.2	1.5	2.1	3.0	3.0
Milk yields[b] (tonnes per cow)					
1880	1.7	1.6	1.7[c]	1.6	n.a.
1910	1.9	n.a	n.a	2.8	n.a
1930	2.0	1.8	2.5[d]	3.3	3.5[d]

Notes
a   Five year average.
b   single year.
c   1890–1900.
d   1934–38 average.

Sources: Wade (1973, Appendices); Tracy (1982); Clark (1960).

Labour-saving technology was slower to be developed, the major constraint being the supply of motive power: horses were not to be replaced by tractors until the 1920s onwards. The main mechanical innovation was the centrifugal cream separator which was adopted rapidly in Denmark, Holland, Germany and France.

Between 1880 and 1930, Denmark, Germany and Holland experienced relatively high rates of growth in agricultural output and productivity, whilst farming in France and the UK showed a poorer productivity record (Table 2.6). In 1880, the UK was to the forefront of agricultural productivity; but subsequently fell behind. In contrast, Germany, starting from a low base, moved forward rapidly. Overall, technological change was largely land saving rather than labour saving.

It would appear that Britain and France lagged behind because they did not adopt the new land saving inputs. A contributory factor to the relative slowness of technological change in these two countries was that they were late in setting up nationwide agriculture research and extension services.[17]

Table 2.6   Agricultural productivity in Western Europe, 1880–1930 (annual average percentage rates of change)

	UK	France	Germany	Denmark	Holland
Agricultural output*	0.21	0.76	1.31	2.07	1.50
Output per hectare	0.14	0.70	1.37	1.83	1.30
Output per worker	0.43	1.16	1.42	1.66	1.20
Land per worker	0.29	0.47	0.04	–0.17	–

Note: *In wheat units except for Holland (real gross value added). One wheat unit equals one tonne of wheat valued at some statistically derived 'representative price'. For the purpose of aggregation across commodities, both wheat and non-wheat, the output of wheat valued in wheat units, is combined with a derived value of other commodities using 'wheat relative prices' as weights. In this way aggregate output of all commodities may be expressed in wheat units. For more detail see Binswanger and Ruttan (1978, App. 3–2, p. 81, notes to Tables 3–11 to 3–16).

Sources: Ruttan et al. (1978); van de Meer and Yamada (1986).

Trade Policy and Market Intervention

Pre 1914

From medieval times through to the mid 1850s, various governments in Western Europe used trade taxes and export bounties as well as regulatory devices to modify the grain trade between their countries. This intervention was mainly for stabilisation purposes but also to give protection, particularly toward the end of the period. The longest and best established grain trade policy was the English Corn Laws dating from the mid-fifteenth century until 1846. Protection against imports under the Corn Laws from 1660 onwards was by means of sliding scale duties: the import tariff was inversely related to the domestic price level. After the repeal of the Corn Laws there was a brief period of free, or nearly free, trade in grain and other products between most European countries. However, from the 1870s onwards cheap grain, principally from the USA but also from Russia, was imported into Europe. Technological change in shipping led to a drastic reduction in transatlantic freight costs and internal transport costs fell within the USA. Grain output expanded in the USA as the land frontier was pushed westwards. These developments drastically reduced natural protection for grain in Europe: for example, the c.i.f. prices of US imports into England through Liverpool halved between the early 1870s and the turn of the century. Competition from imports, coupled with a general economic recession in Europe retarding the growth in demand for agricultural products, led to an agricultural depression between 1870 and the late 1890s. Grain prices recovered from the turn of the century onwards as US export prices rose under a tightening internal supply/demand balance.

Livestock products also felt competition from imports from outside Europe after the mid 1870s as the US and Australia began to export meat and dairy products following the invention and commercial application of the technique of refrigeration. However, prices of livestock products did not fall to the same extent as those of grains: imports did not augment supply to the same degree as with grains whilst a gradual improvement in urban incomes was increasing the demand for livestock products. As a consequence, arable farmers were much more severely affected by the competition from the New World than livestock farmers who derived some benefit from the falling price of grain.

Policy responses to this new situation differed greatly between the European nations. Britain had a comparative advantage in industrial production and cheap food was in the interests of the manufacturing class in keeping down wage costs. These trends reinforced liberal economic attitudes and agriculture suffered from benign neglect under *laissez-faire*. In contrast, the response of Germany and France was protectionist.

British agriculture endured a 'Great Depression' between 1875 to 1895, particularly in arable areas where farmers experienced a cost–price squeeze as the price of inputs such as fertilisers and machinery failed to fall with cereal prices. Although livestock farmers derived some benefit from falling grain prices they did not entirely escape the effects of the depression. Successive governments adhered to the policy of *laissez-faire*, and apart from minor subventions and concessions there was virtually no government intervention on behalf of agriculture between 1846 and the outbreak of the First World War. The effect of exposing British agriculture to the forces of competition was that, by the years 1909–13, more than half the cereals and a third of the carcass meat consumed were imported. Self-sufficiency ratios were also low for bacon and ham, lard and dairy products. Only fresh milk enjoyed the full benefit of natural protection, although being jointly produced with milk sold for manufacture its price was affected by the prices of cheap dairy products (Whetham, 1978, p. 15).

In the recession of the 1870s and 1880s, German industrialists combined with the Junkers in seeking and obtaining protection for both manufactured and agricultural products. Later in the 1890s, tariff rates were reduced and policy was reoriented towards trade expansion (Hayami and Ruttan, 1985, p. 370).[18] Prior to 1870, Germany had been a net exporter of wheat. Thereafter she became a net importer and this trend was enhanced during the 1890s by the introduction of a system of import certificates. Because Prussian wheat was of relatively low quality it had long been the practice to import higher quality wheat to be mixed with domestically produced grain. Although part of the imported grain was re-exported much of it was absorbed by the domestic market (mixed with German grain in both cases). The ostensible purpose of the import certificate system introduced in 1894 was to encourage the admixture of domestic and foreign grain, in order to enhance grain exports. The system entitled grain exporters to obtain exemption from paying duty on grain imports. An exporter's entitlement to import certificates depended directly on the amount of his exports. The certificates were negotiable and could be sold for their face value – the amount of the import duty – less a small deduction for interest and transfer costs. The exporter's total return, therefore, consisted of the export price plus an amount equivalent to most of the duty. The incentive to export remained provided this total return exceeded the domestic grain price. In effect, the value of the import certificate represented an export subsidy. But it also encouraged grain imports. Grain exports from east Germany in fact expanded considerably following the introduction of the system and the domestic price rose above the world price level by approximately the amount of the duty. The system remained in use until the outbreak of the First World War and was revived under the Weimar Republic from 1925 until 1930.[19]

Despite some recovery of world agricultural markets at the turn of the century, the political climate became more favourable to higher agricultural protection as German foreign policy shifted to re-armament and reduced reliance on imports of all strategic goods including food. A new tariff, enacted in 1902, established maximum and minimum rates for grains, but only maximum rates for livestock products. The minimum rates for grain limited the government's ability to make concessions on agriculture in negotiating commercial treaties. Although livestock products were not protected by minimum rates of duty, they were protected in other ways such as sanitary regulations legalised in the 1880s.

The relatively high level of agricultural protection established in Germany at the turn of the century remained intact until the First World War.[20] But despite protection and a relatively high rate of agricultural growth, Germany failed to achieve the objective of agricultural self-sufficiency: when war broke out about one-third of total foodstuffs were still being imported.

A protectionist revival also took place in France during the last quarter of the nineteenth century. This was sparked off mainly by political developments. Nationalist sentiment was fuelled by France's defeat in the Franco-Prussian War in 1870. The monarchy was abolished the same year and the Republicans, who were naturally opposed to the actions of the previous monarchist regime which had encouraged trade liberalisation, held a parliamentary majority from 1879. Higher tariffs on imported manufactured goods were re-imposed in 1881 following a campaign for higher protection by industrialists. Following political pressure from agricultural interests for equality of protection with industry, substantial duty increases were eventually granted on imported livestock and livestock products. But duties on imported cereals remained low (wheat) or zero (other grains).

After 1881, following a succession of bad harvests (as also occurred in Britain) and a growing volume of cheap imports, French agriculturalists, supported by industrialists, intensified their campaign for higher protection. Substantial increases in the duties on wheat, other grains and livestock were eventually granted, first in 1885 and again in 1887. The level of protection was substantially raised, yet again, with the enactment of the so-called Méline Tariff of 1892. Jules Méline, the principal architect and promoter of the 1892 tariff bill, who also piloted it through parliament, was a former Minister of Agriculture, and president both of an all-party parliamentary agricultural group and a special tariff commission appointed to examine the 'tariff question'. Méline campaigned for agriculture and industry to have equality of tariff protection. The new tariff code achieved this but also raised duties considerably on both agricultural and industrial products. As a consequence of the Méline tariff France became one of the most highly protected economies in the world with the exception of Russia and the USA. A notable feature of the new French tariff was that it incorporated a combination of general and minimum rates of duty which limited the freedom of governments to reduce duties by entering into commercial treaties.

Despite the 1892 tariff law, French imports of agricultural products continued to increase, and agriculture entered a further period of depression. The duty on wheat was raised yet again in 1894: duties on livestock followed suit in 1903. Delays in obtaining parliamentary approval for tariff increases became a contentious issue, but in 1897 a law (loi de cadenas) was passed empowering the government to raise duties on major agricultural products without parliament's prior consent (though retrospective consent was still needed). The agricultural situation improved somewhat after 1900, but, in general, the high agricultural duties brought in during the 1890s remained intact up to the outbreak of the First World War.

Denmark and Holland were established agricultural exporting countries in the nineteenth century. They both adopted similar policy stances in the face of foreign competition. These encompassed (a) increasing the production of livestock products using cheap grain imports,[21] and emphasising horticultural products as well in the case of Holland; (b) improving the productivity of agriculture through research and cooperative marketing; (c) standardising products for export and raising quality. Both countries adhered to an open trading policy: restructuring and raising efficiency were favoured rather than erecting barriers to trade as the answer to low-price foreign competition. Exports of livestock products were advantageous on at least three counts. First, production could be based on cheap cereal foodstuffs in the case of Danish and Dutch dairy products and dairy by-products in the case of Danish bacon. Second, because the export products of Denmark and Holland were perishable they enjoyed a transport cost advantage in the European market. Third, the prospective demand for livestock products was better due to the combination of rising per capita incomes and higher income elasticity.

There is a paucity of reliable factual data on European levels of agricultural protection before 1914. However, one estimate of average tariff levels across a sample of 38 different food stuffs, relating to the year 1913, suggested that in France and Germany levels of protection ranged between 20 and 30 per cent above export prices (Tracy, 1989, pp. 22–3 quoting Liepmann, 1938).[22] In contrast to France and Germany, the levels of protection prevailing in *laissez-faire* Britain and net exporting Denmark and Holland were, by definition, negligible.

The First World War and its aftermath

During the First World War, the governments of the main protagonists, Britain, France and Germany, took emergency measures to deal with food shortages and to control food distribution. Denmark and Holland were neutral but cut off from most of their trading links: extensive emergency government regulation of agriculture was undertaken in these countries also. After the war, governments gradually readopted their traditional policy stances; the UK, Denmark and Holland became liberal free traders again whilst France and Germany resorted to tariff protection. However, agricultural prices collapsed in Western Europe in 1929 and extensive intervention into agricultural markets subsequently became the 'norm' in all countries. Here we briefly summarise policy up to 1929.

Britain   When the First World War broke out Britain was a substantial importer of food and also of livestock feedingstuffs. However, although it was recognised that food shortages, particularly of bread, might arise if the war was prolonged, no special measures were taken to increase domestic production until the closing stages of the war. Specifically, in 1917, by which time shipping losses from submarine warfare had become very serious, the Corn Production Act was passed. This Act specified annual minimum guaranteed prices for wheat and oats: the difference between these prices and market prices (if lower) was to be made up by government payments.[23] As a counterpart to the minimum price guarantee, farm workers were guaranteed minimum wages and agricultural landlords were prevented from raising rents. The Act also gave authority to the Board of Agriculture, working through County Executive Committees, to compel farmers to plough up grassland in order to increase the production of wheat and other arable crops.

The average market price of wheat and oats remained above the guaranteed minimum for the remainder of the war. Consequently, the deficiency payment machinery authorised in 1917 was never called into action. When the war ended the government had to formulate its agricultural policy and appointed a Royal Commission to make recommendations. On the strength of the Commission's advice, the government decided to retain minimum guaranteed prices for wheat and oats but, in order to provide flexibility, to base these on average costs of production. This provision was included in the Agriculture Act, 1920. However, the currency of the 1920 Act was very brief as world cereal prices started collapsing almost immediately after it had been passed. The government was so intimidated by estimates of the costs of meeting its cereal price guarantees that it decided to repeal the relevant sections of the 1920 Act. The Corn Production Acts (Repeal) Act of 1921 achieved notoriety as the 'great betrayal' of British agriculture.[24] Minimum agricultural wage guarantees were also abandoned by the 1921 Act.

During the 1920s, British farmers

> were at the mercy of a capricious market. As a result of many years of free trade and her special relationship with the predominantly agricultural Dominions, Britain had become increasingly dependent on imports of agricultural products. Consequently, British farm prices for many products were determined to a large extent by the decisions of foreign producers and foreign governments. (Currie and Rayner, 1979, p. 22)

But the expansion of overseas production, improved international transport facilities and a greater willingness on the part of overseas farmers to improve the marketing, distribution and presentation of their produce, all tended to reduce the competitiveness of British agriculture. The state of the industry was one of almost continual depression throughout the 1920s, as the general level of farm prices exhibited a downward trend, But it was not until 1929 when the situation reached critical proportions that the stance of government policy changed.

The state of government thinking on agricultural policy in the 1920s was revealed by a White Paper published in 1926[25] which expressed strong opposition to agricultural protection either in the form of grain import duties or any kind of production subsidy. The strategic argument for encouraging farmers to produce more in peace-time than could be justified by current market conditions was firmly rejected. Whilst a general attitude of *laissez-faire* prevailed, the British government did make some exceptions in the 1920s. These were:

1. Special measures to foster the development of an indigenous sugar beet industry. The British Sugar Subsidy Act of 1925 provided a sugar beet subsidy (payable to factories) over a period of ten years, as well as capital grants. In addition, farmers were guaranteed a minimum price for beet. By the end of the 1920s, 18 factories were operating.
2. The de-rating of farm buildings and farm land: a concession essentially to landowners rather than farmers *per se*.
3. The promotion of voluntary marketing reform. It was felt that marketing margins were excessive and 'that the farming community could be assisted without any significant burden falling on either the consumers of agricultural products or the exchequer' (Currie and Rayner, 1979, p. 23). Essentially, the government tried to promote, (a) the grading and standardisation of domestic production so enabling British farmers to compete more effectively with their foreign counterparts, and (b) the encouragement of voluntary cooperation which would increase farmers' bargaining power and raise their 'marketing sense'. The policy of voluntary marketing reform was unsuccessful but the policy stance was reinforced with the introduction of marketing board legislation in the early 1930s.

France and Germany   French agriculture was severely hit by the 1914–18 war due to physical destruction in battle areas and shortages of manpower and other resources. Duties on major foodstuffs were suspended for the duration and imports rose dramatically. The state assumed responsibility for purchasing and distributing food. After the war, the food shortage continued for some time and the protection of agriculture was restored only by degrees, but by the mid 1920s the political pressure generated by an agricultural cost–price squeeze was sufficient to induce the governments to raise tariffs on most agricultural products. The traditional policy stance was restored.

Germany, likewise, experienced severe food shortages and rationing during the war. Price controls lasted from 1916 until the early postwar years. Commitments imposed in the Treaty of Versailles mitigated against a restoration of tariffs. However, tariff protection was reintroduced in 1929 after a vigorous debate between left-wing politicians and parties representing the peasants (against import duties on grains) and right-wing conservatives representing large landowners (in favour of protection). At the same time, the pre-war grain import certificate scheme was revived. By 1929, tariffs were back to pre-war levels. However, production levels did not fully recover.

Denmark and Holland   With the cutting off of trading links during the war, Denmark and Holland reduced the livestock sector and increased the production of wheat and potatoes in order to ensure food sufficiency. However, after the war and the resumption of normal trade, there was a switch back to producing livestock products for export. Agricultural trade in volume and value terms increased in the early 1920s, but then began decreasing. As this turned into a slump in the early 1930s, non-intervention was abandoned and producer support measures were introduced.

Matching the lack of reliable factual data on European levels of agricultural protection before the First World War there is a similar paucity of data relating to the postwar period. However, estimates made by Liepmann (1938) and quoted by Tracy (1989), pp. 122–3, suggest that between 1927 and 1931 average levels of protection had risen from the pre-war range of 20–30 per cent of export prices to around 50 per cent in France and as much as 80 per cent in Germany. Although Britain, Denmark and Holland also resorted to protection in the early 1930s, no comparable estimates of average levels of protection are available for these countries.

US POLICY TO 1933

Introduction

In the nineteenth century, the interior of the USA was gradually settled from the east to the west by pioneer farmers. Simultaneously with growth in the economy and the extension of inter-state and rural transport links, subsistence farm households became elementary firms selling surplus produce to local towns and urban areas. By the turn of the century, the land frontier was closed and agriculture was largely commercialised.[26] The fortunes of farmers were dependent upon the state of the market as well as their hard work and technical skills. Over the period from the year of independence (1776) to the early 1930s, farms were transformed from subsistence units into businesses integrated into the economy. The shift from self-sufficient to commercial agriculture is indicated by the decline in the proportion of the population engaged in agriculture. At the time of the first census in 1790, more than 94 per cent of the population was classified as rural (Benedict, 1953, p. 87). By 1933 only 25 per cent of the population derived their livelihood directly from agriculture (Penn, 1984, p. 573).

Agricultural policy over much of this period assisted the development of a free market farm sector. Thus major policy initiatives concerned land settlement and the establishment of a freehold land tenure system, reform of the agricultural credit system, the setting up of an agricultural research and extension system and the improvement of farmers' technical education. However, with the onset of an agricultural recession in the 1920s, pressures arose for active government intervention into commodity markets. The Great Depression of 1929–33 intensified these pressures: domestic deflation and slack export demand led to depressed commodity prices and low resource returns in agriculture. By 1933, the incomes of farm people were scarcely 40 per cent of those in the non-farm sector,[27] farms were 'mostly small and mostly poor' (Lee, 1981, p. 136). A consequence of the severe agricultural recession was that 'farm problems got on the Nation's policy agenda because dissatisfied farmers put them there' (Brandow, 1977, p. 212). As part of President Roosevelt's New Deal of 1933, there was a decisive break in policy: an attitude of *laissez-faire* toward the major agricultural markets was supplanted by government management. The 1933 Agricultural Adjustment Act (AAA), enacted within the first 100 days of Roosevelt's Presidency, established a framework for agricultural policy which persisted until the 1990s.

Property Rights, Land Settlement and Farm Structure

Although during the initial colonisation of America, some land settlements were based upon a communal system, private land ownership soon became the dominant mode for the organisation of agriculture. 'When the colonies declared their independence of the mother country in 1776, colonial farmers had established the rights to alienate and inherit land ... the land owner had basically acquired the right to use land as he saw fit with few restrictions and controls by the government' (Anderson and Hill, 1976, p. 939). The right to private property was embodied in the Constitution[28] and the principle of private property became firmly established in the legal and economic system.

The major concern of agricultural policy in the post independence period was the disposal to farmers of the very large area of land held in the public domain. The American revolution transferred property rights over land from the British Crown and a number of noblemen to the new Eastern states. These states subsequently ceded their land titles to the Federal government whilst new lands were gradually acquired under the national public domain through treaties and settlement with and annexation from other countries. The emphasis of land disposal policy was on the rapid settlement of farmers with land held under private property rights. The major controversy concerned the methods of transfer of the public domain lands into private ownership.

The first major land act was the Ordinance of 1785 which provided for the sale of federal land at public auction in minimum lot sizes of a section of land (640 acres) on strictly cash terms. A reserve price was set at $1.00 per acre. The next Land Act, that of 1796 relating to the North-West Territory, made similar provisions except that the reserve price was set at $2.00 per acre and the purchaser was given a year to pay. The terms for land purchase were, however, outwith the resources of the majority of the pioneer farmers. Land-hungry settlers pressed for sale in small parcels and on easier terms, and for squatter rights. Subsequent Land Acts made concessions in these directions. The Land Act of 1800 allowed sale in half section (320 acre) lots, and included a credit provision allowing the purchaser four years to pay. In the Act passed in 1804 the minimum lot size was further reduced to a quarter section (160 acres), the previous credit provision was retained and the minimum price reduced to $1.64 per acre. The next important Land Act, that of 1820, provided for the sale of public domain land in half and quarter sections at public auction at a minimum price of $1.25 per acre. Private sale was also permitted with a minimum size of 80 acres. The credit provisions of previous Acts were abolished, however, in an attempt to curb land speculation which was prevalent at that time.

The Land Act of 1820 had a stimulating effect on land sales from the public domain, albeit more in the 1830s than in the 1820s. However, neither this Act, nor its predecessors, dealt with the problem of settler-squatters. Heavy migration to the West in the 1830s increased demands for pre-emptive rights. Five laws were passed between 1830 and 1840 giving squatters retrospective rights: if they were already settled on public land, they had the right to purchase it at the minimum price. The Pre-emption Act of 1841 increased these rights: a pioneer was allowed to settle legally on public land and he then had the pre-emptive right to buy a section at the minimum price when land in that area was put up for sale. Finally under the Homestead Act of 1862, free access to public land was granted. Specifically, the Act gave the settler a fee simple title to a section after five years of consecutive residence.[29] By about 1890, there was little good land remaining to be settled: the land frontier was virtually closed. Indeed subsequent policy toward remaining public domain land was concerned with conservation rather than settlement.[30]

The method of disposal of public domain land from 1783 onwards was conducive to the economic development of the USA in the nineteenth century in at least two ways.[31] First, the revenue from disposal was used to fund public education and the building of transport infrastructure was supported by granting public land to public and private transport agencies. Second, the agricultural land resource was eventually settled by family operated freehold farms on units (typically a quarter section) appropriate to the general farming conditions (particularly in the humid areas) of the USA. Land was fairly equitably distributed so avoiding large estates[32] but in units precluding tiny peasant holdings. The typical farm was both efficient in relation to resource constraints[33] and productive in that the owner had the incentives to reap the rewards from his effort.[34] Land settlement on a large number of freehold units was also important in establishing the democratic base of the market economy.

Agriculture's Official Status in Government

The United States Department of Agriculture (USDA) was established in 1862 during the Presidency of Abraham Lincoln. Initially, the USDA was headed by a commissioner without full cabinet status. However, in 1889, the position of head of the USDA was upgraded to Secretary of Agriculture with cabinet status. The initial functions of the USDA were concerned with collecting and publishing statistics, introducing new plants and animals, testing agricultural implements, and initiating, conducting and funding practical and scientific research. The last function became increasingly important, and by the beginning of the twentieth century the USDA had established Bureaux of Plant Industry, Animal Industry, Entomology, Soils, Biological Survey and Weather. In 1922, a Bureau of Agricultural Economics was set up. Basically in the years to

1933, the USDA was 'primarily a fact-finding research and science-producing institution' (Cochrane, 1979, p. 105).

The size of the USDA and its capacity for administration, regulation and control grew during the First World War and the subsequent decade. The number of employees rose from just under 10 000 in 1900 to 20 000 in the early 1920s and 33 000 by 1933.[35]

Farmer Representative Organisations

During the final quarter of the nineteenth century, US farmers began to organise and act collectively in business and politics. This was a period of 'hard times' for US agriculture (Cochrane, 1979, p. 93). In addition, farmers were concerned over what they perceived as high marketing margins stemming from a concentration of power in railroad transportation and grain storage. Agrarian protest movements demanded that 'something be done' to stabilise and improve farm incomes. They also strove to obtain a 'fair share' of the marketing margin via cooperation.

The most important farm organisations during this period were the Grange and the Farmers' Alliances. The National Order of the Patrons of Husbandry, better known as the Grange, and founded by O.H. Kelley in 1867, was primarily concerned in its early days with the public regulation of railroads to lower freight rates. The Grangers were later involved with getting the US Department of Agriculture raised to Cabinet status as well as with the establishment of state agricultural experiment stations (under the Hatch Act of 1887). Many other farm organisations sprang up during the last quarter of the nineteenth century, including the Farmers' Alliance which helped to form the Populist party which in turn attempted to form a united front of farmers and organised labour in other industries. However, the Populists were unsuccessful electorally in 1892 and the Alliance movement went down with the disbandment of the party. At the end of the century, the Grange was the only farm organisation to have survived on a significant scale.

The next major farm organisation to emerge was the Farmers' Union which started in Texas in 1902. By 1907 its membership had expanded to around one million farmers, mainly in the South. The main emphasis was on cooperation, including attempts to raise prices directly by holding farm products off the market. This policy was unsuccessful and was eventually abandoned. However, the Farmers' Union remained as a significant force in agricultural politics.

A new type of general farm organisation developed from the county farm bureaux set up to administer the agricultural extension programme authorised by the Smith-Lever Act of 1913. It was not the original intention that farm bureaux should concern themselves with business and politics. Rather their sole function was seen to be the provision of farmer education and farm demonstrations. But in the event farmer clients of the bureaux pressed for them to assume pressure group functions as well. The county farm bureaux soon formed themselves into state federations and, in 1920, a national Farm Bureau Federation was formed to promote the economic and legislative interests of farmers. In the adverse economic conditions following the First World War the Federation's national membership grew rapidly, particularly amongst better educated and more commercially minded farmers: its stance was middle-class, progressive and mildly conservative (Benedict, 1953, p. 178).

The Grange also became more active after the First World War. Both it and the Farmers' Union were jealous of the prominence achieved by the Farm Bureau movement and critical of its activities. In particular, the rival organisations criticised the Farm Bureau for its close relations with the extension service and the agricultural colleges, who they saw as being the protégés of 'big business'. However, the Farm Bureau continued to attract the support of many farmers due to 'a widespread feeling that agriculture was entitled to a more effective voice in national affairs and [that] the Farm Bureau was particularly well equipped to exploit that interest' (Benedict, 1953, p. 191).

In the middle and late 1920s, the Farm Bureau was broadly supportive of the abortive McNary-Haugen plan for supporting producer prices of exportable farm products by means of an administered 2-tier price system involving an export subsidy or 'equalisation fee'. When the Great Depression struck, the Farm Bureau and other farm organisations supported the raising of tariffs; indeed, they criticised the tariff increases authorised by the Hawley–Smoot Act of 1930 for not going far enough to protect agriculture (Benedict, 1953, p. 269).

Farmer Cooperation

State laws covering the establishment and operation of cooperative business organisations were legislated from the beginning of the twentieth century. Most, though not all, such laws were based on 'Rochdale principles', notwithstanding the fact that these were devised for consumer cooperatives. Most of the early farmer cooperatives in the US were small-scale and confined to local activities such as cooperative grain elevators, creameries and cheese factories. But a few, such as the California Fruit Growers Exchange, founded in 1895, successfully entered major central markets (Benedict, 1953, p. 136).

The period from 1900 to 1915 was one of relative prosperity for US agriculture. This reduced the incentive for farmers to engage in collective action (Anderson and Hill, 1976). However, substantial numbers of local farm cooperative ventures, with a focus on marketing members' produce, had been successfully established during this period. But with the sharp reversal of farm fortunes following the First World War there was a marked revival of interest in collective action in the early 1920s. 'Farmers wanted more from their cooperative marketing associations. Orderly marketing became a popular slogan' (Cochrane, 1979, p. 114). There was also a revival of interest in establishing nationwide associations to exert monopoly power.

The main government response to the renewed interest in cooperative collective action was the enactment of the Capper–Volstead Cooperative Marketing Act of 1922. This tightened the legal definition of the cooperative association but also exempted cooperatives from anti-trust laws as well as providing them with income tax privileges.

Much of the impetus for the revival of interest in cooperatives attempting to exert monopoly marketing power came from the 'Sapiro movement' of the early 1920s.[36] Although Sapiro's grandiose plans for farmer cooperatives to transform themselves into monopoly buying and selling organisations in central markets were a failure, the idea of pushing cooperative marketing beyond the local level to more distant markets persisted.

Agricultural Research, Education, Credit and Technological Change

Farm mechanisation

Between 1820 and 1920, 'the process of farm mechanisation was the principal, almost the exclusive, form of farm technological advance' (Cochrane, 1979, p. 200). This process was sourced by the private 'industrial' sector of the economy. From the years immediately after independence until the closing of the land frontier, US agriculture was land abundant and labour scarce. Machines relieved the labour constraint by substituting horse power for human energy. The period 1820–50 saw the invention and innovation of machines that facilitated the preparation of seed beds and the harvesting of grains;[37] widespread diffusion occurred in the period following the Civil War. The mechanical 'revolution' greatly facilitated an increase in area cultivated per worker or, equivalently, a reduction in labour hours per acre.[38] Technological change then had a machinery-using and labour-saving bias. The new machines were supplied by the manufacturing sector; incentives to the invention and mass production and distribution of the new technology were provided by the patent system.[39]

A second wave of mechanisation occurred after 1910 based on the invention in the late nineteenth century of the farm tractor. The assembly line production of the tractor was in being by 1920; farmer adoption was rapid thereafter (1000 tractors on farms in 1910, 246 000 in 1920, 1 million in 1930). Tractor-based mechanical power displaced horses and released land.[40] USDA indices suggest that the mechanical power and machinery input on farms increased by some 25 per cent whilst labour input declined by 5 per cent between 1920 and 1930 (Penn, 1981, p. 39). Labour productivity increased by about 1.4 per cent per annum over this period.[41]

Over the period 1870 to 1930, the substitution of capital for labour is reflected in a declining proportion of total inputs contributed by labour and a rising proportion contributed by capital. In 1870, labour represented 65 per cent, land 18 per cent and capital 27 per cent of total input. By 1930, the proportions were around 45, 18 and 37 per cent respectively.[42]

The public sector research system, agricultural education and extension

A tripartite system of agricultural higher education, research and extension was institutionalised between 1862 and 1920. In the same year (1862) as the USDA was created, the Morrill Land Grant College Act authorised funding for a college of agriculture in each state. Specifically, under the provisions of the Act, Congress would donate to each state accepting the terms of the Act, public domain land that could be sold for settlement. The receipts were to be used to endow, support and maintain agricultural education in at least one college in each state. Seventeen states used their land grant to support agricultural education at an already established state university; the rest founded separate agricultural and mechanical arts colleges (A&M colleges). Cochrane (1979, p. 293) reports that the growth in agricultural education was slow and uneven during the 1870s and 1880s but by 1900 some of the better agricultural colleges had become effective instruments of agricultural education.

At the time the land grant colleges were being established, scientific leaders, inspired by European experience in applying research to agriculture, pressed for the establishment of agricultural experimental stations (AESs). The first AES was established in Connecticut in 1877; this was independent of the land grant college. Subsequently, certain other states set up AESs, some attached to the colleges. Eventually federal support for the funding of AESs was sought and granted in the Hatch Act of 1887. This Act provided each state with monies from the sale of public lands to support AESs attached in most cases to Land Grant Colleges. This link between station and college facilitated the integration of teaching and research. Research work in agriculture was complemented by USDA activity (the Agricultural Research Service).

The land grant colleges were quickly involved in adult education or extension work as a means of reaching out to the farm community, the constituency that had lent support to their founding. By 1913, colleges in 38 states had extension departments and pressed for federal support. The Smith-Lever Cooperative Extension Act of 1914 made provision for federal funding provided it was matched by state monies. By 1917 this extension system was in place helping with the dissemination of research produced by the colleges as well as upgrading the technical skills of farmers.

The thrust of legislation from 1862 to 1920 led to an integrated science-based research, teaching and extension system: 'by the early 1920s a national agricultural research and extension system had been effectively institutionalised at both the federal and the state levels' (Hayami and Ruttan, 1971, p. 144). However, the funds allocated were comparatively small (see ibid., p. 144). Partly for this reason, and partly because research was necessarily of a basic scientific nature (for example establishing a science of genetics), progress in developing biologically based innovations was slow until the 1920s.

New biological technologies enhancing output per acre and output per unit of breeding stock began to come on stream in the mid-1920s (Ruttan, 1984, p. 557). These developments were to become of commercial importance in future decades and were the culmination of past research activity in the public sector. Institutionalised research was expanded in the period 1910–25 in comparison to previous times; a further major expansion occurred after 1925. The Purnell Act of 1925 provided for more adequate support of the agricultural experiment stations. It also initiated a coordinated national corn improvement research programme and permitted the stations to carry out research into economic and social problems. The hybrid corn programme was of particular significance in the work of the agricultural experiment stations from their instigation. Basic scientific research was conducted in the period 1890–1920 whilst applied research concerned with breeding and trialling hybrid corn was initiated in the 1920s. By the 1930s, hybrid corn was in commercial production on a substantial scale (Hayami and Ruttan, 1971, p. 147).

Agricultural credit

An inadequate system of agricultural credit, particularly long term for land purchase, was a continual problem for farmers during the settlement of the West. Farmers also had a need for short-term credit for the purchase of machinery during the latter part of the nineteenth century. Farmers' organisations complained continuously about the shortcomings of the banking system and farm mortgage credit arrangements for decades prior to public intervention in the early 1900s.

Between 1863 and 1913, a national banking system was in operation whereby chartered national banks issued standard bank notes on the credit of the central government. The national banks were held to be inadequate at providing credit facilities in rural regions – they were too few in number in such areas, unable to lend by law on real estate and had a policy of short-term (60 to 90 days) lending. Consequently, farm credit was largely met by small state banks 'whose interest rates were high and whose financial condition was often precarious' (Faulkner, 1960, p. 525). Mortgage credit was provided by these banks and by farm mortgage corporations. 'Interest rates were high, loans were limited to short periods (three to five years) and many abuses existed' (Benedict, 1953, p. 145).[43] The banking system was improved by the Federal Reserve Act of 1913 which provided for twelve regional reserve banks coordinated and supervised by a central Board. The Federal Reserve System brought greater coordination and enhanced stability to the system. It also permitted national banks to lend money on farm mortgages. Further easement of the agricultural mortgage situation was provided for by the Federal Farm Loan Act of 1916. Under this Act, twelve federal land banks were established as cooperative loan agencies to be owned eventually by the borrowing farmers. They were placed under the supervision of a Federal Farm Loan Board.[44] The banks did not lend directly to farmers but to cooperative borrowing groups called 'National Farm Loan Associations'. The Loan Act also created private joint-stock land banks which could deal directly with individuals.[45] This Act inaugurated an extensive federal farm mortgage credit system allowing farmers to secure long-term loans at reasonable interest rates. It was also a prelude to more extensive governmental involvement in the financial affairs of farmers in later decades.

Further legislation with reference to credit was enacted during the early 1920s. The federally sponsored credit system created in pre-war years was augmented by the Agricultural Credit Act of 1923. 'The Act established a system of twelve intermediate credit banks associated with the twelve federal land banks and under the supervision of the Federal Farm Loan Board' (Benedict, 1953, p. 185). The purpose of the Act was to provide credit facilities for loans made for periods between the short term which were normally supplied by commercial facilities and the long term which were secured by land collateral. However the intermediate credit banks could not lend directly to farmers; loan facilities were available either to cooperative marketing associations or were made available indirectly through a local credit agency such as a country bank. As a consequence, the facilities provided by the Act were little used by farmers.

Productivity growth

Agricultural development during the nineteenth and early twentieth centuries was based on abundant land and was aided by the growth of the transport system and the mechanisation of farms. Government policies toward land settlement, agricultural research and education and the provision of credit helped to foster this development.

Data on the patterns of agricultural development become available from the latter part of the nineteenth century onwards following the foundation of the USDA which collected and published statistics. Salient features of productivity growth for the period 1880–1930 are given in Tables 2.7 and 2.8.

Table 2.7 Agricultural output, inputs and productivity in the US, 1880–1930

	Average annual growth rate (%)
Index of agricultural output (wheat units)*	1.44
Index of total inputs	1.32
Index of total factor productivity	0.015
Output (wheat units) per male worker	1.10
Output (wheat units) per ha agricultural land**	0.16
Agricultural land* (ha) per male worker	0.94
Index of capital per male worker	2.10
Index of output per unit of capital	−0.90

Notes
*See note to Table 2.6 for definition of wheat units.
**Note that agricultural land indicates cropland and permanent pasture.

Sources: Abstracted or derived from Ruttan et al. (1978, p. 48): Hayami and Ruttan (1985, p. 481); Cochrane (1979, p. 329, for capital series).

Table 2.8   Crop yields and fertiliser usage in the US, 1880 and 1930

Year	Corn yield (bushels per harvested acre)	Fertiliser use on arable land (kg nutrients per ha)	Fertiliser use on agricultural land (kg nutrients per ha)	Crop output per ha (index)
1880	25.6	1.0	0.5	100
1930	24.7	5.8	2.9	109

Note: Data are five-year averages centred on year in question except for land (actual figure for the year).

Source: Hayami and Ruttan (1985, p. 481).

Agricultural output doubled over the 50-year period (1870–1930) with an annual average growth rate of 1.44 per cent. Output growth was accompanied by growth of total inputs with total factor productivity barely increasing.[46] The labour force rose by some 30 per cent from 1880 to 1910, peaked and then declined: the land input increased some 40 per cent between 1880 and 1900 and increased only slowly thereafter. The major increase in inputs was accounted for by capital which trebled over the period. A declining price of capital items relative to wage rates stimulated mechanical innovation and capital substitution for labour (Hayami and Ruttan, 1985, ch. 7). Labour productivity measured in terms of output per worker or as acres per worker grew at around 1 per cent per annum. There was little apparent biological innovation with land productivity rising very slowly at just over 0.1 per cent per annum. Table 2.8 indicates that crop yields were fairly static over the period and fertiliser use low. This was despite the fact that fertiliser prices fell in nominal terms over most of the period and fell relative to the price of land over the whole period (Hayami and Ruttan, 1985, ch. 7). A lack of fertiliser responsive crop varieties inhibited the use of fertilisers over the period. The increase in fertiliser use that occurred was concentrated on cotton and tobacco in the South; 'these crops were regarded as "soil depleting" and artificial fertilisers replaced the loss of natural nutrients from the soil' (ibid.).

In short, production growth was based on increasing inputs. Mechanical innovation as represented especially by the introduction of the tractor, and the substitution of capital for labour raised labour productivity substantially. However, crop yields and land productivity virtually stagnated awaiting the innovation and adoption of biological technology.[47]

Trade Policy and Market Intervention

Pre-1920: America the agricultural exporter
The foreign trade of the USA grew slowly and erratically between 1783 and 1815 and then showed a steady upward trend until the Civil War (1861–67). The trade balance was generally negative[48] with imports being mainly of manufactured goods and exports being principally cotton and tobacco from the Southern States. Tariff policy in this period was a compromise between the Southern planters who sought trade expansion and the Northern industrialists who sought protection behind a tariff wall. A number of tariff acts varied the tariff levels and the list of dutiable items over the period with tariff rates being as high as 50–60 per cent and gradually dropping to around 20 per cent by 1860.[49]

During and after the Civil War, as the influence of the Southern planters became negligible, the Northern industrialists pressed for and obtained in Congress a series of highly protectionist tariff acts with rates rising up to 50 per cent on dutiable imports.[50] The various acts also extended the list of dutiable items; in particular the McKinley Tariff of 1890 extended duties to a complete range of farm products. A reduction in tariff levels and a withdrawal of duties on agricultural commodities came about in 1913.

However, whilst industrial protectionism raised the cost of consumer goods and certain inputs purchased by farmers, they had probably had little impact on farm output. During the half century after the Civil War, farm output and agricultural exports increased rapidly. Farm production tripled between 1870 and 1915.[51] This was largely a result of the (westward) expansion of farm land, although the 'frontier' was virtually closed by the turn of the century.[52] Between 1870 and 1900, exports of agricultural products more than doubled in value terms,[53] the main products exported being grains, cotton, tobacco, meat and meat products. However, in the following decade, that is, 1900–1910, grain and meat exports declined although cotton and tobacco exports held up. Consequently, there was a moderate decline in the volume of agricultural exports, although higher prices more than maintained the monetary value of this trade. Over the whole period, 1870–1910, the major overseas market supplied by US agriculture was Western Europe, particularly Great Britain. These European countries had large and fast growing populations and their economies were experiencing rapid industrial growth: they augmented domestic food supplies by imports, particularly from the US.

In the period 1870–90, agricultural exports accounted for over 75 per cent of the total value of US exports. From this high point, the proportion dropped to just over 50 per cent by 1910. The US balance of trade was in surplus over the whole period and there was a substantial inflow of primarily European investment capital. The main imports were raw materials for manufacturing and sugar; US manufacturing industries were protected by high levels of protection so restricting the imports of industrial goods. Aided by foreign capital, spurred by technological change including the development of mass production techniques and protected by tariffs, US manufacturing grew apace over the period. Simultaneously, the population grew rapidly, partly through mass immigration. As a result, the domestic market for agricultural products was greatly expanded and was able to compensate for declining export demand after 1900.

The period 1870–1910 witnessed the commercialisation and maturation of American agriculture. Developments in internal and external transport – the railroad and the steamship – linked farmers to domestic and foreign markets. Farmers produced for the marketplace rather than for self-sufficiency. They purchased an increasing proportion of their inputs and the capital to labour ratio rose. The percentage of the male labour force in agriculture declined continuously; from over 60 per cent in 1870 it declined to 55 per cent in 1880, 43 per cent in 1900 and 34 per cent in 1910 (Hayami and Ruttan, 1970, Appendix B). The absolute size of the agricultural labour force rose over the period but peaked in 1910 and declined thereafter (Wilcox and Cochrane, 1960, p. 32).

Farming fortunes fluctuated considerably between the Civil War and the First World War. Farm prices inevitably fell following the end of the Civil War and continued to decline persistently, if irregularly, in nominal terms until they reached a nadir in 1896.[54] These falling prices were a symptom of production increasing faster on trend than the sum of domestic consumption plus exports.[55] Although non-farm prices also declined between 1866 and 1895, this did not relieve 'hard times' for farmers.[56] During this period of 'agricultural depression', farmers attempted to organise collectively for the first time to redress their income situation.

The period 1897 to 1910 signalled a recovery in farmers' incomes. There was a particularly steep rise in nominal farm prices of 52 per cent in the period 1900–1910 when domestic demand expanded rapidly and the rate of growth of agricultural output was reduced as the expansion of the agricultural frontier came to a close.[57] Farm prices also rose relative to non-farm prices[58] and 'it was the closing years of this prosperous era (the years 1910–14) which later came to be known as the "parity period"' (Benedict, 1953, p. 115). These years have also been called the 'golden age of American agriculture' (ibid). The ratio of farm to non-farm prices (prices received by farmers relative to prices paid by farmers for non-farm inputs and consumption items) at this time had significance for future policy. The ratio – later called the parity ratio – was regarded by farmers in future, less prosperous, years as the normal or proper balance and became a focal point for agricultural income support measures.

The First World War provided an artificial stimulus to European imports of US farm products. From 1915–20 there was a rapid expansion of both industry and agriculture in the US induced by rising European demand and later augmented by American participation in the war. Agricultural prices more than doubled and rose faster than non-agricultural prices. Farm prices peaked in 1919, dropped in 1920 and slumped in 1921.[59] Non-farm prices peaked in 1920 and then declined. However, from 1920 onwards there was a tendency for the ratio of farm to non-farm prices to fall. The major reason for the slump in farm prices was 'a sudden and catastrophic drop in foreign demand for the products of American agriculture which by now had come to be over-expanded' (Benedict, 1953, p. 169). Not only did the end of the war signal economic depression in Europe, the US had become a creditor rather than debtor nation with European countries and it discontinued wartime credits to the Allied countries in 1919 with a consequent impact on their abilities to trade. The weakness of foreign demand was accentuated by a large rise (35–40 per cent) in internal freight rates in 1920. The fall in demand was also augmented by a reduction in domestic demand consequent upon the end of the war. By 1921, the ratio of farm to non-farm prices had dropped to 63 per cent of their 1910–14 value. Agricultural distress was evidenced by farmers in the Dakotas and Nebraska burning corn for fuel. The economic situation of American farmers in 1920–21 was exacerbated by a build-up of farm mortgage debt that had occurred during the war, partly associated with a steep rise in land values. Inevitably, after 1920 land prices fell and farm bankruptcies increased.

1920–33: agricultural depression and the advent of policy intervention
Political pressure for government legislation providing for intervention into agricultural markets built up during the 1920s. As has been indicated, wartime farm prosperity was followed by a sharp fall in the real prices for agricultural commodities in the early 1920s consequent upon reduced export demand from Europe. Tariff protection for agriculture, specifically duties on wheat, corn, meat, wool and sugar, as well as for manufactured goods, was granted in the form of an 'emergency tariff' put through Congress in May 1921.[60] A revised tariff schedule

was ratified as the Fordney–McCumber Tariff in September 1922.[61] However, import tariffs could not raise the prices of exportable agricultural commodities and the general tariff policy tended to inhibit economic growth in the traditional export markets of Europe.

Foreign markets were slack in any case,[62] moreover, agricultural trade was further restricted by the reimposition in many European countries of import tariffs that had been suspended during the war.

Thus, despite the tariff legislation, agricultural incomes fell in contrast to substantial growth in the rest of the economy.[63] Farm organisations gathered strength and gained political influence. A succession of bills, five in total, were sponsored by Senator McNary in the Senate and Congressman Haugen in the House of Representatives between 1924 and 1928 around the idea of 'Equality for Agriculture' (Benedict, 1953, p. 207). Although the first three bills were rejected by Congress and the fourth and fifth were vetoed by President Coolidge, the McNary–Haugen Plan had a substantial formative impact on subsequent legislation. The central proposal of the plan was that a government export corporation be instituted to buy up specified agricultural commodities (the basic commodities of wheat, cotton, corn, rice and hogs) and raise their domestic prices up to their 'ratio price' or pre-war 'real price' in relation to the general wholesale price level. This ratio price was the forerunner of the parity price concept. The surplus over domestic utilisation was to be sold abroad at a loss in conjunction with a protective tariff to prevent re-importation. The plan was to be paid for 'by an initial revolving fund, to be maintained by means of equalisation fees assessed against each of the commodities handled' (Benedict, 1953, p. 225). The equalisation fee was to be a tax levied on the domestic marketing channel.

Over the period 1924–1928 there was a gradual upturn in agricultural prosperity stimulated by internal economic growth rather than recovery in foreign markets.[64] By the end of the 1920s only one-third of the total exports consisted of farm products. The ratio of farm to non-farm prices, with a base of 100 for 1910–14, rose from 84 in 1921 to 94 in 1928. Grain prices remained low but cotton and livestock produce prices recovered to pre-war levels in relation to non-farm prices.

Despite the gradual improvement in farm prices and incomes, the notion of 'Equality for Agriculture' had an influence on the platforms put forward in the 1928 Presidential election. Republican campaign promises to effect 'relief to agriculture' were met soon after the election of President Hoover by the passage of the Agricultural Marketing Act in June 1929. The Act had as objectives the assistance and initiation of farm marketing cooperatives and the stabilisation of market prices. A new institution, the Federal Farm Board, was set up with a $500 million revolving fund with the objective of making loans to cooperatives on favourable terms. The Board also took the initiative in setting up national cooperative agencies overlaying existing marketing cooperatives. These national associations, which had a specific commodity orientation, were to be the instruments of stabilisation, using loans from the Federal Board to purchase and store commodities in times of 'temporary' market surplus. Provision was also made for the direct purchase of commodities by the Board via 'Stabilisation Corporations'.

A number of national farm marketing cooperatives were set up including the Farmers National Grain Corporation handling wheat (October 1929), the National Wool Marketing Corporation (December 1929), and the American Cotton Cooperative Association (January 1930). However, prices of wheat and cotton fell drastically in the marketing year of 1929–30 despite the loan and storage activities of the national cooperatives. The financial burden of these activities proved beyond their funding capacities and the Federal Farm Board took over responsibility for market stabilisation in 1930 via the Grain Stabilisation Corporation and the Cotton Stabilisation Corporation. These corporations became involved in heavy purchasing of the commodities on depressed markets. Wheat was sold on an oversupplied international market at prices below the domestic purchase price. Large stocks of cotton were maintained. However, the fall in domestic prices of grain and cotton could not be checked with the funds available and the activities of the Federal Farm Board came to a halt in 1932.

With hindsight, it is apparent that the Federal Farm Board was instigated at a singularly unpropitious time – four months before the Stock Market collapse of October 1929 and the onset of the Great Depression. The domestic economic slump was quickly transmitted to other countries; domestic and international demands for US agricultural commodities were drastically reduced. Consequently, offsetting purchases by the Federal Farm Board were not a feasible option in view of its limited funding. In its last report, the Board made a recommendation which was to have a major impact in subsequent years: 'no measure for improving the price of farm products other than increasing the demand of consumers can be effective over a period of years *unless it provides a more definite control of production than has been achieved so far,*' (Lesher, 1985, italics added).

The impact of economic depression on trade was magnified by the passage of the Hawley–Smoot Tariff Act of 1930. The Act was initially viewed by President Hoover as a limited revision of tariffs aiding agriculture in particular. In practice, there was a general upward revision of tariffs raising the already high duties established by the Fordney–McCumber Act (1922) on both agricultural and non-agricultural goods.[65] Retaliation and a general wave of protectionism occurred abroad and general US trade declined drastically.[66] 'Beggar my neighbour' trade policies became the order of the day.

International prices of farm products fell sharply between 1929 and 1931; for example, the wheat price fell by almost 50 per cent. European importing countries such as France and Germany reacted by substantially raising tariff levels and introducing non-tariff barriers such as the 'milling ratio' for wheat 'whereby millers were obliged to use a certain minimum percentage of domestically-produced wheat in their grist' (Tracy, 1982, p. 131). European countries also reverted to direct intervention measures; even Great Britain abandoned its traditional policy of *laissez-faire* toward agriculture. European producers 'were to a considerable extent insulated from the fall in (international) prices' (ibid., p. 138). US exports of wheat and pigmeat in particular were badly affected by the depression in Europe and by the restrictions on imports. Overall, the farm sector faced reduced export demand at a time when surplus stocks overhung the domestic market.

Agriculture was in a parlous state between 1930 and 1933. As in previous economic depressions, farm prices fell more than non-farm prices. In particular, farm prices dropped by more than 50 per cent between 1929 and 1932 whilst the prices of goods and services purchased by farmers fell by 32 per cent: the ratio of farm to non-farm prices, with 1910–14 = 100, fell from nearly 100 in 1929 to around 60 in 1932. The gross income of American agriculture was halved between 1929 and 1932, and land prices fell some 30 per cent. Nearly a million farmers were dispossessed between 1930 and 1934 (Benedict, 1953, p. 247). Urban incomes were likewise depressed and urban unemployment became widespread (25 per cent by 1933). New economic policies were called for and were presented in the Presidential campaign of 1932. The Democratic candidate, Franklin D. Roosevelt, promised a 'New Deal'.

The period 1920–33 was significant in the history of US agriculture not just for the depression and the limited government support that heralded the introduction of a widespread government intervention into agricultural markets. It was also a period where secular change associated with technological advances was beginning to impact on the farming sector. Technological developments in the 1920s were characterised by the increased utilisation of tractor-based mechanical power on farms which replaced horses and released land. Labour productivity increased by about 1.4 per cent per annum over the period. However, total output and total factor productivity showed little increase over this period. More portentous factors for raising agriculture's future capacity to produce were the new biological technologies beginning to come on stream in the mid-1920s. Hybrid corn was a notable example. In summary, in the period 1920–1933, US agriculture was adapting and adjusting to available mechanical technology and was about to take up the new biological science technology. E.G. Nourse in a memorable statement wrote in 1927: 'Stated as a paradox, the outlook for agricultural production is so good that the outlook for agricultural prosperity is distinctly bad' (Nourse, 1927, p. 21).

COMMENTARY: AGRICULTURAL POLICY IN WESTERN EUROPE AND THE US, 1880–1930

By the mid-nineteenth century, freehold ownership and private land use rights had been established in agriculture in most of Western Europe but with a diversity of farm structures and tenure arrangements across countries. In the USA, land held in the public domain was transferred into private ownership in the post independence period and the land frontier was closed by the turn of the nineteenth century. The land was settled by family operated freehold farms on units of a size appropriate to the farming conditions. American agriculture in 1880 was land extensive and low yielding compared to European agriculture (see Table 2.9). In relation to available technology, Dutch, British and Danish agricultures were highly productive at that time whilst French and German agriculture were less productive, particularly in relation to the use of labour.

Between circa 1870 and 1914, a more or less nationwide system of agricultural research, education and extension, largely sponsored by government, was set up in Germany, Denmark, Holland and the US. However, these institutions were only put in place in the UK and France after the First World War. In the labour-intensive agricultures of Germany, Denmark and Holland this institutional change led to rising productivity in conjunction with new inputs such as fertilisers, concentrated feed and the mechanical cream separator. These inputs were supplied by the industrial sector at falling real prices over time. Between 1870 and 1914 these countries experienced a 'Green Revolution'. However, in America, the research system had little impact on production, and land-saving technological change was slow in this period; rather, technological change was labour saving based on mechanisation.

Output increased significantly over the 50-year period 1880–1930 in

Table 2.9   Comparison of output* and productivity changes between the United States and Western European countries, 1880 and 1930

	Year	US	UK	France	Germany	Denmark	Holland
Agricultural	1880	100	100	100	100	100	100
output index	1930	204	111	146	192	279	215
							index
Agricultural	1880	13.0	16.2	7.4	7.9	10.6	100
output per	1930	22.5	20.1	13.2	16.0	24.1	187
male worker							
							index
Agricultural	1880	0.51	1.10	1.06	1.25	1.19	100
output per	1930	0.56	1.18	1.50	2.47	2.95	195
ha							
agricultural							
land							
							index
Agricultural	1880	25	15	7	6	9	100
land (ha)	1930	41	17	9	6	8	96
per male worker							

Note: *Agricultural output measured in wheat units except for Holland (real value added). See note to Table 2.6 for a definition of wheat units.

Sources: Ruttan et al. (1978, ch. 3); van de Meer and Yamada (1986) for Holland.

the US (stemming from increases in capital inputs) and in Germany, Denmark and Holland (stemming from the use of new inputs and developments in crop and animal breeding). In contrast, UK agriculture stagnated whilst French agriculture witnessed only modest output increases. The relatively large and land extensive (for Western Europe) British farmers were held back by a lack of labour-saving innovations; French agriculture was retarded by a failure of institutional innovation, disincentives to the labour-intensive livestock sector and a slow growth in the market.[67]

By the late nineteenth century, a district pattern of international trade had emerged: agricultural commodities and raw materials were exported from the recently settled countries of the temperate zone and tropical-colonial countries to Western Europe, whilst industrial products were exported from the developed countries to the primary producing regions. The economic climate for European agricultural producers worsened considerably between the 1870s and the 1890s as the price of cereals declined as a result of sharply increasing exports of grains from the American continent. By 1896, the prices of cereals had halved compared to the early 1870s. After 1896 these prices rose again but remained at low levels. The response of France and Germany to the agricultural depression was protectionist. Tariffs on grain were re-introduced, varied or maintained.[68] However, international competition in livestock products was less intense; moreover, rising incomes in Western Europe stimulated demand. As a consequence the prices of livestock products did not fall to the same extent as those of grains in Western Europe between the 1870s and the Second World War. In addition, domestically produced horticultural products in Western Europe had a natural advantage in trade. Specialisation in livestock and horticulture was a rational response by farmers to the agricultural depression and was witnessed in Denmark and Holland. These countries maintained free trade in agriculture, taking advantage of low cereal prices, and became significant agricultural exporters of their 'high value' products. Significant productivity growth aided this transformation. Britain had a clear comparative advantage in manufacturing and main-tained a free trade stance until the First World War. British agriculture stagnated in the face of import competition from the New World and from the livestock exporters of Europe. By 1910, a substantial pro-portion of British food consumption was supplied by overseas producers. American farmers experienced hard times between 1870 and 1896 as grain prices declined but prospered thereafter in a 'golden age' until 1920 as international grain prices recovered and the internal markets for farm products tightened.

Starting with the First World War, there was a sizeable increase in the capacity of government administration and control. Prior to this time, the tariff was the only practicable tool of intervention to manipu-late agricultural prices and redirect income flows between agriculture and the rest of the economy. Following the collapse of agricultural prices in both Western Europe and the USA in 1929 with the onset of the Great Depression, government utilised this capacity to administer a variety of extensive interventionist measures in an attempt to protect agriculture from market forces.

NOTES

1. In particular, we highlight the UK, France, Germany, Denmark and Holland, these being important economies in the EU.

2. For an extended discussion, see Tracy (1982, Part I).
3. Much land was held also by the church and monasteries.
4. The manorial system prevailed in the north-east arable areas. In the south and west, a different system of agriculture prevailed emphasising vines, fruit and olives, vegetables and livestock. Sharecropping (metayage) predominated and was not abolished by the Revolution, although it gradually evolved into cash rents.
5. Other factors such as estate duty liability, rent control after the Second World War and security of tenure also contributed to the breakup of landed estates.
6. During the 1914–18 war a newly appointed President of the Board of Trade, R.E. Protheroe (later Lord Ernle), was given a seat in the cabinet in recognition of his eminent status as an agriculturalist. But this was exceptional.
7. Except that during the period of French occupation at the end of the eighteenth century, a State Secretary of Agriculture was appointed to collect agricultural statistics, and encourage land reclamation.
8. The unionisation of farm workers paralleled the rise of the NFU. The National Agricultural Labourers' Union was founded by Joseph Arch in 1872. But the movement only extended to parts of England and it was not until 1906 that the National Union of Agricultural Workers (NUAW) was established. In addition, agricultural workers were able to belong to the larger Transport and General Workers Union since its inception in 1922. The status of the farm workers' unions rose during the First World War when a National Agricultural Wages Board was formed, with representatives from the farmers and workers unions as well as independent members, to administer national minimum agricultural wages. This Board was disbanded postwar but revived by a Labour government in 1924. Its purpose was to determine the minimum agricultural wage and the Board has remained in existence ever since.
9. For a history of agricultural cooperation in Britain, see Rayner and Ennew (1987).
10. Note that the cooperative movement dates from the formation of the Rochdale Equitable Pioneers (a consumers' cooperative) in 1844. The cooperative movement in its early years was working class in origin and anti-capitalist in outlook.
11. Another factor contributing to the decline of agricultural cooperatives in the 1920s was the political association of the consumer cooperative movement with the Labour party which was not the natural habitat of most farmers.
12. Some innovations were invented in the USA.
13. Output is measured in wheat units (as defined in note to Table 2.6).
14. During the 1920s, a major programme of state technical aid was formulated and tabled by the Minister of Agriculture. But it was never implemented due to financial stringency and political obstacles (Wright, 1964, p. 34).
15. This section draws on van Zanden (1988) as well as Ruttan et al. (1978).
16. Fertiliser prices dropped by around 40 per cent in Holland between 1880 and 1900; before 1880 fertiliser prices had been rising (van Zanden, 1988, p. 21).
17. van Zanden also hypothesises that other causes of the relatively poor productivity performance of Britain and France during the period 1880–1910 were (i) that the price of land saving inputs relative to land fell much less than in other countries, (ii) the large farm structure in the UK, (iii) the cooperative movement in France and the UK was less developed than in the other countries.
18. Agricultural protection was lowered under commercial treaties with European nations who gave concessions on imports of German manufactures. The treaties included Romania and Russia and concessions were extended to third country grain exporters including the USA through the embodiment in the treaties of the 'most favoured nation' principle (to discourage undercutting of tariff concessions by trading competitors).
19. There are obvious similarities, as well as differences, between the German import certificate system, first introduced before the end of the nineteenth century, and the cereals support system adopted by the architects of the European Community's Common Agricultural Policy in the early 1960s. The main difference is that whereas

under the import certificate system import duty revenue subsidised exports in the private market without public intervention (except to enforce the import duty), under the CAP the collection of import levies and the payment of export subsidies was 'socialised' through the operation of the Community Budget. The idea of using import duty revenue to subsidise exports also crossed the Atlantic Ocean to the USA where, in the 1920s, an Export Debenture Plan was an important feature of the abortive McNary-Haugen Bill proposals. Later, Section 32 of the Agricultural Adjustment Act, as amended in 1935, authorised the use of import duty revenue to subsidise farm product sales on both domestic and export markets.

20. It might appear surprising that once Germany had established itself as an industrial power, agricultural protection persisted. Socio-philosophic arguments against over-industrialisation as advanced by Wagner (1902) give at least part of the answer. Wagner's arguments were: (a) urbanisation had undesirable social consequences; (b) reliance on imported food both threatened national food security and exposed consumers to fluctuating world prices; and (c) the terms of trade might shift to favour agriculture, thus threatening industrial prosperity and undermining the balance of payments.

21. In the case of Denmark this meant a switch away from exporting cereals, as in the eighteenth century and early to mid-nineteenth century. By 1890 Denmark was an importer of all grains except barley.

22. Tracy (1982) emphasises the imprecision of these estimates.

23. This represents a 'deficiency payment' system, later to become the standard support system for UK agriculture, but the term was not used in policy circles during the First World War. The notion of guaranteed minimum prices originated with an Agricultural Consultative Committee which reported in the first month of the war. It appears to have been the first committee in British history to recommend the payment of an agricultural price guarantee (Barnett, 1985, pp. 23–4).

24. There is evidence that at the time farmers' reactions to the 1921 repeal of price guarantees for wheat and oats were mixed. Some farmers apparently welcomed the repeal since it was associated with the decontrol of agricultural wages and the ending of government power to impose maximum price controls (which had been used in 1918). It was only after wheat prices had fallen far below the level guaranteed by the 1920 Agriculture Act that farmers were united in accusing the government of a 'great betrayal' (Brown, 1987, pp. 78–9).

25. Agricultural Policy (Cmnd 2581) 1926.

26. Cochrane (1979, p. 76), notes that even by the 1850s there were broad belts of commercial agriculture east of the Mississippi River.

27. See Penn, 1984, p. 573.

28. The US constitution was drawn up in 1787 by the 'Philadelphia Convention'.

29. As Benedict (1953, p. 19) states, 'The Homestead Act was the logical culmination of the long struggle for freer access to the public domain by pioneer farmers.' However, the Act was loosely drawn up, badly administered and subject to abuse with large acreages of timber and mining lands passing into the hands of large corporations. In addition it was not particularly helpful in settling homesteaders in the West, especially in semi-arid areas (the Great Plains) on economically viable units. Moreover, only about 20 per cent of public domain land disposed of between 1860 and 1900 was acquired by the issue of land titles to homesteaders.

30. The conservation of public domain land starts with the General Revision Act of 1891 which repealed both the 1841 Pre-emption Act and various Timber Acts passed between 1873 and 1878 which had granted private access to public forests.

31. Land disposal and its consequences did not provide gains for all groups in society: the Indian tribes were notable losers (see Cochrane, 1979, ch. 4).

32. Plantation agriculture was important in the Old South prior to the Civil War but largely disappeared when slavery was eliminated.

33. Land was the abundant resource: farming was relatively extensive.

34. Critics of the land disposal policy have pointed to the prevalence of land speculation

and of exploitive agriculture that was associated with settlement of the land base. Thus it can be argued that the rewards structure favoured pioneers who held land for speculation whilst mining the soil. Cochrane (1979, ch. 9), argues that whereas such practices existed, they were the results of abundant land *per se*, not the policies governing the disposal of public lands.

35. Figures relate only to federal government employment.

36. Aaron Sapiro was a lawyer who served as an attorney to several cooperatives in California before leading a nationwide crusade for strongly centralised farm cooperatives to 'capture' agricultural markets for themselves.

37. For example the wrought iron plough (John Deere), the mechanical reaper (Hussey-McCormick), the combine harvester (Pitt, Case), grain drill, harrows, discs, and so on.

38. Between 250 and 300 man hours were required to produce 100 bushels of wheat on 5 acres . . . in 1830. By 1890, some 40 to 50 man hours of labour were required to produce 100 bushels of wheat on 5 acres (Cochrane, 1979, p. 200).

39. Hayami and Ruttan (1971) argue that the direction of technological change was a response to relative input prices in the period under review when labour was expensive relative to land. The economic environment for agriculture was 'characterised by a strong demand for labour-saving mechanical technology and the industrial sector responded by introducing a continuous stream of new mechanical equipment' (p. 141).

40. Between 15 and 25 million acres were transferred from the production of feed for draft animals to production of food and livestock feed between 1918 and 1930 (Saloutos, 1982, p. 3).

41. By 1930 the labour input required to produce 100 bushels of wheat had been reduced to 15–20 man hours compared to 40–50 man hours in 1890 (Cochrane, 1979, p. 200).

42. The 1870 figures are from Cochrane, 1979, p. 205. The 1930 figures are interpolations between 1920 and 1940 figures from the same source.

43. Interest rates were particularly high in the expanding West – 'while 6 or 7 percent might be the usual rates on eastern farm mortgages, farmers in the West were paying 8 to 10 or even 15 percent' (Faulkner, 1960, p. 381).

44. The initial capitalisation of the land banks was provided by the government. They were authorised to secure further funding by issue of bonds secured on farm mortgages to private investors but the federal government was forced to subscribe virtually all the additional monies in the first instance.

45. The joint-stock land banks 'obtained funds by selling mortgage tax exempt farmloan bonds on the market' (Faulkner, 1960, p. 381).

46. Although agricultural experimental stations were established in the late 1880s, it took over 40 years before total factor productivity began to show consistent and sizeable growth. Peterson and Fitzharris (1977) attribute the gestation lag to the fact that it was not until 1925 that real annual research expenditure began to climb sharply as the bulk of research input before 1925 was necessary simply to maintain current crop and livestock productivity: 'research effort during the early years of the experiment station system appears to have been aimed largely at maintaining agricultural productivity in the face of a constant surfacing of new problems'.

47. Cochrane (1979) notes that advances in biological technology were made over the period with respect to breeding resistance to crop diseases (especially wheat rust) and vaccinating against and treating animal diseases (for example hog cholera and tick fever). However, as indicated in the previous endnote, these advances largely maintained crop and livestock productivity rather than dramatically increasing it.

48. The trade deficit was financed by loans from British investors and earnings received by US merchant sailors for shipping services.

49. The first Tariff Act of 1789 set a nominal protection rate of about 5 per cent. The Tariff Act of 1816 raised protection to 20 per cent on some imported items; the tariff on dutiable items was raised to 50–60 per cent by the Tariff Act of 1828 (the 'Tariff of Abominations'). The 1833 Tariff Act (Compromise Tariff) provided for a

reduction of duties over a nine-year period. Subsequent Tariff Acts (1846 and 1857) led to further reduction in duties.

50. The principal tariff acts were the Morill Act of 1861 and the amendment of 1864 (introduced as revenue raising acts to finance the Civil War), the McKinley Tariff of 1890 and the Dingley Tariff of 1897 which remained in force until 1909. Tariff levels on dutiable items averaged over 40 per cent in the early bills, 49 per cent in the McKinley Bill and 57 per cent in the Dingley Bill. The McKinley and Dingley Acts made provision for protective duties on imports of farm products; this had little practical impact. Raw sugar, which had been subject to tariffs since 1789 and had been a major source of tariff revenues, was placed on the free list by the McKinley Act and a subsidy (bounty) granted to domestic producers. However, in 1894 the sugar bounty was repealed and tariff protection resumed. Two further tariff acts were the Payne Aldrich Tariff of 1909 and the Underwood Simmons Act of 1913. The former was little more than a continuation of the Dingley Act; the latter reduced tariff rates considerably and placed many items including most agricultural commodities on the free list but had little impact because of the onset of the First World War.

51. Wheat and corn production doubled over the period, cotton production quadrupled.

52. The acreage in farms more than doubled between 1870 and 1900 with a corresponding increase in the number of farms. 'Over 500 million acres of new land was "brought into cultivation", an area almost as large as that of Western Europe. The number of farms grew from 2 million in 1860 to 6 million in 1910,' (Faulkner, 1960, p. 365).

53. See Faulkner (1960, p. 545).

54. The index of prices received by farmers for all products (1910–14 = 100) fell from 119 in 1869 to 66 in 1878 and to 53 in 1896 (Cochrane, 1979, p. 93).

55. Total farm output increased by 135 per cent between 1870 and 1900 (Cochrane, 1979, p. 92). Wheat output almost quadrupled, corn output more than tripled, cotton increased by nearly five times. Despite rising population and increasing exports, domestic consumption and foreign demand could not keep pace with the increase in domestic production.

56. Cochrane (1979, p. 93) attributes the 'hard times' to a combination of factors: first, a cash flow problem as farmers met interest payments for the purchase of land and machinery out of declining gross returns; second, the fall in prices of non-farm variable input and consumption goods had little consequence since they were not important items in farmers' expenditures; third, railroad freights did not decline *pari passu* with farm prices; fourth, the impact of a series of national calamities (drought, prairie fires, pests) affecting production in the West.

57. It is noticeable that land prices virtually doubled over this period (Hayami and Ruttan, 1971, Appendix C).

58. The index of non-farm prices rose on trend from around 75 in 1870 to 100 in 1910–14 with 1910–14 on the base (see Shepherd, 1963, p. 5).

59. Wheat prices dropped to less than half, corn prices to a third and hog prices to less than half compared to pre-war levels.

60. Normal trade arrangements were non-operable during the war. The tariffs provided for in the 1913 Underwood Simmons Act were lower than traditional levels and did not accord with postwar protectionist sentiment. There was strong pressure for an upward revision of the Underwood rates following the election of the Republican President Harding, in 1920.

61. The Fordney–McCumber Tariff set higher tariff rates on manufactures than those of the Underwood Simmons Act of 1913 and close to the levels of the Payne–Aldrich Act of 1909. Benedict (1953) puts the average tariff level of the Act of 1909 at 41 per cent, that of 1913 at 27 per cent and that of 1922 at 38.5 per cent. The 1922 Act also restored duties on agricultural products. Rather importantly, it raised the tariff rather sharply on goods exported to the US from Europe, thus tending to weaken already slack demand for US farm products. The Fordney–McCumber Act also had

a new feature: the President was given authority to raise or lower tariffs not exceeding 50 per cent.

62.   A major factor inhibiting a resumption of 'normal trade' between Europe and the US was a reversal in international financial relations compared to pre-war years. Traditionally, the US was a debtor to Europe but it was now the world's foremost creditor nation. The European Allies borrowed heavily from the US during the war and were required postwar to make repayment of the principal and interest of the war loans.

63.   By 1922, deflation had run its course and the general economy had adjusted to peacetime conditions. Between 1923 and 1929 there was substantial economic growth in America in contrast to most other countries. Industrial production almost doubled and real income per capita increased substantially. The main boom industries were the manufacture of automobiles and electrical equipment and building construction.

64.   Not only were farm markets in Western Europe slack, but the US faced increased competition in exports of wheat from Canada, Australia and Argentina.

65.   The average rate on dutiable items in the Hawley–Smoot Act was 52.3 per cent compared with 38.5 per cent in the Fordney–McCumber Act. Moreover many items were transferred from the free to the dutiable list. The average rate on agricultural raw materials was raised from 38–48.9 per cent (Faulkner, 1960, p. 647).

66.   US imports and exports in 1932 were only some 30 per cent of their 1929 level. For details see Benedict (1953, p. 252).

67.   See Hayami and Ruttan (1985, ch. 13).

68.   Grain import duties were introduced in Germany by Bismarck in 1879 but lowered in the 1890s. In France tariffs were revived by Móline in 1892, raised in 1895 and raised again after the Second World War.

3. The 1930s: economic crisis and agricultural support policies

INTRODUCTION AND OVERVIEW

In this chapter we review and compare the major agricultural policy adjustments to the world economic depression of the 1930s, both in Western Europe and the United States of America. The economic crisis of the 1930s – the Great Depression – was a worldwide phenomenon. For most of the industrial countries there was a common pattern of economic change prior to and during the crisis. After the First World War, there was a period of adjustment and reconstruction lasting until about 1925 for belligerent and neutral countries alike. Next followed a few years of economic growth but in 1929 and 1930 there was a severe slump in national incomes which lasted until 1933. There was then a gradual if erratic recovery but with a recession in 1937–8. The depression ended with the onset of the Second World War. 'The growth rate of industrial production in the "developed" countries fell from 3.6 per cent in 1883–1913 to 2.7 per cent in 1913–29 and 1.3 per cent in 1929–38' (Reynolds, 1986, p. 35).

World trade volume fell sharply in the inter-war years. In the adjustment period after the First World War, most countries returned to the gold standard for defining the values of their currencies but relative values were not in line with equilibrium levels. Most nations reverted to pre-war currency values which did not reflect changes in fundamentals. This inadequate international monetary mechanism constrained trade. Moreover trade interventions introduced in wartime were not completely dismantled: these mercantilist practices disrupted trade. Bilateral agreements and regional trade blocs proliferated in the absence of a well-functioning multilateral trading system; for example, Britain developed a Commonwealth preferential trading system whilst Germany dominated a central European trading bloc. 'Beggar-thy-neighbour' policies became the order of the day. The US raised the levels of its tariffs notably by passing the Hawley Smoot Tariff Act in 1930. Other nations retaliated by raising protection levels. This reinforced the international depression precipitated by the slump.[1]

Protectionist policies were subsequently re-examined in the US and the Reciprocal Trade Agreements Act of 1934 reversed the trend of ever higher tariffs. The Act authorised the president to enter into mutually advantageous bilateral trade agreements with a 'most favoured nation' provision. The bilateral agreements thus had favourable multi-lateral effects. However, whilst trade in manufactures was encouraged in subsequent years, agricultural trade was curtailed by national support measures.

World agriculture was in a parlous state in the late 1920s. From 1925 to around 1931–33, the world prices of most agricultural commodities declined precipitously[2] and stocks accumulated. The problem appeared to be one of overproduction in relation to the contraction in demand: market gluts were causing price to fall.

Farmers everywhere demanded a restoration of their profits and governments responded. Agricultural exporters such as the US, Denmark and Holland, brought in policies to build up stocks and cut back on production in an attempt to raise prices. Agricultural importing nations in Europe sought to preserve the home market for domestic producers. They adopted far-reaching measures of protection, enacting not only stiff tariffs but also import quotas, direct subsidies and mixing regulations. These stifled trade, harming exporters and injuring domestic consumers. Intervention into agricultural markets became self perpetuating and hampered recovery from the depression. However there was some upturn in agricultural prices in the mid to late 1930s, partly as national incomes recovered and stimulated demand and partly as a result of crop failures in North America in 1931–33 and poor harvests of grain in Europe and Argentina in 1936.

Agrarian fundamentalism flowered during the depression. Small-scale farming was viewed both as a refuge for the unemployed and a repository of idealised values. However, whilst the depression slowed the drift from country to city, the dynamism of the agricultural transformation process could not be reversed. Moreover, the self-sufficient farm was rapidly disappearing in Europe as well as in America; even the French peasant was producing for the market and purchasing input and consumer goods from the industrial sectors of the economy. Technological change initiated in previous decades had its own imperative and was beginning to impact on agriculture during the market recovery of the late 1930s.

AGRICULTURAL PROTECTIONISM IN WESTERN EUROPE

United Kingdom

In the UK the agricultural policy response to the world economic depression of 1929–33 contained several different strands. Despite rapidly falling producer prices, particularly of grains, there was initially a natural reluctance on the part of government to adopt protective measures likely to raise the price of food to consumers. This was the background to efforts to support agriculture through reforms in agricultural marketing. However, by 1933 an interventionist attitude was adopted by government in an effort to restore the fortunes of a distressed farming industry: domestic subsidies (deficiency payments) and import controls were widely used thereafter.

Agricultural marketing acts of 1931 and 1933[3]

The national government which took office in 1931 inherited from its predecessor the Agricultural Marketing Act of 1931. The 1931 Act was the original enabling legislation allowing agricultural producers to form themselves into marketing boards, with extensive compulsory powers over virtually all aspects of marketing, subject to certain conditions. The most important condition was that, before a marketing board could get parliamentary approval, a majority of the producers of the commodity concerned had to signify their approval by voting in a referendum. 'In the event, the leaders of the farming community were not impressed by the 1931 Act. They were preoccupied by the slump in agricultural prices: they wanted import controls' (Currie and Rayner, 1979, p. 26). Only one board – the Hops Marketing Board – was set up under the 1931 Act; this became the monopoly seller of English hops in bargaining with the brewers following the passage of the Hops Marketing Scheme through Parliament in 1932.

In 1933, a new Agricultural Marketing Act was submitted to Parliament and passed which permitted the Board of Trade to restrict imports of any agricultural product, provided a marketing scheme for the equivalent home product was either in existence or in preparation.[4,5] In conjunction with the 1931 Act this provided a mechanism for market management which was acceptable to farmers.

Following the passage of the 1933 Act, marketing schemes were presented and given parliamentary approval for milk (1933), pigs (1933) and potatoes (1934). Four Milk Marketing Boards (MMBs) were set up, one for England and Wales and three for Scotland. Two boards were established to regulate the marketing of bacon pigs in Great Britain, the Pigs Marketing Board and the Bacon Marketing Board. A Potato Marketing Board (PMB) covering Great Britain was instituted. The details of the marketing schemes underlying the activities of these boards differed considerably. Whereas the crucial aspect of the milk scheme was that the MMBs were given power to exercise discriminating monopoly in selling milk for different end uses, the crux of the potato scheme was that PMB had power to limit potato supplies through acreage quotas and regulation of the minimum size of tuber sold for human consumption. Unlike the PMB, the MMBs did not attempt to restrict production but only to maximise the 'pool price' obtained from allocating the aggregate supplies of milk they did not control by price discrimination amongst different markets. For its part, the PMB attempted to support producer prices not by entering the potato market, except as a buyer of last resort, but by restricting production and the quantity of potatoes available for human consumption, according to prevailing market conditions. The Pigs Marketing Board resembled the MMBs in being a trading board. But the Pigs Board encountered serious problems for two interrelated reasons. First, its marketing powers were restricted to pigs sold to bacon factories: they did not extend to pork pigs. Secondly, because the Board lacked power to control the pork market it was also unable to control the notorious 'pig cycle' (the alternation of periods of low supplies and high prices with those of high supplies and low prices).

No additional marketing boards were created between 1934 and the outbreak of the Second World War. This was largely because successive governments were willing to assist farmers by other means, principally via domestic subsidies or import controls. Instead, the government favoured the establishment of independent commodity commissions, without trading powers, to give impartial advice on marketing, not only to producers, but also to market intermediaries and consumers: the commodity commissions also had the task of administering producer subsidies. A Livestock Commission was set up in 1934 to administer the deficiency payment on beef cattle. A Sugar Commission followed in 1935 to administer the subsidy on sugarbeet, renewed in that year for an indefinite period after the original enabling act of 1925 had expired.

Deficiency payments

A second strand of policy to deal with the crisis conditions of the world economic depression was the revival of deficiency payment support of agricultural producer prices.[6] The Wheat Act, 1932, gave British producers of milling wheat a minimum guaranteed price (called the 'standard price') subject to a 'standard quantity' restriction. The device adopted for underwriting the price guarantee was a deficiency payment representing the difference between the guarantee itself and the average market price of milling wheat. The deficiency payment was financed by means of a flour levy, paid by millers regardless of whether the flour was the product of home-grown or imported wheat. A Wheat Commission was set up to collect the flour levy and to distribute deficiency payments to wheat producers. In the immediate aftermath of the Wheat Act there was a substantial increase in the British wheat acreage: there is also evidence of a rising trend in wheat prices, including the deficiency payment (Whetham, 1978, p. 244, Table 44). The application of the principle of deficiency payments was later extended to beef cattle (Cattle Industry (Emergency Provisions) Acts, 1934 and 1936, and Livestock Industry Act, 1937), and barley and oats (Agriculture Act, 1937). A notable feature of the deficiency payments on barley and oats was that the total subsidy payment a farmer was qualified to receive was based not on grain production but on crop acreage. Thus producers of barley and oats did not have to sell their crops to qualify for the deficiency payments. Also the cost of support was met by the Exchequer and not by a levy. Legislation passed in 1939 empowered the Livestock Commission to extend deficiency payment support to producers of fat sheep, but this scheme was never implemented due to the outbreak of war. Despite the fairly widespread use of deficiency payments, 'the cost to the British Exchequer was negligible – no more than 5 per cent of the value of gross output in 1937–8' (Grigg, 1989, p. 24).[7]

Restriction of imports
Protection against imports was a third strand of policy adopted to deal with the crisis caused by the depression. However, in Britain this particular response was much more muted than the corresponding protective measures adopted by the majority of other European countries. Whereas in Britain resorting to protection meant re-adopting a policy measure which had been abandoned nearly a century earlier, most countries were merely reinforcing existing policy by increasing the level of protection.

The Import Duties Act, 1932, imposed a modest *ad valorem* tariff on all classes of goods except that certain types of raw materials and foodstuffs, including grains, meat and wool, were exempted from duty. In the same year, 1932, the principle of discriminating between imports from different sources was introduced and applied through the Ottawa Agreements Act. Under this Act all imports from British Commonwealth countries were allowed to enter Britain duty-free. The Ottawa Agreements Act established the principle of giving 'imperial preference' to imports from the Commonwealth. The counterpart of preference for Commonwealth products in the UK market was increased preferences for British exports in the markets of Commonwealth countries. Agricultural import statistics for the period point strongly to the conclusion that the main effect of combining protection against imports from foreign countries with imperial preference was to divert agricultural imports into the UK from non-Commonwealth to Commonwealth sources. The record shows that between 1932 and 1934 the total volume of food imports into the UK declined by some 6 per cent. However, whereas imports from foreign countries went down by 15 per cent, imports from the Commonwealth increased by about 11 per cent. It is also significant that even in 1934 total food imports were still higher than before the onset of the depression in 1929 (Whetham, 1978, p. 234, Table 40). The evidence that the policy of imperial preference diverted food imports to the Commonwealth, rather than reducing their total volume, points to the conclusion that in attempting to protect domestic agriculture whilst simultaneously protecting consumers from higher food prices and safeguarding the exports of British industry, British policy-makers during the 1930s were attempting the impossible. In the event the policy of protecting domestic agriculture by means of import restrictions was not very effective. Most stringently controlled were imports of maincrop potatoes. These were prohibited, except under special licence of the Board of Trade. Bacon imports were also restricted (from 1933 onwards) to assist the Pig and Bacon Marketing Boards.

Despite the Ottawa Agreements Act and the adoption of imperial preference as a trading strategy, Britain still entered into several bilateral trading agreements with non-Commonwealth countries under which agricultural imports were admitted either duty-free or at a reduced rate. In 1933 an agreement was concluded with Denmark concerning imports of bacon, ham and eggs. In the same year an agreement with Argentina related to imports of beef, maize, wheat and other products. In 1938 concessions were made on imports of a wide range of agricultural products, both crops and livestock, under an agreement with the USA (Tracy, 1982, p. 165). Some of these agreements incorporated the principle of the exporting country voluntarily agreeing to restrict its exports to Britain – as opposed to being subjected to a compulsory import quota. Without entering the argument about the substance of the difference between voluntary agreement and compulsion in this context, 'voluntary export restraints' (VERs) were destined to become a widely used protective device, both by Britain and other countries after the Second World War.

France

In France also, the agricultural policy response to world economic depression contained several strands. Initially, the government relied mainly on the tightening of import controls but, later, intervention extended to domestic supply control and market management for some commodities. From 1930 onwards, tariffs alone proved to be inadequate in maintaining domestic prices when world prices were still falling. It was in this situation that France led the world in resorting to using import quotas to protect agriculture. These were adopted in 1931, first for timber and wine, but shortly afterwards for virtually all agricultural products in quick succession, except wheat for which a different method of protection was adopted. A law passed in 1929 authorised the Minister of Agriculture to prescribe the minimum proportion of French wheat which millers must incorporate in their flour: the 'milling ratio' could be adjusted by the government according to the market situation. Like import quotas, milling ratios were due to be widely adopted as a non-tariff barrier to trade, not only in France but in other countries as well.

Another important policy innovation was that import quotas were to be supplemented not only by a specific tariff but also by a variable import license tax, with the amount of the tax varying directly with the difference between the foreign and domestic prices of the commodity (Tracy, 1982, p. 182). The resemblance of France's pre-war import license tax to the EEC's 'variable import levy' – the principal protective device adopted by the architects of the CAP in the 1960s – is too close to be coincidental.

Even when tariffs had been supplemented by import quotas and other non-tariff barriers, import controls alone proved to be insufficient to maintain domestic agricultural prices at the required level. Thus, during the 1930s the state increasingly intervened to control supplies entering the domestic market, that is, direct intervention in the market replaced indirect control via import regulation. The examples of wheat and wine illustrate the kinds of measures adopted. For wheat, the failure of the milling ratio to maintain producer prices, even when set at 100 per cent, led to the introduction of several other methods of market regulation, including storage subsidies, government intervention buying, an attempt to impose a minimum buying price on merchants, export subsidisation and the denaturing of wheat diverted to livestock feeding.

The budget costs of these measures, none of which was fully successful, were partially covered by levies imposed on both producers and millers. The Popular Front Government which came to power in 1936 adopted an even more radical policy for wheat. Under a law passed in that year, the State acquired full monopoly powers over trade in wheat. These powers were exercised by a specially created body called the Office National Interprofessionel du Blé (ONIB). The ONIB was empowered both to fix wheat prices on the domestic market and to exercise full monopoly powers over foreign trade. At that time France was a net importer of wheat.[8]

Although the Popular Front Government fell from power in 1938 the creation of the ONIB in 1936 was nevertheless a major watershed in French agricultural policy comparable with similar measures of direct government intervention in agricultural trade adopted in many other countries at about the same time, both in Europe and elsewhere in the world such as the USA (Petit, 1985).

For wine, a complex marketing scheme was devised, as early as 1931, under which producers could sell their wine only by permit. The number of permits issued was regulated by the government in order to maintain a minimum price. Under another aspect of the scheme large wine producers could be compelled to sell part of their output for distillation at a very low price. Government subsidies for uprooting vineyards were also brought in.

During the 1930s, the main arguments used in France to justify protection as a long-term policy were:

1. French farmers could not compete with foreigners enjoying benefits such as larger and more mechanised farms (especially in 'new' countries') or cheap labour (as in less industrialised countries).
2. Domestic agriculture had an essential role to play in maintaining national economic and social balance: being less volatile than industrial workers, the peasants who derived the whole of their livelihood from agriculture were an important stabilising factor in French society. Moreover, the peasants would still form the backbone of the army in the event of another war.

When the European Community was formed after the Second World War, similar arguments were used to justify protecting Community farmers from overseas competition with the Common Agricultural Policy. It is also apparent that several of the policy instruments adapted by the architects of the CAP closely resembled instruments tried out in France during the 1930s.

Germany

In Germany, the agricultural policy response to world economic depression was similar to the response in France, that is, tighter border protection combined with domestic market regulation such as a compulsory milling ratio for wheat. But after the Nazis came to power in 1933 they launched a major programme of agricultural reconstruction under which market forces were virtually abandoned in favour of direct control of agricultural production, marketing and trade by the state.

In 1929, the German government obtained powers to adjust tariffs by decree, without waiting for parliamentary approval, and the duties on both grains and livestock products were in fact raised to very high levels compared with world prices. A compulsory milling ratio, initially fixed in 1929 at a minimum level of 30 per cent domestic wheat in the grist, was later raised to 60 per cent and then 97 per cent. The government entered the rye market as a buyer of last resort, and surplus grain was denatured for use as livestock feed. In 1930 a state maize monopoly, trading mainly in imported maize, since little was produced in Germany, was created. Agricultural import quotas were also adopted to a limited extent, but much less so than in France during the same period.

Food import statistics indicate that between 1929 and 1933 there was a major decline in the volume of German food imports (Tracy, 1982, p. 200, Table 9.1). However, farm product prices and incomes continued to decline, indicating that as Germany approached self-sufficiency in major agricultural products, tariff protection became less and less successful in realising its ultimate objective of safeguarding the welfare of the farm population. The hardship resulting from the decline of farm incomes made it easier for Nazi propaganda to take root in the countryside as well as in other sectors (Tracy, 1982, p. 199).

Two major features of the major programme of agricultural reconstructions launched by the Nazis in 1933 were: first, the virtual abandonment of market forces in directing agricultural production, marketing and trade in favour of a system of highly detailed and complex direction by the state; secondly, a renewed emphasis on the unique role of the agricultural population in German society in safeguarding food supplies and national survival.

The main architect of Nazi agricultural policy was Walther Darré who became Minister of Agriculture shortly after Hitler took power in 1933. A basic tenet of Darré's policy was that farmers deserved reasonable prices and a stable income in return for their unique service of providing the nation with its food supply. Darré described the farmer as the 'blood source of the nation'; hence the Nazi slogan 'Blut und

Boden' (Blood and Soil). The Nazis made national self-sufficiency in food an axiomatic principle of agricultural policy. Without food self-sufficiency the nation could not have an effective foreign policy. Although Darré resigned as Minister of Agriculture in 1942 and took no further part in politics after that date, the fact remains that his ideas suited Hitler's aggressive intentions (Tracy, 1982, p. 203).

A law promulgated in 1933 transferred all powers covering agriculture to the Reich government. Two state agencies were newly created to control all agricultural production, marketing and trade:

1. A State Food Corporation (the Reichsnährstand or RNS) controlled all aspects of production and distribution, mainly by means of price controls and regulating supplies in other ways: farmers were guaranteed fixed prices and could be required to deliver crops to authorised market intermediaries by prescribed dates. Subsidies were used to keep consumer prices low relative to higher producer prices (Tangermann, 1982). All farmers, farm workers, processors and traders were required by law to belong to the RNS: farmers' unions and agricultural cooperatives were compulsorily affiliated to it.

2. A number of State Import Boards (Reichstellen) were created with full powers of control over import volumes, import duties and prices of imported goods on the domestic market. The Boards had both regulatory and trading powers, including powers to import on their own account, as well as buying and selling on the domestic market and holding stocks. They were also empowered to regulate trade by deciding: (a) the sources from which imports would be accepted (generally countries prepared to accept German exports) and (b) the allocation of import quotas and the amounts of preferential tariffs. Thus, under the Nazis, Germany abandoned the traditional system of commercial treaties, with 'most favoured nation' provisions, in favour of bilateral arrangements involving import quotas and preferential tariffs.

In view of the infamous deeds and atrocities perpetrated by the Nazis, both before and during the Second World War, it is difficult to be objective in evaluating any aspect of their policy, including their agricultural policy. However, it has been cogently argued that 'the basic ideas of Nazi agricultural policy were already implicit in measures taken previously in Germany and in the action of some other countries during the 1930s' (Tracy, 1982, p. 212). The basic tenets of agricultural policy which commanded widespread support, not only in pre-war Germany but in other European countries as well, included:

1. Strong belief in the social importance of the farm population.
2. Willingness of the non-farm population to protect farmers from market forces by ensuring 'fair prices' for farm products.
3. Desire for national food self-sufficiency.

The difference between Nazi Germany and the majority of her European neighbours lay not in holding to these beliefs, but in the ability of politicians to systematically carry them into practice. Tracy concludes that the formulation and implementation of agricultural policy in Nazi Germany was 'an important event in the history of European agriculture'. Moreover, even though Germany lost the war, many of the ideas about agricultural policy pioneered there during the Nazi regime survived it and 'the methods of market organisation they devised to carry out their policy were the predecessors of those which were widely adopted after the Second World War' (ibid). Subscribing to this view does not imply that National Socialist economic philosophy is not vulnerable to attack, particularly by critics stressing the long-run benefits of free trade and economic liberalism in the widest sense. Particularly telling is the argument that economic autarky, as virtually invented and practised by the Nazis, stifles international trade. This, in the eyes of economic liberals, makes all nations worse off in the long run. Thus, from an economic perspective, the National Socialist objective of complete food self-sufficiency is extremely questionable even in the context of the economic conditions prevailing in the 1930s, as well as in the present day.

Denmark

Danish agriculture was hit by the great depression of the 1930s mainly through the collapse of export market prices, particularly in the UK and Germany. By 1932 the Danish livestock price index had fallen to only 54 per cent of its 1929 level (Friedmann, 1974, p. 229). Various measures were adopted by the Danish government in attempting to raise farm prices. First, in an attempt to maintain the competitiveness of agricultural exports, the Danish krone was devalued to match the devaluation of the pound sterling in September 1931. A Foreign Exchange Control Office was also set up to regulate trade and, in particular, control imports through the allocation of foreign exchange. The export problem was not only low market prices but also import quotas imposed by countries importing Danish farm products. To tackle these problems various commodity-specific marketing boards were set up under the Ministry of Agriculture with powers both to allocate export licenses and provide price equalisation through the pooling of prices obtained in different export markets. Another set of measures was adopted to support prices on the domestic market. These included fixing the price of sugar beet, a butter price subsidy funded by a tax on domestic consumption and a grain price subsidy financed through an import duty. Most significantly, the domestic price of pork was raised through a major cut in Danish pig production engineered by imposing production quotas on individual producers. The feasibility of all such measures was, of course, dependent on the effective control of imports by the Foreign Exchange Control Office (Friedmann, 1974, p. 230).

Thus, in contrast to earlier agricultural depressions, when Denmark had eschewed protection in favour of structural adaptation to economic change, the policy response to the crisis conditions of the early 1930s was fundamentally the same in Denmark as in all other European countries.

Holland

Rather than resorting to tariff protection in reaction to the low prices and depressed trading conditions of the early 1930s, the Netherlands adopted non-tariff barriers to trade such as import quotas, import licence fees, milling ratios and other devices such as requiring margarine producers to incorporate a minimum percentage of butter in their product. Direct subsidies were used to maintain domestic producer prices of products like sugar beet and potatoes, and export subsidies to maintain exports (Tracy, 1982, pp. 131–2). Ad hoc measures of intervention adopted from 1933 onwards were later consolidated into a 'Law on the Agricultural Crisis' and by 1937 budget expenditure on agriculture had reached 4 per cent of Dutch national income (Huizinger and Strijker, 1986).

Domestic marketing and external trade in agricultural products were both closely regulated by the government through commodity specific 'Centrales'. As well as regulating production and distribution on the domestic market, each Centrale had a Purchase and Sale Office to supervise foreign trade in the commodity for which it was responsible by issuing import and export licences, collecting levies, and so on (although actual trading operations remained in private hands) (Organisation of European Economic Co-operation, 1956, p. 158). In 1941 the pre-war Centrales were replaced by semi-official Marketing Boards with compulsory membership and representation on the controlling body for all producers, traders and processors. But the Purchase and Sales Offices remained to exercise commercial functions which the Marketing Boards lacked.

Productivity Growth in Agriculture

With excess supply viewed as the primary cause of the agricultural depression of the late 1920s–early 1930s, policy makers were not inclined to increase publicly funded agricultural research. Institutional changes were also limited but included an expansion of the state extension service in Holland and the setting up of the Agricultural Research Council (ARC) in Britain.[9] Nevertheless the prevalence of agricultural protectionism in Western Europe shielded farmers from the worst effects of the economic crisis and there was a slow diffusion of past innovations. These included the increased use of new crop varieties and fertiliser, improvements in animal breeding and animal health and some replacement of horses by tractors. Private-sector technological break-throughs were also constrained by the economic climate and were sparse.[10]

A dynamism in agricultural productivity growth had been established in Denmark, Holland and Germany in previous decades. In contrast, French and British farming had experienced sluggish productivity growth over the 50 years from 1880 to 1930. The economic climate of the 1930s was particularly harsh for the agricultural exporters. In Denmark and Holland production stagnated and there was a productivity slowdown. The drive for food self-sufficiency in Germany brought about a substantial increase in agricultural output and 'overall production in 1938–9 was reckoned to be 20% above the level of ten years previously' (Tracy, 1982, p. 210). This increase was associated with rising land and labour productivity (see Ruttan et al., 1978). Increased protectionism in France merely preserved the status quo of a predominance of small mixed farms; output and productivity hardly changed during the 1930s (see Wade, 1973). Moreover, effective agricultural research and extension services were not instituted in France until after the Second World War.[11] French politicians were concerned to protect the rural sector from change rather than to induce change. However, in Britain agricultural production rose substantially at a rate of around 1.5 per cent per annum in this decade,[12] whereas production had stagnated in the 1920s. Likewise land and labour productivity increased at rates of around 1.5 per cent and 2.0 per cent per annum. Wade (1973, p. 68) observes that 'soon after 1930 Britain experienced a productivity take-off'. This was associated with the introduction of price supports which brought stability to the farming industry after a decade of almost continual depression and a continuing shift in tenure from tenancy to owner-occupation which provided increased incentives.[13] At a technical level, these productivity gains were associated with the cumulative effect of a number of innovations that were gradually introduced into farming in the 1930s. Thus, for example, new cereal varieties were developed by the agricultural research institutes set up after the First World War, pesticides and herbicides were starting to be used by farmers, fertiliser application increased, farms were being connected to the National Electricity Grid, there were improvements in the breeding and management of dairy cattle and there was a steady increase in mechanisation associated in part with the early (for Western Europe) adoption of the tractor.

US POLICY 1933–40: PRODUCTION CONTROL, PRICE SUPPORT AND STABILISATION POLICIES FOR AGRICULTURE

Introduction

When Franklin D. Roosevelt became President in March 1933 the American economy was in the depths of the depression.[14] The farm sector was in desperate straits as a result not only of a contraction of domestic consumption but also the decline of export demand.[15] Prices received by farmers fell from 148 in 1929 to 65 in 1932 (with 1910–14 = 100), whilst prices paid declined from 150 to 102. Thus the ratio of prices received to paid fell some 35 per cent. Real income from farming fell by some 50 per cent.[16] The value of farm real estate fell by about 30 per cent in nominal terms and capital losses were substantial. Around 40 per cent of farms were mortgaged at the beginning of the 1930s[17] and 'from 1930 through 1934 it is estimated that 45 per cent of the mortgaged farms changed hands through distress transfers' (Benedict, 1955, p. 140). Over a million farmers lost their farms.

Roosevelt's 'New Deal' was a response to this situation of economic collapse. Its objectives were recovery, reform and relief. A large body of legislation was enacted from 1933 to 1935 with the aims of revitalising industry, commerce and agriculture, regulating finance and the labour market, and providing direct help to the less fortunate in society. In this last respect, important policy innovations were public works projects to relieve unemployment, the provision of social security benefits, and the introduction of the dole and 'work relief'. The last item had a particular impact in rural areas.

Direct government intervention became most pronounced in agriculture compared to other sectors of the economy. This was a radical change in the philosophy of agricultural policy. The policies in force before 1933 with respect to farm credit, research and development, education and extension were viewed as self help and efficiency improvement programmes. The new policies were designed to improve the relative prices and incomes of the farm sector via direct government intervention and participation. Farm income policy was consolidated and strengthened by subsequent legislation and became an enduring legacy of the New Deal.[18] Roosevelt's administration instigated new policies toward international finance and trade as well as new domestic policies.

1933–35: Relief and Equality for Agriculture

The legislative programme of 1933
The Roosevelt administration responded very quickly to the desperate financial circumstances of the agricultural sector. In the first three months of office, it passed legislation with the purposes of improving the supply of farm mortgages and raising agricultural prices. In the autumn of 1933, the administration supplemented the legislative measures by setting up two government agencies, the Commodity Credit Corporation (CCC) and the Federal Surplus Relief Corporation (FSRC). These had the respective functions of putting a floor to the market prices of cotton and corn and expanding domestic demand for various farm products by subsidising the food consumption of families on relief.

The first action by the government was to abolish the Federal Farm Board and the Federal Farm Loan Board as legacies of the Hoover period. The powers and duties of these boards were transferred to a new credit organisation, The Farm Credit Administration (FCA). This organisation created for the first time a coordinated and comprehensive system of agricultural credit agencies. Whilst this step was intended mainly to improve efficiency in the supply of credit, more direct action to provide help to agriculture was given by the Agriculture Act of May 1933. The Act consisted of three titles: Title I, the Agricultural Adjustment Act (the AAA); Title II, the Emergency Farm Mortgage Act; and Title III, the Inflation Act (the Thomas amendment to the

Agricultural Act).[19] The major features of the Act and the CCC legislation were:

Farm mortgage relief (Title II)   The Emergency Farm Mortgage Act provided for refinancing through federal land bank loans of farm mortgages held by private lenders and a reduction in the rate of interest payable on all land bank loans. This action was essentially a 'rescue' operation to reduce the rate of farm foreclosures and inject government sponsored credit into agriculture to counteract the withdrawal of private credit.

The AAA and price support (Title I)   The AAA established the Agricultural Adjustment Administration within the USDA and gave far-reaching powers to the Secretary of Agriculture. The objective of the Act was to restore farm prices to parity with their purchasing power in 1910–14, except for tobacco, for which it was August 1919–July 1929. The pre-war base period was chosen as representing a stable period of high employment when farm and non-farm incomes were roughly in equilibrium in a free market. It was also a period when farmers were better off than at any time since the Civil War.

The main powers granted to the Secretary of Agriculture by the Act may be classified into two groups: (see Benedict, 1955, pp. 218–19).

1.   Supply control measures – authority was given to the Secretary of Agriculture to reduce acreage or production for market, or both, of any 'basic', agricultural commodity either through voluntary agreements with producers, or by other methods. To achieve this end, rental or benefit payments could be made as deemed 'fair or reasonable'. These payments were made to compensate producers for reducing the acreage of the specified crops. The basic commodities were initially defined as wheat, cotton, corn, hogs, rice, tobacco and milk and dairy products. (Peanuts were added to the list of basic commodities in 1934 by an Amendment to the AAA.) A base acreage for each basic crop was to be determined for each grower who was obliged not to grow more than an agreed percentage of his base acreage. A hog base was also defined for each pig producer. The rental payments on land taken out of basic commodities were to be supplemented by other compensatory payments. So, for example, growers of cotton and tobacco became eligible to receive 'parity payments' to bridge the gap between the parity price and the price actually received from the market (a form of deficiency payment). For wheat growers, rental payments were supplemented by extra

payments per bushel on the proportion of the crop used for domestic consumption (Benedict, 1953, pp. 306–7). The benefit and rental payments were to be funded eventually by levying processing taxes based on the difference between the average farm price and the parity price. However, initial finance of $100 million for the programme was provided by the government. The crop base for each commodity for each farmer was calculated as the average acreage grown in previous years (for example, 1930–32 for wheat, 1929–33 for corn).

2. Marketing measures – authority was given to the Secretary of Agriculture to enter into marketing agreements with processors or associations of producers in order to control prices paid to producers and margins allowed to handlers and processors. The enforcement of compliance with marketing agreements was provided for by issue of licences to processors or associations of producers. Although the provisions of the marketing agreements legislation were initially available across the spectrum of commodities, they were to become relevant only as an aid to the producers of fluid milk, fruits and vegetables.

Both sets of measures were designed to raise producers' incomes. However, the first set was based on direct government action regulating production with a transfer of income from consumers (via higher prices) and taxpayers. The second set of measures was designed to overcome the inherent weakness of voluntary producer cooperatives – that of the 'free-rider'. The aim was to increase the ability of growers to undertake self regulation of quantity and quality to increase their bargaining power. Efficiency benefits were also expected via improvement of quality, elimination of waste and evening-out of the supply of perishables throughout the marketing season. However, although a large number of marketing agreements were put into effect between 1933 and 1935, most were quickly abandoned due to disagreements with the AAA about their objectives (Benedict, 1953, pp. 303–4).

Stabilisation and the Commodity Credit Corporation   The measures contained in the AAA could not bring immediate relief to the hardpressed farm sector, particularly as large stocks overhung the markets for the major storable products. There was widespread farmer agitation and unrest particularly in the cotton and corn regions in the summer and autumn of 1933. In response to this political pressure, the administration sought to take direct and speedy action to strengthen farm prices and provide credit for farm storage of major crops by setting up the Commodity Credit Corporation. 'The CCC was created in October 1933 to supplement with direct price support the more indirect production control activities of the AAA' (Commodity Credit Corporation, 1964, p. 2). The principal activity of the CCC was to make advance loans to farmers for commodity storage. The commodity, stored in approved facilities on or off the farm, acted as collateral for the loan. The loans were made at a fixed rate – the loan rate – per unit of the commodity. In effect, the loan rate, set at a level determined by the Secretary of Agriculture, provided producers with a price floor. The loans were also non-recourse: the farmer-borrower could elect either to repay the loan within a specified period (usually by August 1st of the following year) and repossess the collateral, or default on the loan with ownership of the commodity passing to the CCC regardless of the market price. If the loan was redeemed, interest charges (at a fixed rate) were added to the face value of the loan.

The CCC loans had the functions of (a) providing cash to farmers that could be used to make payment to creditors whilst retaining control of the commodity; (b) encouraging more even marketing throughout the crop year and thereby strengthening prices especially at harvest time; (c) setting a price floor or safety net protecting participating producers against low prices whilst allowing them to gain from price rises above the loan rate. Non-participating producers would also benefit if the loan operations held market prices above the equilibrium level. Finally, it was envisaged that forfeited stocks held by CCC would be used for stabilisation purposes: the release of stocks would augment supplies in years of short crops or increased demand and dampen upward price movements. Thus, as originally conceived, CCC operations were meant to have a stabilising influence on the market both within and between crop years. Inter-annual stabilisation came later to be linked to the concept of the 'Ever-Normal Granary' and the name of Henry A. Wallace, Roosevelt's charismatic Secretary of Agriculture. Thus loan rates would stop prices falling in high production years and stocks would be accumulated by the CCC. These stocks would then be released in low crop years to hold down rising prices.

Intervention and further legislation

Acreage allotment programmes, with per acre rental payments for land withdrawn from production of programme crops, were introduced for cotton and tobacco in 1933. Producer participation was initially voluntary. The cotton programme also incorporated CCC loans at about 69 per cent of parity for 1933 reduced to 62 per cent for 1935. Production controls on these crops were strengthened by the enactment in 1934 of

the Bankhead Act relating to cotton and the Kerr Smith Act relating
to tobacco. The purpose of these acts was to improve compliance with
supply control measures. The acts provided for marketing quotas, for
all producers. Cotton and tobacco sold in excess of quota was subject
to processing tax; sales within quota were exempt. The imposition of
marketing quotas was subject to the approval of two thirds or more
of the growers voting in a poll. This necessary requirement was met in
polls in 1934.[20] An acreage allotment programme for wheat was applied
only in 1934 because of heavy winterkill of the 1933 and 1935 crops
and the effects of the Dust Bowl created by the droughts of 1934 and
1935. Moreover, compliance with the 1934 wheat programme was only
about 80 per cent and the programme itself called only for a 15 per
cent reduction in base acreage. Production of wheat in the 1933, 1934
and 1935 seasons was well below the 1928–32 average largely because
of the drought conditions. Wheat stocks were substantially reduced and
the US became a net importer for the first time since records had
started in 1866. The main impact of the wheat programme was an
income transfer to producers via rental and benefit payments.

The final major programme instituted by the 1933 AAA related to
corn and hogs. Because much corn was fed to hogs, often on the
same farm, an interrelated adjustment programme was brought in to
be financed by a tax on hogs. The first action was a hog slaughter
campaign in the autumn and winter of 1933/34. Young hogs and brood
sows were purchased by the Agricultural Adjustment Administration
at premium prices: pork was distributed to the needy through the
Federal Surplus Relief Corporation and the non-edible remainder and
small pigs were turned into tankage (grease) and fertiliser. The slaughter
programme caused a public outcry. Supply control measures for subsequent years involved rental payments on a per bushel basis, based on
the estimated normal yield, for land taken out of corn production.
Bonuses were paid also to producers for reducing hog numbers; these
payments were proportionate to the producer's hog base. An important
element of the corn–hog programme was the CCC operation commencing in 1933. Some 13 per cent of the 1933 corn harvest was stored
under CCC loans but, with the severe drought in 1934, it was evident
that the 1934 harvest would be low. Market prices firmed considerably
in the 1933–34 marketing year and in 1934 nearly all the 1933 loans
were repaid and both farmer-borrowers and the CCC made profits from
the loan scheme. The 1933/34 CCC corn operation was regarded as a
success: this was an important factor in establishing the credibility of
price-support loans after the disastrous experience of the Federal Farm
Board.

A dairy programme was initiated under the AAA but no supply control measures were undertaken. A system of licences for fluid milk was introduced. However, the main feature was 'surplus removal' of butter and cheese diverted to FSRC operations.

Political pressures resulted in seven additional commodities being brought under AAA authorisation in 1934. These were cattle, sugar, peanuts, rye, flax, barley and grain sorghums.

The sugar programme (enacted by the Jones–Costigan Sugar Act of 1934) defined production quotas for beet and cane sugar in the (continental) US, and for US territories (Hawaii, Puerto Rico and the Virgin Islands), and import quotas for supplies from the Philippines and Cuba.[21] The aggregate of the quotas was determined in relation to estimated consumption requirements. A processing tax on sugar was imposed and accompanied by a corresponding downward adjustment in the import tariff. The domestic sugar quota was allocated between factory districts and acreage allotments were made to producers.

The main emphasis in the cattle programme (enacted by the Jones–Connally Cattle Act of 1934) was on relief purchases via the FSRC of animals in drought-stricken areas in 1934. The programme also included an extensive disease eradication element involving the slaughter of animals infected by tuberculosis and contagious abortion.

Amendments in 1935 to the AAA
In 1935 a number of amendments to the 1933 AAA were enacted. The most important of these concerned agricultural import quotas and the use of customs revenue to subsidise domestic agricultural programmes.

Section 22: trade controls   Section 22 of the 1935 amendments to the AAA authorised the use of trade controls to underpin domestic price support policy. Specifically, the president could place quotas on imports if foreign supplies impeded programmes for raising the prices of farm products. This provision was rather unimportant in the 1930s but came to have considerable prominence in later decades when it was in conflict with US commitments to freer international trade.[22] We are unaware of any record that the US government consulted international trading partners before enacting Section 22 in 1935.

Section 32: use of customs revenue for surplus removal   Section 32 of the 1935 amendments to the AAA set aside 30 per cent of all import duty revenue for programmes to expand the domestic and foreign demand for US farm products through the use of domestic consumption and export subsidies. Section 32 funds in fact became the major source of finance for the relief distribution operated by the Federal Surplus Commodity Corporation (FSCC).[23] Section 32 funds could also be used to finance supply adjustment programmes. The provisions of Section 32 were of considerable importance because, first, they applied to all commodities and not just 'basic' commodities, and secondly, they set up a specific fund for subsidy programmes.

Summary: impact of the 1933–35 legislation

The 1933 legislation was introduced largely as an emergency measure to relieve hardship and aid recovery in the depressed farm sector that at the time provided a livelihood for more than 25 per cent of the US population. Low prices had led to farm incomes being well below levels in the rest of (employed) society. Farm bankruptcies were widespread and the threat of dispossession hung over the heads of a large number of farmers. The AAA, supplemented by the institution of the CCC, 'gave the Secretary of Agriculture the tools to prop up sagging commodity prices and farm returns and, in the process, protect the sector from collapse. Credit programs were also used to help stem the tide of bankruptcies and enable farm families to stay on the land and in their homes' (Lesher, 1985, p. 43).

The main scheme in the AAA for improving farm incomes was that of voluntary production adjustment designed to produce a supply and demand balance giving remunerative prices. This was aided by benefit payments to farmers who participated in supply control. These provided immediate cash to farmers and were financed partly by government and partly by special excise taxes. Supply control was viewed as a practical and quick method of raising prices and reducing accumulated stocks for the major crops and for supporting the market for hogs.

Other supporting measures were introduced soon after the passage of the AAA. Voluntary supply control was replaced by mandatory participation for cotton and tobacco. The CCC loan operation supported prices for cotton and corn. The list of basic commodities was extended from seven to fifteen. Surplus disposal through relief agencies using domestic subsidies was of importance for some commodities. Finally, the 1935 amendments, particularly Sections 22 and 32 concerned with trade measures, enhanced the ability of government to carry out agricultural price support.

The impact of AAA control measures on production is difficult to evaluate because of the severity of the droughts and dust storms in the period. It is agreed that acreage control measures were more effective for cotton and tobacco than for other crops. (See Benedict, 1953, pp. 312–17). However, there was some reduction in wheat and corn acreages in 1934 and the hog slaughter campaign of 1933/34 brought about a significant reduction in 1934 hog marketings. The CCC operation strengthened corn prices in the marketing year 1933/34 and increased the carryover. The success of this policy laid the basis for future price-support policy.

The impact of the policy measures on farm incomes in the period is also difficult to discern. Not only did the droughts cause farm prices to rise but also general economic recovery strengthened the demand for farm products.[24] Farm prices had reached their lowest point in 1932 at an index level of 62 (1909–14 = 100). They improved to 70 in 1933, 90 in 1934, 109 in 1935 and 184 in 1936 (Benedict, 1953, p. 314). The parity ratio increased from its low point of around 60 per cent in 1932 and 1933 to over 90 per cent in 1935 and 1936. Farm income in 1935 was some 50 per cent higher than in 1932. Rental and benefit payments contributed about 25 per cent of the increase in income of the years 1933–35 compared to 1932 (USDA, 1984, p. 10). Side effects of the programmes began to emerge. Supply control and increases in prices began adversely to affect US exports of cotton in 1934–35 and subsequent years as importers purchased from alternative supply sources. Political pressures built up for widening the scope of the programmes so that income transfers were made to most producers and not just those of the basic commodities. As a result, additional commodities were brought within the scope of the AAA. The aspirations and influence of farmer organisations on the legislature increased.

1936–40: Consolidation of Price-Support for Agriculture

Revision of AAA and associated regulations in 1936 and 1937. The Soil Conservation and Domestic Allotment Act of 1936, the Marketing and Sugar Acts of 1937

In January 1936, an adverse ruling of the US Supreme Court invalidated the powers of the Secretary of Agriculture to levy processing taxes and to enter into acreage reduction contracts.[25] As a result of the Court's decision, the Bankhead (cotton) and Kerr Smith (tobacco) Acts were repealed. However, the Sugar Act remained 'on the books' as did the marketing agreement provisions of the AAA together with the Section 22 and Section 32 amendments of 1935, respectively dealing with import quotas and the use of customs duty revenue to fund farm programmes. Revised legislation with essentially the same philosophy as the AAA, but circumventing the legal objections of the supreme Court was quickly prepared and approved in February 1936 as the Soil Conservation and Domestic Allotment Act (SCDAA). The aim of the new Act remained as before, that is, to control production of the major cash products and transfer income to farmers. However, the objective of parity price was replaced by that of parity of income.[26] But the development of workable methods for applying this principle was to prove difficult and 'Although income parity was the stated goal in this and subsequent programs, price parity remained the operating concept,' (Tweeten, 1970, p. 303).

Rather than directly paying farmers to reduce the acreage of cash crops, the new legislation achieved the same purpose by paying farmers to increase their acreages of non-cash crops.[27] Specifically, crops were classified as either 'soil-depleting' – cash crops such as wheat, cotton, tobacco, corn and sugar beet – or 'soil-conserving' – non-cash crops such as grasses, legumes and forages. Farmers were then paid on a per acre basis for shifting specified percentages of their acreages of soil-depleting crops into soil conserving crops. The payments to producers became known as acreage diversion payments. Diversion payments were only granted to a farmer provided he kept his acreage of soil-depleting crops down to his acreage allotment as specified by the Secretary for Agriculture. In addition, farmers were eligible for subsidies for carrying out specified soil-improving practices. Funds for the programme were appropriated by Congress from the Treasury, rather than being provided by processing taxes. In addition, funds from customs receipts under Section 32 could be assigned for diversion and conservation purposes.

The 1936 Act's emphasis on soil conservation was largely but not wholly an expedient device for retaining an adjustment programme. Public and congressional concern over soil conservation had been aroused by the drought and dust storms of 1934. The passage of the Act was more easily achieved by emphasising soil conservation rather than its principal objective of raising farm prices. Nevertheless, the Act did increase the environmental awareness of farmers.

Two supplemental agricultural acts were passed in 1937, to update the relevant legislation in line with the Supreme Court's judgement of 1936, even though the legislation had not been specifically invalidated. These were the 1937 Agricultural Marketing Act and the 1937 Sugar Act. The latter was similar to the 1934 Act except that an excise tax payable to the Treasury was substituted for the processing tax. Its essential provisions remained in force until 1974 with domestic production and import quotas being the key instruments adopted for giving protection to domestic producers and refiners.[28]

Emphasis on CCC operations: the Agricultural Adjustment Act of 1938

The agricultural policy of the New Deal was consolidated in 1936 not merely by the passing of the SCDAA but, more importantly, by the re-election of Roosevelt in that year. Agricultural policy was a prime issue in the election campaign (see Saloutos, 1982, ch. 16). The Democrats emphasised the benefits that the New Deal had brought to the farm sector, defended the claim that reciprocal trade pacts had revived trade and promised a continuation of the agricultural programme. Stress was placed on proposals by the Secretary for Agriculture, Wallace, for an ever-normal granary and crop insurance. The Democrats won the election easily with a sweep of the farm states. The New Deal for agriculture was vindicated in the sense that farmers voted for its continuation: the Roosevelt administration had a mandate for consolidation of its agricultural policy. However, a change of emphasis was imminent.

Droughts in 1934 and 1936 had highlighted the desirability of supply reserves. But the usually favourable growing conditions of 1937 and the prospects of excellent crops in 1938 exposed the inadequacy of the conservation approach in years of bumper crops, as well as emphasising the need for a broader storage programme to cope with fluctuations of production (Saloutos, 1982, p. 255). A new AAA passed in February 1938 made the CCC loan and storage operation the main instrument of policy and gave area adjustment and conservation a supporting role.

The main new features of the 1938 AAA were that the loan programme was to be integrated with the acreage adjustment programme and that the CCC was obliged to make non-recourse loans on wheat, cotton and corn at specified percentages of parity. Other new aspects were provisions for marketing quotas, for crop insurance and greater emphasis on parity (deficiency) payments.

CCC provisions   The granting of CCC loans was made mandatory for wheat, cotton and corn under specified conditions rather than being left to the discretion of the Secretary for Agriculture.[29] Discretionary loans were to be available for tobacco and a number of other commodities.[30] The CCC loans were available only to producers complying with supply restrictions that were in force.

In 1939, the CCC was placed under the control of the USDA; a move designed to strengthen the tie between price–loan policy and supply control.

Supply control   The supply control provisions of the new Act were of two types: crop diversion and marketing quotas. The main features of the 1936 SCDAA were retained so that the Secretary for Agriculture had the power to allot acreages of the soil-depleting crops and make diversion payments. A national maximum acreage could be specified for allotment crops.[31]

Marketing quotas could be introduced in conjunction with acreage allotments for wheat, cotton, corn, tobacco or rice, if the supply of the crop exceeded 'normal' supply – an amount equal to domestic consumption plus exports plus a safety margin (see Benedict, 1953, p. 377). The marketing quotas would apply to sales in the following season, provided the quota was approved by at least two thirds of producers who voted in a referendum. When marketing quotas were approved, compliance with acreage allotments was compulsory; non-cooperating producers not only lost price supports but were subject to penalties including fines and a loss of future allotments. Quotas were a more stringent application of allotments: both were essentially acreage controls. If allotments were announced, only cooperators were eligible to receive non-recourse loans but there were no penalties for non-compliance unless marketing quotas also applied. Similarly, if growers rejected a quota plan, non-recourse loans were not available for the marketing season in which quotas would have applied. The principal purpose of acreage allotments and marketing quotas was as a backup to the CCC operation and in particular, to prevent large stock accumulation by the CCC.

In the period 1938–40, marketing quotas were applied only to cotton (1938, 1939 and 1940 harvests) and tobacco (1938 and 1940 harvests).

Parity (deficiency) payments Provision was made in the 1938 AAA for parity or deficiency payments equal to the difference between farm price and parity price to be made on a wider range of crops, namely wheat, cotton, corn, rice and tobacco. These payments were conditional on compliance with acreage and quota limitations and were to be based on 'normal' production. They were made from Treasury funds, were additional to other payments and were not to exceed more than 25 per cent of the parity price per unit of commodity. Parity payments were made on wheat (crop-years 1938–43), cotton (crop years 1939–41), rice (crop years 1938–43), corn (crop years 1938–43) and tobacco (crop years 1941–43).

Federal crop insurance Title V of the 1938 AAA specified a crop insurance scheme directed primarily at crop losses of wheat producers in dry areas. The plan was prompted by the distress caused by the droughts of 1934 and 1936. A Federal Crop Insurance Corporation was set up with initial capital funds of $100 million. The Corporation was directed to insure wheat producers against losses in yield caused by natural hazards beginning with the 1939 crop. Insurance was to be based on not less than 50 cent nor more than 75 per cent of average yields. Premiums and indemnities were to be paid in wheat or its cash equivalent. A similar plan for cotton was introduced in June 1941. Participation by producers of both crops was low, the financial results were unsatisfactory, and the programme came to an end in 1943 when the Congress enacted legislation which had the effect of withdrawing financial support.

Research into new uses for farm products   The Act provided for the establishment, under the direction of the USDA, of four regional laboratories that would carry out research into new, particularly industrial, uses for farm products. At the time, particular interest centred on the possibility of producing alcohol from feed grains for use as a motor fuel.

Trade Policy

United States' trade policy was broadly protectionist from the period of the Civil War in the 1860s, until the late 1920s. Then, when the Great Depression struck, and international trade was shrinking throughout the world, US tariffs were raised to a record level by the Hoover administration, with the passage of the Hawley–Smoot Tariff Act of 1930. This legislation was passed in the face of strong criticism by leading US economists. One of the criticisms advanced was that, because of the relative unimportance of agricultural importing, higher tariffs could not possibly benefit US agriculture (Benedict, 1953, p. 251). It was against this background that a sharp reversal of trade policy towards lower tariffs occurred during Roosevelt's first term as president. The US dollar came off the gold standard in April 1933 by presidential order. The dollar depreciated in relation to currencies based on gold but the dollar devaluation did not have much impact on agricultural exports.[32] More important in the longer term was the shift in US policy toward lower tariffs and increased trade. The administration pursued a policy of tariff reductions through reciprocal trade agreeements. The Reciprocal Trade Agreement Act of 1934, an amendment to the Hawley–Smoot Act of 1930 authorised the president for a period of three years to negotiate trade agreements and to raise or lower tariff rates by not more than 50 per cent for the purpose of expanding trade. Significant features of the Act were provisions for reciprocal tariff and quota reductions and the most-favoured nation (MFN) principle. The latter provided that concessions granted to a particular exporter of a specific commodity (or commodities) to the US were automatically given to all similar exporters whose treaties with the US authorised like treatment for imports from the US. The Trade Agreements Act was reviewed in 1937 and then at subsequent intervals to 1952. Sixteen agreements were signed by 1938 and 29 by 1948. Tariffs were reduced in the 1930s as a result of the agreements and there is some evidence that they led to a modest expansion of trade, including some recovery of farm exports.[33] However, the main significance of the Act is that it represented a major reversal of the trend toward higher tariffs that had taken place over the past seventy years. The balance had swung toward freer trade and away from protectionism.[34]

The New Deal for domestic agriculture policy was, in principle, in conflict with this shift toward a more liberal trade policy.[35] Production adjustment and domestic price support for an exporter constitutes an interference with trade as much as tariff protection for an importer. However, in the 1930s this conflict was of little consequence because of the relative unimportance then of exports to US agriculture.

General international trade shrivelled in the depression years; in addition, the US share dropped from 16 per cent to 11 per cent in the five years following the Hawley–Smoot Tariff Act. Exports as a proportion of national income fell from around 6.5 per cent in the 1920s to around 4 per cent in the early 1930s. Some revival of trade occurred in the following years, partly as a result of trade agreements. The US continued to have a positive balance of trade and to accumulate reserve assets (principally gold and silver). Farm exports in value terms were halved in the 1930s compared to the previous decade[36] and took a declining share of total exports. In 1925 agricultural exports had accounted for about 40 per cent of total exports, by 1930 the proportion was down to one-third and was around 20 per cent by 1939 (see Wilcox and Cochrane, 1960, p. 345). The volume of all the main agricultural exports declined. Cotton, wheat, lard and other pork products were badly hit. The decline of the European market was a major factor.[37] However, the contraction of cotton exports was partly a consequence of the cotton programme.[38] Farm exports as a proportion of the value of farm marketings was less than 10 per cent and the percentage of harvested cropland used for exports was only about 5 per cent during the 1930s (Johnson, 1977, p. 299). In summary, the farm commodity programmes were introduced and consolidated during a period when exports, except for cotton, were not an important outlet for US farm produce.

A corollary to domestic intervention and trade interference pro-grammes for agriculture in the US and other countries was a movement to regulate trade through international commodity agreements. All the major wheat exporters (the US, Canada, Australia and Argentina) insti-tuted domestic intervention policies in the 1930s (see Gordon-Ashworth, 1984, ch. 7). An International Wheat Agreement was signed by 22 countries in August 1933. This provided for export quotas and production restraint in importing countries. The agreement proved unworkable. However, a Wheat Advisory Committee was kept in being. Following a large US harvest in 1938 and the prospect of low world prices, the Committee sought a new agreement around US proposals for 'an international granary plan'. No agreement could be reached but the main exporters continued with talks and a draft agreement was in sight by 1939 and completed by 1942. This agreement specified wheat export quotas and a minimum world price for a selected reference wheat. Although wartime controls prevented the implementation of the agreement, an International Wheat Council was created in 1942. This was the forum for postwar discussions leading to an International Wheat Agreement (IWA). The US also participated in discussions leading to the conclusion of an International Sugar Agreement (ISA) between exporters and importers which came into effect in 1937. Export quotas and minimum import commitments were specified. The ISA had little impact pre-war but laid the basis for several postwar agreements.

Use of Section 32 Funds

Section 32 funds were used in three principal ways. First, the FSCC continued its scheme of purchase and distribution to state relief agen-cies. The principal commodities concerned were dairy products, fruits and vegetables. The FSCC was merged with the USDA division of Marketing in 1940 to form the Surplus Marketing Administration. Sec-ondly, a School Lunch Programme was initiated in 1936 and expanded thereafter. Under the plan, surplus commodities were given to schools for lunch provision. Thirdly, a Food Stamp Plan was introduced in 1939. Under this scheme low-income families on relief could purchase stamps (orange-coloured) which could be spent on food. In addition, they were given additional stamps (blue coloured) for the purchase of specified foods (in surplus). The plan was essentially a food subsidy scheme for low-income households. It was abolished in 1943 when the wartime revival of employment and income reduced the number of families on relief and agricultural surpluses were no longer a problem for the administration.

The use of Section 32 funds to subsidise exports was also authorised. However, relatively little use was made of this instrument of surplus disposal during the 1930s. Possible explanations for this include the Roosevelt Administration's adherence to a relatively liberal trading policy, despite economic depression and the priority accorded to using surplus foodstuffs to relieve domestic unemployment and poverty (Benedict, 1955, p. 283). This attitude to the use of export subsidies stands in marked contrast to that adopted by US governments in more recent times.

Technical Change in Agriculture, 1933–40

Federal sponsorship of agricultural research in state experiment stations (SEAs) plus direct USDA appropriations rose annually in real terms from 1925–30, levelled off and fell in the period to 1934 and then climbed sharply in the period to 1940 (see Peterson and Fitzharris, 1977, p. 77). Federal support to the SEAs was boosted in the first instance by the Purnell Act of 1925 and in the second instance by the Bankhead–Jones Act of 1935. USDA spending diminished in the early 1930s and then increased significantly from 1935 onwards. An increased proportion of USDA research was located in the SEAs. The coordinated corn improvement programme established in 1925 was followed by similar projects in the 1930s for the other grains. The coordinated national crop improvement programmes also placed more emphasis on location-specific research. Private sector involvement in crop research developed in the 1930s with respect of hybrid corn. Because of the proprietary nature of hybrid corn seed, the private sector was able to reap a return on its investment in research, multiplication of seed and distribution to farmers.

Another government initiative stimulating agricultural technical change was the rural electrification programme created by the Rural Electrification Act by which cheap credit was made available to electric power companies in rural areas. In 1935, only 11 per cent of farms had electric power. By 1941, 35 per cent of farms were supplied with central station power. The programme was virtually complete by 1955 when over 90 per cent of farms were provided with electricity.

The depression and droughts of the early 1930s held back agriculture's productivity potential. However, a marked and continuing increase in total factor productivity took place from the mid-1930s onwards (see Peterson and Fitzharris, 1977, p. 75). The shift to tractor-based mechanised crop farming that had gathered pace in the 1920s continued in the 1930s and the stock of tractor horsepower doubled over the period (see

Benedict, 1955, p. 32 and Hayami and Ruttan, 1971, p. 339). Combines and cornpickers on farms began to increase rapidly; the mechanisation of cotton farms was a prominent feature of the late 1930s following the introduction of the cotton-picker. Rural electrification permitted the use of milking machines and feed handling equipment. It also revolutionised poultry farming and fostered broiler production. Mechanical power and machinery increased by around 8 per cent between 1930 and 1940 (Penn, 1981, p. 39). The farm labour force declined by about 10 per cent between 1930 and 1940 (see Penn, 1981, p. 39) and the proportion of the total labour force in agriculture fell to about 20 per cent by 1940. The capital-to-labour ratio in agriculture continued to rise in the 1930s. In 1920, labour contributed approximately 50 per cent of total inputs to agriculture, by 1930 the figure was 46 per cent and by 1940 down to 41 per cent whilst capital's share, excluding real estate, rose from 32 per cent to 36 per cent to 41 per cent (see Tweeten, 1970, p. 128).

The replacement of horses and mules by tractor power released land for other uses and was an important source of a 15 per cent increase in farm output between 1930 and 1940 (ibid., p. 129). Yield increasing biological innovations for crops were significant from the late 1930s onwards. The most significant development was the use of hybrid corn varieties in place of open pollinated varieties. Hybrid seeds were first made available in Iowa in the late 1920s. By 1940, over 30 per cent of the total corn area was planted with hybrid varieties. Hybrid seed increased corn yields by about 20 per cent compared to the traditional varieties. Associated with the uptake of hybrid corn was an increase in the utilisation of commercial fertilisers. A major factor in the adoption of hybrid corn was greater responsiveness to improved (higher nutrient) fertilisers which were being supplied at lower real prices. Total fertiliser use increased between 1930 and 1940 by some 30 per cent (Heady and Tweeten, 1963, p. 15) but this only constituted the beginning of the era of chemical innovations in agriculture.

Although the trend of increasing yields stemming from the adoption of hybrid corn is the most widely referenced biological innovation of the 1930s, similar trends for the other grains, cotton and tobacco also begin to appear in the late 1930s. An USDA index of crop production per acre displays a slight upward trend from 1910 to the mid-1930s and then a much steeper trend after that time (see Heady and Tweeten, 1963, p. 95). Efficiency in livestock production also began to increase from the mid-1930s. Technical change indices such as eggs per hen, milk yield per cow, feed per pound of broiler and pigs saved per sow show improvement from that date.

Productivity growth stemming from biological technological change in the late 1930s represented the application of the research programmes initiated by federal funding in earlier years. Adoption was delayed in the early 1930s by the drought, depression and the unfavourable capital and credit situation of farmers. After the mid-1930s, the equity position of farmers improved, price relatives became more favourable and the government support programmes increased price certainty and enhanced incomes. These all favoured the uptake of the available new technology. Finally, the extension services in the 1930s were 'well organised and ably staffed and farmers had become receptive to the recommendations made by them. Thus there was brought about a much wider and faster adoption of improved methods than had occurred in any previous period' (Benedict, 1955, p. 34).

Summary: The New Deal for Agriculture

Saloutos (1982, p. 270), in an appraisal of the New Deal farm policies, concludes that 'with all its limitations and frustrations, the New Deal . . . constituted the greatest innovative epoch in the history of American Agriculture'. Paarlberg (1984, p. 14) in a review of agricultural policy set in a long-term perspective sees 1933 as a watershed: 'Historically, American agricultural policy issues have sprung from three evolving and overlapping agendas: (1) Before 1933: Agricultural development, particularly research and education, (2), Since 1933: Commodity programs and (3) Increasingly since the mid-sixties: issues raised by non-farmers.'

As noted in previous sections, farm policy from 1860 to 1933 was concerned with improving the efficiency and productive base of agriculture. Land settlement, research and education and farm credit programmes had been set in motion and expanded. However, within the legal, technological and credit framework, resource allocation, production and returns to producers were largely determined by the state of domestic and foreign markets. There was little direct government support for farm products, except sugar, in contrast to a policy of high protectionism for manufacturers. The latter, of course, had a negative impact on farm exports. Macro policy was non-interventionist being imbued by the belief that the market economy was self-regulating and self-curing. With the New Deal came a reversal of policy attitudes and the initiation of new policy initiatives. Direct government intervention to improve the relative prices and incomes of farmers via the 'big commodity programmes' (Paarlberg, 1984) became a major feature of agricultural policy. Agricultural production was intentionally reduced and farm price supports were put in place. However, internationally, the government favoured reduced protectionism, a lowering of tariffs and trade liberalisation through the MFN policy. Macro policy had a new direction: government took on the responsibility of stimulating domestic economic activity in the circumstances of the depression. Thus the New Deal created a new farm policy agenda whilst expanding the old. It also initiated new macro and trade policies which had an impact on agriculture.

Since the export demand for agricultural products was small, farm prices and agriculture's internal terms of trade during the 1930s were determined almost entirely by domestic demand and supply factors overlaid by the New Deal programmes. Hathaway (1963) has argued that in the inter-war period, domestic demand for farm products recovered somewhat as the macro economy came out of the slump after 1933. Real national income had contracted between 1929 and 1932 but expanded from 1933 to 1937. There was a short but sharp recession in 1937–8 and an upturn thereafter. However, even by 1940, real national income was only approaching the level of the late 1920s. Given a positive link between changes in real national income and disposable personal income and a positive income elasticity of demand for food, fluctuations in the business cycle shift the demand curve for farm products. Evidence advanced by Hathaway reveals a positive link between the business cycle and both farm price and cash receipts in nominal and real terms (Hathaway, 1963, p. 138).[39] The link between the business cycle and farm prosperity was also argued by Benedict (1955): 'The overriding cause of the (farm) depression of the 1930s was a tremendous shrinkage in demand, both here (domestically) and abroad' (p. 442) and 'the recovery of agriculture was slowed by the severe business recession of 1938. This gives further evidence of the heavy dependency of farm prosperity on high levels of business activity' (p. 444). Benedict argues further that as an emergency device, the institution of production controls under the New Deal programmes was a logical response for effecting relief to agriculture in the situation of depressed demand overlaid by the carryover of large stocks. However, he also argues that the controls were only 'moderately effective' and that the droughts of 1934 and 1936 had a much more dominant impact on the supply situation, particularly in reducing the overhang of stocks.

The domestic demand and supply curves were also shifting to the right during the 1930s because of population growth and technological change. The US population grew by about 8 per cent between 1930 and 1940. Tractors continued to replace draft animals releasing land for the production of cash crops and forage for livestock. The adoption of new biological technologies was in evidence during the late 1930s.

Benedict (1955, ch. 11) argues that the course of farm prices and farm prosperity in the 1930s was largely a result of these demand/supply factors rather than the instruments employed under the Agricultural Adjustment Acts. Farm prices had reached their lowest point in 1932 at an index level of 65 (1910–14 = 100). They rose to 122 in 1937, fell in 1938 and recovered to 100 in 1940. Prices paid by farmers rose between 1932 to 1935 and then remained fairly stable. The index of prices paid was at a low of 102 in 1932 and had moved to 122 by 1937. The parity ratio reached 93 in 1937 from a low of 58 in 1932 but dropped to 78 in 1939.[40] Thus the internal terms of trade for agriculture improved somewhat over the period. Realised net income from farming (including direct government payments) followed a similar pattern. Farm income dropped from just over $6 billion (thousand million) in 1929 to around $2 billion in 1932 and recovered to $4.4 billion in 1939 (see Wilcox and Cochrane, 1960 p. 216).

The impact of the New Deal on farm prosperity was mixed. The voluntary acreage adjustments and marketing quotas constituted moderately successful production controls for cotton and tobacco but were less effective for wheat and corn. However, rising yields put these programmes under pressure by the late 1930s. CCC operations tended to have a stabilising rather than an overall price support function, particularly before 1938 when loan rates were set at the discretion of the Secretary of Agriculture. The 1938 Act made mandatory provisions for loan rates but support levels in 1938 were not unduly high being around or below market prices of the previous years. However in 1939 and 1940, CCC stocks of cotton, corn and wheat became large, indicating that the loan rates were being set above equilibrium levels. The benefit and rental payments were a welcome source of cash to farmers but did not constitute a large element of total income. They contributed around 5 per cent of gross farm income and around 10–15 per cent of net farm income over the 1933–40 period.[41] The emergency credit programme brought quick and vital financial relief to thousands of farmers and prevented a major dislocation of the structure of agriculture.

The expansion of the traditional policy agenda as part of the New Deal was relevant to the era and was important also for the future. The reorganisation of the federally sponsored credit system was a major success giving rise to a comprehensive credit base comparable to that provided to urban business by commercial banks. The federal farm credit agencies instituted long-term amortized loan plans for real-estate mortgages; this was a major innovation compared to the short-term unamortized loans previously available from commercial banks. The Federal Land Banks had, prior to the 1930s, held only a small proportion of total real-estate loans. Now they had become major lenders. The credit base was widened and the provision of production credit greatly strengthened. 'Credit was made available at the lowest possible rate consistent with good market practices' (Saloutos, 1982, p. 269). The research and development programme was also expanded and the rural electrification scheme was a substantial contributor to productivity increase and rural wellbeing. A programme for controlling soil erosion was set in being which was directed at conserving agriculture's productive base. This was to be the forerunner of wider environmental concerns with respect to farm production.

However, the political economy aspects of the New Deal had more significance for the future than its direct effects on farm prosperity or its innovations with regard to agricultural productivity. The programme for agriculture was conceived as an emergency response to the parlous condition of farming. New measures were employed to deal with unprecedented circumstances. Relief came to the farm sector. 'On every hand was visible evidence that the government cared. The Depression dragged on but the mood changed for the better on American farms' (Paarlberg, 1980, p. 24). The farmers voted to re-elect Roosevelt in 1936; recovery in the farm sector was only just beginning and 'the vote indicated that the farmers wanted the federal government to play a positive role in protecting their interests' (Saloutos, 1982, p. 235). The credentials of the mixed economy approach to agriculture had been established. Political opposition to the commodity programmes faded away. The USDA grew in size and influence and became one of the most prestigious federal agencies of cabinet rank. Agricultural policy changed from an emergency action programme to encompass longer-term considerations with emphasis on the twin aspects of agricultural adjustment and stabilisation. The commodity programmes were firmly in place by the late 1930s and a new phase of farm policy had begun. Economic management of agriculture via the use of price instruments and production controls had replaced *laissez-faire*. Despite some obvious economic drawbacks, except possibly in wartime, the new agenda was to prove both durable and flexible.

COMMENTARY: AGRICULTURAL POLICY IN THE 1930s IN WESTERN EUROPE AND THE US

The depression of the 1930s ushered in a new and lasting form of agricultural protectionism involving the direct intervention by governments in commodity markets. This interventionism was designed to stabilise returns and bolster the incomes of farmers. The agricultural importing countries of Western Europe with a history of protection, notably France and Germany, replaced tariffs by a variety of non-tariff barriers (NTBs)[42] which, for the most part insulated domestic markets from foreign competition. Great Britain reversed its commercial policy, abandoned free trade and introduced domestic subsidies via deficiency payments (a form of NTB), marketing schemes, import controls and modest import duties. There was a reversal of policy also in the agricultural exporting nations of Denmark and Holland. These countries utilised devices such as domestic subsidies, quantitative restrictions and duties on imported commodities and the regulation of exports via export licensing schemes to raise returns via price discrimination. Much of the intervention in Western Europe tended to encourage domestic self-sufficiency. In contrast, US policy brought in via the Agricultural Acts of the 1930s was practically unique in that domestic production restrictions were applied alongside price supports.[43] However, in other respects US policy was similar to that in Western Europe in that it attempted to increase returns to producers by direct intervention and through Section 22 of the AAA which authorised the use of NTBs to restrict imports rather than relying on traditional tariffs. Section 32 of the AAA also provided funds for the subsidised expansion of domestic and foreign demand.

The new agricultural protectionism was radically different in orientation and scope from traditional tariff protection. Government intervention into agricultural markets became the norm, domestic production was largely insulated from foreign competition and levels of protection were substantially increased. Disequilibrium in the chaotic and depressed world commodity markets was consequently exacerbated and trade was substantially reduced.[44] Agricultural trade restrictions were an adjunct to domestic farm policies.

The prevalence of widespread government intervention into domestic agriculture in the 1930s might be explained by a number of interrelated factors. First and foremost was the demand by dissatisfied agriculturalists, in the midst of an economic depression accompanied by monetary instability, for action to bolster their sagging returns. As such, much intervention was conceived initially as a temporary response to a 'crisis' situation. Second, was the enhanced capacity of government to deliver more effective protection through an enlarged bureaucracy and improved administrative ability. Third, the political situation of the day encouraged retaliation and defensive trade action. Fourth, agrarian fundamentalism which invoked both a special relationship between man, land and nature and an identity between national and rural interests was conducive to the notion that the rural sector should be sheltered from external forces. Fifth, in Western Europe, there was toward the end of the 1930s a drive for self-sufficiency as part of the preparations for war.

The depressed state of agriculture in the 1930s tended to retard the onset of the agricultural adjustment problem. Agricultural productivity growth started to take off in the US (from the mid-1930s) and in Britain (from the early 1930s) but was largely halted in some European countries, such as Denmark, and was not set in train in France until after 1945. In the post-Second World War period there was an acceleration of technical change in western agriculture coupled with a slow growth in effective demand for agricultural products. The forces requiring agricultural adjustment were largely internal to each country. For Western Europe this was in contrast to the experience of the previous century when external competition provided the challenge to domestic producers and dictated the response of policymakers. In attempting to cope with this agricultural adjustment problem, the postwar policy response in both the US and Western Europe was to rely on the interventionist measures introduced in the 1930s. Direct government involvement in agriculture became a permanent feature of agricultural policy in the industrialised countries.

NOTES

1. In 1929, the US produced over 40 per cent of the world's industrial goods, twice as much as Britain and Germany combined. The US contraction post-1929 had a severe impact on exporters to America and on world trade. US protectionism furthered the contraction of world trade.
2. 'Around 1925 the recovery of agricultural production in countries affected by the (Great) war had upset the balance of supply and demand and started a decline in agricultural prices which since 1934 had become acute' (League of Nations Economic Committee 1935, reported in Tracy, 1982, p. 147).
3. For a review of the Acts see Currie and Rayner (1979, pp. 25–7).
4. Between 1929 and 1933 British food imports rose and agricultural prices continued falling (Whetham, 1978, p. 234, Table 40). Without necessarily implying that imports were the sole reason for low prices, or even a major explanatory factor, this was the background to the passage of the 1933 Act.
5. It is notable that the power to restrict imports was given not to the marketing board itself, or even to the Minister of Agriculture (through whom marketing boards were ultimately responsible to Parliament not to abuse their monopoly powers), but to the Board of Trade.
6. First proposed by the Milner Committee in 1915 and later incorporated in the abortive Agricultural Act of 1920.
7. This figure also suggests that the level of protection afforded to British agriculture was equivalent to a Producer Subsidy Equivalent (PSE) somewhat higher than 5 per cent since producer prices were raised above world levels by the instruments

used by the Marketing Boards and by import restrictions (see Chapter 6 for a discussion of the principle and recent evidence on PSEs).

8. The principle underlying the fixing of the domestic wheat price was historic purchasing power, similar to the parity price concept used in the USA (Petit, 1985, p. 25).

9. The ARC was a purely advisory body without funds to sponsor research until after the Second World War.

10. Two major improvements of tractors were initiated in the 1930s which provided a stimulus to mechanisation of agriculture after 1939: first, the development of satisfactory pneumatic tyres; and, second, the invention of a combined linkage and hydraulic control system by Harry Ferguson in the UK in 1934. The chemical industry also made some limited advances in the 1920s and 1930s in the development of pesticides and herbicides and the production of synthetic fertilisers.

11. The research service set up after the First World War received very limited funding and was abolished in 1935 as an economy measure. A 1927 proposal for an extension service could not get through the legislature.

12. Growth rates presented for Britain are guestimates based on Wade (1973).

13. By 1933 some 35 per cent of farm land was under owner-management compared to 12 per cent in 1915.

14. Industrial production declined by nearly 50 per cent between 1929 and 1932 (see Benedict, 1953, p. 277).

15. The principal reasons for the weakening of export sales were economic depression and agricultural trade restrictions in importing countries and increased competition from countries such as Australia and Canada. The volume of US agricultural exports declined by around 20 per cent between 1929 and 1932. Wheat exports fell off by some 80 per cent, pork exports by some 65 per cent and tobacco by some 24 per cent. Only cotton maintained its volume of exports (Benedict, 1953, p. 277).

16. Net income from farming declined in nominal terms from $6.7 billion in 1929 to $2.3 billion in 1932 (Benedict, 1955, p. 11). The estimate in the text of the decline in real income takes account of the fall in prices paid by farmers.

17. This estimate is based on the figure given by Benedict (1955, p. 139), of 2.5 million mortgaged farms and an estimate taken from Penn (1981) of the number of farms of 6.5 million.

18. In the period preceding the enactment of the New Deal agricultural programme there was a vigorous debate in the US concerning the causes of the agricultural depression. Opinion was divided between (a) those who attributed low farm prices and income to oversupply (with the corollary that the solution to the farm problem was supply control), and (b) those who thought that low prices in agriculture, as well as in other sectors, were due to misconceived monetary policy. The main protagonists in the debate included J.D. Black, of Harvard University, who advocated supply control with acreage allotments, and G.F. Warren, of Cornell University, who thought that prices generally could be restored to the pre-depression level by adjusting the gold parity of the dollar (Paarlberg, 1984). The monetary explanation of the farm problem was undermined in part by the observation that farm prices were more depressed than non-farm prices. For this and other reasons Warren lost and Black won the debate, so paving the way for the New Deal agricultural programme.

19. Title III gave the president powers to require the Federal Reserve Banks to expand credit and to reduce the gold content of the dollar.

20. According to Benedict and Stine (1956), the supply control measures for cotton and tobacco were effective in the period 1933–36: 'the controls held the harvested cotton acreage through the 1933–36 seasons to a level below the acreage harvested in the period of Farm Board operations. In spite of high yields in 1933, offset by drought in 1934, production was reduced by more than 20 per cent. The cutback of production supported prices and provided an opportunity for disposing of the excessive carry-over that had accumulated by 1932' (p. 12). 'The first phase of the AAA programme

for tobacco was ... to bring about a quick adjustment of production. That phase was completed by 1936' (p. 79).

21. There were virtually no imports from elsewhere.

22. It is significant that the enactment of Section 22 is unrecorded by M.R. Benedict in his monumental book *Farm Policies in the United States, 1790–1950*, published in 1953.

23. The Federal Surplus Relief Corporation (FSRC), created in 1933, was so renamed in 1935.

24. National income reached a low of $39.6 billion in 1933. It recovered to $48.6 billion in 1934, reached $56.8 billion in 1935 and stood at $64.7 billion in 1936 (Benedict, 1953, p. 314).

25. The case of US v. Butler et al., Receivers of Hoosac Mills Corporation. The Court adopted a more favourable attitude to Roosevelt's legislation after the replacement of retiring judges by others who were more attuned to the New Deal policies.

26. The stated objective of the 1936 Act was 'to re-establish at as rapid a rate as the Secretary of Agriculture determines to be practicable and in the public interest ... the ratio between the purchasing power of the net income per person on farms and that of the income per person not on farms that prevailed during the five year period August 1909–July 1914'.

27. The SCDAA instituted a change in procedure for contracts between farmers and the administration. Under the AAA, separate adjustment contracts were worked out for each crop. Under the SCDAA the farmer was offered one contract on the basis of a plan to reduce his acreage of soil-depleting crops and increase that of soil-conserving crops. Decentralisation of the USDA administration was introduced along with the SCDAA: an office was opened in each state for the purposes of making and checking compliance with contracts and issuing benefit cheques.

28. These provisions were: (1) estimates of US consumption requirements made annually; (2) allocation of domestic requirements among domestic (continental and offshore) and foreign sources; (3) allotment of 'proportional shares' to domestic growers of beet and cane, these to be the bases for conditional payments and, at the same time, the bases to which acreage restrictions would be applied if necessary; (4) import quotas on raw and refined sugar; (5) limits on shipments of refined sugar from Hawaii and Puerto Rico to continental US; (6) benefit (conditional) payments per hundredweight of raw sugar to domestic producers for complying with the terms of the Sugar Act, which declined with the level of production per farm; (7) a tax of 50 cents per hundredweight on domestic raw sugar; and (8) a tariff of 62.5 cents per hundredweight on imports of raw sugar.

29. For wheat and cotton, loans were to be made available if the farm price on 15 June (1 August for cotton) or at any time thereafter during the marketing year was below 52 per cent of parity or if the July (August) crop estimate indicated a supply in excess of normal annual consumption plus exports. The loan rate for these crops was to be specified by the Secretary within a range of 52–75 per cent of parity. Loans on corn were mandatory in the commercial corn areas if the farm price on 15 November was below 75 per cent of parity or if the November estimate of production exceeded a normal year's domestic consumption and exports. The loan rate was to be 52 to 75 per cent of parity according to a specified scale in inverse relation to the size of the harvest. Thus they could only be 75 per cent of parity if expected production was not more than normal consumption plus exports and could only be 52 per cent of parity if expected production was larger than 125 per cent of normal consumption plus exports.

30. CCC support in 1938–40 was given to butter, grain sorghums, barley, rice, peanuts and a number of fruits and nuts.

31. The national allotted acreage for wheat was to be that which, with average yields, would produce a quantity equal to normal consumption and exports plus 30 per cent. The national corn allotment (in commercial corn areas) was an acreage designed to supply normal feeding requirements plus a reasonable carryover. The allotment for

cotton was expected to produce a quantity equal to normal consumption plus exports with average yields. Allotments for tobacco and for rice were used for the 1939 and 1940 crops.

32. The devaluation of the dollar undermined the London Economic Conference of 1933 and chaos reigned in international markets for a while. However, in 1934 the US implemented a policy of stabilising the exchange rate value of the dollar. The limited impact of the dollar devaluation on farm exports is summarised by Benedict, 1953, pp. 298–9.

33. Saloutos (1982, ch. 10), gives an account of the impact of trade agreements on agricultural trade in the 1930s. The Canadian Trade Treaty of 1934 was of substantial importance in expanding bilateral trade in farm products. However, there was little progress in breaking down barriers in the European farm market where extreme protection was the order of the day. No general agreement could be reached with European countries on a reduction in trade barriers for wheat and flour. However, an agreement was reached with the UK in 1938 on a wide range of agricultural commodities.

34. The Secretary of Agriculture 1933–40, Henry A. Wallace, was an influential figure in determining the shift toward a liberal trade policy. His views were expressed in a pamphlet, 'America Must Choose' (1934), which received widespread public attention and support. Wallace argued that lower US tariffs were a necessary precondition for an expansion of international trade which would allow America to regain its foreign markets. This, he argued, was a necessary complement to domestic agricultural policy.

35. This conflict has been an important issue ever since. See Gale Johnson (1977).

36. In nominal terms, agricultural exports declined from $1.8 billion (thousand million) in 1929 to less than $1 billion in 1932 and remained below this level throughout the 1930s. In real terms, the volume of farm exports in the 1930s was well below the levels attained in the 1920s (see Hathaway, 1963, p. 134).

37. Trade protection in Europe severely aggravated the effects of the depression on US exports. Regulation of imports was increased considerably: the degree of regulation (percentage of agricultural trade subject to non-tariff barriers) increased from 5 per cent in 1929–30 to 55 per cent in 1935 (Heidhues, 1979, p. 121). US exports were also cut back because of the drought and the US was a net importer of wheat in 1932–34.

38. The US share of world cotton trade had declined throughout the early part of this century. It was 50 per cent in 1921, 45 per cent in 1931 and 23 per cent in 1937. However, production control, high prices, and CCC stock purchase in the US undoubtedly accentuated this trend in the 1930s. High cotton prices also stimulated the development of rayon, a synthetic substitute for cotton, during the 1930s. US producers were still dependent on the overseas market: about 50 per cent of domestic production was exported during the 1930s.

39. Hathaway also argues that this link was substantially weaker after the Second World War. Firstly, automatic stabilisers reduced the correlation between changes in NI and DPIs and, secondly, the income elasticity of demand for farm products fell as DPIs rose.

40. Parity prices for individual commodities in August 1939 were beef = 101, corn = 59, cotton = 66, wheat = 50, butterfat = 59, hogs = 60, chickens = 93, eggs = 49 (Saloutos, 1982, p. 256).

41. Based on data from Benedict (1953, p. 315) and Wilcox and Cochrane (1960, p. 216). Note the similarity with Britain.

42. An NTB is 'any government device or practice other than a tariff which directly impedes the entry of imports into a country and which discriminates against imports – that is, does not apply with equal force on domestic production or distribution' (Hillman, 1978, p. 14). More generally, NTBs are practices other than tariffs which distort trade and include (i) devices which restrict imports, (ii) measures which assist

domestic production thereby indirectly reducing imports or increasing exports, and (iii) measures which directly assist exports.
43. Note, however, that limited production controls were applied in Britain (for potatoes) and Denmark (for pork).
44. Yates (1959) provides evidence to show that the volume of world trade in temperate zone products in the mid-1930s was much less than in 1929 and export values for some major products were lower than in 1913.

4. 1940–1973: agricultural adjustment and trade interaction

INTRODUCTION AND OVERVIEW

In this chapter we review and compare the major agricultural policy adjustments in Western Europe and the US which took place between 1940 and 1973. The beginning of this period approximately coincides with the outbreak of the Second World War. Its end was marked by the first enlargement of the EC to include Denmark, Ireland and the UK, and by a marked shift in US policy to protect the interests of food consumers. The chapter refers, in several places, to agricultural aspects of multilateral trade negotiations, including the foundation of the GATT in 1947, and the Dillon and Kennedy Rounds which coincided with the early years of the EC and the formation of the CAP.

General Economic Background

Wartime and immediate postwar period

The Second World War led to devastation and food shortages in Western Europe, partially alleviated by lend–lease shipments from America to the Allies. In the US, there was a high level of economic activity with rapid increases in industrial and agricultural production and a shift in resources to the production of war goods. Economic policy in the US and European Allied countries rested on planning and controls. These were removed in the immediate postwar period. However, subsequent macro policy stances tended to incorporate Keynesian interventionist ideas in an attempt to promote 'full' employment and to stabilise the level of economic activity.

Following the end of the Second World War, the US took action to forestall economic depression in Europe. The main effort came with the Marshall Plan or European Recovery Programme under which US aid was made available to Europe between 1948 and 1952. The aid took the form of gifts of commodities and industrial products and long-term loans. Economic recovery from war occurred in Europe; the GNP of the 16 countries given aid grew by 25 per cent within three and a half years (Faulkner, 1960, p. 27). Aid to Western Europe was channelled via the Organisation of European Economic Cooperation (OEEC)[1] which coordinated reconstruction plans and helped to liberalise intra-European trade. The Marshall Plan assisted economic cooperation in Europe and helped to lay the basis for economic integration. Out of a European desire for rapprochement between France and Germany, came the Schuman Plan of 1950 which led to the formation of the European Iron and Steel Community in 1952. Eventually, in 1957, the European Community (EC) was formed which also led to the setting up of the Common Agricultural Policy (CAP).

American influence was instrumental in initiating certain major institutional developments on the international scene. The United Nations (UN) was founded in 1945 and specialised agencies were attached to it. The most important of these were the Food and Agricultural Organisation (FAO, founded in October 1945), the International Bank for Reconstruction and Development (IBRD, founded December 1945 and now called the World Bank) and the International Monetary Fund (IMF). The IBRD and the IMF, stemmed from the so-called Bretton Woods Conference (July 1944). The IBRD was to facilitate European reconstruction and later to serve as an instrument for enabling economic development. The IMF was to be the central international financial institution promoting cooperation in solving short-term problems connected with international liquidity and balance of payments. An integral and important element of the 'Bretton Woods' system was a commitment to exchange rate stability: exchange rates would be fixed at declared par values and only altered in the event of a fundamental disequilibrium. The 'fixed' exchange rate system prevailed until 1973.

The major trading nations also discussed, in the postwar period, the formation of an institution to promote liberal trading arrangements. Whilst the charter of the International Trading Organisation (ITO) was drawn up in Havana 1947, the organisation never came into being because of the refusal of the US Senate to ratify the ITO.[2] As a substitute, an informal association, the General Agreement on Tariffs and Trade (GATT),[3] was set up to serve as a framework for multinational trade negotiations (MTNs). The original and fundamental aim of the GATT was to liberalise and expand trade; this to be achieved via negotiated reductions in trade barriers.

Postwar boom: 1950–73

The period 1950–73, witnessed a 'boom' in world production and trade: 'a "second golden age" with growth rates well above those of the "first golden age" of 1850–1914' (Reynolds, 1985, p. 36). GNP in the OECD countries grew at an average annual rate of '4.9 per cent compared to an 1870–1913 average of 2.5 per cent and a 1913–50 figure of 1.9 per cent' (ibid). Fast growth combined with a lowering of transport costs led to an even faster rate of growth in the volume of international trade and the export volume of OECD countries rose at 8.6 per cent per year from 1950–73 (ibid); world trade value in current prices expanded tenfold between 1950 and 1972–75 average (Schmidt et al., 1978, p. 75). Much of the increase in trade was between the industrialised nations. However, world trade in agricultural products expanded less rapidly and the share of agricultural commodities in world trade declined from about 34 per cent to about 16 per cent over the period. There was a marked change in the pattern of agricultural trade: '(1) a growing concentration of trade amongst developed countries, (2) growing dependency of LDC, and centrally planned economies upon the developed countries for more of their food imports, and (3) diminishing concentration of trade among centrally planned economies' (ibid, p. 76). The commodity composition of agricultural trade also changed with an increase in the importance of food and feed products and a decline in the proportion of raw materials and other products in commodity trade. Of particular note was the rise in the importance of grains from around 10 per cent in 1955 to about 18 per cent in 1973 and a rapid advance in trade in feed products from around 4 per cent to around 9 per cent over the same period (derived from ibid., Appendix Table 2).

Economic growth per capita in the 1950s and 1960s was faster in Japan and the emerging EC(6) than in the US.[4] Consequently, whilst the US was the dominant economic force in the immediate postwar period, its economic significance gradually declined whilst that of Japan and Western Europe increased. There was also a move to a more integrated trading world as export/GNP ratios generally increased. However, by 1973, this trading world was increasingly centred on the US, Western Europe and Japan rather than on the US alone. Global integration was facilitated by MTNs under the GATT which enhanced trade liberalisation in manufactures in the 1950s and 1960s. However, special rules were applied to agricultural trade under the GATT and agricultural protectionism was largely untouched by multilateral negotiations.

The GATT and Trade Negotiations

The GATT was founded in 1947 to provide multilateral trade rules and to act as a forum for negotiating trade liberalisation. At that time, protectionism was widespread – a legacy of the Great Depression and the Second World War. High tariffs and import quotas restricted trade and bilateral agreements segmented world trade. In the period to 1973, protectionism generally declined. Average tariff levels in the industrialised world were reduced from around 40 per cent at the end of the Second World War to around 12 per cent in the late 1960s as a result of successive rounds or negotiating conferences under the GATT. Import quotas were also largely removed and intra-European trade was facilitated by the creation of the EC and the European Free Trade Association (EFTA).[5]

The basic principles of the GATT which enhance liberalisation are (Moser, 1990, ch. 3):

1. Non-discrimination in trade (Article 1): each member country has to treat the trade of all other contracting parties equally. Equivalently, a country has to extend its most-favoured nation's treatment to all other countries.
2. Open markets: Prohibition of all forms of protection except customs tariffs (Article XI): agreed-upon tariffs bind each contracting party and can only be altered in trade negotiations (Article II).
3. National treatment (Article III): imported goods are afforded the same treatment as domestic goods with regard to non-border taxation and regulation.
4. Transparency: members are required to report regularly on trade policy actions such as the use of subsidies (Article XVI) and on escape clause actions (Article XIX).

Trade negotiations under the GATT are 'based upon the reciprocal exchange of concessions among governments' (ibid., p. 39). This takes many forms from setting the agenda to negotiating multilateral tariff-cutting formulae. In general, reciprocity requires a reduction in the domestic trade barriers of one nation in order to open up foreign markets for that country's exports without matching concessions necessarily being expected or received, sector by sector, or country for country.

A number of protective devices, particularly relating to the protection of agriculture, were either not covered at all by the original General Agreement or were included without any provision for regulating their use. A very conspicuous omission in the light of subsequent development in European agricultural policy was variable import levy protection, which gives domestic producers the most complete and absolute form of protection from outside competition. One reason why

VILs were not covered by the original General Agreement was that they were scarcely in use at the time. It was only later that they were adopted by the EC as the principal instrument of agricultural protection under the CAP. Although the legality of VILs within the GATT has been questioned as, for example, during GATT committee discussions on CAP commodity regulations in the 1960s, the issue remained unresolved until the Uruguay Round Agreement was concluded in 1994.

Another type of protective measure not covered by the GATT is the voluntary export restraint (VER) or voluntary restraint agreement (VRA).[6] VERs began with an informal agreement between the US and Japan in 1957 for limits on exports of cotton textiles from Japan to the US. Although not widely used for agricultural protection, VERs have been used both by the US (to limit meat imports) and the EC (to limit imports of manioc, a cereal substitute).

A further protective device which was not adequately covered by the original General Agreement was the use of producer subsidies, whether to stimulate domestic production (implicitly at the expense of imports) or to facilitate the disposal of export surpluses at a price lower than that prevailing on the domestic market. Far from prohibiting the use of subsidies either to boost domestic production or exports, Article XVI of the original Agreement merely required contracting parties to report their use. As far as the use of domestic subsidies is concerned, the position in GATT has remained essentially unchanged: there are no 'rules' governing their use despite a growing recognition that they impact directly upon trade. But an attempt has been made to devise rules for dealing with export subsidies. In 1955 Article XVI was extended in recognition of the harm that export subsidies could do to the interests of competing exporters (Art. XVI:2). The use of export subsidies was then specifically outlawed for non-primary products (Art. XVI:4). But an exception was made for agricultural and other primary products. Article XVI:3 accordingly laid down that contracting parties should try to avoid using export subsidies even for primary products. But if they nevertheless continued to be used, they should not be used to obtain a 'more than equitable share' of world trade, having regard to historic market shares and other criteria. The interpretation of 'equitable market shares' in the context of Article XVI:3 has been the subject of many subsequent disputes in the GATT (Hathaway, 1987). It is on record that the United States was prominent amongst the GATT member countries who insisted on agricultural commodities being accorded exceptional treatment under the GATT code on export subsidies (Harris et al., 1983, p. 275). A further attempt was made to tighten restrictions on the use of agricultural export subsidies under Article

XVI:3 during the Tokyo negotiations ending in 1979 but the resulting 'Subsidies Code' proved to be largely ineffective (Warley, 1990). The Uruguay Round Agriculture Agreement of 1994 imposed limits on the use of agricultural export subsidies without actually outlawing them (see Chapter 7).

The United States also acted to obtain special concessions for itself regarding the use of agricultural import quotas. Article XI:2 of the General Agreement makes certain agricultural exceptions which effectively permit the use of quantitative restrictions on both exports and imports in defined circumstances. In particular, quantitative import restrictions could be applied only if measures were in force to 'restrict the production or marketing of the like domestic product or a product which is a close substitute' (Hathaway, 1987, p. 108). This part of Article XI:2 did not suit the United States where, under Section 22 of the 1935 amendment of the Agricultural Adjustment Act, the government had obtained the power to restrict by quota imports of any agricultural commodity for which a domestic price support or other government programme existed. The force of Section 22 was re-emphasised in 1951 when the Congress declared 'No trade agreement could be applied in a manner inconsistent with this section' (ibid, p. 109). Accordingly in 1955, when Article XI:2 was added to the General Agreement, the US sought and obtained for itself the famous Section 22 waiver allowing it to apply import quotas to agricultural commodities without taking parallel action to restrict US domestic output. This waiver applied only to the US and not to other members of the GATT, who, in applying agricultural import quotas, continued to be bound by the restrictions of Article XI:2. Agricultural import quotas were finally outlawed by the Uruguay Round Agriculture Agreement of 1994 which made tariffs (including tariff rate quotas) the only legal form of import restriction.

Agricultural Trade and Links between the US and Western Europe[7]

Over the period 1950–73, 'the US played a diminishing role in total world trade but a growing and leading role in agricultural trade', (Schmidt et al., 1978, p. 78). The US share of world total exports declined from 18 per cent in 1951–55 to about 12 per cent in 1971–75 whilst its share of world agricultural exports rose from 12 per cent to over 16 per cent. Major agricultural exports were cereals and soya beans (and products) and the US accounted for around 44 per cent of world grain exports in the early 1970s. Agricultural imports into the US nearly doubled in value from the mid-1950s to the early 1970s but the US share of world agricultural imports declined from 17 per cent to about 9 per cent.

From 1960 onwards, the US had a positive and growing agricultural trade balance. Agricultural exports accounted for some 20 per cent plus of total exports over the period from 1950–73 whilst agricultural imports declined from around 40 per cent to around 11 per cent of total US imports. Agricultural producers in the US became more dependent upon foreign trade over the period under study. In 1950, the value of farm product exports was around 10 per cent of cash receipts from farming; in the early 1970s, the figure was about 15 per cent. For crop farmers, export dependence increased significantly: in the early 1950s, around 12 per cent of crop acreage supplied exports; by the early 1970s this figure had risen to about 26 per cent.

Western Europe was the most important market for US exports in the early fifties (46 per cent of exports in 1951–55), but gradually declined in relative importance. By 1971–75, Asia and Western Europe accounted for approximately one third each of US agricultural exports. Japan was the single largest importer.

Adjustment to Rapid Economic Growth

Rapid economic growth, slow population growth and a technological 'revolution' in agriculture led to an agricultural adjustment problem – a chronic disequilibrium adverse to agriculture – in the 1950s and 1960s in both the US and Western Europe. The relative size of the agricultural sector and the agricultural labour force declined, whilst agricultural production rose. Tables 4.1 and 4.2 indicate the nature of these changes.

The disparity between agriculture's share of GDP and its share of the labour force is indicative of relatively low average incomes in agriculture – the farm income problem. Certainly, the required adjustment of agriculture to economic forces was rapid in the period under study as evidenced by the decline in the agricultural labour force in the different countries. A major and, probably overriding, concern of agricultural policy makers in the US and in Western Europe (particularly in the EC(6)) was to moderate the apparent frenzied pace of agricultural adjustment and provide support for farm incomes. The notion of an 'equitable' income for persons engaged in agriculture was at the heart of most policy statements. The conservative social welfare function (CSWF) embraces the belief that governments seek to prevent events that cut the welfare of any particular group of society (see Corden, 1974). Thus it was possible to rationalise government support for well-being in agriculture on the grounds of 'fairness' especially as the

*Table 4.1   Agriculture's share of GDP and civilian employment in
Western Europe and the US, 1955–70*

	1955		1960		1965		1970	
	% empl.	% GDP	% empl.	% GDP	% empl.	% GDP	% empl.	% GDP
Belgium	9.3	7.9	7.6	7.3	6.4	6.3	4.7	4.9
Luxembourg	19.4	9.3	16.4	7.6	13.7	6.3	9.5	4.9
France	26.9	11.4	22.4	9.7	18.2	7.7	13.9	6.6
Germany	18.5	8.0	14.0	6.0	11.1	4.4	8.6	3.8
Italy	40.0	20.7	32.8	15.1	26.1	13.3	20.2	10.3
Netherlands	13.2	11.4	11.5	10.5	8.8	8.3	7.2	6.2
EEC-6	26.1	11.6	20.9	9.0	16.5	7.4	12.3	6.1
UK	4.6	4.8	4.3	4.0	3.4	3.4	3.2	3.0
US	9.8	4.7	8.3	4.0	6.1	3.4	4.5	3.0

Source: OECD Agricultural Statistics.

*Table 4.2   Agricultural production index (1952–56 = 100) and the
agricultural labour force index (1955 = 100) in Western Europe and
the US, 1955–70*

	1955		1960		1965		1970	
	P	L	P	L	P	L	P	L
Belg/Lux	106	100	115	91.2	117	70.1	143	52.6
France	102	100	124	82.7	141	68.5	158	56.6
Germany	101	100	121	83.9	118	66.6	143	52.4
Italy	105	100	109	93.8	126	70.0	141	51.6
Netherlands	106	100	125	98.9	128	82.6	161	70.0
EEC-6	–	100	–	89.4	–	72.2	–	58.6
UK	99	100	121	98.0	143	82.3	152	67.8
US	101	100	110	84.6	118	67.6	124	36.7

Notes: P = agricultural production index, L = agricultural labour force index.

Sources: Production indices: FAO, *Yearbook of Food and Agricultural Statistics*,
various issues; labour force indices: Eurostat Population and Employment (numbers
employed in agriculture). Agriculture defined as agriculture, hunting, forestry and fishing. US agricultural employment data from OECD Agricultural Statistics (include
fishing).

adjustment of the farm sector to technological change was contributing to general welfare. In addition, agricultural support could be expected to win political aquiescence from the farm lobby. Against the background of intervention into agricultural markets in the pre-war period, it is perhaps understandable that inherited policy instruments were employed in modified forms in the postwar period. Vested agricultural interests were also in a strong position to organise to avert adjustment and secure income transfers whilst the agricultural bureaucracies reacted positively to this sectional interest. Furthermore, in Continental Europe, support for the 'farm lobby' was forthcoming from the population at large with memories of wartime privation, and for many who had an attachment to farming, being only a single generation away from working on the land themselves.

Intervention into agricultural markets was accompanied by protection for domestic producers against foreign traders, particularly in the EC. In the period from the mid-1950s to the late-1960s there was, in fact, a decline in protection rates for US export crops whilst for US commodities subject to competition from imports, such as sugar and dairy products, and for EC farm products in general, protectionism was entrenched and largely on the increase. As noted by Johnson (1973a, p. 861) 'there was the undocumented fear that adding freer trade in farm products to the existing requirements for adjustment would impose burdens greater than the social and political fabric could stand'. This made it difficult for governments to pursue agricultural trade liberalisation.

By the early 1970s, the agricultural adjustment problem had largely run its course in the US and the wealthier areas of Western Europe. The farm population was increasingly integrated into the economy and society through improvements in the ease, speed and cost of communications and better access to education. However, divergences in Western Europe continued to present EC policy makers with the problem of coping with the agricultural transformation process in many regions. Furthermore, slow structural adjustment within agriculture presented a social problem of many small-scale producers who, particularly in 'disadvantaged' localities, eked out a living from the land.

POLICY IN WESTERN EUROPE

The UK

Agricultural policy in the immediate postwar period

The first postwar government's plans for agricultural policy were written into the Agriculture Act, 1947, which stipulated both the objectives of the policy and the means of their implementation. In very broad terms there were two major objectives, namely to (a) substantially increase domestic agricultural production, and (b) support farm incomes at a level consistent with 'proper remuneration and living conditions' for both farmers and farmworkers together with 'an adequate return on capital invested'. However, the architects of the 1947 Act also clearly envisaged that Britain would continue to obtain a proportion of her total food supplies from abroad, and the government reserved the right to determine the relative market shares of home producers and overseas suppliers.

The preamble to the Act also laid down that the principal means of realising these objectives was to be minimum government guaranteed prices for the major agricultural products. Price guarantees were limited to 'review commodities', but in practice nearly all the main agricultural (but not horticultural) products were included. The minister was empowered to add to the list of review commodities. (Wool was added in 1950, when a Wool Marketing Board was also established.) The Act also imposed upon the Minister of Agriculture a statutory obligation to conduct an annual review of the economic condition of agriculture in consultation with farmer representative organisations (thus formalising an ongoing practice which had started during the war).

During the first few years of the recovery period, the output objective comprised the general expansion of agricultural production virtually regardless of either the commodity composition of the extra output, or the costs and efficiency of expansion. In 1947, an official target of increasing the net output[8] of UK agriculture by 50 per cent compared with pre-war within five years was set (since net output was already about 30 per cent above pre-war in 1947, the target increment over five years was only about 20 per cent). The main policy instruments at this time were fixed guaranteed prices for all 'review commodities' combined with the retention (from the war) of state trading. The Ministry of Food continued as the sole first-hand buyer of major foodstuffs. Farm product prices were deliberately fixed at a 'high' level, not only to provide farmers with a short-term incentive to raise output, but also to encourage them to invest for the long term, that is, price guarantees included an allowance for 'capital injection'.

Between 1950 and 1954, there was some shift in the objective of production policy away from general expansion regardless of efficiency to expansion combined with improved efficiency. To this end, fixed product price guarantees were supplemented by production grants, or input subsidies, to encourage the adoption of more efficient methods of production: examples included fertiliser purchase and calf-rearing subsidies. However, the incentive to expand production remained quite generalised. The 1947 production target of a 50 per cent increase in agricultural net output above pre-war within five years had actually been realised by 1952 and, in that year, the target was raised by a further 10 per cent, to 60 per cent above the pre-war level of net output over five years. This target was reached ahead of schedule, so much so that by 1954, when food rationing finally ended, the production of some commodities such as milk and pig meat already exceeded market requirements – at the ruling-fixed guaranteed prices – especially during seasonal production peaks. An additional factor contributing to the greatly eased agricultural supply situation towards the end of the second sub-period was that the availability of overseas supplies of agricultural commodities had recovered more quickly than expected from the disruption caused by the war.

Despite a change of government at the end of 1951, from Labour to Conservative, agricultural policy remained broadly bipartisan and there were no abrupt changes. However, towards the end of the 1945–54 period, the system of state trading in agricultural products at fixed guaranteed prices, inherited from the war, was gradually abandoned. Starting with cereals in 1953, fixed guaranteed prices were replaced by minimum guaranteed prices, backed by deficiency payments. Thus new markets were partially de-controlled to permit market prices to be determined by market forces down to the minimum guarantee level. At the same time, the pre-war agricultural marketing boards recovered their trading powers (except for the Pigs and Bacon Marketing Boards, which were not revived). With the end of state trading and rationing the main raison d'être of the Ministry of Food disappeared and in 1955 it was merged with the Ministry of Agriculture and Fisheries to form the Ministry of Agriculture, Fisheries and Food.

Agricultural adjustment, 1955–73

Macroeconomic policy objectives, trade policy and the balance of payments The dominant characteristic of the period of agricultural adjustment, 1955–73, was relatively plentiful supplies of virtually all agricultural products both from domestic sources and from abroad. Against this changed scenario, there was soon a marked shift in the objectives of British agricultural policy away from the unselective expansion of output which had characterised the immediate postwar period. The new objective, from the mid-1950s onwards, was selective expansion, mainly of products with an import-saving potential. With improving the balance of payments being a major objective of British macroeconomic policy during most of this period, the case for expanding domestic agriculture in order to relieve the balance of payments attracted a lot of attention.

During virtually the whole of the period between the end of the Second World War and accession to the EC, the UK had a balance of payments problem. With hindsight, it is tempting to argue that the root cause of this problem was the overvaluation of sterling and that the only correct and effective solution was currency devaluation. However, prior to the abandonment of the Bretton Woods agreement on fixed exchange rates in 1971, governments were reluctant to resort to this solution, not only in the UK, but in most other countries as well.

In the early postwar years there were two main pressures on Britain's balance of payments. First, there was the 'dollar gap' problem *vis-à-vis* essential imports from North America. This problem was resolved by the late 1950s due largely to growing dollar reserves held outside the US. Second, there was the problem that the UK lacked gold and dollar reserves adequate to cover the sterling area debt largely built up during the war and held by Commonwealth and other Sterling Area countries. The seriousness of this problem lessened as the US dollar gradually took over from sterling as the world's major trading currency.

Regardless of the general case for expanding domestic agricultural production to reduce imports and so assist the balance of payments (to be considered later), an agricultural solution to these two particular problems of the immediate postwar period seemed unlikely (McCrone, 1962, ch. 5). The potential for closing the dollar gap by expanding home agricultural production was greatly limited by the low elasticity of substitution between agricultural imports from the dollar bloc and their nearest domestically produced equivalents. So, for example, due to the peculiarities of the British loaf (reflecting consumer preference) the scope for substituting British-grown soft wheat for North American hard wheat in the UK miller's grist was very limited. The scope for ameliorating the Sterling Area Debt problem through agricultural expansion was limited by the comparatively large share of UK food imports held by Commonwealth countries (approximately 50 per cent around 1960 according to McCrone). It was argued that import-substituting agricultural expansion by the UK would result in lower UK exports of non-agricultural goods to the Commonwealth, due to adverse effects on purchasing power and/or the risk of retaliation.[9]

The duration of these highly specific early postwar pressures on the British balance of payments did not extend much beyond the period of food scarcity when the main objective of agricultural policy was non-selective expansion of domestic output and food imports were controlled by the Ministry of Food. But even after markets were de-controlled, deficiency payments substituted for fixed price guarantees, and excess supplies of certain commodities began to appear, the case for expanding agricultural production in the UK to benefit the balance of payments continued to be pressed, not only by vested interests but also by some academic economists. The case was made out in two main forms. First, there was the argument that due to the immobility of agricultural resources and the difficulties which exporters might have in adapting to the requirements of new overseas markets, it might be easier and more certain in the short run to improve the balance of payments by saving imports through the expansion of domestic agriculture than by attempting to increase exports (Sharpe and Capstick, 1966).

The second, and more academically respectable, argument for encouraging domestic agricultural expansion to save imports, and so benefit the balance of payments, came from optimum tariff theorists. The crux of the 'optimum tariff' argument, applied to UK agriculture's balance of payments contribution in the 1950s and 1960s, was that as a major exporter of manufactures and a major importer of agricultural products, the UK might shift the terms of trade in her own favour by producing more at home, particularly of agricultural products, and importing less.

A number of empirical estimates were made of how the British balance of payments in the 1950s and 1960s would have been affected by marginal adjustments in domestic agricultural production. None of these studies allowed for the possibility of trade repercussions and all were also open to both theoretical and methodological criticisms. (Moore and Peters, 1965; *House of Commons Select Committee on Agriculture, 1968–9*). Although the quantitative results of these studies were subject to wide margins of error, they all pointed to the same qualitative conclusion. This was that, in the 1950s and 1960s, British agricultural expansion was making some positive net contribution to the balance of payments. To the extent that expansion was the result of government policy this might have been regarded as a positive vindication of that policy.

The government's policy of selective agricultural expansion undoubtedly emphasised import saving, particularly the reduction of the import content of domestic agricultural output. So, for example, the reduction of imported animal feedingstuffs received considerable emphasis as a policy objective. The 1965 National Plan for Economic Development confronted agricultural import saving more directly by requiring domestic agriculture to meet most of the expected increase in demand for temperate climate foodstuffs (up to 1970) plus a large proportion of the extra cereals needed for livestock feeding. This programme was later extended for 2/3 years, with special emphasis on wheat, barley, beef and pig-meat. By 1970, selective expansion was seen not only as a means of 'saving imports now' but also as a means of reducing the agricultural import levies which the UK would have to pay into the Common Agricultural Fund (FEOGA) if she joined the EC.

As during the 1930s, Britain's ability to restrict or reduce imports of agricultural products was limited by long-term commitments to Commonwealth and other overseas suppliers. So, for example, in 1962 New Zealand and Ireland were given specified minimum allocations under a butter import quota system intended to protect traditional overseas suppliers from the effects of dumping on the British butter market by 'new' foreign suppliers. In 1964, bilateral marketing sharing agreements with a number of overseas cereal suppliers, which also specified minimum import prices, paralleled the imposition of standard quantity restrictions on domestic producers. In the same year, 1964, a Bacon Market Sharing Understanding was entered into with Denmark and other foreign suppliers. The Anglo-Irish Free Trade Area Agreement of 1965 prolonged Ireland's longstanding rights of unrestricted and duty-free access to the UK market for a wide range of commodities and restricted access for others such as butter and bacon. As a final example, since the early 1950s the Commonwealth Sugar Agreement had given Commonwealth sugar producers guaranteed access to the British market for fixed quantities of sugar.

Despite the adoption during the 1960s of limited measures, such as minimum import prices, to restrict competitive imports of agricultural products, the UK's agricultural trading policy remained relatively liberal right up to the eve of EC accession and the obligation to abide by the provisions of the Common Agricultural Policy. In particular, traditional agricultural trading links with Commonwealth countries were maintained. On the eve of EC entry, the UK was fully self-sufficient in a number of temperate agricultural products, such as liquid milk, pork, poultry meat and eggs, due to natural production advantage or for other reasons. For other commodities, the degree of self-sufficiency ranged down from about 90 per cent for barley to 16 per cent for butter. Overall, Britain derived about two-thirds of indigenous supplies from domestic production. This degree of self-sufficiency was only marginally higher than in the mid 1950s despite the selective expansion programme. However, it was substantially higher than the pre-war level of around one-half.

Agricultural adjustment policies　Despite the change from acute scarcity of food supplies immediately after the war to a period of relative plenty, and the shift from unlimited output expansion to selective expansion to improve the balance of payments, the 1947 Agriculture Act, which pledged the government to maintaining 'proper remuneration and living conditions' for farmers remained on the statute book. Thus farm income support continued as a major policy objective. Although the 1947 Act gave the government sufficient flexibility in determining and administering the precise form of price guarantees to accommodate the switch from fixed prices to deficiency payments without new legislation (Williams, 1960, p. 45), the National Farmers Union (NFU) pressed the case for giving producers firmer long-term price guarantees.

The new policy of selective agricultural expansion implied that minimum price guarantees would not necessarily be increased at successive price reviews and might even be reduced. Selective price reductions actually occurred from 1954 onwards, starting with cereals, pigs and milk in that year. Whilst the NFU was understandably hostile to price reductions, rather than confront that issue head-on, it chose rather to press for firm and meaningful long-term price guarantees.[10] It was argued that farmers needed realistic price guarantees more than one year ahead to permit efficient farm planning and resource allocation. The government eventually responded to this pressure by accepting statutory limits to the rates at which price guarantees could be reduced in the short term. Under the Agriculture Act, 1957, it was stipulated that:

1. No commodity would have its minimum guaranteed price reduced by more than 4 per cent per year.
2. No livestock or livestock products would have their guaranteed prices cut by more than 9 per cent over three consecutive years.
3. The total value of all the guarantees taken together (after adjustment for cost changes since the last price review) would not be reduced by more than 2.5 per cent per year.[11]

Although the limits to the government's ability to lower guaranteed prices which were written into the 1957 Act probably increased the bargaining strength of the farmers unions at the annual price review, the real gain in farmers' security was less than the apparent gain due to inflation.

Although deficiency payments were reinstated as a policy instrument as early as 1953, they were not formally embodied in postwar legislation until the 1957 Agriculture Act (which, inter alia, repealed the Wheat Act, 1932 and other items of pre-war legislation). Compared with other instruments of agricultural price support, deficiency payments were deemed to possess a number of economic virtues. At the time of their re-introduction after the war, the British government of the day stressed that they encouraged the improvement of farmers' marketing efficiency since the individual farmer's total return consisted of the best market price he could achieve plus a deficiency payment which was the same for all farmers. Another notable virtue of the system is that it combines producer price support with enabling markets to clear whilst consumers procure supplies at market prices. Thus, the accumulation of stocks associated with other systems of price support is avoided. The system also possessed the merit of enabling the UK to continue importing agricultural products from the Commonwealth and other traditional suppliers. Commonwealth ties were still strong after two world wars, and national sentiment favoured the maintenance of trading links as a desirable objective of commercial policy.

But quite apart from giving rise to resource use disequilibrium deficiency payments also have at least one other notable drawback, especially for net food importing countries. This is that if imports are unrestricted the exchequer cost of the deficiency payment bill remains uncontrolled and is liable to rise unpredictably if there are exogenous downward shocks to the price of imports. Moreover, for a large importer the import price is in part endogenous, and if in the longer term the increased confidence engendered by price support induces domestic producers to expand their output at the guaranteed price – through technological innovation for example – then the import price may well fall as a direct consequence of deficiency payment support. In principle, a government confronted by a rising deficiency payment bill, and wishing to control it, can adopt any or all of three classes of counter-measures. First, it can restrict imports, either by controlling their volume or their price. Second, it can reduce the level of the domestic price guarantees. Third, it can limit the quantity of domestic output qualifying for the price guarantee. Faced with a rising deficiency payment bill, particularly for cereals and fatstock during the middle and late 1950s and the early 1960s,[12] British governments adopted all of these courses.

Minimum price guarantees were reduced from as early as 1954, starting with the prices of cereals, fat pigs and milk in that year. In the same year, 1954, the guaranteed price for milk was restricted to a 'standard quantity'. The amount of the standard quantity was initially the amount of total milk sales off farms in the year before the restriction was imposed. Subsequently, the standard quantity was increased in line with any increase in sales of milk for liquid consumption. Standard quantity restrictions were extended to cereal price guarantees in 1964 but were lifted for wheat in 1968 to encourage farmers to switch resources to wheat from other cereals, particularly barley. A variety of instruments was used for restricting imports. Imports of potatoes, for example, were controlled by the Board of Trade. But the principal innovative device for restricting imports, first introduced during the 1960s, was the minimum import price (MIP). The principle of the MIP is that overseas suppliers are invited to charge a minimum price for their exports. The MIP is set by the importing country at a level which is high enough to 'protect' the domestic support price of the commodity concerned. Should any exporter decline to charge the MIP, then the (lower) import price is brought up to that level by the imposition of a variable import levy (VIL). Thus MIP = PI + VIL, where VIL > 0 unless PI = MIP.

Cereal imports were subjected to minimum import price controls from 1964, the year in which cereal standard quantities were also introduced.[13] The timing of the introduction of both measures occurred shortly after the UK's first, abortive attempt to join the EC, in 1961/2, but some years before the successful application preceding actual entry in 1973. The substantial problems of harmonising the UK's system of agricultural support with that of the EC(6) were anticipated, and these measures, particularly the adoption of MIPs, were seen as moving in that direction. Minimum import prices were extended to eggs in 1970 and to beef and veal in 1971.

Costs of agricultural protection and distribution of its benefits   During the 1950s and 1960s a vigorous debate developed concerning the competitiveness of UK agriculture and the real costs of agricultural support. It was argued not only that the total costs of support exceeded the Exchequer costs, due to additional (and concealed) costs borne by consumers, but also that the budget costs of support failed to show the degree to which UK agriculture was protected from overseas competition. At that time, the consumer costs of agricultural support derived partly from tariffs and import quota restriction applied, for example, to some horticultural products, and partly from the monopoly powers exercised by certain marketing boards. Although the Milk Marketing Board failed to regain its price fixing powers after the Second World War, it did retain the power to segregate the liquid and manufacturing milk markets. It was maintained that having regard to the size of the manufacturing milk surplus, and regardless of the government-determined maximum retail price of liquid milk, this segregation inevitably resulted in the liquid milk price being higher than it would have been in a 'free market' (Nash, 1955).

The pioneering empirical work to estimate the total cost of agricultural support in the UK was conducted by Nash, who compared domestic price support levels with current import prices on a commodity-by-commodity basis. Using this method, he estimated that in 1955–56 the total cost of agricultural support in the UK amounted to £294.5 million (Nash, 1956). This figure exceeded the estimated costs of Exchequer support for the same year by about £90 million. Nash also observed that on this basis, UK farmers were deriving a very high proportion of their farming net income – officially estimated at £350 million in 1955–56 – from protection. However, he was careful to add that his calculation did not indicate what aggregate net farming income would have been in the absence of protection, due to the substantial reallocation of resources which the withdrawal of support would necessarily cause.[14] McCrone used Nash's method to estimate the total cost of supporting agriculture a few years later (1960–61) and reached a similar conclusion regarding the degree of support (McCrone, 1962, ch. 2). He also extended his analysis to twelve other West European countries. In doing so he estimated each country's aggregate level of agricultural output, in 1956, at both national prices and 'common European import prices'. The national price valuation exceeded the common import price valuation in all cases and McCrone used the difference between them as an approximate measure of the cost of price support.[15] The cost of price support expressed as a percentage of aggregate agricultural output at national prices gave what McCrone called the 'level of price support'. The estimated levels of protection ranged from 42 per cent (Finland) to 3 per cent (Denmark) about a 13 country mean of 16 per cent: the UK came out above the mean at 24 per cent. Critics of Nash and other users of the import parity price method of assessing the competitiveness of domestic agriculture, concentrated upon the implicit assumption that non-marginal adjustments in quantities of agricultural imports would not affect the terms of trade. More specifically, the critics questioned the relevance of current import prices to what the marginal costs of agricultural imports would be if support were absent, domestic production much lower and the volume of imports much higher than their current levels. In effect, the critics were arguing that Nash's methodology overstated the uncompetitiveness of domestic agriculture and the real costs of support. Whilst accepting that this criticism had some substance, Nash countered by arguing that it would not apply to commodities being produced in excess of domestic consumption requirements, like liquid milk, as a consequence of government agricultural policy (Nash, 1955, pp. 240–41).

A related debating issue concerned the distribution of support payments within the farm sector. Defenders of government policy tended to argue that income support under the 1947 Agriculture Act had been distributed using a combination of commodity subsidies – representing 'payment by results' – and targeted production grants, such as hill farming subsidies – representing 'payment by need' (Kirk, 1958). But critics of UK agricultural income support policy on the grounds of its inequity remained unconvinced by this argument, partly due to the lack of evidence that production grants were efficiently targeted on 'needy' groups of farmers. The critics argued, on welfare grounds, for a major shift away from commodity price supports to direct income payments based on the needs of individual farmers, combined with redoubled efforts and more resources to encourage sub-marginal farmers to retire early or retrain for a non-farm occupation. The fact that the government introduced the Small Farmer Scheme in 1959 and the Payment to Outgoers Scheme under the 1967 Agriculture Act, was an acknowledgement of these criticisms, even though neither scheme was very successful.

The hypothesis that the income distribution effect of the deficiency payment system was highly inequitable was confirmed by a path-breaking study which investigated the distribution of exchequer support payments (including production grants) amongst different standard-man-day and type-of-farming groups in England and Wales (Josling and Hamway, 1972). The results, relating to 1969, confirmed that the proprietors of the largest farms received the largest absolute payments per farm. Moreover, because deficiency payments tended to be concentrated on cereals and fatstock and large farmers specialised in producing these commodities, the proprietors of the largest farms also obtained the highest proportion of their farming net income from exchequer payments. Josling and Hamway also undertook a purely static analysis of the differential effect on large and small farmers' incomes of the complete withdrawal of exchequer support payments. Their results showed that large farmers' incomes would still have been more than double those of small farmers, contrary to the sometimes heard argument that large farmers would be even more adversely affected than small farmers, in terms of residual income, by the cessation of support payments.

Trends in agricultural output, productivity and farm incomes

Between the late 1930s and the early 1970s, when the UK acceded to the EC, the volume of aggregate agricultural gross output at constant prices increased almost threefold. Only a quite small proportion of the increase in output occurred immediately before and during the Second World War, the vast majority occurred after 1947. During the same period the volume of gross inputs, representing agricultural inputs purchased from the non-farm sector, increased somewhat more slowly and in a lower proportion. Between the late 1940s and the early 1970s the volume of gross inputs only about doubled. These figures imply that total factor productivity increased at a rate of around 1 per cent per annum from the late 1930s to the early 1970s. A similar rate was found for the period 1965–79 (Rayner et al., 1986).

In marked contrast is the lack of any discernible trend in farming net income at constant prices over the same period. Available data on UK farming net income at constant prices goes back only to the year 1946/7. The data suggest that from that year onwards aggregate real farming income rose to a peak in the late 1940s and thereafter gradually fell away to a trough in the late 1950s. Thereafter, the level of farming net income at constant prices recovered slightly, particularly during the five or so years immediately preceding Britain's accession to the EC. But by 1972 aggregate farming net income in real terms appears to have been barely back to the level it had reached in the late 1950s. But this observation needs to be qualified in two respects. First, since during the period under discussion aggregate farming net income was calculated on a tenant farmer basis, the figures take no account of rising agricultural land values, or the increase in wealth which owner-occupier farmers (including sitting tenants who bought their farms from their landlords) derived from this source. The second qualification of the apparent stagnation in the level of real aggregate farming net income during the 25 or so years following the Second World War is that, since the number of farmers declined, the level of real farming net income per farmer almost certainly went up. Due to a serious gap in historical statistics pertaining to British agriculture there is no reliable record of numbers of farmers before 1971 when the figure stood at 298 000 for the UK as a whole. This may be compared with the 290 000 agricultural holdings of five acres and above in England and Wales alone recorded in 1941 by the National Farm Survey (Ministry of Agriculture and Fisheries, 1946). Allowing both for farmers in Scotland and Northern

Ireland and for holdings of less than five acres in England and Wales, this is evidence of a substantial, though unquantifiable, reduction in the number of UK farmers in the quarter century following the Second World War. The extent of the corresponding increase in real farming net income per farmer, which appears likely to have occurred, is also unquantifiable.

Public expenditure on agricultural research
After the Second World War the agricultural expansion programme was accompanied by substantially increased public expenditure on agricultural R&D. Although a proportion of the research was conducted by the agricultural departments themselves and another part by universities and agricultural colleges (often with funds provided by the agricultural departments), a major share of the responsibility was taken over by a much expanded Agricultural Research Council. A substantial number of new ARC research institutes and research units were added to those established with Development Commission Funds before the First World War and for which the ARC took responsibility in 1933. Although the institutes and research units were often located near to universities with which they formed and maintained academic links, they were independently administered and funded.

Up to 1956, the ARC was funded through the agricultural departments to whom it was answerable for the use of public funds. But under the Agricultural Research Act, 1956, the ARC was made directly answerable to Parliament for the use of funds devoted to it. At the same time, the Council was enlarged to provide seats for representatives of the agricultural departments. In addition to receiving public funds, the ARC continued to receive substantial research donations from other sources including foreign governments, international organisations and agricultural marketing boards (Cooke, 1981). Following the publication in 1971 of the Rothschild Report on the organisation of publicly funded R&D, the disposition of part of the ARC's research budget was placed in the hands of the MAFF in application of the so-called customer/ contractor principle.

There appears to be no published official statistical series of UK public expenditure on agricultural R&D. However, unofficial figures suggest that such expenditure increased from between £4m and £6m per year in the early 1950s to around £30m per year in the years immediately preceding the UK's accession to the EC. After allowing for inflation during this period, it would appear that there was still an increase of around 250 per cent in real terms. In the mid 1950s, when the exchequer costs of agricultural price guarantees and production grants totalled around £250 million per year, public expenditure on agricultural R&D was running at around £7 million per year. By the late 1960s and early 1970s, when the costs of price guarantees and production grants were approaching £300 million per year or more, the increase in expenditure on agricultural R&D to about £30 million per year was proportionately higher. But, even then, public expenditure on agricultural R&D amounted to only about 10 per cent of total exchequer costs of agricultural price guarantees and production grants.

A further item of public expenditure on agriculture during this period was the cost of the national agricultural advisory service (NAAS) set up in 1946. Published details of this expenditure are not readily available. However, it can be deduced from figures quoted by McCrone for the years 1954–60 and derived from Hansard, that at that time agricultural advisory expenditure amounted to no more than about 10 per cent of the amount of public expenditure on agricultural R&D (McCrone, 1962, p. 46, Table 1). Thus, compared with other items of public expenditure in support of agriculture, the costs of the state agricultural advisory service appear to have been quite minor.

Denmark

After being occupied by the Germans during the Second World War, Denmark attempted, after the war, to return to a non-interventionist agricultural policy. But this policy encountered serious difficulties from the late 1950s onwards as long-term export contracts with the UK ran out for supplies of bacon, dairy products and eggs. Although increased export of agricultural commodities to Germany partially compensated for reduced exports to Britain, market intervention was gradually reintroduced from the late 1950s onwards. The forms of intervention included minimum milling ratios to maintain the domestic prices of bread wheat and rye, and minimum import prices (maintained by import levies) for feedgrains. Measures were also introduced to maintain the domestic prices of dairy products and pigmeat above their export price equivalents, as well as providing fertiliser subsidies and public funds for promoting export and for agricultural R&D (Tracy, 1982, pp. 242–3). A contemporary study of Anglo–Danish trade emphasised Denmark's overwhelming dependence on agricultural exports to Britain, even after undertaking a measure of export market diversification especially to Germany. The strength of the bilateral trading links between the UK and Denmark was the major factor which prevented Denmark from applying for EEC membership until Britain also applied. The study also produced evidence of Danish agriculture's superior efficiency *vis à vis*

British agriculture, at least with respect to producing the commodities exported by Denmark to Britain, and pressed the case for reducing the gap between British and Danish producer price levels for those commodities (Nash and Attwood, 1961).

France

French agriculture was badly hit by the Second World War despite being put on a wartime footing by the Vichy government. By 1945, agricultural production was down to only about two-thirds of the pre-war level (Tracy, 1982, p. 231).

After the war, France embraced the practice of indicative economic planning with enthusiasm, and the first modernisation plan included, amongst its objectives, both the rapid expansion of agricultural production to relieve food shortages and improved agricultural labour productivity to release more labour for industry. However, as in most other West European countries, agricultural surpluses began to reappear from 1950 onwards, and pre-war methods of attempting to curb excess production, discourage imports and assist exports were revived. The pre-war Wheat Board (ONIB) was not only revived but extended to other cereals and re-named Office National Interprofessional des Cereales (ONIC). New boards were created to regulate other products, including dairy, meat and livestock. Then, in the early 1960s the separate boards for individual commodities were merged into a single, multi-commodity organisation called Fonds d'Orientation et de Regularisation des Marches Agricoles (FORMA).

Despite these developments, average farm incomes remained relatively low and farmer organisations were united in pressing for government measures to provide parity of farmer incomes with those of non-farmers. Two Agricultural Orientation Laws passed in 1960 and 1962 conceded the principle of farm income parity, but also emphasised agricultural productivity improvement and farm structural reform (Petit, 1985, p. 31; Tracy, 1982, pp. 237–9).

Farm organisations remained politically divided but still managed to exert considerable pressure on governments, increasingly through violent and illegal demonstrations (ibid., p. 250).

France played a leading role in the abortive attempt to create a European Agricultural Community (or 'Green Pool') in the early 1950s (the Netherlands being the other leading protagonist). After that, French agriculture policy was mainly concerned with issues arising from the formation of the European Economic Community – with France one of the six founding members – and the evolution of the Common Agricultural Policy.

Germany

The Nazis succeeded in maintaining food production reasonably well for most of the war, despite serious shortages of manpower and other inputs. However, during the final stages of the war there was a serious deterioration in the food situation and, in the immediate postwar years, Western Germany was on the verge of starvation. The food shortage was exacerbated by the division of pre-war Germany into eastern and western zones, respectively occupied by the forces of the Soviet Union and the Allies, since East Germany had been the primary source of bread grains.

Following the constitution of the Federal Republic of Germany in 1949, a policy of government intervention to maintain domestic agricultural prices and control imports was re-established through the installation of import and storage boards for major agricultural products. These resembled the boards established before the war by the Nazis. The Federal Government supported domestic agricultural prices at well above world market levels (Tracy, 1982, p. 239).

A new German Farmers' Union, claiming to represent a large majority of farmers in the Federal Republic of Germany, was established after the war, and this organisation demanded parity of income between farmers and non-farmers. The Agriculture Act of 1955 committed the government to pursuing a number of specific policy objectives for agriculture though without conceding the principle of income parity. These commitments did include achieving a reasonable standard of living for people working on well-managed farms. In addition, the government was committed to producing two annual documents, the one to monitor past agricultural progress and the other to detail plans for future improvement. The annual 'Green Report' was to be based on the analysis of sample farm data to enable the economic and social situation of the farm population to be compared with that of people working in similar professions. The second document, the 'Green Plan', was to be based directly on the preceding Green Report, and was required to detail the policy measures the government intended to adopt to achieve the policy objectives laid down by the Agricultural Law of 1955. That piece of legislation, the provisions of which have survived to the present day, also committed the government to transferring resources from better off to more backward agricultural areas (Cecil, 1979, pp. 50–51; Tangermann, 1982, p. 16).

The German Farmers' Union was closely allied with the Christian Democratic Union (CDU) which dominated the political coalition ruling West Germany during the period leading up to the formation of the EEC. The CDU also had a high proportion of farmers amongst its parliamentary members (Tracy, 1982, p. 251).

When the European Economic Community was formed, with West Germany as a foundation member, German agricultural prices tended to be higher than in other members' states, particularly France, for most commodities. From the date of the foundation of the EC, German agricultural policy was therefore dominated by problems of adjusting to the common price level of the CAP.

Movement towards European Integration

Belgium and Luxembourg formed a customs union (BLEU) as long ago as 1922. After the Second World War, BLEU became Benelux with the accession of the Netherlands to the customs union in 1948. The Benelux countries were later to play a leading role in the creation of the EEC.

For the subject matter of this book it is especially significant that part of the initial impetus for broader West European integration after the Second World War came from the United States. Although the primary motivation for the giving of Marshall Aid may have been more political than economic – to provide a bulwark against the spread of communism from Eastern Europe – the most obvious effect was to hasten economic recovery from the war. The Organisation of European Economic Cooperation (OEEC) was established in 1948, with a membership of 16 countries, to administer the Marshall Plan at the European end. An important part of the OEEC's mandate was the liberalisation of industrial trade. This was facilitated by the formation of the European Payments Union (EPU), but parallel progress with the lowering of barriers to agricultural trade was conspicuously lacking (Pollard, 1981; Griffiths and Mildward, 1986; Kock, 1969).

In 1950, the French government published a plan to internationalise the coal and steel industries of Western Europe (the Schuman Plan). This initiative, inspired in part by the ideal of making a future war between France and Germany impossible, quickly led to the formation of the European Coal and Steel Community (ECSC) in 1951. This integrated the coal and steel industries of West Germany, France, Italy and the Benelux countries under a controlling High Authority with supranational powers.

The architects of the ECSC clearly had more ambitious plans for advancing the cause of economic integration and, in June 1955, the foreign ministers of ECSC member states meeting at Messina in Italy adopted a Benelux resolution declaring their intention to work for a united Europe, including the creation of a common market. An inter-governmental committee was immediately set up, under the chairmanship of the Belgian Foreign Minister, Paul-Henri Spaak, to draft treaties to that end. The Spaak Report, presented in April 1956 and approved by the foreign ministers of the ECSC member states at a meeting in Venice shortly thereafter, formed the basis of the enabling legislation which brought the European Economic Community (EEC) into being. The Treaty of Rome came into effect after ratification by the legislatures of the six founding member states on 1 January 1958, and committed its signatories to forming a customs union, with complete freedom of trade on the internal market and a common external tariff, within twelve years. The common market provisions were clearly intended to include agriculture and the adoption of a common agricul-tural policy was stipulated. However, the details of how this was to be organised were not spelled out in the treaty.

The United Kingdom was not a founder member of the EC. The British government of the day took the view that although the liberalis-ation of industrial product trade with Europe was to be welcomed, there were serious objections to free trade in agricultural products and to the harmonisation of trade policies *vis à vis* the rest of the world. This attitude could largely be explained by Britain's unique position as an agricultural importing country with a low self-sufficiency ratio, and by the magnitude and long-standing of trading links with Commonwealth countries. The British attitude was also influenced by the fact that in recent history most of her trade had been with countries outside Europe, including North America as well as the Commonwealth. The mainten-ance and, if possible, the expansion of trade with these traditional British trading partners was considered to be vital. Thus, when the ECSC countries were moving towards the formation of the EC(6), following the completion of the Spaak Report, the UK worked through the OEEC to try to stimulate interest in the formation of a European free trade area with a much wider membership than that of the six prospective members of the EC. The essence of this proposal was the liberalisation of intra-European trade in industrial products combined with the retention of agricultural trade barriers and the maintenance of national autonomy with respect to external protection. This early British attempt to capture some of the benefits of European Community mem-bership without paying the full price, in terms of the loss of national autonomy with respect to agricultural trade with the Community and all trade with the rest of the world, was unsuccessful. The French were particularly hostile to the idea after de Gaulle returned to power as president in 1958. But, despite this rebuff, the UK continued to work for the liberalisation of industrial trade amongst western European countries who remained outside the EC(6). This effort culminated in the creation of the European Free Trade Area (EFTA), under the Stockholm Convention of 1959, with a membership of seven countries (UK, Denmark, Norway, Sweden, Austria, Switzerland and Portugal).

The birth of EFTA did not kill off the British ambition to join the EC if membership could be obtained on acceptable terms. The remaining EFTA countries did not oppose the UK holding exploratory talks with the EC(6) and when the first formal bid for British membership was made in 1961, Denmark and Ireland also tendered applications as major trading partners of the UK.

The UK's first application for EC membership was unsuccessful, the coup de grace being given by President de Gaulle's famous 'veto' of 1963. In the French President's view, England was not yet ready for Community membership: she still had too many non-European ties. In 1967, a second British membership application suffered the same fate at the hands of de Gaulle. But in 1969 the French Presidency passed from de Gaulle to Georges Pompidou who was more sympathetic to the idea of British membership. At a summit meeting of the Six held at the Hague in December 1969, new ground rules were agreed for the admission of new EC members and this provided the catalyst for the UK, Denmark, Ireland and Norway to re-enter their applications shortly afterwards. Agreement on all aspects of the negotiations was finally reached in January 1972 which provided for the four candidate countries to become members of the EC on 1 January 1973.[16]

The remaining five EFTA countries (including Norway) were able to negotiate a series of agreements with the EC for free trade in industrial products: but no substantive agreements were entered into regarding agricultural trade or the harmonisation of agricultural policies (Tracy, 1982, pp. 308–9).

The preamble to the Treaty of Rome invited other European countries who shared the Community's ideal of pooling resources to 'preserve and strengthen peace and liberty' to apply for membership (Hill, 1984, p. 143). The first enlargement of 1973 which brought in three new members from northern Europe was shortly followed by applications from three southern European countries. Greece applied in 1975, and Spain and Portugal in 1977.

It was recognised that the admission to the Community of relatively poor countries from the Mediterranean region would pose serious initial problems of economic disequilibrium and disharmony. The assimilation of the applicant countries' agricultures into the CAP was going to be doubly difficult due to the relatively greater importance of agriculture in their economies and the backwardness of the farming sector compared with northern European countries. But despite these difficulties, entry negotiations were completed in time for Greece to be admitted to full membership on 1 January 1981. By comparison, the negotiations with Spain and Portugal were more protracted. The delay was not wholly due to the inherent problems of admitting two more members from the southern European region but also to the Community's efforts to solve its own mounting internal problems, relating particularly to the budget, agriculture and fishing, during the early 1980s (Swann, 1988, p. 41). But Spain and Portugal were finally admitted to membership on 1 January 1986.

In 1958, the EC started with only six members and a total population of 169 million: by 1986, the six had expanded to twelve and the total population was 321 million (Statistical Office of the European Community, 1968, Table 1; Swann, 1988, p. 42).

Origins and Foundation of the Common Agricultural Policy

The foundation of the EEC and the formation of the CAP were preceded by some largely abortive attempts to liberalise intra-European trade and reform national agricultural policies for the 'common good'. The most important of these initiatives was the attempt to create a European Agricultural Community or 'Green Pool', with supranational authority, to supervise trade amongst the participant countries. The initial impetus came in 1950 from the Consultative Assembly of the Council of Europe, with France playing a leading role. French agriculture had quickly recovered from the effects of the Second World War and, by the late 1940s, France was already anticipating the emergence of a substantial agricultural surplus for export disposal.[17]

France's enthusiasm for liberalising European agricultural trade was shared by the Netherlands. As a small country with a liberal trading tradition, the Netherlands was interested in the overall liberalisation of intra-European trade, including industrial trade, and saw the freeing of trade in agricultural products as an important step in that direction (Griffiths and Mildward, 1986, p. 55).

Several proposals were tabled by the Council of Europe's Special Committee on Agriculture, including two drawn up by the French (the Charpentier and Pflimlin Plans), one by the Dutch (the Mansholt Plan) and one by the British (the Eccles Plan). Whereas both the French plans and the Dutch plan placed considerable emphasis on the transfer of mandatory powers to a supranational authority, the British plan envisaged that the authority would be limited to making recommendations to national governments. Between 1952 and 1954 a series of conferences was held in Paris, independently of the Council of Europe, to discuss these proposals and at which fifteen western European countries were represented. Many difficulties were encountered on the details of the organisation of agricultural trade. There was considerable disagreement on whether members of the agricultural community would be obliged to give preference to the exports of fellow members (analogous to the 'Community preference' which was later to become a central principle of the CAP) and the nature and extent of powers to be accorded to the supranational authority. In the end, the talks failed in the sense that they did not lead to the establishment of a separate European agricultural community. But the experience of dealing with problems uncovered by the talks, such as the difficulties of harmonising agricultural markets, were later turned to good account by the founder members of the EEC in drafting relevant parts of the Treaty of Rome, as well as in evolving the stucture and organisation of the CAP.

The collapse of the talks on the creation of a European Agricultural Community was followed, in 1955, by the formation in the OEEC of a Ministerial Committee for Agriculture and Food. The purpose of this body was to encourage the 'confrontation' of national agricultural policies amongst the countries belonging to the OEEC in the hope that this would lead to policy reforms favourable to the liberalisation of agricultural trade. But the Committee possessed no supranational power and could reach decisions only by unanimous voting. The main format of the Committee's work was a series of comprehensive reports on agricultural policies in Europe and North America. However despite the effort put into their preparation, it is doubtful whether these reports had any real impact on agricultural policy in the countries concerned (Tracy, 1982, pp. 263–6).

With the signing of the Treaty of Rome in 1957 and the establishment of the EC(6) from 1 January 1958, the initiative for the integration of western European agriculture passed to the six founder members of the European Community. Agriculture is the subject of Articles 38 to 47 of the Treaty of Rome. Whereas Article 38 declared that a common agricultural policy would be established, Article 39 specified its objectives in very general terms. The wording of the article is open to various interpretations, but it has been held that the foremost of the declared aims was that of 'ensuring a fair standard of living for the agricultural population'. This was to be accomplished by increasing agricultural productivity through technical progress and by increasing the individual earnings of persons engaged in agriculture (Tracy, 1982, p. 239).

The clause specifying increased agricultural productivity through technical progress also referred to the 'rational' development of agriculture and the optimum utilisation of factors of production, particularly labour. The other objectives specified were to:

- stabilise markets,
- assure the availability of supplies,
- ensure reasonable consumer prices.

This statement of EC policy objectives for agriculture was unremarkable in that, to a considerable degree, it reflected the goals implicit in the current agricultural policies of the constituent member states. It was unremarkable even relative to the policy objectives of the UK, a non-member state, except that Article 39 made no reference to sharing the domestic market for agricultural products with third country suppliers, as the 1947 Agriculture Act did. Article 40 stipulated that the Common Agricultural Policy should be fully phased in amongst the member states over a transitional period and that a 'common organisation of agricultural markets' was to be effected. Article 43 stipulated the convening of a conference of member states to formulate guidelines for use by the Commission in submitting detailed proposals for the Common Agricultural Policy within two years. The Commission accordingly convened a conference which met at Stresa in July 1958. But wide differences of view between member states emerged at this conference, which was consequently able to agree only upon a set of very general and rather vague 'guidelines' which really amounted to little more than a restatement of the objectives of the Common Agricultural Policy rather than a statement of the means to be employed in attaining those objectives. So it was effectively left to the Commission to work out the details without much guidance from the national representatives of the member states.

The problems confronting the architects of the European Communities' Common Agricultural Policy (CAP) were numerous and difficult to resolve. The existing national agricultural policies of 'the Six' were anything but uniform. In particular, different price levels prevailed for major commodities, maintained by strict controls on external trade. Thus, for example, in the case of soft wheat, the price in Germany, a net importer, was considerably higher than in France, a net exporter, with the prices in other member states lying in between (Hill, 1984, p. 23). These price differences were maintained by strict controls on external trade. The harmonisation of prices needed to give effect to the 'common organisation of agricultural markets' required by the Treaty of Rome would clearly give rise to serious transitional problems.

More fundamental and long-term problems derived from the size, structure and economic situation of the agricultural sector in the member states. The farm population was large, consisting of a total of more than six million holdings in 1960 with around 20 per cent of the total working population of the Community dependent on agriculture for its livelihood (Swann, 1988, pp. 20–26). Further important character-istics were the predominance of small farms – a majority under five hectares – and of low-income farmers. To a considerable degree the problem of low incomes was the consequence of the small average farm size. Relative to the current level of aggregate farm output and income there were too many farms, and they were too fragmented to yield a per capita income level comparable with that of other occupations. Moreover, in many regions of the EC(6) farming was characterised by technological backwardness (linked with the unfavourable structure) and the rural sector by infrastructural deficiencies. The rural population also tended to be socially deprived in certain respects, like educational opportunities.

The Commission decided to develop policy proposals to tackle these problems on two fronts. First there had to be a price policy, and second, a structural policy. In the event, structural policy was to play only a subordinate role in terms of the Community's agricultural budget, but it is not clear that this was the original intention. We deal first with price policy.

With the benefit of hindsight, it is possible to identify three general principles underlying the European Community's policy on agricultural prices as developed during the early transitional period. These were: (a) common prices, (b) common financing and (c) Community prefer-ence.[18] The principle of common agricultural product prices followed logically from the removal of all barriers to intra-EEC agricultural trade. Although it might have been foreseen that, since the Community lacked a common currency, adherence to this principle might be seriously compromised by exchange rate adjustments, this prospect apparently did not worry the architects of the CAP at the time (they were working in a period of virtually fixed exchange rates which had prevailed since the Bretton Woods Agreement of 1944 and could scarcely be expected to have foreseen the collapse of that agreement in 1971). The principle of common financing followed from the proposal (subsequently endorsed by the Council) that all agricultural support measures would be jointly financed by the Community budget. The principle of Community preference, to which net agricultural exporting countries like France attached particular importance, was a natural consequence of agreeing to regulate trade with third countries. Third country suppliers must always be at a competitive disadvantage compared with Community suppliers in selling on Community markets for regulated commodities, that is, third country suppliers must suffer a price penalty.

The principles of common pricing, common financing and Community preference underlay the choice of price policy instruments. The Treaty of Rome permitted a transitional period of twelve years for the harmonisation of national agricultural and trade policies with the common policy, the establishment of common trading rules and bringing common prices into effect. Harmonisation of national price levels meant adjusting to a single Community price, for each 'regulated' commodity, within that period. In order to maintain common prices, there was a choice in principle between either some form of import regulation (given that the EC(6) was a net importer of several major commodities), or domestic market intervention (as practised in the USA), or a deficiency payment system (as then practised in the UK and later, from the early 1970s, by the USA). In the event, the architects of the CAP adopted all of these instruments of price support, either singly or in combination for different commodities. But, in view of the national agricultural policy histories of EC(6) member states during the first half of the twentieth century, it was virtually inevitable that import regulation would be chosen as the principal instrument.

Although the Treaty of Rome had set a deadline on formulation of the details of the CAP, the end of 1961 arrived without agreement having been reached on the regulation of any commodity. The Council was still in session at the end of the year, trying to resolve outstanding problems and resorted, for the first time, to the device of 'stopping the clock'. Finally, on 14 January 1962 the Council reached agreement on a 'package' of regulations for cereals, and cereal-based livestock products, pigmeat and poultry and eggs, as well as for fruit and vegetables. Tentative arrangements were also made for wine. Details of the price support regimes for each of these various commodities were far from uniform. However, for cereals, the variable import levy was adopted as the main instrument of support combined with a system of intervention buying to smooth seasonal fluctuations of supplies and prices and export refunds to dispose of structural surpluses.[19]

The import levy bridges the difference between the minimum import price – termed the 'threshold price' – and the lowest price on the world market of the commodity concerned. As such it is subject to frequent adjustment as the world price varies. For cereals, the national producer price – termed the 'target price' – was set somewhat above the threshold price, the difference representing slightly more than the notional cost of transporting the commodity from the port to the inland market with the maximum deficit between local consumption and local production (Duisberg, in West Germany, in the case of cereals). Thus, 'intervention price' is the price at which national intervention agencies acting on behalf of the Commission are required to purchase eligible grain from producers in order to support the market. The difference between the intervention price and the target price is based on the application of a complicated formula involving the costs of transport from Duisberg to the area of maximum surplus of local production over local consumption (the city of Ormes, near Paris) and the expected relationship between the local market price in that area and the intervention price in a normal year (Fennell, 1987, p. 113). Since producers selling grain into intervention have to deliver to the intervention store at their own expense, the intervention price is a minimum wholesale price, not a minimum farm-gate price.

The final basic element of the cereals regulation is the 'export refund'. This is analogous to the import levy which brings the world price of imports up to the level of the threshold price. The export refund is paid to Community exporters by the intervention agencies to enable commodity surpluses to be exported to the world market at the world price.

The regulations for the other commodities included in the January 1962 package differed from the cereals regulation in several details. So, for example, for pigmeat there is a target price, and an intervention price and an export refund but no threshold price. Instead there is a minimum import price called a 'sluice-gate' price based on production costs (primarily the cost of feeding stuffs). It would be tedious to catalogue the details of the regulations for other commodities.

Consolidation of the CAP, by extension of the basic principles of common prices, common financing and Community preference to other regulated commodities took place between 1962 and 1967. The principal commodities concerned were beef and veal, milk and dairy products, sugar, olive oil and oilseeds.

Despite numerous disputes, disagreements and hiccups on the way, including the celebrated episode in 1965 when France withdrew from all Community activities for six months (ostensibly on the issue of agricultural financing but also for political reasons) at the behest of President de Gaulle, Community agricultural prices and policies were fully harmonised by the beginning of 1968, two years earlier than the original target laid down by the Treaty of Rome.

In determining the levels at which the common prices of regulated commodities were initially set the principal decision-making body was the Council of Agricultural Ministers. The strongest political pressures upon Ministers of Agriculture tend to come from farmers through their representative organisations, rather than from consumers or even taxpayers. The crux of the problem of agreeing on common price levels, therefore, lay in persuading countries with relative high national prices to move down to a lower level. Countries with relatively low national prices did not need persuading to move up to a higher level. So, taking cereals as an example, national prices initially ranged, at the beginning of the harmonisation period, from the highest level in Germany to the lowest level in France, and it is unsurprising that the common prices were initially fixed nearer to the 'high' German level than the 'low' French one. The same principles tended to apply in fixing the common prices of other regulated commodities, though the German and French prices did not necessarily define the extremes in all cases. There was naturally a 'knock on' effect from the relatively high common prices of cereals to the prices set for other commodities, particularly cereals-fed livestock and livestock products like pigs, poultry meat, eggs, milk and other dairy products.

With the advantage of hindsight, it is easy to see that the decision to set the common prices of virtually all regulated commodities at a high level, not only relative to world prices but also to the costs of low-cost EC producers, was likely to lead eventually to serious problems of overproduction and the accumulation of structural surpluses. But there is little or no evidence that CAP decision makers anticipated such problems at the time. Even if they had done so, political pressures for keeping prices high might have been irresistible (Tracy, 1982, p. 287).

Turning from price policy to structural policy, the adoption of the principle of common financing of the CAP was complemented in January 1962 by a Council Resolution establishing a European Agricultural Guidance and Guarantee Fund to finance export refunds, market intervention and structural reform. The English-language title of the fund is rarely used: rather the acronym FEOGA, derived from its French language title is used instead. FEOGA was set up with separate Guarantee and Guidance Sections. It appears to have been anticipated that if Guarantee Section expenditure was unconstrained, it would swallow the lion's share of FEOGA. Consequently, a Guidance Section target of one-third of Guarantee Section expenditure was initially set. But, in practice, that target was never met (Fennell, 1987, p. 77).

The arrangements for financing FEOGA during the early years of the CAP were highly controversial and a major source of friction amongst the EC(6) member states and the Council of Ministers. However, the temporary financial arrangements during the early life of the Community (that is the 1960s) are of little permanent interest. We will return later to the post-1970 arrangements, after the principle of a fully-fledged Community Budget with its 'own resources' had become established.

Post-foundation Evolution of the Common Agricultural Policy up to 1973

In this section we sketch the evolution of the CAP from about 1967 until the enlargement from EC(6) to EC(9) in 1973. We start with the earliest proposals for farm structural reform (the so-called Mansholt Plan). We then go on to the problem of reconciling common commodity prices with variable exchange rates and the introduction of monetary compensatory amounts (MCAs) and the question of the absorption of FEOGA into a wider Community Budget with its 'own resources'.

Measures of farm structural reform

Most of the countries comprising the EC(6) had national policies of structural reform through land consolidation in place prior to the formation of the Community (Organisation of European Economic Cooperation 1956, p. 332). In France, for example, the main vehicle of land consolidation was Land Improvement and Rural Equipment Societies (or 'SAFER') set up under the 1960 Agricultural Law. The SAFER were parastatal organisations with power to acquire and hold land or farms for resale expressly for the purpose of amalgamation to create viable-sized holdings. But progress with consolidation was still quite slow, both in France and elsewhere in Western Europe, so that when the EC(6) was formed much remained to be done.

In the early days of the CAP, Community policy for farm structural reform was passive rather than active. The Guidance Section of FEOGA existed to help finance national programmes. The decision to leave responsibility for initiating new programmes to the member states was rationalised in part by arguing that national governments had to bear the political repercussions of unpopular policies. But a more immediate reason for the lack of a Community initiative was the shortage of funds in the Guidance Section of FEOGA – due to the insatiable appetite of the Guarantee Section. But this passive attitude was eventually questioned by the Commission under the dynamic leadership of the first

Commissioner for Agriculture, Dr Sicco Mansholt. Dr Mansholt took the view that the solution to the farm income problem lay not in enhanced commodity price supports, but in an accelerated programme of farm structural reform. The aggregate production of most major commodities was already close to domestic consumption needs and serious surpluses threatened. Higher product prices would merely exacerbate the surplus problem without significantly improving the incomes of farmers with inadequately-sized or over-fragmented holdings. The root of the problem of low average farm incomes was simply that there was insufficient land to go round amongst all those trying to make their livelihood from farming. The obvious solution to the problem was the adoption of measures to reduce the number of farmers.

The Council of Agriculture Ministers was sufficiently impressed by Mansholt's case to authorise a detailed report by the Commission. The result was a Memorandum on the Reform of Agriculture in the EEC, presented by the Commission in December 1968, which became better known as the 'Mansholt Plan'.[20] Although the main thrust of the Mansholt Plan was farm structural reform and land retirement, it did not neglect price policy. Rather, the argument was that structural reform to create larger more efficient farms would permit prices to be reduced nearer to the market clearing level so that the risks of surplus accumulation would be greatly reduced and the efficiency of EC agriculture improved relative to potential world market competitors. Thus, part of the philosophy of the Mansholt Plan was that farm product prices should be shorn of their income supporting function in order to free them to perform their neoclassical roles of allocating resources and clearing markets.

The key proposal of structural reform was the creation of a new class of larger, more efficient farms – termed 'modern agricultural enterprises'. It was envisaged that these would comprise at least 80–120 hectares of arable land and/or 40–60 dairy cows. Such minimum-sized units would permit the application of modern technology and farming methods and enable those remaining in agriculture to enjoy better working and living conditions and, above all, better incomes. It was recognised that the transformation from the present farming structure, with a predominance of small farms, to the new, modern structure would entail a substantial reduction in the size of the farm workforce. So it was proposed that between 1970 and 1980 about five million people should be encouraged to leave agriculture with incentives for early retirement or retraining. But it was envisaged that as a consequence of the structural revolution and farm productivity gains anticipated by the Plan, other resources would be in excess supply as well. So, it was thought that by 1980 about five million hectares of land would need to be transferred out of agriculture to alternative uses such as forestry and recreation. Similarly, it was suggested that the size of the Community's dairy herd would need to be cut by about three million cows and that landowners should be offered a 'slaughter premium' to encourage this.

Unsurprisingly, the Mansholt Plan encountered considerable political opposition, particularly from farmers' representative organisations. Mansholt himself was dubbed the 'peasant killer' (Hill, 1984 p. 125). Particular exception was taken not only to reducing the number of farmers but also to the retirement of agricultural land.[21] In the face of this opposition the Council of Ministers took no action on the December 1968 Memorandum for more than two years. In the meantime, two modified versions of the original Mansholt Plan were published, together with an official document on structural reform in France (the Vedel Report) which was in broad agreement with the line taken by Mansholt, particularly on the need for land retirement (French Ministry of Agriculture, Paris, 1969).

Early in 1971, the Council's deliberations on the Commission's proposals for structural reform became enmeshed with equally difficult negotiations on prices during which there were violent farmer demonstrations in Paris. Finally, in March 1971 the Council agreed on a Resolution which accepted, in principle, the adoption of a Community-wide programme of structural reform financed by FEOGA. The programme finally agreed was much less radical and ambitious than the original Mansholt Plan. It contained no references to 'modern agricultural enterprises' or to widespread land retirement. The main elements of the programme were:

1. Assistance for people leaving agriculture – for older farmers, a combination of pensions and lump-sum payments for those prepared to retire early and give up their land: for younger farmers, vocational retraining grants, including a maintenance allowance during training. State scholarships were also made available for the children of smaller farmers.
2. Farm improvement measures for those remaining in agriculture – farmers with adequate professional training were eligible to receive a Community grant to help finance an approved farm development programme, to be completed in six years. Those qualifying for assistance were also eligible to buy land released by retiring farmers for farm enlargement with Community guaranteed loans at a subsidised rate of interest.

3. Information and training services to assist farmers in deciding whether or not to remain in agriculture.

The costs of the programme were to be shared between the Community and national governments according to an underlying principle of the FEOGA Guidance Section. In the following year, 1972, three Directives based on these elements were adopted. These were: Dir. 72/159 on the modernisation of farms; Dir. 72/160 on the cessation of farming; Dir. 72/161 on socioeconomic guidance of farmers.[22]

Agri-monetary problems

Very soon after it came into being the European Community adopted a special unit of account (UA) for use in denominating its financial transactions. The exchange value of the UA was originally set equal to the US dollar (that is 1UA = $1.00 US) when the dollar was convertible into gold at a fixed rate. The common prices of all agricultural commodities regulated under the CAP were initially determined in terms of UAs. They were then converted to the national currencies of the Member States at prevailing exchange rates. Thus, common prices, denominated in UAs, remained 'common' even after conversion to national currencies, provided that exchange rates remained fixed. After some years, a special Agricultural Unit of Account (AUA) with a different parity from that of the UA was adopted for agricultural transactions.

In August 1969, the French franc was devalued by approximately 11 per cent in response to a high rate of inflation and a growing balance of payments deficit. If the CAP rules on common pricing had been strictly followed, the devaluation should have led to an 11 per cent increase in commodity support price levels, denominated in francs, guaranteed to French farmers. But the French government wished to avoid sudden and large commodity price increases which might exacerbate inflation. But it was also recognised that if agricultural prices in France were not adjusted, intra-Community trade would be destabilised, that is, the devaluation gave French agricultural exports an 'unfair' advantage in the markets of other Member States which had not devalued their currencies. It was, therefore, agreed by the Community that farm prices in France would stay temporarily at their pre-devaluation level but also that trade destabilisation would be avoided by taxing exports and subsidising imports at the French frontier. These taxes/subsidies were termed 'monetary compensatory amounts' (MCAs). When Germany revalued the DM a few months later (October 1969) similar action was taken, except that in the German case exports were subsidised and imports taxed. MCAs were also applied to trade with third countries so that, in effect, variable import levies and export restitution payments became supplemented with MCAs. The rationale of extending MCAs to external trade was that without them third country exporters of agricultural products to the EEC would gain an 'unfair advantage' following currency revaluations in Member States, despite import levies denominated in UAs. By the same token, devaluing Member States would be unfairly advantaged in exporting to third countries.

Although, when it was first introduced in 1969, the MCA system was intended only as a temporary measure, it in fact became a persistent feature of the CAP, despite its anomalous character.[23] If common agricultural prices expressed in national currencies are not adjusted to reflect exchange rate movements, then clearly they are no longer 'common'. Thus, the persistence of MCAs is clearly inconsistent with the maintenance of the ideals of a single market with common prices, that is, it distorts competition. The most damning criticism of MCAs, from a 'first-best' perspective, is that they inhibit trade.

Adjustments in FEOGA financing before the first enlargement

Arrangements for the financing of FEOGA were the source of considerable friction amongst the Member States of the Community from the outset of the fund's creation in 1962. A major difficulty in the early days was technical: namely, that rather than possessing its own funds, FEOGA was dependent on the contributions of member states (the so-called 'national budget contributions'). The Commission's objective, therefore, was to change the legal status of FEOGA, and of the Community Budget of which it formed a major part, so that it commanded its 'own resources'. It was hoped that once accomplished, this change would take the heat out of the issue of how the costs (and benefits) of FEOGA's operations were shared amongst the Member States. This hope proved to be over-sanguine.

When agreeing on interim FEOGA financing arrangements in 1966, the Council had agreed that permanent arrangements must be in place by the beginning of 1970. Under the new, definitive system of financing, agreed by the Council with only a few days to spare at the end of 1969, the Community Budget was to obtain its own independent revenue (or 'own resources') from two sources:

1. Ninety per cent of agricultural import levy and custom duty revenues (mainly on industrial products) as collected at the Community's 'frontier' with the rest of the world; member states were

entitled to retain the remaining 10 per cent of such revenues to cover collection costs.

2. A notional value added tax (VAT) of up to 1 per cent of a 'common assessment base' to cover any shortfall between budget expenditure and budget receipts from the other sources, that is, import levy and custom duty revenues. The common assessment base was (and still is) an agreed common collection of goods and services upon which VAT up to an agreed rate is levied (see Swann, 1988, p. 67).

The new system was to be brought into operation in stages, partly because when the agreement was reached the VAT systems of the EC(6) Member States had not been harmonised. The target date set for complete harmonisation and the full operation of the new system was 1975. In the event this target was not achieved and the new system of financing, including VAT-based contributions, did not become fully operational – for the enlarged EC(9) Community – until 1979. Between 1970 and 1979 interim arrangements prevailed, similar to the 'old' arrangements but complicated by the accession to the Community of three new member states – Denmark, Ireland and the United Kingdom – in 1973 (Hill, 1984, pp. 37–8).

Going back to the formulation of the Community's 'own resources' budget, as devised at the end of 1969, some comment is needed to explain why the VAT contribution was brought in to supplement import levy and customs duty revenues. The explanation is that contrary to hopes and expectations prevailing when the interim budget arrangements were set up in 1962, by 1969 the growth of agricultural import levy revenues was already lagging behind the growth of intervention and export restitution payments. This was largely a consequence of the EC(6)'s growing degree of self-sufficiency in the majority of regulated commodities. For some commodities like sugar and dairy products, the EC(6) had been self-sufficient from the beginning and, by the early 1970s, large export surpluses existed not only for these commodities but for others, such as wheat and barley, as well (Tracy, 1982, p. 289). The disposal of surpluses imposed a growing burden of export restitution payments on the budget. Although later it was hoped that the accession of the UK, as a net importer of most agricultural products, would help to relieve this problem, any respite was short-lived, and the problem of dwindling import levy revenues and growing export restitutions intensified in the late 1970s and early 1980s.

Multilateral Trade Negotiations in the GATT and the CAP

Apart from providing a forum in which bilateral trade disputes can be discussed and, on occasion, resolved, the GATT also organised a series of multilateral trade bargaining sessions in which tariff reductions could be negotiated within the context of the principles of non-discrimination and reciprocity. In more recent times these sessions also provided a forum within which the lowering or removal of import quotas and other NTBs could be discussed.

The first round of multilateral tariff negotiations coincided with the signing of the General Agreement in Geneva in 1947. Three further rounds were held between 1949 and 1956 in Annecy, Torquay and again in Geneva. These early rounds of negotiations resulted in substantial tariff reductions for industrial goods but virtually none on agricultural products.

The Dillon and Kennedy Rounds

The impetus for the next round of tariff negotiations came partly from the formation of the EC(6) in 1957. Under Article XXIV:6 the GATT is required to examine the impact of any new customs union or free trade area on third countries, and this examination was supplemented by a round of full-scale tariff negotiations, christened the Dillon Round, in 1960–61. Up to the end of the 1960s one further major round of MTNs under the GATT was held, the Kennedy Round (1964/67). Considering the fruits of these rounds of negotiations as a whole, considerable progress was made with reducing tariffs on non-agricultural goods. By comparison progress with the reduction of trade barriers on all kinds of agricultural goods, and the lessening of NTBs on trade in all classes of goods, was much smaller. We confine our remarks on the details of these negotiations to trade in agricultural products, and particularly to the negotiating position adopted by the EC and the USA.

The crux of the Dillon Round was that in the EC the switch from specific rates of import duty, bound under GATT by individual member states, to variable import levies was expected to reduce access to the EC market for third country exporters, such as the US. The US tried but failed to obtain from the EC guaranteed access for its existing level of agricultural exports. But bilateral standstill agreements, effectively freezing current levels of trade, were obtained by the US for particular commodities, including wheat, maize and poultry. Even more importantly, with the benefit of hindsight, the US and other agricultural exporters obtained from the EC the binding of duty rates at low or zero levels for oilseeds, oilseed products (such as oil and meal) and cereal substitutes (such as tapioca and corn gluten feed). The common external tariff for sheepmeat (for which no Community Regulation existed or was contemplated) was also bound at 20 per cent (Harris et al., 1983, p. 276). These duty bindings on commodities in which the EC was, at the time, far from self-sufficient, later re-emerged as serious constraints on the EC's ability to modify the CAP in response to budgetary and political pressures.

Apart from the binding of the low or zero duty on cereal substitutes, oilseeds and oilseed products, the US benefited little from the Dillon Round in purely trading terms. Even the bilateral standstill agreement on US exports of poultry (as well as other agricultural products) came unstuck in the so-called 'chicken war' in the early 1960s.[24] The main explanation of why the US gave way to the EC in the Dillon Round appears to have been that for political reasons the US did not wish to seriously impede the progress of West European economic integration (ibid., quoting Warley, 1976, p. 379).

During the Kennedy Round (1964/67) attempting to liberalise agricultural trade was closer to the centre of the stage than it had been in earlier rounds of MTNs. The EC's use of the variable import levy was a particular bone of contention: the US was keen to see this system of support modified to remove the absolute protection it provides. The negotiations were also complicated by the growing use throughout the world of non-tariff barriers to agricultural trade (such as import quotas) and the growing realisation that domestic support policies impacted directly upon exporters' access to markets.

The EC's Kennedy Round negotiating position had two main planks. The first of these did concern levels of agricultural protection. The Community proposed that all agricultural support measures be reduced to a common denominator[25] and that it might then be feasible to bind the margin of support (termed the 'montant de soutien'). The second main plank in the EC's negotiating position was to press for concerted market organisation and market sharing amongst major agricultural exporters. Thus, a 'World Commodity Agreement' was proposed, covering cereals, beef and veal, some dairy products and sugar, to stabilise prices at fair and remunerative levels and control product surpluses (Tracy, 1982, p. 376).

These EC proposals were rejected by the US and other exporters of temperate agricultural products, ostensibly on the grounds that they failed to offer any lowering of levels of agricultural protection. But a more fundamental reason for the rejection may have been that the countries concerned were not willing to accept constraints on their domestic agricultural policies (ibid., p. 277, quoting Warley, 1976, p. 385).

Apart from minor concessions on certain agricultural duties, the main agricultural achievement of the Kennedy Round was the negotiation of the 1967 International Grains Agreement. The intention of the IGA, which succeeded an earlier, longstanding International Wheat Agreement, was to raise the floor price of wheat below which participating importing and exporting countries agreed not to buy or sell the grain. Also linked with the IGA was a Food Aid Convention (FAC) under which aid donors committed themselves to releasing a minimum global quantity of grain for distribution as food aid each year, with the costs being shared amongst the donors. As major wheat exporters and food aid donors, the US and the EC both had their vested interests in seeing the 1967 IGA work as intended. In the event, however, its price supporting element never got off the ground. Due to the growing pressure of supplies on an already glutted market, the world price of wheat fell below the IGA floor price within a year. Only the FAC remained.

As far as the EC and the US were concerned, the main upshot of the Kennedy Round was that the EC could claim that it had successfully defended the CAP. But, for its part, the US could claim that it had 'avoided legitimising the CAP' (Harris et al., 1983, p. 277).

US POLICY: POSTWAR TO 1973

Introduction

Our review of US agricultural policy in this chapter is divided into three chronological periods. First, we briefly consider the period immediately following the Second World War, from 1948–53, when policy adjustments were only minimal. Second, we review developments in the middle and late 1950s (1954–60), when pre-war problems of excess capacity and over-abundant agricultural supplies re-emerged. Third, we examine compromises made on the basis of the agricultural policy debate during the 1960s and early 1970s (1961–73). In all three periods we briefly review major changes in agricultural legislation, and their underlying rationale, together with the main policy issues taken up for debate by professional agricultural economists.

1948–53: Fixed Price Supports for Agriculture

Introduction

The US emerged from the Second World War as the most powerful economy in the world. Having eschewed the option of retreating into isolationism, America sought to restore and enhance the economies of 'friendly' nations for a mixture of commercial and strategic motives. Thus, the US was the principal contributor to the UN Relief and Rehabilitation Administration (UNRRA) which provided emergency postwar relief and aid. Shortly afterwards the Marshall Plan was launched to provide the basis for long-term economic recovery in Western Europe. The US was also influential in the establishment of new institutions for reviving world trade, such as the World Bank, the IMF and the GATT. Also symbolic of American commitment to the cause of world trade liberalisation was the renewal in 1945, and at subsequent three-yearly intervals, of the 1934 Reciprocal Trade Agreements Act. By 1947, the average US tariff level was down 25 per cent compared with 1934 (Robertson, 1973, p. 664). This period has been identified as marking the high point of US trade liberalisation (Cochrane, 1979, p. 295). But as non-tariff barriers to trade began to be seen increasingly as the major obstacles to trade liberalisation, so policy attention gradually shifted away from bilateral reciprocal trade agreements on tariffs to multilateral negotiations under the GATT.

The farm policy debate

In the immediate postwar period, agricultural policy analysis was dominated by T.W. Schultz's diagnosis of the 'farm problem' (Schultz, 1945). The crux of Schultz's analysis was the persistent tendency for the aggregate supply of agricultural commodities to grow faster than the aggregate demand for them, so that agriculture is 'burdened constantly with an excess supply of labour even when business is expanding and there are brisk job opportunities in non-agricultural industries' (ibid., p. 82). Schultz identified the influence of exogenous technological advance on agricultural supply as a major contributing factor to the persistent disequilibrium of supply and demand growth rates. This diagnosis pointed to the conclusion that a constant redistribution of the national labour force was required with relatively fewer workers engaged in agriculture as the economy developed (ibid., p. 82). But outmigration of labour from agriculture was slow, depending more upon the availability of jobs outside agriculture than upon farm prices and incomes.

Schultz achieved a broad consensus amongst fellow agricultural economists of the day over the fundamental causes of the agricultural adjustment problem (Brandow, 1977). Policy proposals of the profession between 1943 and 1948 reflected both Schultz's analysis and agriculture's experience during the 1930s. It was stressed that prices should follow the long-run market equilibrium path, but that supplementary government intervention was required to stabilise farm prices and incomes, using either direct income payments or compensating price subsidies during recession. Fixed support prices as a percentage of parity were rejected in favour of flexible prices related to market trends. Forward pricing was advocated as part of the compensatory price package (Johnson, 1947). Policies were also proposed for facilitating the mobility of agricultural labour and for increasing the demand for food with consumption subsidies (Brandow, 1977, pp. 237–41).

Legislative developments

Wartime level price supports expired at the end of 1948, but the 1948 Agriculture Act extended them for a further year, at 90 per cent of parity, for most major commodities. Thereafter, flexible price supports were to become effective (Cochrane and Ryan, 1976, p. 27).

The farm policy debate reopened in Congress in 1949, following the re-election of Truman as President and a Democratic majority in both houses of Congress resulting from the previous year's elections. Truman's Secretary of Agriculture, Charles Brannan presented to Congress a revolutionary set of agricultural price policy proposals. The nub of the Brannan Plan was mandatory support at virtually 100 per cent of parity for basic commodities (corn, wheat, cotton, tobacco, rice and peanuts) plus certain livestock commodities. But rigorous production controls would be needed to maintain the high prices. The most revolutionary feature of Brannan's proposal, however, was that income supports for producers of other commodities (mainly perishables) would be given via direct payments (that is, deficiency payments in modern parlance) to bridge any gap between support price levels and average market prices. Advocates of the Brannan Plan stressed that direct payments would enable 'fair' prices for producers to be combined with relatively 'low' prices to consumers. However, to the extent that supply controls had to be invoked to limit the budget cost of direct payments (and provision was made for doing this) consumers would be adversely affected by higher prices. The Plan also proposed a ceiling on direct payments per farm regardless of the level of production, the limit to be determined by the size of the typical family farm.

The Brannan Plan encountered a hostile reception in Congress and was finally defeated in both houses in the summer of 1949. The reasons for its defeat included farmer opposition to the explicit subsidy inherent in direct payments and to the limitation on payments per farm. There was also widespread Congressional opposition to the implied budgetary cost of the Plan and the Republican minority feared that the intrinsic appeal to voters of combining high prices for farmers with low prices to consumers, for perishable commodities, might damage their electoral prospects (Cochrane and Ryan, 1976, pp. 88–9; Cochrane, 1979, p. 145).

Following the defeat of the Brannan Plan in 1949, no further attempt was made to incorporate overt deficiency payments in US farm legislation until the early 1970s (with the successful passage of the Agriculture and Consumer Protection Act of 1973). In place of a bill based on the Brannan Plan, the Agriculture Act of 1949 as enacted represented a broad continuation of previous legislation from the 1930s, with some modification of the provisions of the 1948 Act. Prices of basic commodities were maintained at 90 per cent of parity subject to some supply constraints: but in practice the supply triggers were higher than previously and largely ineffective. From 1949 through to 1953, there was little change in farm legislation.

State of agriculture[26]
The farm price parity ratio peaked at 115 in 1947, before dropping to 101 in 1950 and rising again to 107 in 1951 with the onset of the Korean war: by 1953 it had fallen again to a ratio of 92. Net farm income followed a similar path, peaking in 1947, dropping by 20–25 per cent in 1949 and 1950, recovering again in 1951, and declining again in 1952 and 1953. Despite this variability, US agriculture was in a much healthier state after the war than it had been during the 1930s. In 1950, real net farm income was 50 per cent higher than in 1940 and at the level of 1930.

Agricultural production rose rapidly during the war and immediate postwar period to reach 25 per cent above the 1940 level in 1947. Production then remained static until 1951, before climbing again through 1952 and 1953. During the war and immediately afterwards the high production was fully absorbed by domestic demand and exports, including special government export programmes of postwar relief. But during the mild recession of 1948–49 commercial export growth slackened, farm prices sagged, and the CCC began to accumulate stocks of cotton, wheat and corn. The onset of postwar adjustment was temporarily relieved by the Korean War which revived both domestic and export demand and caused a reduction of CCC stocks. But by 1953 and 1954 the surplus problem had re-emerged, reflecting a decline in exports caused, in part, by the recovery of European and world agricultural output. The reversion of commercial farm exports to pre-war levels also signified a return to the secular downward trend of agricultural exports as a percentage of total US merchandise exports which had taken place since the turn of the century. By the early 1950s this ratio was down to only 15–20 per cent compared with nearly 60 per cent during the period 1900–1910. The relative importance of farm export revenue had also declined. By 1953, only about 10 per cent of farm cash receipts were accounted for by exports which accounted for less than 10 per cent of the total cropland harvested acreage.

Summary
After the war, farmers' organisations and Congress were apprehensive that agriculture would return to a depression as in the 1920s and 1930s. Following the sweeping Democratic Party victory in 1948 there was an intense debate concerning instruments to be used for market management and farm income support centred on the Brannan Plan for direct (deficiency) payment support of perishable commodities. The Brannan Plan failed: farmers were not prepared to exchange parity price support (an implicit subsidy) for deficiency payments (an explicit subsidy), and the budgetary implication of shifting the costs of support from consumers to taxpayers was also a major stumbling block. The 1949 Agriculture Act represented a continuation of the 1938 Act with parity-based price supports, acreage allotments and marketing quotas as the main instruments of market adjustment and CCC loans providing a floor to the market. High demand for farm commodities during the Korean War alleviated farm income and surplus problems and the policy instruments were little used, but by 1953–54, surging production and slackening foreign demand resulted in the re-appearance of commodity surpluses. The postwar adjustment of US agriculture had been postponed for nearly a decade by a combination of special circumstances, but with the return to normality surpluses and excess capacity were to be highly visible symptoms of the retention of a system of price support designed for the depression of the 1930s, allied to the persistence of forces tending to produce chronic agricultural disequilibrium, as so brilliantly analysed by T.W. Schultz.

1954–60: Excess Capacity and a Crisis of Abundance in Agriculture

Introduction
The presidency passed from the Democrats to the Republicans with the election of President Eisenhower in 1952 and his re-election in 1956. But Congress continued to be controlled by the Democrats for all but

two of Eisenhower's eight years as President, and the interventionist character of domestic macroeconomic and foreign policies remained in place. Although the macroeconomy grew steadily during the Eisenhower era, with real GNP rising at around 4.5 per cent per year, high government spending on defence and foreign economic and military aid, coupled with large US private business investment abroad, led to a growing balance of payments deficit and rising foreign ownership of dollar assets. By the late 1950s the postwar world dollar shortage was over.

Legislative developments
Despite the change of presidency in 1952 existing farm legislation continued in force until 1954. But in preparation for new legislation in the latter year, Eisenhower's Secretary of Agriculture, Ezra Benson attempted to re-orientate agricultural policy towards the free market. Benson proposed so-called 'flexible price supports', ranging from 75 per cent to 90 per cent of parity, whereby the level of support would decline as supplies increased: a further element of the plan was the expansion of agricultural exports. It was envisaged that lowering support prices and expanding foreign demand would stem the emerging tide of surpluses via market forces. The flexible price supports proposal encountered considerable opposition in Congress and the bill which was actually passed, the 1954 Agricultural Act, was a watered down version of the Benson plan. However, compared to the fixed high price supports of previous administrations, the Eisenhower administration did succeed, to a degree, in making price supports more flexible and generally lower.

The objective of expanding foreign demand was met by the passage, in 1954, of the Agricultural Trade Development and Assistance Act, better known subsequently as PL480. This Act, which received bipartisan support in Congress, was viewed as successfully combining the realisation of a foreign policy objective with advancing the aims of domestic agricultural policy. The institutionalisation of substantial food aid to 'friendly' developing countries was allied to the disposal abroad of embarrassing agricultural surpluses. The centrepiece of PL480 was Title I, 'Sales for Foreign Currency', whereby agricultural commodities were sold abroad in exchange for foreign currency (to circumvent the problem of dollar scarcity in aid recipient countries). Shipping costs were met by the US and sales revenue payments in the currency of the recipient country were deposited to the account of the US government in that country. These payments were available for specified purposes, including development loans to the government of the country concerned (the major use). The main recipients of aid under Title I were India and Pakistan; the major commodity shipped was wheat.

The PL480 programme did not start to have an impact until 1956. In the meantime farm commodity stocks increased and farm incomes fell. Farm organisations (the Farm Bureau and Farmers Union) sought production controls. The Eisenhower Administration's response was a cropland diversion programme introduced via the Agricultural Act of 1956. In paying farmers to divert land from the production of surplus commodities and practise soil conservation measures, the Soil Bank programme of 1956 had its roots in pre-war legislation enacted to combat soil erosion (1936 Soil Conservation and Domestic Allotment Act). The Soil Bank consisted of two parts, a short-term acreage reserve and a more long-term conservation reserve. Under the acreage reserve programme (ARP) farmers could let up to 50 per cent of their allotted acreage of basic crops to the government in return for a rent. Land placed in the Soil Bank could be used for soil conservation, but no crop could be harvested nor could the land be pastured (except in drought areas). The ARP operated on an annual basis. Under the conservation reserve programme (CRP) farmers could receive annual payments for shifting cropland to long-term conservation. Participants were required to sign a contract retiring land from crop production for a minimum of three years or a maximum of fifteen years if the land was planted with trees.

The ARP was discontinued in 1958, having proved to be costly ($600 million per annum in 1956 and 1957) and relatively ineffective in the preceding two years: crop production reached an all-time high in 1958. The CRP was also costly (some $300 million per annum), ineffective in controlling production and much criticised by rural areas experiencing the spillover effects of taking whole farms out of production. No further contracts for the CRP were entered into after 1960. Despite the ex post criticism of the Soil Bank that US agricultural production continued rising in the face of its existence, the rate of production might have been even higher without it and all other things being equal.

In sum, the lower commodity support prices and land retirement which characterised the era of Eisenhower's two successive presidential terms did not prevent an unprecedented rate of production growth as biological, chemical and mechanical technical change proceeded apace in agriculture. Yields of basic crops and dairy products increased (for example, by some 25 per cent for corn, 33 per cent for wheat and 30 per cent for milk yield per cow between 1954 and 1960). Production of other (non-basic) commodities also expanded, for example the soybean acreage expanded by around one-third between 1954 and 1960, mostly onto land taken out of basic crops because of acreage allotments. Demand expansion measures had little effect and excess supply increased to such an extent that 'by 1960 the surplus problem had reached crisis proportions' (USDA, 1984, p. 23). The budgetary costs of farm programmes had not been reduced by Benson's policy changes nor had farm incomes shown any real improvement. Indeed, in 1960, net farm income was no higher than it had been in 1954 and lower than it had been in the immediate post-Second World War and Korean War periods. The end of the Eisenhower era was marked by a crisis in agriculture and farm policy in which 'agricultural distress and discontent were widespread and the agricultural administration was near a state of shambles as the year 1960 drew to a close' (Cochrane and Ryan, 1976, p. 92).

Developments in analysing the 'farm problem'

T.W. Schultz's analysis of the reasons for chronic disequilibrium in agriculture was developed by other agricultural economists to explain excess capacity and low resource returns in agriculture in the 1950s (and 1960s). Earl Heady and his colleagues at Iowa State University stressed that adjustment in agriculture is implicit in the process of economic growth (Heady, 1966). The crux of Heady's analysis was that the twin problems of (a) agricultural surplus creation and (b) structural adjustment involving labour displacement and the transition to a smaller number of larger farms, could be attributed to the combined effects of four factors:

1. the low income elasticity of demand for farm products;
2. the determination of the prices of purchased farm capital inputs primarily by economic forces in the non-farm sector;
3. continual decline in the price of capital inputs relative to the price of labour resulting in declining demand for agricultural labour due to factor substitution;
4. the development of new forms of capital, via technological change, which relax the constraints on food production imposed by 'fixed' agricultural resources, particularly land.

Heady viewed labour displacement as the major problem of agricultural adjustment. Moreover, he saw barriers to the outflow of labour from agriculture as the main reason for relatively low farm incomes under economic growth. The reasons for low agricultural labour mobility identified by Heady included:

1. lack of non-farm employment opportunities,
2. lack of industrial employment skills,
3. attachment to the rural way of life,
4. unacceptable costs of migration,
5. lack of knowledge about alternatives.

A major outcome of Heady's analysis was the establishment, at Iowa State University, of a Centre for Agricultural and Economic Adjustment. The primary purpose of this institution was to educate farmers and the United States public at large about the nature of the 'farm problem', and the types of adjustment policies needed to resolve it, by closing the gap in resource returns between agriculture and other industries.

Another major contribution to the analysis of the farm problem in the 1950s was Cochrane's technological treadmill hypothesis (Cochrane, 1958, pp. 105–7; Cochrane and Ryan, 1976, p. 15). The crux of this hypothesis was that farmers are compelled by economic forces to adopt unit cost reducing and total output increasing new technologies in order to remain in business. Moreover, the adoption of new agricultural technology is not one-off but a continuous process. Having stepped onto the 'technological treadmill' farmers must keep pedalling in order to avoid falling off. The main points of treadmill theory are: (a) society at large supports the public funding of agricultural R&D; (b) since individual farmers face perfectly elastic demand curves for their products they adopt new technology eagerly and rapidly; (c) once innovations have been successfully pioneered by early adopters, other producers have to take up the new technology in order to maintain their incomes as prices fall due to increasing supply pressing against a severely price inelastic demand curve; (d) a cycle of new innovations, adoption by farmers, increased aggregate output, falling prices and the further adoption of new technology in an attempt to maintain income places farmers on a treadmill from which it is virtually impossible to escape and survive economically.

Cochrane also stressed that, as well as continually shifting to the right due to the impact of technological innovation, the short-run supply curve for farm products is also severely inelastic 'and provides no brake to falling prices in a surplus situation' (Cochrane and Ryan, 1976, p. 17). The reasons given for supply inelasticity included the immobility of farm labour and the lack of alternative uses for land and capital assets such as buildings and farm machinery.

Two main criticisms were leveled at treadmill theory (Hathaway, 1963, ch. 4). First, it was argued that far from being exogenous to agriculture, the rate at which new practices were adopted was related to price and income levels. Second, rational farmers would purchase output increasing inputs only if the expected marginal revenue exceeded the marginal cost. Moreover, in driving the returns to labour in agriculture substantially below returns to human resources elsewhere, the behaviour of treadmill farmers was difficult to reconcile even with static economic theory (ibid., p. 104).

As an alternative explanation of large and persistent disequilibrium in agriculture resulting in chronically low returns for some resources in the industry, Hathaway emphasised the importance of the notion of asset fixity in explaining resource immobility. The theory of asset fixity was originally developed by Glenn Johnson (1960). Johnson argued that because of resource immobility and/or transport and transactions costs, the 'salvage value' of a durable farm asset is invariably below its 'acquisition cost'. Moreover, should the marginal value product (MVP) of the service flow provided by the asset fall below its acquisition cost, the asset is effectively trapped in agriculture so long as its MVP remains between the acquisition cost and the salvage value. Johnson also maintained that like durable assets, labour also became trapped in agriculture due to the 'moving disruption and retraining cost involved in changing occupations'.

In the Hathaway synthesis of the theory of asset fixity, new resources were brought into agriculture when they were profitable at their acquisition prices but became trapped with falling output prices because their salvage values were substantially below acquisition costs. For the industry as a whole it appeared that substantial divergencies between acquisition costs and salvage values were most likely for the resources of human labour, land and durable capital. But low returns on durable capital inputs did not persist due to depreciation. To Hathaway this explained why, in agriculture, returns to labour were low relative to returns on investments in land, machinery and working capital, which were approximately the same as returns to capital elsewhere in the economy (ibid., p. 138). It followed that the major problem of agricultural adjustment concerned farm labour.

Tweeten (1970) questioned whether the earnings disequilibrium between agriculture and non-agriculture was as chronic as was implied by fixed asset theory. Tweeten cited evidence to show that rewards to labour in agriculture were consistent with earning potential as evidenced by length of schooling: also that there was a rapid rate of adjustment for farm labour and that since farmers engaged in much job experimentation, the labour market worked efficiently. Thus, under Tweeten's alternative hypothesis (termed the 'flip-flop' antithesis) dynamic disequilibrium 'is alleviated quickly enough by out-migration to keep farm earnings on a par with non-farm earnings. If farm earnings appear low it is only because economists have imputed too high an opportunity cost' (ibid., p. 176).

Tweeten suggested that the labour market worked most efficiently for the young and out-migration of this group of workers provided the major equilibriating force in the adjustment process. But older farmers and associated family workers constituted a sizeable reservoir of redundant labour (ibid., p. 177). Tweeten concluded that (at the time of writing) the problem of surplus labour was diminishing and that the farm problem would increasingly be one of low absolute returns to labour, rather than low relative returns, with the policy implication that priority should be given to 'raising the opportunity price of labour through education and training' (ibid., p. 193).

Johnson (1958) noted a net migration from farm to non-farm employment of some 13.7 million persons between 1940 and 1956, representing a reduction in farm employment of over 30 per cent. Although this out-migration had resulted in farm people obtaining increases in per capita income comparable with those of the non-farm population, an income gap of some 56 per cent remained in 1956 for labour of equivalent earning ability (after allowing for differences in age, sex and education). Johnson concluded that 'there is no satisfactory alternative to greater mobility of labour if agricultural incomes are to be increased relative to non-agriculture. Labour must be made more expensive by making it scarcer' (ibid., p. 171). The measures pinpointed by Johnson for increasing mobility were: (a) improved school education in rural areas; (b) improved provision of job information; (c) investment in employment and training agencies and (d) grants or loans to migrants for resettlement.

Brandow (1977) noted that much of the transfer from farm to non-farm sector employment occurs when young people decide not to follow their parents in farming. However, considerable inertia remains in the system so that although 'adjustment of the farm labour force can be speeded up or slowed down . . . large changes cannot be expected in a few years and great changes require the turnover of generations' (ibid., p. 229).

Developments in the farm policy debate
During the 1950s there was an intense and, at times, acrimonious debate amongst agricultural economists over farm policy. As the decade progressed, and existing farm policy was perceived by many to have failed, opinion tended to become divided between two main schools of

thought. First, there were those such as O.B. Jesness and M. Clawson, who advocated greater market liberalisation via lower and more flexible price supports, possibly supplemented by limited direct income supports. Then there were those, like Willard Cochrane and George Brandow, advancing the case for direct supply control with individual production quotas.

Jesness (1958) directed attention to the policy emphasis, since the 1933 AAA, on 'prices and price relationships'. He saw this as the natural corollary of the importance attached to prices by farmers in determining their incomes, as well as the appeal to politicians of fixing prices to gain favour with farm voters. He also noted that downward adjustments in production did not have the same appeal as 'better prices' and that farmers had little enthusiasm for production constraints. But the continuation of 'price incentives' from the 1930s had priced some products out of the market. US cotton had been replaced by expanded overseas production in the export market; price support for cotton and wool had stimulated the development and expansion of synthetic fibres and, similarly, margarine had increasingly substituted for butter and wheat substitutes for wheat in the feed grains market. Jesness conceded that there was a real cost/price squeeze in agriculture and that farmers had not fully shared in the boom enjoyed by the rest of the economy in recent years. Moreover, 60 per cent of US farmers derived little benefit from government programmes through having insufficient to sell. In general, Jesness advocated policy reforms to increase reliance on market prices, coupled with government aid to encourage out-migration. He was against the extension of supply control.

In surveying the prospects for US agriculture over the next 25 years, Clawson (1958) foresaw 'a persistent tendency for agricultural output to outrun agricultural requirements' with technological change being the major driving force (p. 271). He criticised past agricultural programmes for being 'obsessed with land as if it were the only factor of production' in attempting to adjust output, and concluded that the acreage adjustment programmes of the past 25 years had had comparatively little effect on total agricultural output (ibid., p. 272). Clawson proposed that agricultural adjustment policy should focus on encouraging out-migration with cash subsidies and provision for retraining. He also advocated that farm prices be 'established entirely in the market place' (ibid., p. 274) in order to fulfil their resource allocating and market clearing roles, and that the farm income problem be tackled with direct income supports. Specifically, Clawson proposed supplemental income payments to producers in years of low income.

In sum, Jesness and Clawson both advocated the abolition of price supports and production controls in favour of a return to market prices. They were also agreed on the need for policy to emphasise the withdrawal of resources from agriculture, with appropriate subsidies. Clawson alone advocated supplemental direct income payments for farmers remaining in agriculture.

Turning to the second school of thought concerning the solution to the farm problem, Cochrane was particularly prominent in opposing the free market solution. He believed that the price reductions needed to bring production into line with demand were so great that no government could live with the attendant social and economic unrest (Cochrane and Ryan, 1976, p. 37). Cochrane's cure for agricultural disequilibrium was supply control, which he defined as 'the conscious adjustment of supply to demand commodity by commodity, year after year, to yield prices in the market that have already been determined as fair by some responsible agency' (Cochrane, 1959, p. 698). He criticised previous attempts at supply control for (1) restricting only land and then being ineffective as capital substituted for land, and (2) applying only to certain commodities and not preventing resources being shifted to substitute commodities. To be effective, supply control had to be all embracing and enforced with mandatory, but negotiable, marketing quotas. The national sales quota for a commodity would clear the market at a 'fair' or parity price. The initial allocation of individual quotas would be a pro rata share of the national sales quota based on recent historic production. Cochrane recognised that the 'fair' price would have to be determined by Congress but proposed that it be based on returns to capital and labour on representative farms comparable to resource returns outside agriculture. Finally, it was to be expected that the fair price would decline with technological advance in agriculture. Cochrane also argued that, by stabilising prices, his proposal would mitigate the problem that farm income depended upon the date of entry into farming: those who entered during a farm depression when land prices were low gained substantially in any subsequent boom, whilst those who entered during a boom would find it difficult to survive in a depression without price support. More succinctly, Cochrane stated that, in a free market agriculture, 'it is important to be born at the right time'. Cochrane also challenged the equity of attempting to solve the farm problem through a policy of aiding out-migration to reduce the farm labour supply (the Chicago School solution). Specifically, he argued that this policy was unfair to the farm population for three interrelated reasons: (1) before labour remaining in agriculture could reap any gain, the decrease in the labour supply must more than offset increases in product resulting from technological advance; (2) the migrants must consequently bear the cost of improving the economic well-being of those that remained; and (3) the farm population, in the main, did not want to solve their income problem by leaving agriculture and their preferences merited some consideration (ibid., p. 705).

Whilst the adoption of Cochrane's supply control plan might have enhanced the survival of the present generation of farmers, it faced at least two major problems: first mandatory supply control was unlikely to be welcomed by farmers themselves and, second, despite the transferability of quotas, the capitalisation of their benefits would discourage the entry of new producers.

The impact of advancing technology in reducing land and labour requirements in agriculture and in depressing farm prices, was also emphasised by Brandow (1960), who argued that, for this reason, there was little prospect for a prosperous agriculture in free markets. Brandow therefore saw merit in applying the principle of supply control to administratively adjust supply to demand. In his view this would not affect labour mobility, possibly not affect farm consolidation, probably not affect technological progress in agriculture, and not affect income distribution amongst farmers (ibid., p. 1171). However, he favoured selective rather than comprehensive supply control which he considered to be impracticable, although some means of checking the diversion of acreage from controlled to uncontrolled products was of vital importance. Sales quotas were considered suitable for livestock products and for crops grown for processing such as cotton, soybeans and tobacco. But acreage controls were judged to be more suitable for feed grains.

Brandow had earlier proposed combining individual production quotas with direct payments. But such payments would be restricted to a portion of the quota only, so that at the margin of production the producer's return would be no more than the market price (Brandow, 1955 and 1960).[27]

An illuminating review of the costs and benefits of agricultural supply control, including undesirable impacts on the non-farm economy and the international economy, was undertaken by Hathaway (1960). He maintained that although supply control would lower Treasury payments, it would increase costs to consumers and that the main benefits would accrue to the larger, more efficient farmers. Moreover it was doubtful if the public would support transferring income from lower income consumers to the higher end of the farm income scale (ibid., p. 1192). Note that Hathaway ignored the option of combining supply control with deficiency payment support, as proposed by Brandow. Hathaway also drew attention to certain costly side effects of supply control, including: (a) the link between higher food prices and inflation;

(b) the undesirable impact of export subsidies and import quotas, adopted as an essential adjunct of supply control, on the international trading stance of the US; and (c) the costs of political opposition to supply control from input suppliers, trading intermediaries, consumers and numerous farmers.

Hathaway returned to the issue of agricultural policy options in his influential 1963 textbook (Hathaway, 1963). Here he identified five major options (not necessarily mutually exclusive). These were:

1. returning to the market as a solution,
2. policies to increase product demand,
3. supply control,
4. direct compensation for low or unstable farm prices and incomes,
5. programmes outside agriculture.

Hathaway rejected relying solely on the market solution, not only for its political infeasibility but also for its neglect of genuine poverty amongst a section of the farm population.

Policies to increase farm product demand included loan storage programmes of the type inherited from the 1930s, as well as market discrimination and demand expansion both at home and abroad. Although a case might be made for continuing commodity loans in order to smooth short-term price and income instability, this instrument was not suitable for dealing with longer-term shifts in demand. The option of market discrimination both domestically and in overseas markets was largely rejected, due not only to numerous problems of maintaining separate markets, but also because it did not offer a solution to the basic problem of too many resources being committed to agriculture relative to the demand for its products and the desire for equitable price and incomes. Similarly, the option of overall demand expansion, including PL480, was not adequate for dealing with the problem of disequilibrium. On the supply control option, Hathaway considered both the traditional instrument of attempting to control crop output by means of acreage restriction and Cochrane's proposal of direct production quotas. On the effectiveness of acreage restriction, he concluded that the historical record in the US had ranged from tolerable to disastrous. A constant problem had been the rapid rise in land substitutes which, by increasing yields per acre, had forced continuous reductions in acreage allotments. Land retirement tended to reduce the returns to capital and labour, but increase the value of land, so that landowners were the major beneficiaries. There was also the fundamental criticism that by removing an input which, according to

Hathaway, had little or no productive value elsewhere in the economy, land retirement constituted a serious misallocation of resources.[28] On the production quota alternative, as proposed by Cochrane, Hathaway foresaw that due to continuing technological progress, regular quota reductions would be needed to maintain the effectiveness of the programme, otherwise the net marginal returns to labour would eventually be no higher than without the programme. In the long run, the benefits of quota restrictions could accrue wholly to landowners or other holders of the 'right to produce'. Hathaway judged that, quite apart from the a priori objections to supply control, there was serious doubt about the political feasibility of a land retirement or marketing quota programme sufficiently restrictive to deal effectively with the disequilibrium problem in US agriculture (ibid, p. 330).

On the option of direct compensation for low or unstable farm prices and incomes, Hathaway considered both deficiency payments (termed 'direct payments') and direct income payments (or income insurance) for farmers. His main objection to deficiency payments was that, because they compensated producers without curbing production, they did nothing to solve the disequilibrium problem. He maintained this criticism despite acknowledging that Brandow's proposal of combining deficiency payments with individual production quotas, in order to match production at the margin with the market price, would go some way towards meeting this objection to deficiency payments. However, he granted that the Brandow proposal was superior to most alternatives for dealing with disequilibrium, including land retirement. On the direct income payments option – to compensate farmers when their earnings fell below some pre-determined percentage of recent average earnings, for example – Hathaway made the same criticism that such schemes did not tackle the fundamental problem of agricultural disequilibrium.

On the final option of seeking a solution to the farm problem outside agriculture, Hathaway emphasised the benefits of all policies encouraging the out migration of agricultural labour, such as full employment, increased expenditure on education and vocational training for rural youth, and industrial development in 'suitable' rural areas.[29]

In sum, Hathaway's textbook review of policy options for remedying the US 'farm problem', as perceived in the early 1960s, was critical in varying degrees of all proposals confined to tackling the problem from within agriculture. Rather, he saw the best hope for correcting chronic agricultural disequilibrium in the adoption of appropriate microeconomic policies elsewhere in the economy to attract excess resources, particularly labour, away from agriculture. But land retirement was not to be recommended on grounds of opportunity cost and resource allocation efficiency.

More generally, Hathaway's perspective on agricultural policy emphasised four major aspects: first, the multiplicity of farm policy objectives and the impossibility of attaining all of them simultaneously; second, the need to continue encouraging the withdrawal of labour from agriculture; third, income transfers to farmers must continue to be limited by budget constraints; and fourth, farmers must expect the increased use of restrictive devices limiting their freedom of action.

State of the US farm policy debate around 1960

Looking back on the state of the US farm policy debate around 1960, four salient points emerge. First, there was a growing academic consensus that the root cause of the farm problem was a chronic disequilibrium between inelastic demand and a burgeoning supply of farm products. Technological innovation was recognised as the major driving force on the supply side. Second, there was a marked division of opinion on the choice of remedies for dealing with the problem. At one extreme were those who saw the solution in the withdrawal of all government price support and production intervention to liberalise agricultural markets. At the other extreme were the advocates of comprehensive supply control to match aggregate production with demand at a 'fair' price to producers. In between were those who advocated compromise solutions borrowing and combining elements from both extremes. Third, there was a growing emphasis on seeking a solution to the farm problem outside agriculture itself. The removal of excess labour from agriculture was seen as crucial for restoring agricultural equilibrium, but appropriate policy measures were needed in the broader economy to ensure adequate non-agricultural employment opportunities for migrants from the agricultural sector. Measures were also needed to ensure that potential migrants were adequately informed about non-agricultural job opportunities as well as being trained to fill them. Finally, despite the postwar renewal of the Reciprocal Trade Agreements Act of 1934, the farm policy debate in the US remained largely isolated from developments in the rest of the world. This comment applies particularly to those who advocated more government intervention, rather than less, to solve the farm problem. By and large, agricultural trade policy, including competition between the US and other countries for export market shares, and the interaction between trade policy and domestic agricultural policy, remained at the margin of the debate.

1961–73: Compromise and Consolidation of Agricultural Policy Formation

Introduction

During the 1960s, US agricultural policy evolved against a background of moderate growth in real GNP and labour productivity (around 4 per cent and 3 per cent per annum, respectively), falling unemployment and gradually rising inflation. US performance on economic growth and productivity was only moderate compared with most West European countries and Japan. US economic performance during this period was also marked by growing balance of payments deficits reaching more than $3 billion per annum by the late 1960s. Economic aid and military expenditures abroad, including NATO commitments and financing of the Vietnam war, were major contributory causes to the deterioration in the balance of payments which culminated with the Smithsonian realignment of 1971, under which the dollar was devalued by 8 per cent. This was shortly followed, in 1973, by the adoption of a system of managed floating exchange rates following the demise of the Bretton Woods Agreement of 1944.

The direction of farm policy during this period was influenced by these macroeconomic trends. It was also affected by two domestic concerns and a foreign one. On the domestic front, poverty and environmental conservation emerged as major policy issues. On the foreign front, the advent of the European Community and the formation of the Common Agricultural Policy brought to the fore a divergence of views between the US and West European countries on the issue of agricultural trade. The poverty issue was epitomised by the 'War on Poverty' launched by President Johnson in 1964. This had a direct impact on domestic food programmes, especially the Food Stamp Programme. From 1969 to 1977, federal expenditures for domestic food assistance increased from $250 million to $3600 million – larger than the combined expenditures of the USDA on research, education, conservation and commodity programmes (Paarlberg, 1980, p. 102). We deal separately with environmental conservation below.

On the issue of agricultural trade, the 1960s witnessed two rounds of multilateral trade negotiations in the GATT, the Dillon Round (1960–61) and the Kennedy Round (1963–68). As briefly discussed earlier in this chapter, conflict between the United States and the EC on the issue of the liberalisation of agricultural trade were important features of both rounds. The US was largely unsuccessful in gaining improved access to the EC market for its agricultural exports.

Agricultural policy adjustments: 1961–69
Following the debate in the 1960s on the means for solving the farm problem, the Kennedy Administration, on assuming office in 1961, was inclined to opt for supply management. The new Secretary for Agriculture, Orville Freeman, had three priorities: first, to effect an immediate increase in farm income; second, to reverse the nine-year build-up in stocks of feed grains; third, to undertake a major revision of policy by enacting comprehensive supply management instruments. Price supports for over a dozen commodities were immediately raised by more than 10 per cent in implementation of the first priority. The 1961 Feed Grains Bill, which sought to lower stocks of feed grains by paying farmers to voluntarily idle corn and grain sorghum acreage was intended to implement the second priority. Unlike the other two, the third and most radical priority of introducing mandatory production controls encountered major Congressional opposition, based in part on a fear that supply control would raise food prices: unwillingness to yield political power to the administration *vis-à-vis* the management of agriculture may also have been a decisive factor (Cochrane and Ryan, 1976, p. 93). The feed grains provision of the 1962 Food and Agriculture Act broke new ground by giving producers deficiency payment support for the first time ever in the US. The loan rate for feed grains was dropped close to the level of the world price but deficiency payments, or 'direct payments' in US parlance, were introduced to bridge the gap between the old, higher loan rate and the new one. In addition, diversion payments were made for land withdrawn from production by feed grain programme participants. The basic components of the 1963 feed grains programme – loan rate at or below world prices, direct price support payments and diversion payments – continued for the next eleven years.

Despite the opposition of Congress, the Kennedy administration persevered in attempting to impose mandatory supply controls. The next step was to seek the support of producers. The 1962 Food and Agriculture Act also included provision for a wheat referendum to be conducted in 1963. The referendum invited wheat producers to choose between the alternatives of:

1. mandatory programme of acreage control combined with a comparatively high support price (based on parity) for the share of the crop used for domestic consumption. Heavy penalties would be imposed for the 'overplanting' of acreage allotments.
2. No acreage control combined with a much lower support price level (50 per cent of parity).

The first alternative was defeated by the result of the referendum.[30] This result effectively killed the Kennedy administration's bid to introduce mandatory supply controls. Following the result of the 1963 referendum, legislation on agricultural policy represented a compromise between the extremes of market liberalisation and mandatory supply control.

A notable feature of the 1964 Agricultural Act was the introduction of direct payments to wheat programme participants who received wheat certificates corresponding with the whole of their crop. The face value of the certificates was the support price. Wheat processors and exporters were required by law to honour certificates at their face value in exchange for deliveries of grain, but were free to recoup the extra cost partly from domestic consumers and partly from the exchequer. Under the original scheme, certificates consisted of a domestic element (approximately 45 per cent of the total allotment), an export element (approximately 40 per cent) and an acreage diversion element (approximately 15 per cent). Whereas the cost of the domestic element was passed on to consumers via processors, the costs of the export and acreage diversion elements were borne by the exchequer.[31] These details of the scheme were subsequently modified several times, as explained below.

The Food and Agricultural Act of 1965 consolidated the compromise policies by continuing wheat certificate payments for four more years and by extending similar schemes of support to feed grains and cotton. However, the details were modified for all crops from the pattern set for wheat in 1964. For wheat, from 1966–70, the cost of financing the domestic element was shared between domestic consumers and the exchequer. Even more importantly, the export element was discontinued. Thus, during this period the wheat certificate payment programme in the US was effectively a two-tier pricing scheme with the upper tier price, corresponding with domestic usage, set at the support price level, and the lower tier price corresponding with exports determined by world market forces.[32] Between 1971 and 1973 direct payments were again confined to the domestic wheat allotment, but no limit was imposed on total wheat planting. However, programme participants were required to divert a proportion of their cropland to conserving uses (later termed 'set-aside'). In contrast to wheat, the costs of certificate payments support for feedgrains and cotton were met wholly by taxpayers throughout the life of the scheme. Thus, for these commodities, the US scheme during this period closely resembled the archetypal system of deficiency payments under which costs of support are borne wholly by the exchequer and consumers pay no more than the price determined by free market forces.

The term 'deficiency payments' was not used in the US until 1973. In fact, the true nature of the certificate payment programme introduced during the 1960s appears to have been cloaked in obscurity. A possible explanation of this ambiguity is that had the true nature of the policy been more open, increased producer opposition might have been provoked. Farmer opposition to the notion of being identified as recipients of 'state welfare' was (and probably still is) very strong in the US.

The reason underlying the decision to exclude wheat exports from direct payments support between 1966 and 1973 is also obscure. From the perspective of the late 1980s it might be thought that policymakers were attempting to purge domestic agricultural support of its trade-distorting element. But it seems very doubtful whether this issue exercised the minds of policymakers in the 1960s. The most plausible explanation would seem to be that this measure helped to curb the exchequer costs of agricultural support.[33]

The farm policy debate: 1961–69

Domestic policy   The academic debate on the best approach to solving the price and income problems of commercial agriculture spilled over from the 1950s to the 1960s. Advocates of both the free market solution and of supply management continued to be vocal.

The newly appointed Secretary for Agriculture, Orville Freeman, set the scene for the debate at an American Farm Economics Association Conference in 1962. Freeman declared that US agriculture had reached a crossroads with one direction marked 'the free market' and the other 'supply management'. Given this choice, the administration's farm policy would be based on supply management coupled with trade expansion legislation to maintain US farm exports at historic levels, particularly in Europe 'where protectionism was becoming entrenched within the EC' (Freeman, 1962, p. 1160). In response to Freeman, Paarlberg commented that whilst the administration deserved praise for its trade expansion measures, it warranted criticism for advocating supply management (Paarlberg, 1962). As well as rehearsing well-known neoclassical arguments against production quotas, including the one that they are difficult to remove once in place, Paarlberg asserted that in a growing economy agricultural incomes can be maintained in real terms only if the supply curve of farm labour shifts to the left at a high enough rate. Farm incomes will be 'unsatisfactory' if the rate is 'too low' and the appropriate remedial policy in this case is to increase it. At a later conference, D. Gale Johnson also restated the neoclassical view that the most appropriate farm policy was market liberalisation plus government aid to enhance labour mobility. He estimated that total resources committed to US agriculture were 6–8 per cent above the level required to produce the output 'that could be sold at the average level of prices in recent years' (Johnson, 1963, p. 342). He concluded that 'the possibilities of increasing the average and marginal returns to labour are much greater through reducing the quantity of labour engaged in agriculture and through increasing its quality and skill than through increasing commodity prices' (ibid.).

The supply management option was defended by John Schnittker, then with the USDA, on largely pragmatic grounds. Schnittker maintained that criticism of farm policy had become somewhat muted, for three reasons (Schnittker, 1963, p. 358). First, an 'uneasy political consensus' had been reached that some form of supply management, particularly acreage diversion, was here to stay; second, there was concern over the work prospects for displaced farmers if the free market option were adopted; third, a growing consensus took the view that the rate at which the farm population declined depended more upon overall economic policy than upon farm policy as such (with the implication that the former was slow to change).

In a perceptive paper presented to the 1962 Conference of the AFEA, G.E. Brandow made the point that the choice of farm policy options depended upon a prior choice of farm income goals. More specifically, Brandow distinguished between a 'minimum income goal' and a 'comparable earning goal' for agricultural price policy. He asserted that if minimum income were the chosen goal, then 'strong efforts are justified to hold farm income up to the proposed minimum'. But if comparable earnings is the goal then 'the public's obligation to farmers is much weaker' (Brandow, 1962, p. 153). Brandow also suggested that if minimum income were the goal, then instruments like limited direct payments and voluntary land retirement, coupled with modest price supports and domestic and foreign food disposal, were appropriate. But, in contrast, if comparable earnings were the goal, then supply management was the appropriate instrument since price incentives for resource allocation would be lacking. Thus, Brandow advocated that agricultural policy should have a clear income goal and adopt appropriate instruments accordingly. But he also stressed the federal budget constraint on the selection of farm programmes and that farm policy should be compatible with comparative advantage in commercial foreign trade. In a retrospective review of actual policy developments, Brandow later identified the middle and late 1960s as a period of relatively settled farm policy in which a compromise was struck between the extremes of supply management and a free market in pursuit of the 'minimum income' option (Brandow, 1977).

Trade policy   The early 1960s witnessed a revival of interest in agricultural trade policy, which had been largely in abeyance since 1933. With farm exports accounting for about a quarter of total exports, the US was the world's largest exporter and second largest importer of farm products (about 60 per cent non-competing). The main exports were wheat (and flour), feed grains, cotton, oilseeds (and products), fruits and vegetables, tobacco, rice and dairy products. The main export destinations were Western Europe and Asia. Around one-third of all exports took the form of non-dollar food aid and a further fifth received subsidies (Mehren, 1963). Exports were recognised as a cheap method of surplus disposal provided the gap between domestic producer and export prices could be closed, or at least narrowed. But agricultural policies on both sides of the Atlantic were seen to be in conflict with the drive for freer trade. It was foreseen that EC agricultural expansion would adversely affect US exports of wheat, feed grains, tobacco, fruits and vegetables and olive oil: but the prospects for exports of cotton and soybeans were better due to their duty-free access to the EC (Learn, 1963). But the US stance on agricultural trade policy remained ambivalent. It was noted that between 1935 and 1962 Section 22 of the AAA as amended had been used to restrict imports of ten major product groups. Moreover, restrictive measures against imports had been reinforced by the 1955 waiver in GATT absolving the US from the obligation to match import quotas with corresponding restrictions on domestic commodity supplies (Menzie, 1963). It was suggested that Section 22 should be terminated to smooth the path of trade negotiations since the benefits of import restriction were minuscule compared with the benefits of trade expansion (Fuller and Menzie, 1964). There was also a growing interest in and awareness of the impact of domestic agricultural protection and surplus disposal as food aid on the welfare of recipient LDCs, including their export earnings. The question of shifting the emphasis of PL480 away from domestic surplus disposal to the economic development of the recipient countries was posed as an important policy issue (Mackie, 1966).

In 1967, the report of the National Advisory Commission on Food and Fibre, appointed by the president in 1965 to give a long-range appraisal of agricultural policy, brought together the twin threads of domestic agricultural policy and agricultural trade policy. On domestic policy the Commission recommended a transition to a fully market-orientated agricultural price policy, but with direct payments to protect farm incomes. But the Commission linked domestic price liberalisation with the adoption of trade liberalisation, including the elimination of import quotas and export subsidies (Hillman, 1967).

Policy developments: 1969–72

In 1969, the presidency passed from the Democrats to the Republicans following the election of President Nixon. The new Secretary for Agriculture, Clifford Hardin, adopted a low-key approach to agricultural policy. Thus, despite the change of administration, the 1970 Agriculture Act incorporated no really fundamental changes. Rather, compared with the 1965 Act (which had been extended for one year in 1969) there was little more than tinkering at the margin of commodity programmes. The major innovation in 1970 was one of nomenclature. Short-term cropland acreage restrictions, with which producers had to comply in order to benefit from government price support were renamed 'set-aside'. Previously such restrictions had been termed (specific) crop acreage diversion programmes. The underlying rationale and operation of the set-aside programme introduced in 1970 was much the same as with schemes it replaced except that set-aside did not specifically restrict the acreage of any crop. Provided a farmer idled the required percentage of the farm's total acreage allotment, the remaining land could be planted to any crop or combination of crops. This change was intended to give market prices a greater role in planting decisions (Harwood and Young, 1989). There were also marginal adjustments in other commodity programme details, such as the limitation of total payments to individual producers. In 1971, Hardin was replaced as Secretary for Agriculture by Earl Butz who was soon advocating higher farm prices in preparation for the 1972 presidential campaign. However, the Nixon administration also based its agricultural policy strategy for the 1972 presidential election campaign on expanding agricultural exports. The US also played a leading role during 1972 in inaugurating the Tokyo Round of multilateral trade negotiations under the auspices of GATT which began in 1973. The obvious inconsistency between raising domestic support whilst simultaneously preaching external liberalisation was masked by the worldwide and largely fortuitous surge in the market prices of cereals and other commodities which occurred in 1972. Rising market prices won the farm vote for Nixon who was victorious in November 1972.

Considering the whole of the short period between the mid-1960s and 1972, it may be argued with some credibility that during this time US governments may have thought that they had 'solved' the farm surplus problem. Market prices were relatively high and stocks substantially reduced, largely due to the relative buoyancy of farm exports during this period and the belief that the Third World was on the brink of starvation. In 1972, the worldwide commodity price explosion abruptly switched attention from expanding commercial farm exports to containing domestic food price inflation and confronting the spectre of hunger on a world scale. Also during this period, commodity loan rates for wheat, feed grains and cotton were reduced near to the level of world prices and direct payments (that is deficiency payments), partially financed by taxpayers, replaced indirect support via high consumer prices. For a short time a two-tier pricing system, anticipating the Producer Entitlement Guarantee (PEG) proposal of the late 1980s, actually operated in the US. However, this innovation was overwhelmed by the food scarcity syndrome which briefly dominated policy in the early 1970s and disappeared with the passage of Agriculture and Consumer Protection Act of 1973.

The farm policy debate: 1969–72

During this period the specifics of the commodity programmes were overshadowed by three more general issues in the farm policy debate. These were, first, inflation and stabilisation; second, the prospects for trade liberalisation; third, agriculture and the environment. Here we deal only with the first two of these issues, the third being dealt with later.

On the issue of inflation and stabilisation, there was a clash between conflicting interpretations of the food price inflation which marked the early 1970s. The dramatic rise in food prices in 1972 was discussed by Brandow (1973) as 'The Food Price Problem'. Food prices had risen faster than at any time since 1951. 'In seven months (to January 1973) retail food prices had risen 4.6 per cent, wholesale prices of processed foods and feeds 11.0 per cent and farm food prices 13.0 per cent' (ibid., p. 389). Agricultural economists tended to be guarded in their interpretation of the implications of the sudden surge in food prices for agricultural policy. Was the inflation of food prices primarily due to shifts on the supply-side or the demand-side? In particular, did it mark the end of chronic excess capacity in US agriculture? Brandow hedged his bets by advising that 'since the future is highly uncertain, American agricultural policy should incorporate strategy capable of dealing with any situation likely to develop; commitment to an assumption of either excess or deficient capacity could be badly mistaken' (ibid., p. 390). But policy makers appeared to be less guarded in their interpretation of events. It was argued that, for them, Hathaway's explanation of excess capacity and chronic disequilibrium in agriculture, which held sway in the 1960s, was no longer a major influence on policy. On taking office after the 1972 Presidential Election, the Nixon administration had assumed 'a permanent change in the economic characteristics of agriculture' (Bonnen, 1973, p. 394). This change in policy stance was shortly to be reflected in the Agriculture and Consumer Protection Act of 1973.

Bonnen's own interpretation of the sudden rise in food prices and its policy implications was quite different. Having noted and analysed movements on both sides of the market, he concluded that

> much of the current change is short-run and that the discipline of the post-1960s economic model of agriculture has not been discarded. Until demonstrated otherwise, the prudent analyst must assume that entry is being made to yet another boom and bust cycle in agriculture in which farmers are now being induced to build additional production capacity in excess of some future period's needs. (ibid., p. 395)

On the issue of agricultural trade policy, Johnson (1970) made the important point that with the US farm economy increasingly integrated into trade, attempting to raise farm incomes by land withdrawal was unlikely to be successful for two reasons. First, the direct price effect would be small and most of the US supply contraction would be eroded by output expansion in other countries. Second, the general willingness of the US to contract supply had probably encouraged output expansion by other countries. A similar point was made by Cochrane (1970) who argued that the US would find itself in the impossible position of trying to support world farm commodity prices by controlling or reducing production within its borders alone.

The standing of the US as the world's largest agricultural exporter was again emphasised together with the proportion of total farm receipts derived from export sales – 14 per cent in 1972 (West, 1972, p. 827). Other notable shifts in the pattern of agricultural trade on a world scale were the growing proportions of total trade accounted for by trade amongst developed countries and of LDC food imports from the developed world (ibid., p. 828). However, there were reasons for doubting whether the buoyancy of farm exports could be sustained. It was noted that for some products, such as feed grains, nominal protection rates had fallen during the 1960s. But, due to the reduction of loan rates, effective protection rates had remained high due to direct payments (Wipf, 1970). The difficulties of negotiating agricultural trade liberalisation through the GATT were discussed by Bergsten (1973) and Schnittker (1973) in anticipation of the Tokyo Round of MTNs. Bergsten asserted that protectionism for farm products was strongly entrenched: it had been barely reduced by the Kennedy Round. The liberalisation of agricultural trade could be negotiated only within a broader, overall trade-liberalising framework. The US could get major foreign concessions on agriculture only by extending concessions of its own in the industrial sector. However, on the specific issue of US–EC trade relations, Bergsten doubted whether Europe was sufficiently interested in US concessions on industrial trade to make the tough internal decisions needed to liberalise the CAP. But without a 'cooperative stance' by the EC and other nations, it would be difficult for the US government to withstand internal interest group pressures for increased protection against foreign competition. Bergsten concluded that the outlook for freer farm trade was close to zero in the short run (ibid., p. 288).

Schnittker shared Bergsten's pessimism on the prospects for trade liberalisation, identifying the political leverage of farm groups with a vested interest in excluding imports, such as dairy producers, as well as the EC and Japan, as barriers to freer trade. But, despite his pessimism on liberalisation, Schnittker was optimistic that agricultural trade would be expanded in the 1970s for five reasons: (a) rising incomes and increasing demand for livestock products; (b) increased Japanese imports of grain and oilseeds; (c) continuing production problems in the USSR and failure to meet domestic meat production targets; (d) opening of the Chinese economy for trade; and (e) growing LDC food import needs despite the success of the Green Revolution (Schnittker, 1973, p. 289). On the issue of trade liberalisation, Schnittker concluded that 'only when nations decide that agricultural protection costs too much will freer trade be realised on a faster timetable' (ibid., p. 293).

Developments in Farm Policy Analysis

The stock of social science knowledge relating to farm policy analysis was increased substantially during the period under review. A number of advances were to have a significant impact on both the issues examined and the frames of reference used by agricultural economists in subsequent years. Five aspects stand out: first, the placing of the agricultural policy within an international context; second, the adoption of the concept of economic surplus for quantifying the static efficiency implications of farm programmes; third, the identification of the long-run effects of policy with asset values in agriculture; fourth, the examination of the link between public sector research and development and agricultural productivity and of the relationship between technological change and welfare gains in the farm sector; fifth, a growing awareness of the environmental impacts of high technology – intensive farming and of the requirement that the policy agenda be broadened to incorporate environmental concerns.

The international context of farm policy

Johnson (1973a) placed the agricultural adjustment problem within an international context. He noted that freer trade would add to the social and political costs of adjustment and this could impede the pursuit of agricultural trade liberalisation. However, adjustment was inevitable in the long run because government price support and protection could have only a once-and-for-all impact on the demand for agricultural labour. In the long run, reduced demand for labour could not be averted due to continuous decline in the relative importance of agriculture in the economy, and the continuing erosion of the farmer's share of consumer food expenditure accounted for by the 'urbanisation effect', and the persistent substitution of purchased inputs for agricultural labour. The major impact of protection on the one hand, and trade liberalisation on the other, must be on the value of the least elastic resource, land.

Schuh (1974) challenged the conventional explanation of the farm problem in the 1950s and 1960s by pointing to the impact of exchange-rate policy on the farm sector. The main thrust of Schuh's thesis was that persistent overvaluation of the US dollar had undermined the performance of US agriculture, and greatly added to the costs of support, through its depressing effect on exports. Overvaluation of the dollar meant that domestic agricultural resources were undervalued compared to a situation where the exchange rate was in market equilibrium. This analysis cast new light on the reasons for low resource returns in agriculture. Schuh also maintained that the undervaluation of agricultural resources (caused by overvaluation of the exchange rate) tended to speed up the rate of technical change. He argued that financial stress is an important motivation for technical change.

Schuh was careful to qualify his thesis by granting that exchange rate overvaluation was not the only reason for the farm problem in the 1950s and 1960s. Other contributory factors included the prevalence of restrictions on international trade and economic development in general. However, the performance of the agricultural sector could not be understoood fully without adequate consideration of the exchange rate. That was the crux of Schuh's argument.

The importance of the contributions of Johnson and Schuh to policy analysis cannot be understated. Johnson coined the memorable phrase 'World Agriculture in Disarray' (Johnson, 1973b) to describe the resource misallocation implications stemming from the prevalence of government intervention into agriculture worldwide. It became widely recognised that protection policies distort the location of production and the extent and patterns of trade flows in agricultural commodities so restricting the gains from trade to world consumers. Schuh highlighted the interaction between macroeconomic policy and farm policy; this was to become of considerable importance in future years when exchange rates were allowed to float and financial liberalisation gave a more prominent role to monetary policy.

Farm programmes and static welfare analysis
A number of studies popularised the use of static partial equilibrium welfare analysis of farm support programmes. Such analysis attempts to quantify the transfers in economic surplus between the three groups of producers, consumers and taxpayers brought about by government intervention into agricultural markets. In addition, it provides estimates of the social cost of distortions – the deadweight costs – induced by such intervention relative to the perfectly competitive norm. Specific studies were by Wallace (1962), Johnson (1965), Dardis and Dennison (1969), and Hushak (1971) in the American literature, and by Josling (1969) in the European literature. General conclusions were that the social costs were small but that the transfers were large. Notwithstanding Brandow's (1977, p. 271) comment that 'the basic theory is invaluable in providing a conceptual orientation for the analysis of programs but the assumptions implicit in the literal forms of it for policy conclusions are breathtakingly heroic', this frame of reference was to become the norm for policy impact analysis in subsequent decades. It was to become particularly useful for multi-country, multi-commodity analysis of the likely implications of policy reform under multilateral negotiations.

Farm programmes and the functional distribution of income
A central conclusion of the farm policy literature was that income benefits from farm programmes tend to be capitalised into the value of resources in inelastic supply, principally land or a supply control instrument such as a sales quota or crop allotment. Such capitalisation means higher costs for incoming farmers. Furthermore, little income benefit accrues to labour in the long run. In the short run, for farmers who own their own farms, the distinction between factor returns is not important. However, part-owners and tenants benefit less than landowners. Important studies were by Johnson (1963) and Floyd (1965). These stimulated subsequent econometric analyses of the relationship between farm support and asset values in agriculture as well as providing a frame of reference for examining the ultimate beneficiaries from agricultural protection.

Technological progress in agriculture

At least up to about 1970, most of the literature dealing with technological change in agriculture was concerned with its consequences rather
than its origins. T.W. Schultz and E.O. Heady emphasised the role
of technological change in their writings developing, explaining and
popularising the nature of the agricultural adjustment problem. Central
to their policy analysis and prescription was the notion that economy-
wide gains from technological change in agriculture (principally to food
consumers) outweighed the losses (principally borne by the suppliers
of agricultural labour, that is, farmers). Moreover, the payment of compensation to the losers would still leave considerable gains to the
economy as a whole. Both maintained that agriculture's continuing
contribution to general economic progress via the process of technological change was both desirable and inevitable. Further, one of the
objectives of agricultural policy should be to encourage agriculture's
contribution to economic growth by not inhibiting technological change.
Indeed, Schultz argued that the rate of return on agricultural R&D was
high (50 per cent at the margin). Four main consequences of technological change were identified:

1. the real price of farm products falls to the benefit of consumers;
2. because technological change in agriculture is biased towards the
   substitution of non-land inputs (such as fertilisers) for land, the real
   value of land falls to the disadvantage of landowners (or would do
   so under *laissez-faire*);
3. less labour is required in agriculture and, due to a lag in adjustment,
   the reward to farm labour is depressed, particularly for the self-
   employed;
4. the burden of the negative outcome from the technical advance of
   agriculture falls on a particular segment of farmers 'which is
   restrained by funds, farm size, managerial ability or age' (Heady,
   1966, p. 33).

In modelling its effects, technological change was usually treated as an
exogenous shift variable operating on the agricultural supply curve.
However, Brandow (1977, p. 274) suggested that in agriculture the rate
of technological change is endogenous, at least in part. Farm programmes speed up the adoption of technology by putting farmers in a
better position to finance required investments and reducing risk.
Brandow also noted that in the past agricultural economists had paid
little attention to analysing technical progress – they had merely noted
the presence of advancing technology and its dramatic consequences.

He suggested that the reason for this lack of analysis was that betweeen 1920 and 1970 US agriculture had a high rate of progressiveness, so inadequate progressiveness was not a problem during this period (ibid., p. 274).

Kendrick (1965) considered the gains and losses from technological change in a general theoretical sense, emphasising its effects upon resource productivity. Tweeten and Plaxico (1964) showed that gains in agricultural productivity between 1930 and 1960 had saved a large portion of the inputs that would otherwise have been required to produce the farm output of 1960. The gains in agricultural productivity were attributed to past R&D, but with a considerable time lag between 'the application of basic inputs and the realisation of the full output potential' (ibid., p. 44). Tweeten and Tyner (1965) discussed criteria for judging what might be an optimum rate of technological change in agriculture in terms of commitments to providing the basic inputs of R&D. They noted that the share of federal funds denoted to agricultural research had fallen from nearly 40 per cent in 1940 to around 1 per cent in the 1960s (63 per cent to 13 per cent with space and defence research expenditures excluded). However, the absolute magnitude of federal spending on agriculture had been growing rapidly – at a rate of 11 per cent per annum in the 1960s. They estimated in a crude manner that the rate of return on agricultural research expenditures was around 100 per cent. This high return justified future investment but did not indicate how research funds should be allocated between the farm and non-farm sectors.

Evenson (1967) attempted to quantify the contribution of public sector agricultural research to production. He postulated a research production function with lags. He also postulated that extension activity increased the speed with which existing knowledge or quality changes actually came into use. Evenson then estimated two time-series equations (1938–63) in order to quantify the impact of research expenditures on agricultural output. He found through experimentation with lag lengths, that the 'best' model indicated a mean lag length of 6–7 years between research expenditures and the effect on production. The long-run elasticity of research expenditure came out at 0.21. Bieri, de Janvry and Schmitz (1972) analysed the welfare implications of different types of technological change in agriculture, using the partial equilibrium economic surplus approach. They also discussed the biases inherent in technological change, distinguishing in particular between land-saving capital (biochemicals) and labour-saving capital (machinery). They then postulated an aggregate production function for agriculture embodying this distinction and also incorporating an index of Hicks-neutral technological change. Subject to certain limiting assumptions concerning resource substitution elasticities, Bieri, de Janvry and Schmitz asserted that 'mechanisation is purely cost reducing and the resulting net social gains accrue wholly to landowners in both closed and open economies since welfare gains are capitalised in land values' (ibid., p. 805). In contrast, 'the net social gains from (the use of) biochemicals accrue to consumers under perfect competition in a closed economy' but 'they benefit landowners in an open or in a farm price supported economy' (ibid., p. 806). The Schuh–de Janvry model of induced technical change in agriculture, reported in Schuh (1974), was distinctive in explicitly linking the adoption of technological innovations with the financial stress caused by exchange rate over-valuation.

Looking back on the objectives and findings of research on technological change in agriculture up to about 1970, a noticeable feature is the paucity of systematic work on the economics of agricultural R&D. Although a direct link between the rate of technological change and the rate of investment in R&D was clearly recognised, there were few, if any, attempts to articulate a theory explaining the rate of investment. Moreover, there was little attempt to refine methods of estimating rates of return on agricultural R&D with a view to evaluating the efficiency of investment in that area, either with respect to the total amount invested per unit of time, or its allocation between different sectors of agricultural research. Some of these gaps in knowledge of the economics of agricultural R&D were remedied during the 1970s.

Agriculture and the environment
In 1969 the programme for the annual meeting of the American Agricultural Economics Association included papers on the application of environmental economics to agriculture for the first time. Taylor (1969) drew attention to increasing anxiety about environmental pollution among the general public and sought to identify the main agriculturally related pollutants. These were 'pesticides, animal wastes, sediments, plant nutrients, inorganic salts and minerals, forest and crop residues, agricultural processing wastes and smoke, dusts and other air pollutants' (ibid., pp. 1182–3). Langham and Edwards (1969) considered specific problems involved in measuring the costs of externalities stemming from the use of pesticides (organic phosphates and chlorinated hydrocarbons).

Rachel Carson's book *Silent Spring* (1963) was a catalyst to the environmental movement in the US and encapsulated the mood of future concerns. Major legislation for environmental protection was passed in the 1970s which directly affected agriculture. This included the establishment of the Environmental Protection Agency (EPA) in 1970 with overall responsibility for the abatement of air, soil and water pollution. 'With this legislation the federal government was given sweeping powers to restrict the pollution of soil, water and air, the three elements essential to agricultural production' (Paarlberg, 1980, p. 122).

Professor Vernon W. Ruttan set the scene for the analytical modelling of the impact of agriculture on the environment in his Presidential Address to the AAEA in 1971. Ruttan (1971) emphasised that the production of food necessarily involves the production and disposal of 'residuals'. The efficient management of agricultural residuals disposal had been a challenge to mankind throughout history. Ruttan then proceeded to argue that as well as being associated with declining income elasticity of demand for food, rising per capita incomes, denoting economic growth, are also associated with an increasing demand for environmental amenities. The increased demand for such amenities is in turn associated with rising economic values of common property resources, such as air, water and recreational space, formerly regarded as 'free goods'. The provision of 'environmental services' includes the enhancement of environmental amenities by the more effective disposal of residuals. However, under the free enterprise system, environmental services tend to be undervalued due to market failure. This results in 'the direction of technical effort toward excessive production of a wide range of residuals and spillover effects . . . and away from increasing efficiency in the supply of resource amenities' (ibid., p. 712). So, for example, where the overvaluation of land has been induced by 'inappropriate' agricultural policy, scientific and technical innovation in agriculture has been biased towards the development of inputs which substitute for land, such as higher yielding crop varieties and plant protection chemicals. However, the use of such land substitutes has frequently yielded residuals with very high social costs of disposal.

On the question of policy innovations to deal with the environmental problems he had identified, Ruttan favoured 'pollution user charges over standards and regulation, private property rights wherever possible over the common property situation, and the enlargement of the scale of the firm (or government authority) to manage resources to account for externalities' (Schmid, 1972, p. 893). In other words, Ruttan advocated application of the 'classic' principle of 'internalising the externality' in tackling problems of agricultural pollution.

COMMENTARY: AGRICULTURAL POLICY IN WESTERN EUROPE AND THE US: 1945–73

Agricultural policy was conducted in this period against the background of a high rate of economic growth and the expansion of trade in the industrialised world. Important institutional innovations included the creation of the EC, which led to the setting up of the CAP, and the foundation of the GATT, from which stemmed successive rounds of multilateral negotiations aimed at reducing barriers to trade.

Although agricultural trade featured on the agenda of both the Dillon and Kennedy rounds of trade negotiations in the GATT, little was achieved in liberalising trade in farm products. Reasons for this lack of success included:

1. Article XI:2 of the GATT permitted quantitative restriction of agricultural imports provided domestic production controls were also in place. Furthermore, the US in 1955 obtained for itself the so-called section 22 waiver allowing quantitative restraint on imports of farm products that interfere with the operation of its domestic farm programmes without parallel action to restrict domestic production. Strictly speaking, the 1955 waiver applied only to the US but it was a continuing source of resentment by other countries.
2. The introduction of the protectionist Common Agricultural Policy (CAP) of the EC was not effectively challenged in the GATT, in part because of US political support for the formation of the EC. As a result, the bargaining power of the Community countries in the world trade arena was increased and they were in a stronger position to resist pressure for agricultural trade liberalisation.
3. The post-1947 success of the GATT in liberalising trade in industrial products by reducing mutually offsetting trade barriers, largely tariffs, reflected the interests of the industrial sector itself in expanding trade. However, the agricultural sector in many industrialised countries felt threatened by trade reform. Together with many developing countries they opposed efforts to liberalise trade in farm products and instead advocated the establishment of international commodity agreements to manage trade.

The main thrust of policy in both Western Europe and the US was in coping with a perceived agricultural adjustment problem in a largely domestic context and without regard to international trade implications. EC policy makers were also preoccupied with the problems of integrating their agricultural economies and harmonising the farm policies of the founding members. The CAP was inward looking and gave both protection and insulation to domestic farmers from third country suppliers including the US. The development of the CAP was hampered by agrimonetary problems and by disputes over the financing of expenditures.

Theodore Schultz and Earl Heady were both prominent in explaining and popularising the nature of the agricultural adjustment problem, as well as in developing ideas for its solution. In particular they advocated, first, measures to accelerate the adjustment process, and, secondly, measures to provide the losers from that process with compensation. Central to their policy analysis was the notion that the economy-wide gains (principally to food consumers) from technological progress in agriculture outweighed the losses (principally borne by agricultural producers) and that the payment of compensation to the losers would still leave major gains to the economy as a whole. Schultz (1961) held that a rapid rate of technological innovation in agriculture was maintained by a high rate of return on agricultural R&D (50 per cent at the margin). Three major consequences resulted from the rapid adoption of new output increasing technology: (1) the real prices of farm products fell to the general benefit of consumers; (2) the real value of land fell to the disadvantage of landowners; and (3) due to less labour being required in agriculture and a lag in adjustment, the rewards to farm labour fell relative to other sections of the population, especially amongst the self-employed. Schultz also noted the link between the rate of agricultural adjustment and non-farm employment opportunities. The adjustment process was halted with unemployment at 5–7 per cent, but was large when unemployment was only 3–4 per cent, but adjustment could be accelerated by public funding to assist the retraining and relocation of persons willing to leave agriculture. To help older farmers to leave, Schultz advocated government intervention to rent farms and purchase farm assets. Also, to compensate the farm population for losses sustained due to technological progress, Schultz advocated limited direct income payments, payable only when general unemployment was above 4 per cent.

Heady (1966) concurred in broad outline with the Schultz diagnosis of gains and losses from technological progress in agriculture, but added the caveat that some farmers – those with sufficient skills and capital to increase output in a much larger proportion and at a lower cost than the industry as a whole – might actually gain. Thus, the burden of the negative outcome from the technical advance of agriculture tended to fall on 'that segment of farmers which is restrained by funds, farm size, managerial ability or age' (ibid., p. 33).

Heady prescribed three goals for agricultural policy: (a) to provide conditions ensuring agriculture's continuing contribution to economic progress; (b) to provide price, income and other compensation conditions which guarantee a positive income and welfare outcome to farmers; and (c) to provide equality of opportunity for the farm population, especially youth, to participate in the benefits of economic growth (ibid., p. 39).

Heady's proposals for compensating the losers from the agricultural adjustment process were similar to those of Schultz. But Heady stressed that participation in compensation programmes must be voluntary: some might judge themselves to be better off by not participating. Finally, Heady stressed that in a situation where the future would allow only about 5 per cent of farm youth to remain in agriculture, farming could no longer be regarded as being uniquely different from other occupations: rather it must be considered as an integral part of the economic and social structure of society. For Heady this broader social policy for ensuring job mobility was as important as agricultural compensation policy.

In some respects the agricultural policy prescriptions of Schultz and Heady during the 1960s were similar to views being voiced in Europe about the same time, most notably by Sicco Mansholt, author of the Mansholt Plan. On both sides of the Atlantic, there was much emphasis on moving people out of agriculture as a means of remedying earnings disequilibrium between farming and non-farming. On the other hand, although they did not rule out the diversion of agricultural land to other uses, such as forestry and public recreation, Schultz and Heady put less emphasis than Mansholt on the need for land retirement to solve problems of disequilibrium. Heady, in particular, took the view that opportunities for solving the problem of agricultural surplus by land diversion were greater in small and densely populated countries, such as Holland and Belgium, than in 'large' countries like the US with special problems of remoteness and an uneven distribution of the population (Heady, 1966, p. 63).

On the specific issue of land retirement, governments tended to ignore professional advice on both sides of the Atlantic. In the United States, the Soil Bank programme introduced in 1954 was followed by further voluntary, cropland retirement schemes in the 1960s. In the European Community, on the other hand, the land retirement recommendations of the Mansholt Plan (1968) were virtually ignored by the Council of Ministers.

In the years subsequent to 1973, the agricultural adjustment problem became much less pressing and the concerns of analysts and policy makers turned towards the domestic budgetary and social costs of agricultural intervention and to its distorting effects on international trade. The agenda for farm policy was also widened to embrace environmental issues.

NOTES

1. The OEEC was to evolve into the Organisation for Economic Cooperation and Development (OECD), which comprises Western European nations plus the US, Canada, Japan, Australia and New Zealand and a number of other countries. It is essentially a coordinative and consultative agency of the industrialised nations.
2. The US delegation to the ITO conference recognised that the US Senate would not ratify an international agreement that would have forced the US to dismantle its agricultural programmes or which would have made its programmes inoperable (see Hathaway, 1987, p. 103).
3. The GATT was an offshoot of ITO discussions in 1947 and comprised the commercial trade section of the Havana charter.
4. Annual average real GDP per capita growth rates: 1.1 per cent for the US, 7.3 per cent for Japan and 4.4 per cent for the EC(6) in the 1950s and 3.3 per cent for the US, 10.4 per cent for Japan and 4.1 per cent for the EC(6) in the 1960s. Source: UN National Accounts Statistics.
5. EFTA comprised Austria, Denmark, the UK, Norway, Portugal, Sweden and Switzerland at that time.
6. The protective impact of a VER or VRA is similar to that of an import quota, but the former instruments had the advantage, from the protecting country's point of view, of bypassing GATT Article XI. VERs and VRAs now have to be phased out under the terms of the 1994 Uruguay Round Agreement.
7. Data from this subsection are drawn from Schmidt et al. (1978).
8. At that time, agricultural net output was defined as the value of gross output less the cost of imported feedingstuffs, seeds and livestock.
9. Phillips and Ritson (1969) refer to these effects as 'trade reciprocity' but the term reciprocity is reserved in this text for its more common usage in the context of trade negotiations.
10. A system of announcing minimum prices for 2–4 years ahead had in fact been introduced by the government soon after the war. But since government prudence had kept these long-term guarantees at rather low levels, they had failed to give farmers as much security as they wanted (Kirk, 1979, pp. 65–6).
11. Broadly defined, the total value of the guarantees was the sum of the minimum guaranteed price times the output of each commodity, plus the value of production grants and subsidies.
12. The exchequer cost of agricultural support increased from around £200 million in the mid-1950s to around £300 million in the early 1960s.
13. The enabling legislation covering the imposition of minimum import prices was the Agriculture and Horticulture Act, 1964.
14. It can be shown theoretically that, following the removal of government support, aggregate producer revenue would fall by less than the former Exchequer cost of support, although not much less if supply was very inelastic.
15. The more normal measure of the nominal protection rate is to express the difference between domestic and import prices as a proportion of the import price. By comparison, McCrone's method underestimates the level or degree of protection.
16. The Norwegian application was subsequently withdrawn following rejection of the terms of entry in a referendum.

17. There is even evidence that early in the postwar period the production of agricultural surpluses for export was deliberately planned by the French government as part of a broader strategy to hasten economic recovery particularly through measures to strengthen the balance of payments (Griffiths and Mildward, 1986, p. 55).

18. An alternative version of this trilogy of CAP principles is (a) market unity, (b) financial solidarity and (c) Community preference. However, since market unity and financial solidarity clearly imply common pricing and common financing, the two versions are to all intents and purposes identical, although we think the one we have used is clearer and more explicit.

19. Before the import levy was adopted as the principle instrument for regulating imports entering the EC from the rest of the world, it was used to regulate intra-Community agricultural trade during the transitional period. Thus, during this period, in transacting trade between member states, remaining differences in national commodity prices were bridged by means of import levies (called transitional compensatory amounts (TCAs)). In effect, the levies were export taxes paid by exporters in countries with relatively low national prices wishing to export to other member states with higher prices. By the same token, exporters in the higher price countries were able to export to lower price member states with the aid of a positive MCA, or export subsidy, to bridge the price gap. The TCAs were progressively removed as common prices became established through the harmonisation of national prices (Tracy, 1982, pp. 271–4).

20. Commission of the European Community (1968), COM(68) 100.

21. With the benefit of hindsight, it is interesting that there was apparently no opposition to the Mansholt Plan from guardians of environmental conservation.

22. The story of the Mansholt Plan is incomplete without its author's famous 'recantation' a decade or so later. The Plan was published in the late 1960s when Western Europe was still enjoying rapid economic growth and growing employment sparked off by the postwar recovery starting in the early 1950s. Mansholt wanted to speed the exodus of people from agriculture even though the size of the agricultural labour force was already diminishing quite rapidly. Between 1958, the foundation year of the EC(6) and 1972, the year preceding expansion from EC(6) to EC(9), total employment in agriculture within the 'Six' countries declined from over 16 million to only about 8.5 million persons, that is a decline of nearly 50 per cent (Statistical Office of the European Community, 1968; Eurostat, 1975). But the economic climate changed abruptly in 1973, from boom to recession, sparked off by the Arab–Israeli war and the ensuing energy crisis. Thereafter, stagnation and growing unemployment prevailed for the remainder of the 1970s. It was against this background that Mansholt, after he had retired from office, expressed the opinion that given the alternatives of becoming unemployed or remaining in farming, it was better for small farmers to opt for the latter (Mansholt, 1979).

23. One reason for the persistence of MCAs is that different economic interest groups acquire vested interests in retaining them. Thus, whereas agricultural producers have a vested interest in the retention of positive MCAs (and in campaigning for the removal of negative MCAs), the best interest of food consumers is exactly the opposite (since, *ceteris paribus*, negative MCAs keep food prices 'low').

24. This trade conflict between the US and the EC resulted from switching from a fixed import duty (bound in GATT) to a variable levy on US poultry exports to West Germany. Following arbitration in the GATT, the US obtained compensation from the EC for its loss of poultry exports. This took the form of the US withdrawing concessions on a number of items exported there by the EC and adding up to a similar value.

25. The *montant de soutien* was defined similarly to the Producer Subsidy Equivalent (PSE) developed in the early 1980s for use in the GATT Uruguay Round. The margin of support proposed by the EC during the Kennedy Round was to be the difference between the domestic producer price of a commodity, however maintained, and a world 'reference price'.

26. Sources used for this subsection include Benedict (1955) and Wilcox and Cochrane (1960).
27. Note the similarity of this proposal to the so-called production entitlement guarantee (PEG) proposal, advanced in the late 1980s (see Chapter 6).
28. Note that, writing in the early 1960s, Hathaway made a reference to how the retirement of agricultural land might contribute to environmental conservation either by preventing soil erosion or in other ways.
29. Hathaway argued that in a large and relatively sparsely populated country like the United States, geographical remoteness ruled out industrial development as a viable policy option for some rural areas.
30. The defeat of the first alternative did not necessarily imply that producers preferred the second alternative (Cochrane and Ryan, 1976, p. 81).
31. The method of financing the domestic element earned the scheme the sobriquet of the 'bread tax'.
32. The loan rate was generally below the export price during this period.
33. We gratefully acknowledge the guidance of Professors Willard W. Cochrane and James T. Bonnen in articulating the arguments of this paragraph.

5. 1973–1980s: agricultural expansion and the rise of trade policy issues

INTRODUCTION AND OVERVIEW

General Economic Background

The 1970s and 1980s witnessed the consolidation of a trilateral trading world based largely on the US, the EC and Japan. Three regions dominated world trade: North America, Western Europe and the Asia-Pacific region. These accounted for nearly 90 per cent of world trade.

Growth in production and trade was considerably lower than in the 'golden age' from 1950–73. The median average annual growth rate of real GDP in OECD countries was about 2.7 per cent for 1973–79[1] (2.6 per cent for the US, 2.5 per cent for the EC and 3.6 per cent for Japan). There was a recession in 1980–82 with OECD growth averaging less than 1 per cent per annum and a sustained recovery from 1983 onwards with annual growth rates averaging around 4 per cent for the US, 2.7 per cent for the EC(10) and over 4 per cent for Japan for the period 1983–89. World trade in real terms grew at around 4 per cent per annum over the period 1973–79, stagnated from 1980–82, and grew again at a rate around 5 per cent per annum over the period 1983–88.[2]

Non-tariff barriers (NTBs) were increasingly employed as trade restriction devices after the mid-1970s. The proportion of world trade subject to import and/or export controls rose from 40 per cent in 1974 to 48 per cent in 1980 (Hine, 1985, p. 224). The Tokyo Round of GATT negotiations launched in 1973 discussed the issue of NTBs as well as tariff reductions. However, reductions in tariffs provided the main outcome although certain codes of conduct were agreed for specific non-tariff practices. The world economic recession in the early 1980s increased trading tensions and an increase in protectionist tendencies. The 'new protectionism' exemplified by NTBs increased. Under pressure from a large trade deficit, protectionist sentiment was prominent in the US in the 1980s. Protectionist sentiment was also strong in the EC.[3]

The 1980s saw an increase in NTBs and a proliferation of trade disputes. Complaints to GATT over NTBs increased and weakened its ability to oversee a liberal trading system. In the US, there were increasing calls for new protectionist measures. To counter the rise in protectionist sentiment, the US administration, under the authority of the 1984 Tariff and Trade Act, called for a new round of multinational trade negotiations to begin 1987. This round of GATT negotiations – the Uruguay Round – was launched in 1986.

Agricultural Trade[4]

Hathaway (1987, p. 7) notes that during 1973–74 there was a perceived food crisis, whilst by 1986 there was a perceived agricultural trade crisis. In the early 1970s there was a commodity price boom: the prices of grains doubled in nominal dollar terms between 1971/72 and 1972/3. 'By 1974, the prices of wheat and corn were over two and one half times their 1972 level. The IMF index of food commodity prices rose 80 per cent in nominal dollar terms and 54 per cent in real terms' (ibid., p. 12). In the mid-1980s, following stagnation of exports and rising production, there were falling commodity prices, rising stocks and increased use of subsidies by many exporters. A trade crisis in both political and economic terms arose.

There is a general tendency for agricultural trade to grow more slowly than world trade in general and hence for agriculture's share of world trade to decline. However, the period from 1973 to the early 1980s was rather unusual in that agricultural trade expanded at a rate nearly equal to that in manufactures (in volume terms, 3.5 per cent per annum and 4 per cent per annum). During the 1980s, there was a reversion to trend; the volume of agricultural trade grew at about half the rate for industrial goods (in volume terms, 1.5 per cent per annum compared to 3 per cent per annum) and in both areas the growth of world trade was slower.

Behind these changes in agricultural trade volumes lay shifts in trade patterns. As Hathaway (p. 8) observes

> Rapid population growth and strong economic growth combined to increase demand for food faster than agricultural production in many developing countries in the 1960s, a trend that accelerated in the 1970s. In the early 1970s, the Soviet Union became a major factor in the world market for grains, when in a basic policy change, it began to use imports to offset its internal production shortfalls. Other centrally planned economies followed a similar course.

Strong demand coupled with a modest decline in world production of grain in 1972/3 and low stocks led to the commodity price boom. Thereafter, demand growth tended to be matched by export expansion. As a generalisation, the food trade balance of both developing countries and Eastern European non-market economies turned negative whilst that of the industrial economies became positive. In the early to mid-1980s, however, the growth in import demand from developing countries slowed partly as a result of recession and debt-induced cutbacks in imports, and partly because of production expansion. In the industrial-ised world, output expansion gave rise to excess supplies which could not find a ready market.

The grain trade in the 1970s and 1980s exemplified changes in the growth and pattern of agricultural trade. Total trade in cereals doubled between the early 1970s and 1980 (from around 110 million tonnes to around 220 million tonnes) but then fluctuated without any discernible trend in the 1980s. Western Europe was a major importer at the start of this period (around 40 per cent of trade) but its import share fell to about 17 per cent in the 1980s. Conversely the import shares of the developing countries and the CPEs rose from 30 per cent to 40 per cent and from 20 per cent to 27 per cent respectively between the early 1970s and the mid- to late 1980s. Japan also became a major importer (of coarse grain). The major shift in export patterns was the emergence of the EC as a major net exporter. In 1970, the EC was a net importer of circa 20 million tonnes; by 1980 its net trade was around zero and by the mid- to late 1980s, its net exports were circa 20 million tonnes. The other major and traditional exporters are the USA, Canada, Australia and Argentina. Approximate import and export shares for major regions in recent years are given in Tables 5.1. and 5.2.

Table 5.1   Importer shares of the world cereals market, average 1984/5 to 1988/9

	Wheat %	Coarse grains %
USSR and Eastern Europe	24	23
China	12	–
Japan	6	23
Central and South America	10	10
Near East	10	13
Far East	14	13
Africa	18	7
EC(12)	3	6

Table 5.2   Exporter shares of the world cereals market, average
1984/5 to 1988/9

	Wheat %	Coarse grains %
USA	36	55
EC(12)	16	10
Canada	20	5
Australia	15	4
Argentina	6	7

Source: IWC (annual), *World Grain Statistics*, London: International Wheat Council.

The emergence of the EC as a major net exporter stems from increasing production and static demand. As described later in this chapter, production growth arose from a combination of strong technical advances increasing yields and support policies which kept producer prices well above world (trade) prices whilst insulating them from world price fluctuations. On the demand side, high internal prices restricted usage of domestically produced coarse grains whilst encouraging the importation of grain substitutes and soybeans for utilisation in animal feed. These feed constituents were imported without imposition of import duties into the EC since the GATT binding in the early 1960s. As a result, until the mid-1980s, much of the increase in Community grain production was channelled into subsidised exports rather than being consumed domestically.

For the traditional exporters, the strong grains market of the 1970s encouraged grain production whilst domestic use was rising only slowly. In the early 1980s, farm policies in the USA and Canada were supportive of production and grain available for exports outstripped the growth of import demand.

Trade pressures were intensified in the early to mid-1980s by the rise in the value of the US dollar from 1980 to 1985. US grain prices denominated in the ECU and in the Australian and Canadian dollar were rising and the US lost market share. Internal prices to EC producers were not directly affected by the rise in the dollar but the resultant reduction in the unit export subsidy reduced pressures for changes in the common agricultural policy (CAP). For Canadian and Australian producers, internal grain prices increased as the dollar rose.

Agriculture, GATT and the Tokyo Round

The Tokyo Round (1973/79) of GATT negotiations was launched against a background of increasing resort to non-tariff protective barriers and a primary focus of the negotiations was to devise rules to bring these under international control. But as far as agricultural trade was concerned the agenda was little changed from the preceding Kennedy Round. The US and other agricultural exporting countries were still trying to improve their access to the EC market, whereas the EC continued to defend using the CAP to protect farmers from the pressures of outside competition. On this occasion the EC's negotiating mandate was quite explicit in insisting that the CAP's 'principles and mechanisms shall not be called into question and therefore do not constitute a matter for negotiation' (Harris et al., 1983, p. 278). With the CAP firmly established, the EC no longer showed any willingness to bind levels of agricultural protection resembling the *montant de soutien* proposal it had put forward during the Kennedy Round. Rather, the EC revived its ideas for stabilising commodity prices and expanding agricultural trade through international agreements to manage markets, whilst leaving domestic agricultural policies intact. In the event, virtually no progress was made during the Tokyo Round to resolve the basic disagreements between the EC and the US on the objectives of agricultural MTNs under the GATT. Success was limited to trading concessions on a limited number of commodities, mainly on a bilateral basis. Thus, the EC afforded concessions to the US on admitting imports of high quality beef, turkey, pork, prunes, rice and tobacco, whereas the US gained concessions from the EC on cheese, alcoholic spirits, beef and veal. Mutually beneficial bilateral deals on specific commodities were also agreed between the EC and Australia, New Zealand and Canada (Tracy, 1982, p. 378).

Another aspect of the Tokyo Round negotiations, which it was hoped at the time would benefit agricultural trade, was agreement on a Code on Subsidies and Countervailing Duties to strengthen the application of Article XVI (GATT, 1986b, Agreement on Interpretation and Application of Articles VI, XVI and XXIII, pp. 51–80). But the code discussions were not sharply focused upon agricultural subsidies and competition between agricultural exporters in third country markets. In the event the code which was agreed on fell far short of effectively controlling the use of either domestic agricultural subsidies or export subsidies in primary product trade. The fundamental weaknesses of the code were quickly revealed when it was invoked in agricultural trade disputes and 'it was found wanting insofar as every one of the key terms of the code and the articles it amplified were found to lack legal precision' (Warley, 1988).

The Tokyo Round ended in 1979 with no major advances made either in the liberalisation of agricultural trade or agreement upon controlling trade-distorting domestic production subsidies. No progress had been made in defining the status within the GATT of newer trade policy instruments such as variable import levies and voluntary export restraints, and the use of older instruments such as import quotas and variable export subsidies was not effectively controlled despite the existence of articles covering their use.

Certain agreements were reached, however, on international market organisation for dairy products and bovine meats. The International Dairy Arrangement, involving mainly New Zealand, the EEC and the US, was established as of 1 January 1980 with the objective of bringing stability and firmer prices to the world dairy market. More specifically, it set minimum international prices (in US$) for butter, milk powder and certain cheeses, but it did not provide for explicit trade quotas or for coordination of stockholding. An International Dairy Products Council was set up within GATT to review the functioning of the arrangement and to evaluate developments within the world dairy market. The Bovine Meat Arrangement, involving mainly Australia and the EEC, was more modest in scope providing for regular consultation and the provision of information. An International Meat Council was established within GATT to oversee the arrangement. Finally, negotiations on an international wheat agreement followed on from the Tokyo Round. The objective was to establish internationally coordinated reserves of wheat with a view to enhancing world food security and stabilising international wheat prices. However, the negotiations came to naught because of dissatisfaction by developing countries over the price triggers proposed under the negotiations.

Secular Change in US and EC Agriculture[5]

Agricultural adjustment continued throughout the 1970s and 1980s. Major features were rising yields of crops and livestock, rising herd sizes, a declining labour force and a concentration of production on larger farms coupled with an increasing importance of off-farm income in the total income of small scale farmers.

Table 5.3 presents certain indicators of technical change in US and EC agriculture over the period 1973–85. Crop yields increased rapidly, particularly for wheat in the EC (at an annual average rate of over 2.5 per cent per annum). Herd sizes also increased at a high rate.

Table 5.3   Selected agricultural technical change indicators in the EC(10) and the US, 1973 and 1985

	Corn yield (bu/ac)		Wheat yield (bu/ac)		Dairy yield (t/cow)		Average dairy herd size number		Average pig herd size number	
	1973	1985	1973	1985	1973	1985	1973	1985	1973	1985
US	91	118	32	38	3.4	4.6	23	41	82	134
EC(10)	87	107	60	84	3.0	3.6	11	18	25	58

Note: bu/ac = bushels per acre; t/cow = tonnes per cow.

Sources: Newman et al. (1987), Johnson (1985a).

Total factor productivity growth rates are much harder to come by but Ball (1985) estimates an annual average growth rate of 2 per cent for the US (1973–79) and Thirtle and Bottomley (1992) estimate an annual average growth rate of 3.3 per cent for the UK (1975–84).

The labour force in EC agriculture declined at a much faster rate than in US agriculture (Table 5.4), which was partly a reflection of substantial excess labour in EC agriculture at the beginning of the period.

Table 5.4   Agricultural employment in the EC(10) and the US, 1975 and 1985 (millions)

	US	EC
1975	3.41	9.87
1985	3.18	7.67
Annual average per cent rate of change	–0.70	–2.50

Source: Newman et al., 1987.

Average farm size grew and the concentration of production on large farms increased: by the early 1980s, about 30 per cent of farms in the US produced 90 per cent of output (Penn, 1984, p. 574) and one quarter of farms in the EC produced three-quarters of total agricultural output (Lardinois, 1985, p. 109). Part-time farming, which allows the supplementation of farm income and participation in the gains from economic growth, increased through the 1970s and 1980s. The proportion of net income earned from non-farm sources in the US was about 55 per cent in the mid-1980s probably somewhat higher than in the EC during the same period.

Agricultural adjustment is indicated by the falling share of agriculture's contribution to GDP and total employment as indicated in Table 5.5. The ratio of the GDP share to the employment share indicates that whilst the adjustment problem was largely over in the US from the beginning of the period, agricultural transformation continued to create a problem for many regions in the EC.

Table 5.5   Agriculture's share of GDP and employment (%) in the EC(10) and the US, 1975 and 1984

	Agriculture's share of GDP		Agriculture's share of employment	
	1975	1984	1975	1984
US	3.6	2.5	4.0	3.2
EC(10)	4.3	3.3	9.4	7.2

Source: Newman et al., 1987.

THE COMMON AGRICULTURAL POLICY 1973–88: SURPLUSES AND BUDGETARY PROBLEMS

Consequences of Enlargement from EC(6) to EC(9)

New members' terms of entry: the British problem

Britain's first and unsuccessful application to join the EC was made before the form of the CAP had been spelled out precisely. In contrast, before serious negotiations began leading to the second and successful application, the details of the CAP system had been settled by the founding member states of the Community. Thus, by the time Britain's second application was submitted it had become quite clear that the CAP was not negotiable, that is, to be admitted to the EC, Britain and the other applicant countries would have to accept the CAP in its entirety. However, the UK was successful in negotiating limited concessions relating to agriculture and food on two fronts. These concerned imports of dairy products from New Zealand and sugar from less developed Commonwealth countries.

A further consequence of the first enlargement of the EC was that the British problem highlighted the dominance of agricultural spending in the EC budget (Rayner, 1982). The crux of the British problem was that as a large food importer from outside the EC, the UK's prospective transfers of import levy payments to the budget greatly exceeded prospective inward transfers from the budget to cover domestic market intervention and FEOGA Guidance Section subsidies. Thus, a large and unacceptable inequitable net contribution to the Community budget was in prospect for the UK. The Act of Accession recognised and acted upon this problem to the extent of placing limits on the budget contributions of new member states until 1977 plus special arrangements for 1978 and 1979. But the British budget contribution continued to be a contentious issue and between 1975 and 1988 various corrections and 'adjustments' were successfully negotiated by British governments of different political complexions. These adjustments were made within the context of continuing friction amongst EC member states concerning the system of financing the budget.

Continued budget disputes
The 'own resources' system of financing the General Budget of the EC, including FEOGA, first agreed by the Council at the end of 1969, was unsuccessful in ending serious disputes amongst member states concerning the relative and absolute magnitudes of 'national contributions'. The crux of the problem was that although under the new system the Community had a legal right to its 'own resources', each individual member state still had to bear the balance of payments and taxpayer costs of its annual settlement with FEOGA. Without going into the technical details of how the net national contributions to the budget were determined under the new system, knowledge of the basic price support mechanisms of the CAP make it obvious that because import levy revenues are payable to FEOGA, whereas export restitution payments are refundable from it, net agricultural importers were bound to bear a disproportionate share of the costs of financing the budget compared with net exporters. Thus, before the first enlargement, the costs of financing were borne disproportionately by Germany and Italy, whereas France and the Netherlands were the main net beneficiaries. With the enlargement from EC(6) to EC(9) in 1973, Denmark and Ireland joined the net exporters, whereas the UK came in as a substantial net importer. Although the UK's budget contribution was 'corrected' by applying a method agreed during the renegotiation in 1975 of the terms of her accession, by 1979 her net contribution was nearly as great as that of Germany, a much larger country in terms of GNP per head. A new British government elected to office in 1979 demanded a revision of the budgetary arrangements to make them less

inequitable and this pressure eventually resulted in the Council adopting a 3-year formula to reduce the UK's budget contribution up to and including 1982. But this was only an interim settlement. It was simultaneously agreed that by mid-1981 the Commission would advance proposals to resolve the problem of inequitable budget shares by means of 'structural changes', but without calling into question either the principle of common financing with the Community's own resources or the CAP itself. Although the Commission did publish three major documents over the next two years, in response to the 1981 Mandate, actual settlement of the problem was delayed even longer. From 1982 onwards finding a lasting solution to the problem of the UK's budgetary contribution became enmeshed in negotiations on raising the ceiling on the VAT contribution element of the formula used to determine the amount of the Community's 'own resources'.

The breakthrough eventually came early in 1984 when, at the Dublin Summit, measures for curbing farm expenditure were agreed including quotas on milk production. This was followed by a budgetary settlement at the Fontainebleau Summit, later the same year, under which the VAT contribution ceiling was raised from 1 to 1.4 per cent and it was agreed that the UK's share of VAT payments would in future not be allowed to get much out of line with her share of total budgetary expenditure. More precisely, it was agreed that from 1985 onwards the UK would receive back two-thirds of any difference between her VAT share and her expenditure share, in the form of a rebate (Swann, 1988, p. 83). At the Brussels Summit in February 1988, when fresh measures were agreed to curb agricultural spending – including cereal and oil-seed 'stabilisers' and a voluntary acreage 'set-aside' scheme for cereal producers – a GNP percentage key was re-introduced as an additional source of budget revenue (to supplement import levy, customs duty and VAT revenues). Due to this reform, the formula used in calculating the UK's budget rebate was further modified to allow for any difference between GNP-related payments and benefits (Swann, 1988, p. 310).

The MCA problem: 'green' exchange rates
Although the European Community took steps to limit internal exchange rate movements, that is, amongst the ECU currencies, most notably by the creation of the European Monetary System (EMS) in 1979, considerable exchange instability remained within the Community itself, partly because the UK remained outside the ERM until 1990. One reason for the persistence of MCAs was that different economic interest groups acquired vested interests in retaining them. Thus, whereas agricultural producers had a vested interest in the retention of

positive MCAs (and in campaigning for the removal of negative MCAs), the best interest of food consumers was exactly the opposite (since, *ceteris paribus*, negative MCAs keep food prices 'low'). Governments might also choose to maintain negative MCAs as a means of curbing inflation. Although the elimination of MCAs was for long one objective of reforming the CAP, and some success was achieved in reducing positive MCAs, the successful realisation of that objective, at least in the 1980s, proved elusive. However, in the 1990s MCAs fell largely into disuse due to the constraints imposed on exchange rate movements by the EMS.

Due to their persistence, MCAs became institutionalised within the CAP in the form of 'green' exchange rates. Whereas ordinary exchange rates are determined by national governments and central banks, green rates are determined annually by the Council of Agricultural Ministers as part of the package which also fixes the common prices of regulated commodities denominated in ECUs, for the coming year. In effect, a given country's MCA at a particular time, is the difference between its ordinary and green exchange rates, that is, the green rate equals the market rate plus or minus the MCA. If the green rate is higher than the ordinary rate a negative MCA is implied which can be removed by devaluation of the green rate. Similarly, if the green rate is lower than the market rate, revaluation is needed to remove the implied positive MCA. A given country's MCA at a particular time is usually expressed as a percentage of the ordinary exchange rate, either positive or negative.

With the common prices of all CAP-regulated commodities being initially denominated in terms of a common unit of account (now the ECU), it follows that even if there is no change in common, ECU-denominated prices there may still be major changes in the prices received by producers in terms of their own national currencies, due to differential rates of green currency devaluation or revaluation. Thus, in themselves, changes in common prices, denominated in ECUs, tended to be virtually meaningless to producers (or consumers) in particular member states of the community, even in nominal terms.

Although MCAs were collected and disbursed by national intervention authorities, acting on behalf of the Commission, 90 per cent of all MCA revenues were payable to the EC budget. The intervention authorities retained the remaining 10 per cent as a 'collection fee'. Together with variable import levy revenues, MCA revenues were an important element of the contributions to the EC Budget of some member states at various times. Similarly, the budget contributions of other member states were significantly reduced, not only by the receipt of export restitution payments, but also by the subsidies implicit in MCAs.[6]

To bring the account of policy on MCAs further up to date, the failure of earlier efforts to at least phase out positive MCAs led, in 1984, to a different approach to the problem. It was decided that, for a trial period, the creation of new positive MCAs would be prevented. Under Reg. No. 855/84 green rates of exchange were to be aligned with the strongest community currency, the Deutschmark (DM), to produce what was called the 'strong currency system'. Under this system 'no new positive MCAs were created and the entire currency adjustment was achieved by increases in the negative MCAs' (Fennell, 1987, p. 90). In effect, if the DM were to be revalued, agricultural price support levels in Germany would remain unchanged, so no new positive MCAs would be created there. But in other, weaker currency member states, the German revaluation would convert directly into a green rate devaluation and either higher market prices or new negative MCAs. A further change in 1984 was that a new Agricultural ECU was created which was set 3 per cent higher than the old EMS ECU. Thus, all existing negative MCAs were increased by this proportion whereas existing positive MCAs were similarly reduced (referred to as the 'Switchover system').

The economic rationale underlying these changes was that negative MCAs would be easier to get rid of over time than positive MCAs, since removal of the former would involve raising national support price levels instead of lowering them which would be much more difficult. In the event the results of the experiment initiated in 1984 to get rid of MCAs ran foul of other CAP objectives, particularly the objective of damping increased production by following a 'prudent price policy'. The price increases generated by reducing negative MCAs in weaker currency member states encouraged unwanted increases in production. In the strong currency countries attempts to get rid of existing positive MCAs tended to be frustrated by the political costs of producer opposition to lower prices. The MCA system was consequently modified yet again in 1987 (Reg. No. 1889/87). The effect of the modifications was to retain the strong currency system introduced in 1984 but with numerous detailed adjustments intended to reduce negative MCAs without encouraging increased production in weak currency countries. Parallel adjustments were adopted to reduce the amount of positive MCAs in strong currency countries. So, for example, the amount of the 'Switchover coefficient' introduced in 1984 to convert a part of existing positive MCAs to negative MCAs through the re-introduction of a special Agricultural ECU worth more than the EMS ECU, was increased from 3 per cent in 1984 to nearly 14 per cent in 1987. But the implied increase in negative MCAs was offset in part by simultaneous green rate devaluations in negative MCA member states (Fulton, 1988, p. 32).

At the 1988 price-fixing, the Council and the Commission stated that it was their intention to dismantle by 1992 the existing monetary gaps for EC member states with fixed MCAs (those adhering to narrow ERM fluctuations). This was consistent with the spirit of the Single European Act of 1987 which came fully into force with the establishment of a 'frontier-free Europe' at the beginning of 1993. There were bound to be strong political pressures on CAP policy makers by committed Europeans and Community institutions such as the Commission, for real progress to be made in re-harmonising the prices of agricultural products amongst member states to permit the final abolition of separate green exchange rates and MCAs before 1993. However, even if agreement could be reached by the CAP policy makers that the re-harmonisation of prices was desirable in principle, deciding upon the appropriate common price level was again likely to be a very contentious issue as it was during the initial negotiations leading to the formation of the CAP in the early and mid-1960s. The main difference was that, since the 1960s, production quotas and other 'stabilisers' had been institutionalised within the CAP to offset the undesirable effect of setting prices 'too high'.

Recapitulating on how the Community's agri-monetary system worked, if a particular member state's green exchange rate (with the ECU) was below the ordinary rate, then the intervention prices of CAP-regulated commodities in the state would be above the corresponding common price levels and positive MCAs would apply not only to all intra-Community trade but also to that country's trade with third countries. The only exception, as far as intra-Community trade was concerned, was that net positive MCAs would not apply to trade between the state concerned and any other member country with a still higher positive MCA percentage. Regarding trade with third countries, the positive MCA tax/subsidy effectively supplemented the ordinary import levies/export restitution payments.

In states with negative MCAs – because the green exchange rate was above the ordinary rate, so that intervention prices were below the common price level – the mechanism worked in reverse. That is, net negative MCAs applied both to all intra-Community trade, and to trade with third countries, except for trade with other member states with equal or even lower negative MCA percentages. Regarding trade with third countries, the negative MCA tax/subsidy effectively lowered both ordinary import levies and export restitution payments.

Containment and Disposal of Agricultural Surpluses

In the parlance of economics, the existence of an agricultural surplus signifies an excess supply of agricultural products, that is, the amount by which aggregate supply exceeds aggregate demand at the prevailing market price. The persistence of a surplus signifies some degree of market rigidity and price inflexibility. For some reason the market does not clear. Since the pre-1992 CAP system of threshold prices and import levies generally maintained the EC's internal prices of agricultural commodities well above the world level, so that surpluses to internal market requirements could be exported only with the assistance of a subsidy, changes in the Community's agricultural product self-sufficiency ratios are a useful indicator of the magnitude of the 'surplus problem'. In the base period 1956–60, before the CAP existed, the EC(6) countries as a group were self-sufficient, or more than self-sufficient, only in sugar, potatoes, butter and pork. By 1972 (the last year preceding enlargement to EC(9)) the sugar and butter self-sufficiency ratios both exceeded 120 per cent and there were also significant surpluses of wheat and barley. Because the UK was a net importer of most major foodstuffs, enlargement from EC(6) to EC(9) temporarily alleviated the surplus problem for some commodities, but by 1980, the year preceding enlargement from EC(9) to EC(10) with the accession of Greece, the whole of this temporary gain had been lost. Moreover, by 1980, wine and beef had been added to the list of commodities in which the Community was more than self-sufficient. By then, maize was the only major commodity in which the Community was not self-sufficient (Hill, 1984, p. 75, Table 5.2). After 1980, the wheat, barley, butter and beef surpluses substantially increased, and the maize self-sufficiency ratio moved higher (CEC, 1986, pp. 344–5, Table 3.7.3).

We briefly consider three aspects of the EC's agricultural surplus problem:

1. Why the surpluses emerged.
2. The measures adopted in attempting to contain their size.
3. The measures adopted to dispose of them.

Why surpluses emerged

The emergence of the surpluses can be attributed first, to the maintenance of producer prices above the market clearing level and, second, to technical progress in agriculture. As previously remarked in Chapter 4, at the foundation of the CAP the common prices of virtually all regulated commodities were set at a high level relative not only to the world market price but also to the costs of low-cost EC producers. The reasons for setting prices so high were largely political.

It is quite difficult to make representative quantitative comparisons between EC prices and world prices of agricultural products. Even if attention is confined to common CAP prices denominated in ECUs (thus avoiding the effects of MCAs on the prices producers actually receive in national currencies) the ratio of the EC price to the world price for any particular commodity is subject to substantial variations particularly in the short-term, due to fluctuations in the ECU exchange rate (particularly with regard to the $US), as well as to changes in the world price itself. But, despite these complications, until 1980/81 the SOEC regularly published annual data on the ratios of the EC 'entry price' to the world market price of all the major products covered by the CAP. These data established that with minor exceptions of particular products in particular years, EC prices were consistently well above world prices with the ratio commonly exceeding 1.5 for most commodities and going as high as 4 or 5 for some products in some years. The price ratios of dairy products (butter and SMP) and sugar stand out as being particularly high in most years (Swann, 1988, p. 221, Table 20).

Another measure of the 'protectiveness' of the CAP is the producer subsidy equivalent (PSE) of all forms of assistance to agriculture. The OECD attempted to calculate PSEs relative to average world market prices and levels of support during the 3-year period 1979–81 both by commodities and by countries, including the EC. For the EC the average PSE over all commodities came out at 42.8 per cent with individual commodities ranging from 68.8 per cent (dairy products) to 13.6 per cent (rice) (OECD, 1987, Table 2, pp. 11–18). These PSE estimates provide further evidence of why agricultural markets in the EC failed to clear and why surpluses accumulated.[7]

The volume of aggregate agricultural production in the European Community was increasing, not only in response to high incentive prices for producers and enlargement from 6 member states to 9, 10 and 12, but also to rising productivity due to technical change.

Official EC statistics on the volume of final production at constant (1970) prices indicate a positive growth rate for the EC(10) countries as a whole, for the period 1973–83, of 1.8 per cent per annum. The rate of growth in the volume of gross value added, on the same constant price base, was identical. During the same period, total employment in agriculture, forestry and fishing was falling at just under 3 per cent per annum. Thus, compared with volumes of final production and gross value added growing at less than 2 per cent per annum, agricultural labour productivity (gross) was growing at getting on for 5 per cent per annum during this period. Over the same period the total utilised agricultural area (UAA) of the EC(10) countries was slowly declining at a rate of some 0.2 per cent per annum. In association with the rates of growth in the volumes of final production and gross value added, this implies a (gross) land productivity growth rate of 2 per cent per annum. Comparison of these data with similar data for EC(9) countries excepting the UK, during 1968–73, indicates some slowing down in the later period of rates of growth in final production and gross value added, and in the rates of decline in agricultural employment and utilised agricultural area. It follows that the rates of growth in the productivity of agricultural labour and land also declined somewhat in the 1973–83 period compared with 1968–73. These changes are readily explained by the economic turmoil following the Arab–Israeli War and the OPEC oil price increases of 1973, and the world economic recession of the middle and late 1970s. However, the main point is that despite the industrial recession and stagflation which characterised much of the 1973–83 period, the volume of agricultural production in the EC continued to rise, whereas total agricultural employment and the utilised agricultural area both continued to fall. Thus, even under relatively unfavourable economic conditions, EC agriculture continued to exhibit substantial rates of growth in the productivities of both labour and land (Table 5.6).

Compared with monitoring agricultural productivity growth as such, identifying its causes is much more difficult. But there can be little doubt that continued rapid technical progress stemming from both agricultural R&D and technological innovation by farmers was the major factor. Technical progress is very difficult to measure directly, but proxy measures such as crop yields per hectare, particularly of cereals, and livestock product yields, such as milk yield per cow, all indicate relatively rapid rates of advance. So, for example, in the EC(9) countries as a whole between 1960 and 1979, average wheat yields nearly doubled (from 2.39 to 4.75 tonnes per ha) whereas the average milk yield increased by a third from 2943 kg to 4041 kg per cow (Hill, 1984, p. 74, Table 5.1). Agricultural labour productivity is also affected by farm mechanisation. There is a dearth of comprehensive data on the use of agricultural machinery in the EC, but some information is available for individual member states. Thus, for example, between 1965 and 1985 the number of tractors per 100 ha increased from 3.9 to 8.2 in Belgium, from 5.4 to 5.9 in Denmark, from 8.4 to 12.4 in West Germany, from 2.9 to 5.1 in France, from 4.6 to 5.1 in the Netherlands and from 2.4 to 3.1 in the UK (Agra Europe, *CAP Monitor*, Table 6.1.4, 23.5.88).

Table 5.6   Growth in production, employment and productivity in EC agriculture, 1968–73 and 1973–83 (per cent per annum)

	EC(6)[a] 1968–73	EC(10) 1973–83
Final production (at 1970 prices)	3.0	1.8
Employment	–4.9	–2.8[b]
Utilised agricultural area (UAA)	–0.7	–0.2
Labour productivity (final production per labour unit)	7.6	4.7
Land productivity (final production per ha of UAA)	3.7	2.0

Notes
a   EC(6) plus Denmark and Ireland.
b   1977–83.

Source: Agra Europe, *CAP Monitor*, Table 6.1.6, 23.5.88.

The growing volume of EC agricultural production would have been absorbed by the internal market without the appearance of excess supplies and accumulating surpluses had domestic demand and food consumption been growing sufficiently rapidly. But this was not the case. The principal determinants of demand are population and per capita income. The Community's population growth rate was very low. Between 1973 and 1985 the total population of the EC(10) countries increased from 265 million to only 273 million, a growth rate (over 12 years) of only 0.25 per cent per year. In mid-1984, the projected rise in the EC(10) population to the year 2000 was only 1.8 per cent (over 15 years) (Eurostat, 1986, Table 1 and p. 30).

Real per capita incomes in the Community were growing, despite a world economic recession lasting from the mid-1970s to the early 1980s. Between 1972 and 1982 the annual rates of GDP growth at constant prices in the EC(10) country group were 2.2 per cent (aggregate) and 1.9 per cent (per capita) (Eurostat, 1985, Table 2.4). Thus, the rate of per capita income growth was very close to the 1.8 per cent per annum growth rate of the final production of EC agriculture during approximately the same period (Table 5.5). Ignoring the effect on demand of the minuscule population growth rate, the approximate equality of the agricultural production and consumer income growth rates implies excess production or supply, unless the income elasticity of demand for food and other agricultural products parameter value approaches unity.

In reality, of course, the income elasticity of demand for most individual foodstuffs, as well as for food in the aggregate, is known to be substantially less than unity in developed countries, such as those comprising the EC. So, for example, the income elasticity of total food expenditure in Great Britain in 1981 was estimated to be 0.21 (s.e. 0.02) (MAFF, 1983, Appendix B, Table 2). The corresponding quantity elasticity was probably even lower since, a priori, the demand for a better quality diet is expected to be more income elastic than the demand for a greater physical intake.

Finally, official EC statistics of food consumption reveal that per capita consumption of staple foodstuffs, such as cereals, potatoes and sugar, were declining: also of wine. Increases in per capita consumption were largely confined to vegetables, fresh fruit and some kinds of meat, that is, white meat, not red (Table 5.7).

Table 5.7 Changes in per capita consumption of major foodstuffs, EC(10), 1973 and 1983 (kg/head)

	1973	1983	% change
Total cereals (excl. rice)	85	84	−1.2
Potatoes	82	75	−8.5
Sugar	37	34	−8.1
Total vegetables	100	109	+9.0
Total fresh fruit (excl. citrus)	60	62	+3.3
Wine (litres/head)	50	44	−12.0
Fresh milk products (excl. cream)	97	102	+5.2
Eggs	14	14	0.0
Total meat	75	84	+12.0
Total oils and fat	21*	25	+19.0

Note: * EC(9) 1974

Source: European Commission, *The Agricultural Situation in the Community*, 1986 Report, Brussels/Luxembourg 1987.

Choice of measures to contain surpluses

Faced with the problem of growing agricultural surpluses which were increasingly costly to dispose of, the Commission and Council were confronted with a choice of remedial policy instruments. Basically, the choice lay between:

1. Reduction of minimum product price guarantees (or, possibly increasing the prices of production inputs).
2. Bribing producers to retire land from agricultural production or reduce capital inputs.
3. Subjecting producers to production quotas

During the first 20 years of the CAP, each of these instruments was in fact adopted, either singly or in combination, for different commodities at different times.

Reduction of producer prices   Individual farmers tend to view their total output and costs as being virtually fixed in the short term. Their level of farm income therefore depends directly on the prices they receive for their products: the higher the price level the higher the income, and vice versa. Any government attempt to reduce minimum product price guarantees therefore invariably provokes the bitter opposition of farmers and their representative organisations. The history of the CAP has been punctuated by farmer demonstrations both in Brussels and in the capital cities of EC member states, particularly during annual farm price reviews.

Quite apart from political pressure from producers against price reductions, inflation and the agri-monetary system have militated against even attempting to freeze prices at the current level. Trying to freeze real price levels would be hard enough, even if rates of inflation were uniform amongst member states, but in reality inflation rates are not uniform and, quite apart from the inflation of prices denominated in national currencies, the unit of account in which common agricultural prices are denominated (the ECU) is itself subject to inflationary bias. This is because the central value of the 'snake' which, from 1973, limited permissible exchange rate fluctuations amongst member states adhering to the European Monetary System (EMS), was heavily weighted in favour of the German mark and other stronger currencies such as the Dutch guilder. This means that converted to national currencies at prevailing green rates, ECU denominated common agricultural prices in weaker currency member states contained an element of built-in inflation (Tracy, 1982, p. 331).

Due to the inherent problems of making open and direct product price reductions in an effort to contain the production of surpluses, agricultural authorities in the EC resorted to covert price reductions like 'co-responsibility levies' and 'stabilisers'. The principle of the co-responsibility levy is that if aggregate production exceeds a predetermined threshold, producers should bear part or the whole of the cost of disposing of the surplus through an implicit reduction in the support price for the whole crop. Thus, the co-responsibility levy is conceptually very similar to the old UK system of subjecting deficiency payment guarantees to standard quantity limitations.

In the EC the principle of penalising producers for over-producing was first applied to sugar. From the outset of the first sugar regulation, in 1968, production was limited by quota, and a so-called 'producer levy' was imposed to assist with subsidising the disposal of quota sugar on the world market. But, at that time, sugar was unique amongst CAP commodities in being subject to quota regulation, and the first non-quota commodity to become subject to a co-responsibility levy as such was milk in 1977. In trying to contain growing surpluses of butter, skimmed milk powder and other dairy products, the Council decided on the advice of the Commission to impose a levy of 1.5 per cent (on the milk intervention price) in 1977/78 with similar rates in the three subsequent years. These rates of levy were low and it is doubtful whether they had any perceptible effect on production. Although there was a nil increase in the target price of milk in 1979/80 (Tracy, 1982, p. 341), the price-reducing effect of a co-responsibility levy could, in principle, be completely negated by the upward adjustment of the support price level from which it was deducted. At least until the introduction of 'stabilisers' in 1988 there was no formal link between decisions on levels of prices and co-responsibility levies.

In the case of milk, the ineffectiveness of the co-responsibility levy in reducing surplus production eventually led, in 1984, to the introduction of production quotas. We defer discussion of the production quota approach to surplus containment until later in the chapter. In the meantime, we briefly consider the history and evolution of the co-responsibility levy approach for a second major commodity, cereals. The first attempt to penalise producers for over-producing cereals took the form of the so-called 'guarantee threshold', first introduced in 1982. This was replaced in 1986 by something called a co-responsibility levy. Then, in 1988, the co-responsibility levy was modified under the so-called 'stabiliser' provisions which also affected other commodities.

Under the 1982 guarantee threshold (GT) scheme, a threshold quantity was set annually by the Council for each of the major cereal crops. The threshold quantity was set in relation to a medium-term production target (originally 1988), assuming a constant volume of exports, and that any additional internal demand would be met by Community supplies rather than by imported cereal substitutes. If actual Community production averaged over the preceding three years exceeded the threshold quantity, the following year's intervention price would be reduced by 1 per cent for every million tonnes of excess production, subject to a maximum reduction of 5 per cent. A major loophole was that the GT provision did not place any limit on the level at which the intervention price might be set before the imposition of the penalty for excess production. Thus, for political reasons, the effectiveness of the measure was always suspect.

Whereas the intention of the GT mechanism was to lower the intervention price retrospectively if actual production exceeded the threshold, the co-responsibility (CRL) system, which replaced it in 1986, applied without any time-lag. The levy was fixed annually by the Council, in the light of the expected budget cost of disposing of the expected surplus of production above a 'reference level' (based on internal consumption plus imports of cereal substitutes) and was deducted from the price that growers received at the first stage of processing (processors were responsible for collecting the levy). In the first year the CRL was set at 3 per cent of the intervention price of common wheat of bread-making quality. The CRL did not apply to unprocessed grain, such as grain grown for seed or to be fed to livestock without off-farm processing, or to small producers. Moreover, although it effectively reduced the producer price, the CRL introduced in 1986 did not affect the intervention price or other institutional prices. However, this changed with the introduction of the 'stabiliser' scheme in 1988.

The effect of the new co-responsibility levy with stabiliser (CRLS) arrangement was that under certain circumstances the 'basic' co-responsibility levy (as determined under the earlier 1986 scheme) could be supplemented by an additional levy if actual production exceeded the maximum guaranteed quantity (MGQ) – similar in concept to the old guarantee threshold – by more than 3 per cent. The full CRLS, including the additional levy, was collected on all sales of grain for processing from the beginning of the marketing season, but the additional levy was refundable, either in part or in full, if actual production turned out to be less than 3 per cent above the MGQ. However, if the 3 per cent limit was breached, the incidence of the additional levy was cumulative in the sense that if, in a given year, the MGQ was exceeded by more than 3 per cent, the following year's intervention price was automatically cut by the amount of the additional levy.

Bribing producers to reduce inputs   Compared with imposing product price penalties for overproduction, the alternative of paying producers to reduce or limit agricultural production inputs was relatively little used by the CAP policy makers. However, a subsidy scheme to encourage dairy producers to reduce their herd size, or even cease milk production altogether, involving the payment of 'cow slaughter premiums', was introduced as early as 1969 (shortly after the publication of the Mansholt Report). The beef conversion premium scheme of 1974 and the non-marketing and herd conversion schemes of 1977 had a similar intent, that is, to persuade dairy farmers with financial inducements to give up milk production, at least for a stipulated minimum period, either by slaughtering their cows or by converting from the production of milk to the production of beef. For budgetary reasons, the finance for these schemes was always of limited duration, and, by the early 1980s, they were discontinued because of doubts about their cost-effectiveness and the suspicion that the main beneficiaries had been dairy farmers who would have ceased milk production even had the subsidy not been available. Thus, for most, the subsidy had been a 'windfall gain' (Harris et al., 1983, p. 104).

By far the most important instance of bribing producers to reduce production inputs was the arable land 'set-aside' scheme introduced in 1988 (Reg. 1272/88). This scheme was intended to reduce the area planted to arable crops, particularly cereals, by paying farmers to divert arable land to alternative uses. The crux of the scheme was that participants had to undertake to set-aside (that is, withdraw from arable crop production) at least 20 per cent of their arable land for five years (but with the option of withdrawal from the scheme after three years). The alternative uses to which land set aside could be diverted were restricted to fallow, planting with trees, or non-agricultural uses such as playing fields or golf courses. Fallow land had to be covered with a green crop and might either be permanent or rotated round the farm. The Community regulation permitted land which was set aside to be grazed by livestock. Producer participation in set-aside was voluntary but participants qualified for annual compensatory payments per hectare of land set aside within a broad range (denominated in ECUs) specified in the regulation. The rates of compensation paid were supposed to reflect costs (for example of fallowing cultivations) and income loss resulting from reduced arable crop production. Rates also varied according to the alternative use to which the land was put; for example the rate for rotational fallow was lower than for permanent fallow.

Although Regulation 1272/88 applied to the whole Community from 1988/89 onwards (apart from Portugal where the scheme was phased in gradually), the actual rates of payment were left to the discretion of the member states. Moreover, each member state was required to draw up its own national set-aside scheme, consistent with Reg. 1272/88, and submit it for approval by the Commission. Member states could exercise discretion, not only regarding rates of compensation, but in certain other respects as well. For example, the UK set-aside scheme did not permit set-aside fallow land to be grazed.

The success of set-aside in reducing the budget cost of surplus disposal, particularly of cereals, was clearly going to depend on how the budgetary costs of the scheme compared with the budgetary savings. Whereas the total costs would clearly depend on the number of farmers who volunteered to participate, which would in turn determine the area of land which was set aside, the total savings would depend on the impact of the scheme on the amount of intervention and export restitution payments. Although both the total costs and the total budget savings derived from the scheme would almost certainly be directly proportional to the participation rate, the relationship between the reduction of the arable area and the corresponding reduction in the production of arable crops was virtually impossible to forecast. Common sense and experience with set-aside in the USA over many years, both pointed to individual farmer participants setting aside their worst (that is, their least-productive) land. Moreover, there was the possibility that, as a direct consequence of set-aside, yields of arable crops on the remaining land might be deliberately increased through more intensive cultivation. Rising yields could in any case be expected, due to technological advances in plant breeding. Thus, it was most unlikely that the reduction in the area of arable crops due to set-aside would be matched by a corresponding proportional reduction in arable crop production. Indeed, the reduction in production could be negligible, or even zero, particularly if the set-aside participation rate was low. It would have been surprising, therefore, if the original voluntary scheme later gave way to a mandatory one (as actually occurred under the 1992 reform of the CAP).

There is logic in the argument that CAP policy makers preferred the co-responsibility levy approach to curbing production, compared with bribing producers to lower the level of inputs, because levy revenue accrued to the budget. By comparison, cow slaughter premiums and set-aside payments appeared on the debit side of the budget, and the counterpart savings in the costs of intervention and export restitution, which were supposed to result from their application, were highly uncertain and problematical. Thus, with the budget cost being the most transparent component of the total costs of the CAP (which also include resource and consumer costs), policy makers' tardiness in resorting to set-aside was understandable. However, although co-responsibility revenues accrued to the budget, the levies themselves did not necessarily have much, if any, impact on production and the magnitude of surpluses. Until 'stabilisers' were introduced in 1988, rates of co-responsibility levy had mostly been quite low, and the apparent impact on production negligible. This may help to explain, though not necessarily justify, the adoption of set-aside and higher rate of co-responsibility levy in the same year, 1988. Although the authorities appear to have adopted two policy instruments to achieve the single objective of containing the budget costs of the CAP, particularly relating to cereals, it remained to be seen whether this 'belt and braces' approach worked in practice.

Production quotas As already remarked, sugar is unique amongst CAP-regulated commodities in having its production regulated by quota from the outset. The basic regulation which, inter alia, allocated a Community production quota amongst the EC(6) member states, came into force in 1968. Whether it is produced from sugar beet or sugar cane, sugar is notorious for its cyclical instability under free market conditions, and quota systems combined with substantial protection from outside competition were in force in most member states before the Community was formed. Thus the notion and practice of restricting the production of sugar in Europe by means of quotas was already familiar. However, the ostensible reason for incorporating quotas in the first CAP regulation was that some means had to be found for curbing excess production, particularly by the more efficient producers and, without quotas, levels of producer price support would have had to be considerably lowered, and many less efficient producers would have been forced to cease production. It was later estimated by the Commission that without quotas it would have been necessary to lower the support price level by 25 per cent in order to achieve adequate control over production in the mid-1970s (Harris et al., 1983, p. 128). Despite these factors pre-disposing the architects of the 1968 sugar regulation towards opting for a quota system, the regulation stated that quotas were being adopted only as a temporary measure, indicating that at that time the opposition to quotas was quite strong. However, although the life of sugar regulations is limited to five years, with the possibility of renewal and extension, and despite the fact that the 1968 Regulation has been substantially revised in other respects (in 1975 and 1981), the continuance of the quota system has not been questioned.

Sugar is relatively well adapted to quota regulation in that sugar beet and sugar cane are the raw materials of the sugar processing industry which is relatively highly concentrated (sugar production is capital intensive and subject to increasing returns to scale). Thus, the monitoring of production is relatively easy. Few other agricultural commodities produced in the EC are as well adapted to quota regulation. This may be one practical reason why quotas have not been more widely adopted in the EC as an instrument of production control and surplus containment. However, in terms of FEOGA guarantee section expenditure, milk continued to be the foremost surplus commodity for the EC, despite the imposition of co-responsibility levies on producers from 1977. Throughout the period 1975–85, milk and milk products accounted for a higher proportion of total FEOGA guarantee expenditure than any other single commodity or commodity group. This proportion varied between years from rather more than a quarter to well over half of total guarantee expenditure (Table 5.8).

Table 5.8   FEOGA guarantee expenditure on milk and milk products, 1975–85

Financial year	Milk and milk products	%	Total all products	%
	m. ua		m. ua	
1975	1 150	29	3 906	100
1976	2 052	44	4 705	100
1977	2 545	50	5 118	100
	m. EUA		m. UEA	
1978	4 105	52	7 765	100
1979	4 420	46	9 544	100
	m. ECU		m. ECU	
1980	4 752	43	11 017	100
1981	3 343	31	10 903	100
1982	4 019	31	13 042	100
1983	4 396	28	15 431	100
1984	5 811	32	17 991	100
1985	6 602	33	19 899	100

Source: Agra Europe, *CAP Monitor*, Section 6.5.7.

Meeting in Stuttgart in June, 1983 the Community heads of state were confronted with the prospect of the budget cost of agricultural market intervention shortly exceeding the Community's own resources. It was clear that fresh action to curb agricultural budget expenditure was urgently required and the Summit instructed the Commission to prepare and submit proposals for dealing with the crisis. The Commission responded in little more than one month with a document entitled 'Common Agricultural Policy – Proposals of the Commission'.

Although this document contained proposals for limiting budget expenditure in all agricultural product sectors accounting for more than 2 per cent of total guarantee expenditure, the milk sector was singled out as presenting the most urgent problem. The Commission contrasted a trend growth rate of about 3.5 per cent per year for milk deliveries with one of only about 0.5 per cent per year at most for consumption. The milk sector was identified as being unique in the magnitude of the divergence between production and consumption trends. The document observed that, for milk, price decisions over the last ten years had not been sufficient to redress the market balance. Regarding a 'market' solution to the problem, the Commission estimated that to be effective in restricting production to a guarantee threshold closely reflecting consumption needs, the milk support price for the year 1984/85 might have to be lowered by as much as 12 per cent compared with the previous year. This would be unduly harsh on producers as well as being too slow in reducing production to the desired level. A comparable increase in the co-responsibility levy would suffer from the same disadvantages.

Having considered several options the Commission proceeded to recommend that 'the principle of the guarantee threshold in (the milk) sector should be implemented through a quota system accompanied by a restrictive price policy' (Section 4, para. (i)). It observed that milk quotas had 'worked' in other countries and defended using a non-market solution to the problem by observing that it might be 'politically easier to bring about'. Quotas were to be based on actual deliveries to dairies in 1981, and all deliveries in excess of quota were to be subject to a supplementary levy (later termed the 'super levy') large enough to cover the full cost of disposing of the extra milk. Dairies would pass the levy on to individual milk producers.

The Commission's milk quota proposal was first discussed by the Council of Agricultural Ministers, together with the proposals for curbing expenditure in other sectors, at the end of July. The milk quota issue later became tied in with issues relating to other agricultural commodities as well as the general budget and the British rebate. The issue was not resolved until after the complete 'package', in which milk quotas and other agricultural reforms were but a part, had been considered and modified by two Heads of State Summit meetings (Athens, December 1989 and Brussels, March 1984). However, the Council of Agricultural Ministers finally reached a general agreement on agricultural policies, including the adoption of milk quotas, on 31 March 1984. The quota scheme finally adopted was virtually identical with the one proposed by the Commission. The scheme agreed in 1984 was limited to five years, but the 'stabiliser package' agreed by the Council in February, 1988 extended its life for a further three years until 1992.

Special case of oilseeds   In discussing measures to contain agricultural surpluses in the EC, oilseeds constitute a special case. The basic regulation on the establishment of a common market in oils and fats (Reg. No. 136/66) provided support for colza, rape and sunflower seeds. When the regulation was first introduced, in the mid-1960s, the Community was only 20 per cent self-sufficient in all protein sources used for livestock feeding stuffs, and its large oilseed crushing industry used imported oilseeds as its primary raw material. It was consequently decided under the basic regulation to accord imported oilseeds and oilcakes duty-free entry under the Common External Tariff, and to protect domestic oilseeds producers not by import regulation but by means of a system of 'production aids'. Under this system, which was really one of deficiency payments, oilseed target prices were determined each year and any difference between target prices and world prices was made up to oilseed crushers in the form of a crushing subsidy. Thus, in principle at least, Community oilseed producers should always receive the target price. Quite apart from the effects of Community enlargement on oilseeds production, the generosity of the support regime resulted in a rapid increase both in the volume of EC production and the budget cost of support. The breakdown of total FEOGA guarantee expenditure by commodities is not readily available for years prior to 1975, but from the mid-1970s to the early 1980s the share of colza, rape and sunflower seeds increased from less than 2 per cent to nearly 10 per cent. The increased supply of EC-produced oilseeds was not matched by an equally rapid increase in Community market demand for oil and meal.

The overproduction of oilseeds led, in 1982/83, to the introduction of production thresholds to limit the volume qualifying for production aid. The production threshold was set on a gradually rising scale relative to a 1988 target production level. If actual production averaged over the preceding three years exceeded the threshold then the target price in the following year would be reduced proportionately with the production excess. This trend led the Commission, in tabling its farm price proposals for 1987, to resurrect the idea of limiting the budget cost of the oils and fats regime by taxing the consumption of vegetable oils. The proposal was to impose a tax on all oilseeds going for crushing, regardless of whether they were EC produced or imported, with the expectation that the crushers would pass the tax on to consumers. However, EC producers would be protected from the impact of the tax with a deficiency payment of equal magnitude. In effect, therefore, the price paid to crushers of domestically produced oilseeds would remain unchanged, whereas the price of imports would be increased by the amount of the tax (assuming a completely inelastic import supply). Countries making substantial oilseed exports to the EC, such as the USA, had been very critical of the oilseeds regime, even before this new proposal, on the grounds that the deficiency payment system gave Community producers an unfair advantage in the market. But the consumption tax proposal drew an extremely vehement denunciation on the grounds that it clearly violated the EC's binding in GATT of the CET on oilseeds at zero, dating back to the introduction of the basic regulation in 1966. Spokesmen for the Commission countered this criticism by arguing that since the production tax applied to all oilseeds, both imported and home grown, it was not discriminatory and did not contravene GATT. Oilseed processors within the Community were also very critical of the proposal because of the adverse effect which they thought the tax would have on the consumption of vegetable oils and byproducts. The Council's reaction to the oilseeds consumption tax proposal appears to have been mixed. It is thought that the Netherlands and the UK were particularly hostile to the idea. The Community acknowledged that its oilseeds regime would have to be modified in the light of a GATT panel ruling, delivered at the end of 1989, that the existing system of deficiency payment support was 'unfair'.

Choice of measures to dispose of surpluses

Once Community self-sufficiency had been reached in nearly all temperate agricultural products, the CAP system of supporting agricultural incomes through high and inflexible farm product prices was bound to result in excess supplies and surpluses of most products. The appearance of surpluses then posed the problem of how to dispose of them.

Broadly speaking, there were four options for surplus disposal. First, the intervention agencies could purchase the surpluses for storage and resale at a later date. Second, they could be physically destroyed, or rendered unfit for human consumption and diverted to some alternative food use such as animal feeding. Third, surpluses of some products might be converted from food to industrial uses, such as wine into alcohol. Fourth, sales of surpluses might be subsidised either within the Community or outside. The Community authorities in fact resorted to all of these options for different commodities at different times. But the first and last options were the most favoured. Before proceeding to discuss these in more detail, we briefly comment on the limitations of the second and third options.

The physical destruction of food is an emotive issue in a world where malnutrition and even starvation are rife and, therefore, tends to provoke political hostility of the electorate. In the Community, the only group of commodities for which this method of surplus disposal has been widely used is fresh fruit and vegetables. Reg. 1035/72 authorises producers' organisations to fix a 'withdrawal price' below which they will not offer produce for sale. The regulation also stipulates the uses to which produce withdrawn from the market may be put, including free distribution to selected categories of consumers, use as animal feed and 'use for non-food purposes'. Due to the perishability of horticultural produce, this last use is frequently the only feasible option. In practice, it often means that produce is ploughed in or left to rot (Fennell, 1987, p. 159). The free distribution of surplus food to 'deserving' or 'needy' groups of consumers always runs the risk of undermining prices on the ordinary commercial market, due to leakages of various kinds from target to non-target consumers. For this reason, the 'denaturing' of foodstuffs to render them unfit for human consumption, though still acceptable as livestock feed, has sometimes been the preferred option.[8]

Turning to the option of converting agricultural surpluses into industrial byproducts, the principal example in the EC is the conversion of table wine into alcohol. Under the first wine regulation (Reg. 337/79), the main support measures for wine producers were storage aids and distillation. The aim of both measures was to maintain the internal market price at or above a minimum guaranteed level. Several types of distillation measures were provided for, the principal one being 'preventive distillation designed to bring demand and supply into balance at the support price level at the beginning of each season, by removing from the market surplus stocks remaining from the previous season'. The distillation measures were considerably strengthened in 1982, in preparation for the entry of Spain and Portugal into the Community. The main innovation then was the addition of so-called 'obligatory distillation' under which, in seasons of unusually large harvests, surplus production could be removed from the market for distillation – at a guaranteed buying-in price – before the end of the season (Harris et al., 1983, pp. 168–70).[9]

For the reasons just discussed, the second and third options for surplus disposal have serious drawbacks and limitations, which explains their very limited use in the EC. We are left with the first and the last options – purchase for storage and subsidised sale – which have, in fact, been much the most frequently used methods of disposal in the EC. Policy analysis is complicated by the fact that these are not mutually exclusive options. Intervention authorities use two methods of subsidising exports.

On the one hand, they invite exporters to tender for the disposal abroad of intervention stocks. In this case, the export refund consists of the difference between the tender price and the intervention price. On the other hand, exporters may export non-intervention grain at the best price available outside the Community and afterwards claim the 'pre-fixed' export refund. Thus, budget expenditure on storage does not pre-empt expenditure on export refunds, or vice versa.

Furthermore, storage is only a temporary expedient for dealing with a 'permanent' surplus, although it could be potentially useful as a stabilisation device. If attention is confined to the choice between options for surplus disposal (that is, not storage), it is easy to show that export disposal with the aid of a subsidy will generally be cheaper than either subsidising consumption on the internal market or purchase and destruction of the surplus.

The breakdown of FEOGA guarantee expenditure between 1975–87 shows that on average over that period approximately 40 per cent of annual guarantee expenditure was accounted for by export refunds. Of the remaining 60 per cent of expenditure, broadly classified as 'intervention', only about two-fifths was for 'storage'. In most years export refund expenditure exceeded expenditure on storage by a substantial margin. However, a substantial proportion of guarantee expenditure was accounted for by forms of intervention likely to encourage the production of surpluses (broadly categorised as 'price subsidies') rather than by measures of surplus disposal as such (Table 5.9).

The EC's heavy use of export refunds in disposing of its agricultural surpluses naturally attracted considerable international hostility. Other countries with a major interest in agricultural exports accused the EC of using export refunds to undercut competing exports on world markets in order to increase the EC's market share. The EC strenuously denied these allegations whilst simultaneously arguing that export refunds were an integral part of the mechanism of the CAP which was non-negotiable in international trade negotiations. The EC would also claim to have successfully defended the CAP system of agricultural price support during the Kennedy Round of multilateral trade negotiations in GATT from 1963 to 1967.

During the negotiations the USA, in particular, pressed for, but failed to obtain, agreement on the modification of the EC's variable import levy system in order to reduce the Community's level of protection. Whether the outcome of the Kennedy Round negotiations did, in fact, legitimise the CAP in the eyes of the rest of the world is open to argument. But a more important point now is that since the mid-

Table 5.9 Division of FEOGA guarantee expenditure between export refunds and intervention, 1975–87

Financial year	Export refunds		Price subsidies		Other		Total intervention		FEOGA
	m. ua	%	m. ua	%	m. ua	%	m. ua	%	m. ua
1975	968.9	24.8	1 933.1	49.5	1 003.8	25.7	2 937.3	75.2	3 906.1
1976	1 474.3	31.3	1 705.3	36.2	1 525.3	32.4	3 230.6	68.6	4 705.3
1977	2 287.2	44.7	1 639.5	32.0	1 191.4	23.3	2 830.9	55.3	5 118.1
1978	3 538.6	45.5	2 018.8	26.0	2 207.8	28.4	4 226.6	54.4	7 765.2
1979	4 698.5	49.2	3 119.2	32.7	1 726.4	18.1	4 845.6	50.8	9 544.1
	m. ECU		m. ECU		m. ECU		m. ECU		m. ECU
1980	5 452.4	49.5	3 448.3	31.3	2 116.0	19.2	5 364.3	50.3	11 016.7
1981	4 938.5	45.3	3 663.6	33.6	2 300.7	21.1	5 964.3	54.7	10 902.8
1982	6 054.2	46.4	4 646.7	35.7	2 341.2	17.9	6 987.9	53.6	13 042.1
1983	5 220.5	33.8	6 409.8	41.5	3 800.8	24.7	10 210.6	66.2	15 431.1
1984	6 362.5	35.4	6 742.1	37.5	4 886.3	27.1	11 628.4	64.6	17 990.9
1985	6 711.5	33.7	7 332.5	36.9	5 885.1	29.4	13 187.6	66.3	19 899.1
1986	7 239.2	33.5	7 960.1	36.9	6 398.2	29.6	14 358.3	66.5	21 597.5
1987	9 066.0	39.8	8 762.4	38.5	4 948.3	21.7	13 710.7	60.2	22 776.7

Sources: Agra Europe, *CAP Monitor*, Section 6.5.7. European Commission, The Agricultural Situation in the Community, Financial Statistics.

1960s the Community has become self-sufficient in most temperate agricultural commodities, and the main focus of trade conflict between the EC and other countries shifted from access to the EC's internal market to competition in the world market. This shift in emphasis was reflected in the changed ratio of export refund expenditure to variable levy revenue. The relevant financial magnitudes are not readily available for years before 1973. However, over the five years 1973–77, export refund expenditure was less than double variable levy revenue, but ten years later, in the 1983–87 period, the ratio had increased to more than five.[10]

The EC's preferred solution to problems of international agricultural trade was the conclusion of international commodity agreements to maintain prices by market management, including agreement on market shares. But the EC was generally resolutely opposed to externally imposed export quotas.

Consequences of Enlargement to Include Mediterranean Countries: the Background to the Southern European Enlargement

Greece, Spain and Portugal are all Southern European countries with similar climates and agricultures. It is therefore convenient to treat the enlargement of the Community to bring these three additional members in as if they had joined at the same time, even though Greece's accession (in 1981) in fact preceded that of Spain and Portugal by five years.

The Southern European enlargement from EC(9) to EC(12) was preceded by a number of Association Agreements expressing the Community's Mediterranean policy. The primary motivation for this policy appears to have been political and strategic rather than economic. The earliest such agreements were with Greece (1962) and Turkey (1964), but a new and revised Global Mediterranean policy was enunciated at the Paris Summit in October 1972. The main provisions of this policy were the phasing-in of free trade in industrial goods between the EC and Mediterranean countries, some limited liberalisation of agricultural trade on a reciprocal basis, despite the CAP, and the promotion of technical and industrial cooperation assisted by Community financial aid. There followed a number of new association agreements with Mediterranean countries, starting with Cyprus in 1973, Israel in 1975, the Mashreq countries (Egypt, Jordan, Lebanon and Syria) in 1976, the Maghreb countries (Algeria, Morocco and Tunisia) in 1977, and Yugoslavia in 1980. All of these agreements gave duty-free access to the EC market for industrial goods, though with minor exceptions for particular products, and tariff preferences for selected agricultural products

(Koliris, 1984, p. 321). It is notable that none of these agreements included Greece, Spain or Portugal, but the implications of Community enlargement to include these countries needs to be viewed against their existence.

Problems posed by enlargement

Community enlargement to bring in Greece, Spain and Portugal posed a number of problems both for the existing EC member states and for trading partner countries both inside and outside the Mediterranean region. To begin with, all three applicant countries were at a less advanced stage of economic development and poorer than the existing members: they would add approximately 20 per cent to the Community's aggregate population but only about 10 per cent to its aggregate GDP (Swann, 1988, p. 38). Moreover, the economies of the relatively poor new member states were each more dependent on agriculture than amongst the existing members, except for Ireland. This was bound to impose severe extra strain on the Community budget, especially for agricultural spending. Higher budget expenditure would have been implied even if farmers in the applicant countries had been as well off, on average, as farmers in the EC(9). But, in reality, whilst the accession of Greece, Spain and Portugal would more than double the Community's total agricultural population, the total number of agricultural holdings would increase by more than two-thirds. Thus, enlargement must inevitably reduce both the Community's average holding size and, by implication, the average level of farm incomes – a retrograde shift *vis à vis* the objectives of the CAP.

A second batch of problems was concerned with agricultural trade, both within the Community and outside. Whereas Greece's external trade in food and other agricultural products was broadly in balance, Spain and Portugal both had quite large agricultural import deficits, consisting predominantly of food and feed grains. But, at the same time, all three applicant countries had large export surpluses of Mediterranean-type products such as citrus fruit, processed tomatoes, olive oil and wine. Thus, enlargement afforded considerable scope for the diversion of agricultural trade away from the applicant countries traditional trading partners outside the EC. But it also promised to intensify competition between producers of Mediterranean-type products within the EC itself, that is, between producers in the newly acceding countries and those in Italy and the South of France in particular.

Reverting to the problem of the impact of enlargement on agricultural budget expenditure, it seemed likely that, due to enlargement, EC surpluses of Mediterranean-type products – such as olive oil, fruit and vegetables, and wine – would grow considerably above previous levels. The CAP system of support for fruit and vegetables relies mainly on protection at the border – through the combination of customs duties and 'reference' or minimum import prices – and relatively little on intervention buying to maintain floor prices (which, in any case, tend to be low). It therefore seemed likely that, as a result of the removal of border controls between the new member countries and the EC(9), the growing pressure of supplies of fruit and vegetables and other Mediterranean-type products on the internal market would lower market prices considerably, with unwelcome consequences for producers (especially in Italy and the South of France) as well as for the costs of intervention and budget expenditure. There was also the danger that producers in the newly acceding countries would actually expand crop production in response to price support levels which tended to be higher than those to which they had been accustomed. Spain, in particular, was thought to have a substantially under-utilised agricultural production potential, waiting to be mobilised in response to improved price incentives.[11]

Another problem was that if the Community authorities' response to the growing surpluses of Mediterranean products was increased resort to production controls – such as guarantee thresholds and quotas – this would pose severe problems of agricultural adjustment in areas already characterised by low farm incomes and a paucity of production alternatives.

A final problem implicit in enlargement from nine to twelve member states was the political one that decision making at all levels would be more complicated and agreement made more difficult to reach (particularly in view of the unanimity rule, resulting from the Luxembourg Compromise of 1965).

Solutions adopted for overcoming enlargement problems

The negotiators sought to minimise the adverse agricultural impacts of enlargement, on both the agricultures of the new entrants and those of the existing member states, in four main ways.

First, relatively long transitional periods were agreed during which the agricultures of the applicant countries would be gradually integrated into the CAP. For example, Spain was granted periods of 7–10 years, varying between commodities, in which to harmonise domestic agricultural prices with those of CAP, whilst adopting the CAP system of price support (that is, border measures and intervention) immediately. During the harmonisation period, temporary accessionary compensatory amounts (ACAs) were to be used to maintain price differences between the markets of the new entrants and the rest of the EC.

Secondly, as a temporary measure, 'indicative import ceilings' were established to enable intra-EC imports from the new entrants to be suspended if the ceilings based on recent historic trade flows were exceeded.

Thirdly, an Integrated Mediterranean Programme, also applicable to Italy and some regions of France, was negotiated to assist with the financing of regional development projects. In addition, the full benefits of the EC's structural aids programme, financed by the FEOGA Guidance Section, were made available to new members from the date of entry.

Lastly, before the Spanish and Portuguese accession negotiations were completed, the EC(10) agreed upon changes in the CAP which were likely to benefit the new entrants, for example improved support for producer groups, additions to the list of horticultural products receiving support and a strengthening of supply control measures for wine.

Foreign reactions to enlargement
The enlargement of a customs union naturally affects third countries because of trade diversion. In the case of the 1986 enlargement of the EC to admit Spain and Portugal the threat of a transatlantic trade war was provoked by the issue of Spanish imports of maize and sorghum. The US complained that the introduction by Spain of EC levies on imports of these grains would result in US exporters losing their share of the Spanish market for these commodities. The US government threatened to retaliate by imposing punitive duties on a wide range of EC exports of processed foods. Following prolonged bilateral negotiations, the EC and the USA finally reached an agreement in January 1987 under GATT Article XXIV6. Under the agreement, the EC consented to allow reduced levy import quotas of maize and sorghum into Spain from non-EC sources until 1990. Provision was also made for the agreement to be reviewed and possibly renewed in 1990 in the light of circumstances then prevailing.

The 1987 agreement also stipulated that the reduced levy quota grain must remain in Spain and not be re-exported to other EC countries. This aspect initially caused the Spanish government to enter a strong objection to the agreement on the grounds that 'cheap' imports would disrupt the market for domestic producers. But Spain eventually accepted assurances that the Spanish market for the two grains would be adequately protected.

Commission Proposals for the Reform of the Common Agricultural Policy

From quite early in the life of the CAP the Commission was active in analysing its defects and formulating proposals for its reform. Two main periods may be identified during which the Commission was particularly active in this respect: first, during the early 1970s coinciding with a number of destabilising events on the international scene, such as the change from fixed to floating exchange rates and the energy crisis resulting from the first OPEC oil price rise; also, the first enlargement of the Community from EC(6) to EC(9). During this first period, the main impetus for CAP reform came from the Commission itself. Second, in May 1980, the Commission was mandated by the Council to examine the development of Community policies and to make proposals for structural changes in the budget. Growing EC budget pressures in the wake of inflationary pressures exerted by the 1979 oil price rise and other forces, and dissatisfaction within the EC of the distribution of the costs of the budget between the member states, were amongst the primary reasons which compelled the Council to treat the issue of reforming the CAP more seriously during this later period. Budget pressures temporarily abated somewhat in the early 1980s, but were renewed in 1983 combined with further pressure from the UK for a final settlement of her budget contribution problem. This resulted in the Commission's being instructed to re-examine the CAP yet again with a view to bringing agricultural expenditure under more effective control.

Soon after a new Commission took office in 1985, it decided to prepare and publish a consultative green paper on the future of European agriculture and the CAP. The resultant *Perspectives for the Common Agricultural Policy* (CEC, 1985a) was shortly followed by a further document, *A Future for Community Agriculture* (CEC, 1985b), in which the Commission tabled further proposals for dealing with the continuing problem of imbalance between the supply of and demand for certain products of EC agriculture. Although some action was taken on these proposals at the 1986 Price Review, the agricultural surplus and budget problems continued to simmer for a further two years until the Brussels Summit of February 1988 at which 'stabilisers' and a voluntary acreage 'set-aside' scheme were added to the armoury of weapons to be deployed in containing agricultural expenditure: the size of the agricultural budget relative to the total EC budget, and the amount of the Community's own resources, were also 'capped' at the same meeting.

Early reform proposals: 1973–75

Apart from the 1958 Mansholt Plan (see Chapter 4), the Commission's earliest major set of proposals for the reform of the CAP appeared in 1973 with the title *Memorandum Agriculture 1973–1978* (CEC, 1973). Whilst giving credit to the CAP for a number of advances in the agricultural sector, this document also directed attention to various weaknesses. The advances included a sharp increase in agricultural trade between the member states, an expansion of trade with non-member countries, greater internal market stability and substantial improvement in the structure of agriculture through a quite rapid decline in the number of farms. The main problems were the persistence of wide income disparities within agriculture, growing expenditure in the Guarantee Section of FEOGA and the adverse impact of exchange rate instability and MCAs on the unity of the single market. The growing budget expenditure was euphemistically attributed to 'disequilibria on certain agricultural markets'. The facts were that large and mounting structural surpluses, particularly of milk, had already accumulated, even though the first enlargement had for a time reduced the Community's self-sufficiency in some commodities. The Commission's advice on methods of dealing with the structural surplus problem included the proposal that the farmers themselves should bear a proportion of the financial responsibility for disposing of them. In particular, the Commission proposed that milk producers should be subject to a temporary production levy on milk delivered to the dairy in excess of a levy-free quota (of uniform size for all producers regardless of their scale of production). A number of other proposals was also made, relating both to milk and other regulated commodities, directed to the reduction of FEOGA Guarantee Section expenditure. Despite having drawn attention to the growing income disparity within Community agriculture, the Commission did not propose any increase in FEOGA Guidance Section expenditure. CEC, 1973 was also notable for the emphasis which the Commission gave to the need for simultaneous action both to improve the CAP and further progress toward the goal of full economic and monetary union provided for by a Council resolution of 22 March 1971 and confirmed as a firm policy goal by the Summit Conference of October 1972.

To deal with the problem of the disruption of the single market by MCAs, the Commission declared that 'the restoration of a single market not later than 31 December 1977 . . . must remain a fundamental objective of the Common Agricultural Policy' (CEC, 1973, para. 24).

The year in which the memorandum was published (1973) turned out to be a year in which, due to the coincidence of poor harvests in Europe and North America and for other reasons, steep rises in the world prices of grains and other commodities occurred. Due to their negative effect on export restitution payments, these world price movements reduced the pressure of FEOGA Guarantee Section expenditure on the budget. For this reason, the Commission's first attempt to reform the CAP, as represented by the COM (73) 1850 proposals did not result in any immediate action by the Council. But by late 1974 the pressures were building up again, and in October of that year the Council requested the Commission to prepare a 'stocktaking' of the CAP. This led, in March 1975, to the presentation by the Commission to the Council of a follow-up set of proposals for reforming the CAP under the title *Stocktaking of the Common Agricultural Policy* (CEC, 1975). The substance of the Commission's diagnosis of the defects of the CAP and its proposals for remedying these were little changed from the arguments already advanced in the earlier COM(73) 1850 document. The diagnosis again emphasised that since the CAP alone could not solve all of agriculture's economic and social problems, complementary regional and social policies needed to be developed and implemented. The distorting effects of MCAs were again highlighted and progress towards economic and monetary union was advocated to help get rid of them. Under-expenditure on structural reform (relative to expenditure on commodity price support) was criticised on the ground that the 'modernisation of farms', enabling full income parity of farmers and non-farmers to be achieved, had been consequently delayed. The Commission's 1975 'Stocktaking' was long on diagnosis but somewhat short on effective remedies for the ills of the CAP. The principle that producers should 'share responsibility for surpluses' was again mentioned, together with a recommendation that it should be applied to milk production (para. 106). But this was no advance on a virtually identical recommendation in COM(73) 1850. A co-responsibility levy on milk was, in fact, approved by the Council with effect from 1977 onwards. The introduction in 1975 of supplementary income aids for farmers in 'less-favoured areas' might also be interpreted as a Council response to Commission pressure for measures to reduce income inequality within agriculture. Apart from these measures, the short-term impact of the 1975 'Stocktaking' document on the evolution of the CAP was negligible, as it had been to *Memorandum Agriculture 1973–1978*.

However, in the later 1970s budgetary pressures increased due to growing commodity surpluses and declining world prices exacerbated by unfavourable exchange-rate movements, particularly with the $US. Thus, in May 1980, the Commission was mandated by the Council to come forward with proposals for curbing the agricultural budget. Over the next couple of years, the Commission published three documents in response to the 1980 mandate: *Reflections on the Common Agricultural Policy* (CEC, 1980) in December 1980, *Report on the Mandate* (CEC, 1981a) in June 1981, and *Guidelines for European Agriculture* (CEC, 1981b) in October 1981. After a comparative lull of nearly two years, in June 1983 the Commission was instructed by the Stuttgart Summit Meeting, to re-examine the CAP, taking account of its specific elements, with a view to tabling proposals to enable it to fulfil its aims in a more coherent manner and to ensure, inter alia, effective control of agricultural expenditure. The Commission's response to this instruction was *Common Agricultural Policy: Proposals of the Commission* (CEC, 1983), published in July 1983. Shortly after a new Commission took office in January 1985, it decided to publish a green paper on European agricultural policy to clarify policy options and so prepare the way for further reforms. The green paper shortly appeared under the title *Perspectives for the Common Agricultural Policy* (CEC, 1985a) in July 1985. Following consultations on the green paper, the Commission published a further document with the title *A Future for Community Agriculture* (CEC, 1985b) in which it put forward more specific guidelines for CAP policy adjustments. No further major sets of proposals for reforming the CAP were published by the Commission before the February 1988 Summit Meeting at which the decision was taken to 'cap' the rate of growth of agricultural budget expenditure and, as a complementary measure, to impose 'stabilisers' (mainly in the form of steep reductions in producer prices) on the production of virtually all commodities in structural surplus.

In this section we are less concerned with the actual enactment of CAP policy reforms through Council decisions than with the evolution of the Commission's ideas about the nature of the problems underlying the need for reform, the objectives of reform and the choice of policy instruments to give them effect. Consequently, in dealing with the proposals for reform between 1980 (the year of the Mandate) and 1985 (the year of the 'Perspectives' green paper) we choose to review the development of Commission thinking on the reform of the CAP under these three headings, that is, 'problems', 'objectives' and 'choice of instruments', based on the contents of documents already mentioned, rather than attempting to deal with the whole of each document in turn on a chronological basis.

Commission reform proposals: 1980–85

Problems In the 1980 'Reflections' document the Commission identified four major problems deriving from the working of the CAP. First,
there was the problem of growing 'excess supplies' of most major
agricultural commodities produced in the community, leading to uncontrollable budget expenditure on intervention and export refund
payments. That the underlying cause of excess supplies was guaranteed
prices above the market-clearing level was frankly admitted. However,
the Commission also maintained that the size of the agricultural budget
was 'not unreasonable' relative either to Community GDP or levels of
agricultural support in other industrial countries.

The second major problem was the producer inequity resulting from
the CAP guarantee system of supporting farm incomes indirectly via
product prices, so that the bulk of state support was going to a section
of the farmer population which 'needed' it least, that is, the larger-scale
farmers.

The third problem identified by the Commission was regional
inequity. This problem was clearly associated with the second one, since,
due to different rates of structural change, small farms tended to be
concentrated in particular regions of the Community. Another cause of
regional inequality was the unequal degrees of support accorded to
different commodities. So, for example, producers of fruit and vegetables, and other Mediterranean-type products, received much lower
and less certain priced 'guarantees' than the price supports enjoyed by
producers of cereals and other Northern European products.

The fourth problem identified by the 'Reflections' document was that
of the financial inequities which had arisen amongst the member states
in defraying the budget costs of agricultural support. This problem
derived from the second and third ones, in that smaller and regionally
disadvantaged farmers tended to be unequally distributed amongst the
member states. The net result was that the income transfers implicit in
the CAP were going primarily from poor farmers and regions to rich
farmers and regions. The poorer countries were obviously dissatisfied
with a situation in which they were net contributors to the budget costs
of the CAP, rather than being net beneficiaries.

The 1981 *Report on the Mandate* took a wider-ranging view of the
problems of Community development, including the energy crisis, rising
unemployment and other consequences of the world economic recession
which was then current. But little or nothing was added on the problems
of the CAP *per se*, either in the *Report on the Mandate* or in the
'Guidelines' document issued later the same year. By 1983, when

the *Common Agricultural Policy: Proposals of the Commission* document proposing inter alia the introduction of milk quotas was presented to the Council, agricultural budget pressures had re-intensified after a short pause. Thus, the main drift of the 1983 document was to re-emphasise the budget problem arising as a consequence of Community production continuing to grow more rapidly than Community consumption for most farm products, resulting in ever-growing expenditure on intervention storage and export restitution.

The 'Perspectives' green paper, published by the new Commission shortly after taking office in 1985, did add some new dimensions to the problems of the CAP. Although the problem of disequilibrium between supply and demand leading to intense budget pressure was still paramount, the problem of external trade disequilibrium, resulting from the gap between internal Community prices and world prices, was clearly articulated. The green paper stated that 'agricultural policy must take account of international realities'. Another new dimension was the proposition that over-rapid farm structural change, resulting in excessive rural depopulation and the demise of the family farm, posed a potential 'social problem' which should, if possible, be avoided. Similarly, the adverse effects of certain aspects of modern agricultural technology on conservation of the natural environment posed another problem of growing significance. The problem of 'low' farm incomes was now seen to be most acute on small farms with substantial disguised unemployment. On full-time farms, the adverse effects of a cost/price squeeze on farm incomes was at least partially offset by the favourable effect of technical progress on productivity. But, overall, a farm/non-farm income disparity continued to persist, according to the Commission. However, the growing importance in the Community of part-time farming, combined with gainful outside activities, was an encouraging trend.

The problems highlighted in the 1985 'Perspectives' green paper were reiterated in the white paper published later the same year under the title *A Future for Community Agriculture* (CEC, 1985b). The only significant addition was the emphasis given to the increasingly strained relations with agricultural trading partners caused by the working of the CAP.

Objectives   In 1980, the 'Reflections' document emphasised four major CAP reform objectives:

1.   Maintain the positive aspects of the CAP specified as consumers' security of supply and stable prices, farm income support, free

internal trade and the retention of agriculture's contribution to external trade.

2. Achieve better control of the budgetary costs of production surpluses.
3. Improve the regional distribution of the benefits of the CAP to farmers.
4. Reorganise CAP financing to minimise disputes on this issue between Member States.

The 1981 *Report on the Mandate* was more explicit about the objective of improved budgetary control. It proposed that the rate of growth in agricultural spending should be kept below the rate of growth in the Community's own resources. This proposal was an early expression of the principle later termed 'budgetary discipline'. Another objective advanced in this document was to make agricultural prices reflect 'market realities' (an imprecise concept) more than in the past.

The 'Guidelines' document which shortly followed the *Report on the Mandate* added, as further objectives, the avoidance of increased unemployment, agricultural export expansion (to maintain the Community's market share), environmental protection and natural resource conservation.

The publication of the *'Common Agricultural Policy: Proposals of the Commission'* document in 1983 coincided with re-intensification of pressure to restrict price guarantees in order to relieve pressures on the budget. Against this background, the need to protect the incomes of small producers against the adverse effects of a restrictive price policy and similar measures was added to the list of reform objectives. On the issue of external trade, the objective of negotiating revisions of the Community's external protection system, particularly in relation to commodities for which measures had already been taken to restrain internal production (such as the guarantee threshold for cereals introduced in 1982), was also included at this stage, as well as a restatement of the Community's commitment to the principle of 'community preference'.

In restating the objectives of the CAP in the 'Perspectives' green paper of 1985 the new Commission emphasised that Article 39 of the Treaty of Rome remained fully valid: no revision or reinterpretation of the objectives stated there was required. But, at the same time, the CAP could not remain insulated from the influence of world markets where competition formed the framework within which European agriculture had to operate. Thus a more market-oriented approach to pricing and other aspects of the CAP was essential to keep agricultural expenditure within the financial guidelines laid down at the Dublin

Summit in December 1984. The objective of aligning the Community's support price levels with those of competing exporters was recommended as being consistent with this approach, but only in the long term with appropriate complementary measures to safeguard producer incomes. Minimisation of the budget costs of export disposal without disrupting world markets was put forward as an export policy objective. The objective of achieving more 'balanced' levels of protection amongst different commodities, in order to reduce the overall budget costs of support, was reiterated in the 1985 green paper, specifically relative to cereals and livestock (highly protected) and oilseeds and cereals substitutes (zero or very low protection). The difficulty of negotiating such a deal was recognised despite the argument that the Community had already imposed stricter output disciplines on its own producers. The green paper also reiterated the need for the CAP to continue fulfilling the social objective of assuring a fair standard of living for the agricultural population, as well as maintaining a minimum viable population on the land. However, the Commission also recognised the difficulty of satisfying the Community's goals of containing the agricultural budget and supporting farm incomes simultaneously. Thus, historically, the relative priorities accorded to these two major goals had tended to alternate according to the relative strengths of the political pressures to trim the budget and bolster farm incomes.

In *A Future for Community Agriculture*, the white paper which followed in the wake of the 'Perspectives' document, the Commission succinctly summarised the priority objectives of CAP reform, as follows:

1. Gradually to reduce production in surplus sectors.
2. To increase the diversity and improve the quality of agricultural production.
3. To deal more effectively and systematically with the income problems of small family farms.
4. To continue to support agriculture in areas where its survival is essential for land use planning, maintaining the social balance and protecting the environment.
5. To make farmers more aware of environmental issues.
6. To encourage EC development of 'high-tech' industries using agricultural raw materials.

Choice of instruments In the 1980 'Reflections' document, the Commission proposed using three main policy instruments to solve the problems of the CAP through achieving the objectives of reform. These were, first, to extend the application of the principle of producer co-responsibility in order to reduce the budget costs of disposing of structural surpluses from sugar and milk, as already in force, to other commodities. The Commission thought that this principle should be a permanent feature of the CAP. Whilst recognising that the principle could be applied in various different ways, the Commission at this stage expressed a strong preference for a co-responsibility levy deductible from a single guaranteed price, but without a quota, to a dual price system combined with a quota (based, for example, on domestic consumption). The policy to be followed in setting the support price levies from which co-responsibility levels would be deducted if production thresholds were exceeded was vague. The eventual alignment of Community prices on world prices, at least for some commodities such as cereals, was proposed as an objective, but neither the means nor the timescale for achieving this were spelled out. Secondly and thirdly on the achievement of external trade objectives, the 'Reflections' document proposed using two instruments: first, specifically to control imports of cereal substitutes and protein supplements incorporated in animal feedingstuffs, the conclusion of VER agreements with the supplying countries; second, the negotiation of long-term agricultural export agreements, particularly with LDCs.

In 1981, the *Report on the Mandate* and the linked 'Guidelines' document both reiterated the Commission's opposition to the extension of quota controls from sugar to other commodities regulated by the CAP. The 'Guidelines' also set production targets for major commodities relative to a 1988 planning horizon, but also for intervening years, with provision for price support levels to be diminished if the targets were exceeded. The Commission reserved the right to vary production targets in the light of technological, administrative or economic changes. For cereals, a progressive reduction in the gap between EC intervention and US cereal prices over the period to 1988 was proposed. But Community preference was to be retained by keeping the threshold price above the intervention price. The cereals production target set for 1988 was based on the twin assumptions that (a) EC cereal exports would remain at the current (1982/3) level, and (b) no increase in imports of cereal substitutes would occur so that any additional demand for feed cereals would be met by increased domestic supplies. A cereals co-responsibility levy was proposed under which producers would be penalised for exceeding the annual production targets, but only by deducting the levy from the intervention price in the following season. Thus the 1981 'Guidelines' document proposed subjecting EC cereals producers to two kinds of pressure: first, a gradual alignment of the intervention price on the (lower) US price (approximating to the world price); and, secondly, a co-responsibility levy penalty for exceeding the production target. Similar measures were proposed for milk with a production target based on domestic consumption only, and a supplementary levy on top of the existing co-responsibility levy to penalise producers for exceeding the annual production target. It was suggested that the amount of the supplementary levy be sufficient to defray the costs of disposing of surplus milk. It was also suggested that in order to favour small milk producers, producers should be exempted from the payment of any levy (basic or supplementary) on the first 30 000 kgs of milk delivered.

The Commission's proposal for a cereals co-responsibility levy if actual production exceeded a pre-determined production threshold was, in fact, adopted by the Council from the year 1982/83. But the proposal for a supplementary milk levy was not adopted until after the introduction of milk quotas in 1984. In 1982/83 a production threshold was also introduced for rapeseed with provision for lowering the support price (by reducing the deficiency payment) if the threshold was exceeded.

By the time it published the *Common Agricultural Policy: Proposals of the Commission* document in 1983, the Commission had dropped its hitherto implacable opposition to the extension of supply control by means of quotas to other commodities. With the pressure to keep agricultural expenditure within the budget again rising, the need to reduce the surplus of milk was particularly acute. The Commission maintained that for milk the restrictive price policy, which had been in operation for several years, had not worked. The 1983 production threshold was expected to be exceeded by 6 per cent, and the Commission estimated that the 1983/4 support price level would need to be reduced by 12 per cent to offset the additional costs of surplus disposal. The Commission further considered that even with special relief for small producers, a price cut of such a magnitude was likely to result in unacceptable inequalities between Member States and could even 'compromise the unity of the price mechanism' (para. 4.9). Therefore, largely for political expediency the Commission advocated the adoption of the alternative instrument of the production quota, combined with the continuance of a restrictive price policy, to enforce producer compliance with the milk guarantee threshold. The advice was that the quotas should operate at the micro level, applying either to individual producers or processing dairies. Milk quotas were in fact adopted by the Council, as part of the 1984/85 price review package, in the Spring of 1984.

In the 1985 'Perspectives' green paper, the new Commission stressed that, in order to successfully accomplish the transition to a more market-oriented price policy, policy instruments needed to be applied consistently over a long period. Restrictive price policy combined with guarantee thresholds was still the Commission's preferred instrument for products in surplus. The option of attempting to satisfy both the budget and farm income goals of agricultural policy by means of quotas, combined with relatively high prices for within-quota production, was still rejected. The new Commission persisted with its opposition to the extension of the quota system, despite admitting the superiority of quotas to other methods of supply control in producing 'quick results' and the fact that the old Commission had only recently been responsible for introducing milk quotas: milk was considered to be an 'exceptional' case. A number of new policy options were proposed for cereals. First, the existing guarantee threshold system, which deferred penalising producers for exceeding the threshold until the following season, could be modified to apply the price penalty immediately in the same season. Secondly, instead of applying the production threshold only at the aggregate level, a co-responsibility levy might be collected from individual producers at the first point of sale for off-farm processing or consumption. Such a levy could be pitched at the level needed to cover part or all of the costs of cereal export refunds, as well as bringing home to individual producers the consequences and costs of over-production. Thirdly, the intervention system might be modified in various ways to limit its budgetary cost as, for example, by restricting intervention purchases to a shorter season, or by raising minimum quality standards. Fourthly, the Commission put forward land diversion, or 'set-aside', as a feasible option for reducing the cereals surplus, despite drawbacks including high administrative costs and 'slippage' (resulting, in particular, from producers setting aside their least productive land) as already experienced under the operation of set-aside schemes in the USA.

Two further sets of policy instrument proposals in the 1985 green paper concerned export policy adjustment and direct income aids (DIAs). On export policy, the Commission made three proposals for limiting the costs of export refunds: first, by extending the use of tendering procedures (as a substitute for pre-fixed limit export refunds) from cereals and sugar to other commodities; secondly, by changing the method of calculating refunds, especially in relation to commodities for which representative world prices were difficult to determine; thirdly, by varying the amount of unit refunds more according to the quality of the product and its intended use or destination. On the options for direct income aids, the Commission saw a revised programme of such aids as being desirable to further advance agricultural structural adjustment as well as advancing environmental conservation and regional development. Four basic options were canvassed for a new DIA programme:

1.   'pre-pension' scheme for farmers aged 55 or over who were prepared to retire from farming. This scheme would replace the earlier 1972 scheme (Dir. 72/160) which the Commission judged to have been unsuccessful 'due to the inadequacy of the pension offered'.
2.   A scheme of temporary and degressive financial relief for professional farmers with 'low' incomes.
3.   A scheme of basic social security confined to the poorest farmers without realistic alternative options for earning an adequate living.
4.   A 'buy-out' scheme under which farmers would give up the right to produce agricultural products in return for an annual income proportional to the volume of production abandoned. The land so released from agricultural production could be bought or rented long term for various non-agricultural uses, including nature reserves, leisure parks or afforestation.

The Commission stressed the need to keep DIAs 'production-neutral' in order to avoid exacerbation of the structural surplus problem.

The 1985 'Perspectives' green paper contained a number of prophetic policy proposals for agriculture, some of which were taken up in the *A Future for Community Agriculture* white paper published later the same year. The policy instruments proposed in the latter document were very much along the lines of the Commission's 'preferred options' as expressed in the preceding green paper. Thus, in the white paper, although the Commission again posed restrictive pricing and the extension of production quotas as policy options, it continued to argue unambiguously in favour of price restraint and against the extension of quota restrictions. Thus, a rigorous prices policy combined with the continued application of the principle of producer co-responsibility in one or other of several practical forms was advocated, together with an increase in direct aids to target groups of farmers to sharpen the selectivity of price restrictions. The Commission's most recent thinking on modification of the intervention system was that the system needed to be restored to performing the function it had performed before the Community reached self-sufficiency in most agricultural products, that is, the function of providing a short-term price safety net for producers (instead of providing producers with an alternative to ordinary commercial market outlets under normal conditions). In other words, producers should be strongly discouraged from deliberately producing for sale into intervention.

On agricultural trade and external relations, the Commission repeated the case (already made in the green paper) for the pursuit of an active export policy based on the twin principles of (a) greater transparency, and (b) greater diversity of instruments used, to put the Community's agricultural exports on an equal footing with those of competing exporters. The Commission hoped to convince trading partners of the need for better organisation of world markets to the general benefit of all countries, including LDCs, and to avoid the 'unjustified costs of cutthroat competition'. The white paper also acknowledged that the Community's bargaining position in the next round of international trade negotiations, particularly regarding its longstanding wish for a 'more balanced' form of external protection amongst different commodities (already referred to earlier in this section) might well depend on its demonstrated ability to solve its internal agricultural problems, especially the 'surplus problem'. On structural policy, the white paper advocated the revival of early retirement schemes for farmers partially financed by the Guidance Section of the Community Budget, as foreshadowed by the green paper. But, in the white paper, the Commission also advocated improvements in measures to assist farmers in 'less favoured' areas (including mountain and hill farming areas). The objective of such improvement schemes might be to encourage increased production, as well as farm incomes, where this was judged to be desirable and beneficial either socially (for example to prevent or retard rural depopulation) or environmentally (for example to conserve landscape values). On the question of environmental protection, the Commission also gave notice of its intention to propose a common framework for encouraging conservation of the rural environment and protection of specific sites. The granting of income support for farmers agreeable to using methods of production compatible with protection of the natural habitat was proposed.

Aftermath of 1980–85 Reform Proposals

Several of the Commission 'Guidelines' proposals for more restrictive pricing were in fact quite rapidly implemented by the Council. So, for example, the 1986 price review package included a cereals co-responsibility levy, payable by individual producers at the first point of sale off the farm to a merchant or processor, but with concessions to very small producers. Also in 1986, intervention arrangements were modified to reduce the volume of sales into intervention, mainly by not opening the intervention stores until after the end of the harvesting season: the new arrangements applied both to cereals and livestock products. Further modifications of the cereals intervention arrangements followed in 1987 from when intervention purchases were further limited to periods in which market prices were below the intervention level and even then, the price actually paid was limited to 94 per cent of the intervention price.

In June 1987 the European Council meeting in Brussels mandated the Commission to produce a further review of the CAP, including proposals for 'action to ensure full compliance with budgetary discipline'. The Commission responded with the document *Review of Action Taken to Control the Agricultural Markets and Outlook for the CAP* (CEC, 1987a) issued in August 1987. In this document the term 'stabilisers' was used to describe all policy instruments deployed to control the agricultural budget. The document argued that although a number of stabilisers were already in use, such as restrictive pricing, limited intervention and the enforcement of guarantee thresholds and quotas, these instruments needed to be modified or supplemented in order to tighten budgetary discipline. The Commission made a number of suggestions for new policy instruments to achieve this end, including a modification of the cereals co-responsibility arrangements to add a supplementary levy on to the basic levy already payable by producers if a pre-determined maximum annual production quantity was breached. The Commission also promised to look for viable schemes of compensating farmers for taking land out of production, possibly including a US style 'set-aside' scheme. But the review document also argued that the application of budget stabilisers was subject to two important provisos. First, the European pattern of agriculture as typified by 'family farms' must be preserved. Second, the Community's position as a major exporter of agricultural products must be defended.

The CEC, 1987a document was followed by the publication of a further document, COM (87) 452 (CEC, 1987b) in which the Commission further elaborated its proposals for extending new or modified stabilisers to most regulated commodities, including more precise proposals in the form of the new cereals stabiliser. The Commission's proposals for a farmland set-aside scheme were published in January 1988 (CEC, 1988). The central feature of this voluntary scheme was that participating farmers would commit themselves to taking a minimum of 20 per cent of their arable land out of production for at least 5 years in return for compensation based on the farm income foregone. A set-aside scheme with 50 per cent Community financing up to a ceiling level of compensation per hectare of land withdrawn was actually approved at the Brussels Summit of February 1988 as part of a much larger 'stabiliser' package. Although producer participation in set-aside was voluntary, the adoption of the scheme by member states was mandatory (with considerable flexibility for varying levels of compensation according to national circumstances), apart from a temporary waiver granted to Portugal (Reg. No. 1272/88).[12]

We have already referred to the details of the cereals stabiliser arrangements, as agreed at the Brussels Summit Meeting in February 1988 as part of the much larger package of stabiliser measures then adopted. Despite some changes of detail, the package was clearly closely modelled on the proposals advanced by the Commission in August 1987 (CEC, 1987a) and the subsequent documents to which we have referred. But much of the impetus for the measures taken in February 1988 came from the Commission's 'Perspectives' and 'Future for Community Agriculture' documents of 1985. Indeed, the measures taken in February 1988 can now be seen as the culmination of the Commission's efforts to reform the CAP, particularly with respect to controlling the size of the agricultural budget, at least from the date of the publication of the 'Reflections' document in 1980. However, in February 1988 the European Council drew attention to two items of 'unfinished business' on CAP reform. The Agricultural Council was called upon to reach rapid decisions on Community arrangements for (1) a new scheme to encourage the early retirement of farmers and (2) a scheme of direct income aids for disadvantaged farmers. The Council was given deadlines of 1 April and 1 July 1988 respectively for reaching these decisions.

The Commission's initial proposals both for encouraging the early retirement of farmers and for a scheme of direct income aids for disadvantaged farmers appeared in the Spring of 1987 (CEC, 1987c). Dealing first with the proposals for direct income aids, it was argued that Community action to reform agricultural markets would be more effective and consistent if it was supported by instruments allowing direct and selective support to the incomes of those groups of farmers who were suffering most from the ongoing adjustments to markets. But such support must avoid giving an incentive to increased production for all the farmers in a given agricultural sector or region. The scheme of income aids now being proposed differed from the existing scheme of assistance to farmers in mountain, hill and other less favoured areas in that these latter schemes applied to all farmers in the affected areas with the amount of compensation per farmer being linked to his production (para. 7). The purpose of the new scheme was 'to facilitate transition [to the status of "modern" farmers] for "main occupation" farmers placed in difficulties by current adjustments as regards the markets but which are, in fact, potentially viable . . .'. Income payments under the scheme would be limited to five years and would be degressive (para. 10).

The Commission's direct income aids proposals were the cause of much discussion in the Agricultural Council and, despite the earlier deadline set by the 1988 Brussels Summit, final agreement was not reached until January 1989. The Council then approved a scheme of production-neutral support of the incomes of poorer farmers, much revised from the original scheme proposed by the Commission. Whereas the Commission wanted implementation to be mandatory in all member states, the scheme actually approved allowed dissidents to opt out in order to gain the acquiescence of countries like the UK and Denmark, who considered that the whole scheme was misconceived and might otherwise have blocked it. The principal 'rules' resembled those proposed in the COM(87) 166 document. That is:

1. Aid must be degressive over a maximum of five years and not linked to either production or prices.
2. Only 'low income' farmers qualify, the relevant income being total farm household income from all sources which must not exceed a given threshold – to be set by member states but linked to regional GDP per head, subject to an absolute maximum per man-work unit denominated in ECUs.
3. Aid limited to 'main occupation' farmers.
4. The amount of aid per farm household subject to an absolute ECU limit based on several criteria.
5. The Community budget contribution limited to 70 per cent of the eligible amount in less-developed regions and 25 per cent in other regions.

Although Community financing of the direct income aids scheme was covered by a 'special budget line' agreed at the February 1988 Brussels Summit, total expenditure on the scheme was limited by an annual ceiling (expressed relative to 1992).

The implementation of a new scheme to encourage farmers to retire early, to replace the 'failed' 1972 scheme, had an easier passage through the Council. The COM(87) 166 document contained a draft regulation granting an annual pension both to 'main occupation farmers and full-time farm workers aged over 55', provided that they gave up farming. The payment of the pension would be limited to a maximum of ten years. The land given up could either be diverted to forestry or another non-agricultural use, or it might be maintained by the farmer to 'preserve the countryside', provided all commercial production ceased. The Community's contribution to funding the scheme would be 50 per cent of all eligible expenditure up to a ceiling amount per farmer or farm-worker, the remainder of the cost being borne by member states. The Commission also proposed that implementation of the scheme should be at the discretion of member states, that is, they should be able to opt out.

An early retirement scheme based on the Commission's 1987 proposals was finally approved by the Council in April 1988 (Reg. No. 1096/88 establishing a Community scheme to encourage the cessation of farming).

The scheme encountered strong opposition within the Council, particularly from the UK and the Netherlands, and was approved only by a qualified majority vote. Implementation was indeed left to the discretion of member states. Payment of retirement premiums was 'limited to a minimum of five and a maximum ten years to farmers and farm-workers between 55 and 70 years of age'. The land given up by retirees might either be transferred to forestry or other non-agricultural use (under an 'abandonment' scheme) or to another farmer (under a 'restructuring' scheme). The amount of the pension payable was subject to an ECU denominated 'ceiling' with the Community's contribution varying between the abandonment and restructuring options, but with a maximum of 50 per cent under either scheme.

Non-official Critiques of the CAP and Proposals for Reform

Almost from the beginning the CAP has attracted considerable economic criticism from independent observers, and many reform proposals have been made. Many of the criticisms have later reappeared in the Commission's own policy reviews and reform proposals, as discussed in the previous section. To the extent that external critics have influenced the Commission's policy reform proposals, and as far as reforms proposed by the Commission have actually been accepted and implemented by the Council of Ministers, it might be claimed that the critics have actually influenced policy. However, it is recognised that economists' ability to influence agricultural policy from an economic point of view is severely limited by the impact of political forces on the Council's policy decisions.

Direct income payments

One of the earliest critiques of the CAP was issued in 1973 by a group of distinguished agricultural economists drawn from most of the member states after a meeting in the Netherlands (Wageningen Memorandum, 1973). The Wageningen group met when surpluses of certain agricultural commodities, such as bread grains and milk, were already threatening, but self-sufficiency in other commodities, such as beef, had not yet been reached. The group therefore stressed the need for relative price adjustments to divert resources from surplus to non-surplus products. But, around the same time, other critics were already urging the necessity of a lower general level of product price support, to contain surplus accumulation and budget expenditure, as well as benefiting consumers, combined with a system of direct income support to safeguard farm incomes (Josling, 1973). The feasibility of direct income payments, either to complement agricultural product price support in the EC, or even eventually to replace it altogether, was further explored by Koester and Tangermann (1977). These authors reported the results of a cost–benefit analysis of alternative farm price policies applied to West German agriculture which indicated a positive potential social benefit from a reduction of price support in favour of direct income support under a fairly wide range of scenarios. Recognising that a major shift in emphasis away from price support to direct income payments would greatly expand the size of the agricultural budget, Koester and Tangermann also suggested that, as an alternative to funding direct income payments from general tax revenue, a special consumer food tax, equivalent to a VAT, might be imposed instead. Whilst recognising that the transparency of such a food tax would very likely provoke the opposition of farmers, these authors continued to press the claim that this proposed means of combining direct income payments with lower producer prices and a smaller budget deserved to be taken seriously.

Tangermann returned to the case for giving direct income support a pivotal role in the reform of the CAP in the evidence he gave in 1980 to the House of Lords Select Committee of the European Communities (House of Lords Select Committee on the European Communities; 1981). He observed that a reduction in the level of producer price support would redistribute income in favour of net importing countries and consumers at the expense of net exporters and producers. It followed that price cuts would be politically feasible only in combination with the use of instruments to compensate the 'losers'. Direct income transfers were well suited to this purpose, provided that, in the case of direct payments to farmers, these were divorced from either current or future production levels. For this reason, the substitution of a deficiency payment system of price support for the present border protection/ intervention system would not be appropriate. Tangermann also proposed that to accommodate the wide variability of agricultural and economic structures amongst EC member states, direct income payments should be nationally differentiated (with a common system of administration).

Josling also gave evidence to the House of Lords Select Committee and, in doing so, reiterated the theoretical benefits of reduced commodity price levels combined with direct income transfers to farmers 'in need'. But he also recognised and gave weight to the practical problem of reaching agreement amongst the member states on an equitable distribution of Community budget shares, even with lower common price levels. Dominance of the desire to protect national interests over Community interests was also likely to vitiate the adoption of possible reform measures such as quota schemes requiring agreement on quota allocations. To quote Josling verbatim, 'The problem for the reformer is . . . that no scheme can at the same time cost less, relieve the burden on consumers, be consistent with trading interests, and preserve the present income position of EC agriculture' (House of Lords Select Committee Report, Session 79/80 HL 156, p. 98). Owing to the political process followed in reaching CAP price decisions, Josling was not optimistic that rapid progress could be made with radical reforms of the type he and other agricultural economists were recommending, that is, lower price support combined with direct income payments. He therefore reasoned that, at least in the short term, 'control of the budget offers the best hope of progress' (ibid.). This was, in fact, the main objective of reform followed by the Commission, and eventually by Council as well, in the early and mid-1980s.

Partial renationalisation of the CAP

A different line of CAP reform, addressed particularly to easing the 'budget problem', was to advocate partial renationalisation of agricultural policy within the EC. Thus, in the mid-1970s a reform proposal was advanced to effectively legitimise monetary compensatory amounts (MCAs), but with the costs of deviating from Community prices falling on national budgets rather than upon FEOGA (Marsh, 1977). The proposed scheme envisaged that the Council of Ministers would agree upon a 'Community trading price', denominated in UAs,[13] and that member states would agree to trade at this price, both within the Community itself and with third world countries. Variable levies and export refunds would continue to bridge any gap between world prices and the CTP. But as far as domestic markets were concerned, considerable flexibility might be permitted in methods of price support. So, for example, a country wishing to pay its farmers more than the CTP could supplement their incomes with deficiency payments or in some other way. Another country wanting to lower the price of food to its own consumers below the CTP could inject consumer subsidies or other welfare payments. The central point of the Marsh proposal was that all such subventions would be funded by national exchequers and not by FEOGA. Marsh considered that his reform proposals promised two important advantages if adopted. First, it would be easier to negotiate a price at which internal competition worked to the advantage of the whole Community. Because the costs of protecting especially vulnerable groups could be clearly seen to fall on national budgets, there would be no need to raise EC support prices for purely social reasons, and Marsh clearly thought that agreement could be reached on a relatively low CTP. Second, with the effective abolition of MCAs (domestic price differentiation taking their place), FEOGA expenditure could either be reduced overall or reallocated in order to channel extra funds into the Guidance Section.

In 1980, Marsh represented his CAP reform proposals, in a slightly modified form, to the House of Lords Select Committee examination of the CAP. The main changes from the earlier proposal were that supplementary agricultural support was visualised mainly in terms of direct income payments to farmers under a set of commonly determined Community rules, but differentially administered between Member States and at least partly nationally financed. It was proposed that the direct income payments adopted to supplement the support given by a relatively low CTP should be for a limited period only and financed by the Community only *vis-à-vis* the costs of disposing of net exports at below the CTP. The costs of DIPs or any other device to raise domestic producer prices above CTPs would again fall solely on national exchequers.[14]

The critics of Marsh's CTP proposal stressed that Council agreement on a common trading price, particularly a lower price than hitherto, would be inherently difficult to reach. Owing to the intra-Community income transfers inherent in the CAP, the net exporting countries would be bound to hold out for a higher CTP than the one preferred by the net importers. Another inevitable criticism, advanced particularly by those who regard the CAP as an expression of West European 'unity', is that any reversion towards renationalising agricultural policy not only threatens the survival of the CAP but is also a betrayal of the ideals which inspired the formation of the European Community.

Quotas and quasi-quotas

As a broad generalisation, economist critics of the CAP, as well as the Commission, have been opposed to the use of production quotas as an instrument of CAP reform. The economic arguments against quotas are familiar, that is, that they inhibit resource mobility and stifle competition, create windfall capital gains for the original holders, increase the costs of entry for new producers, and so on. However, believing that 'first best' reform of the CAP, involving the alignment of EC producer-prices with world prices is politically unattainable, a few economists have put forward serious proposals for quota or quasi-quota schemes, as a 'second-best' option. It is generally argued that in order to minimise their adverse effects on resource mobility and competition amongst producers, quotas must be both saleable and released for resale at regular intervals. Farmers and their representative organisations have not been implacably opposed to quota restrictions, provided support prices are maintained at a high enough level to protect farm incomes. A study published shortly before the actual introduction of milk quotas in 1984 concluded that, in theory, and for most commodities, a system of saleable quotas with within-quota production supported at a relatively high price (but with no support for above-quota production) could be effective in (a) reducing EC production of surplus commodities and (b) reducing FEOGA guarantee expenditure (Harvey, 1984). This study and its conclusions allowed for the dynamic effects of technical change on unit costs of production and profit-maximising levels of output. It was argued that productivity improvements implicit in technical change would be reflected in quota purchase prices. Harvey acknowledged the practical problems of implementing quota schemes, such as high administrative costs. He also recognised the particular difficulties of applying quotas to cereal production, such as the many alternative uses and market outlets available to producers. But he argued that in the EC these difficulties might be surmounted by switching from the current method of support to a deficiency payment system, combined with crop area quotas. The prospect of heavy fines for quota infringement plus exclusion from future support benefits, combined with spot checks, ought to be sufficient to ensure an adequate compliance rate.

Some of Harvey's ideas about the merits of quotas as an instrument of agricultural policy reappeared later in a modified form. A study of EC cereals policy published in 1986 by the Centre for Agricultural Strategy proposed a 'limited loan rates scheme' for cereals (Beard, 1986). The crux of this proposal was the introduction of a two-tier pricing scheme for cereals within an intervention framework. Every producer's eligibility for selling into intervention at a 'high' price would be limited by quota. The size of the quota would be uniform for all producers regardless of the scale of their cereals enterprise. Thus, the proposed scheme was deliberately biased in favour of 'small' cereal producers who might expect to sell the bulk or even the whole of their output at the 'high' price. In contrast, 'large' producers would have relatively little protection from intervention purchases and would therefore be obliged to sell most of their output on the open market. This idea was later taken up by the North American-based 'International Agricultural Trade Research Consortium' (IATRC) (of which David Harvey is a member) in formulating proposals for agricultural trade and policy reform in the GATT Uruguay Round (IATRC, 1988). The essence of the IATRC proposal was that the entitlement of individual producers to agricultural price support should be restricted by means of quotas called 'production entitlement guarantees' (PEGs).

A PEG is defined as a pre-specified limit on the quantity of production eligible to receive support. Deficiency payments (DPs) are normally advocated as the means of support. PEGs are administered at the level of the individual producer and marginal production in excess of the PEG attracts only the open market (or world) price. Consumers under a PEG scheme pay no more than the equivalent of the world producer price (after allowing for storage, processing and distribution).

Provided the aggregate PEG is set lower than the initial level of output, the scheme is clearly successful in reducing (a) total output and (b) total support costs. If the PEG is set to equate with domestic consumption, the support cost saving is effectively the saving derived from ceasing to subsidise exports. The PEG does not have to equate with domestic consumption: it could be set lower or higher. But setting it higher not only increases the costs of support, it also exacerbates the distortion of world trade.

Under a DP system covering total output, including exports, producers would have received the DP on export production in lieu of an explicit export subsidy. Under the CAP system of border protection an explicit export subsidy was paid. The adoption of a PEG system of farm income support in the EC would have entailed the partial or complete abandonment of border protection. Although switching from border protection to a PEG scheme would have clearly benefited taxpayers, and left domestic consumers unaffected under a DP system, producers would have stood to lose income, particularly on production for export. EC producers could therefore have been expected to oppose the substitution of PEG support for the present system of border protection and, if this strategy had failed, they would have continued to exert pressure for their PEGs to be as 'generous' as possible.

Various options suggest themselves for setting PEGs at the level of the individual producer. They could be related in some way to each individual's past production in a base period: or they could be uniform for all producers, regardless of past production, as under the 'limited loan rate' proposal. Most commentators were agreed that PEGs should be 'decoupled' from current production. Target groups of producers, such as small farmers in less-favoured or environmentally sensitive areas could, of course, be partially or wholly protected from the impact of the scheme on farm incomes.

As with true quota schemes, the efficiency of PEGs would be improved by (a) making them transferable amongst producers, preferably through an open market bidding system, and (b) by the government retaining a pool of PEGs for allocation to new entrants. The pool could be replenished by preemptive government repurchases of unused or unwanted PEGs.

Like other CAP reform proposals, the PEG scheme suffers from some major drawbacks. The major economic drawback is that like other schemes of producer price support, it would tend to distort domestic resource allocation by keeping sub-marginal producers in business who might otherwise be squeezed out by the forces of competition. The force of this objection to PEGs could be minimised by making them transferable by sale to the highest bidder, thus enabling sub-marginal producers to be bought out. Other drawbacks are political and administrative rather than strictly economic: these include (a) the budgetary implications of transferring the costs of (limited) farm income support from consumers to taxpayers; (b) the hostility of producers to the greater visibility of such transfers; (c) high costs of administration. However, in the long run, budget savings and the benefits of more open international agricultural trade, particularly through the abolition of export subsidies, might more than compensate for the short-run costs of these disadvantages.

The input quota is, in principle, an alternative supply control instrument to the output quota. In the context of CAP reform most interest has focused on land input restrictions, as exemplified by the 1968 Mansholt Plan proposal of a major withdrawal of land from agricultural production of any kind, and the more recent set-aside programme aimed at reducing the arable crops land input. But some interest has also been shown in the feasibility of applying fertiliser quotas in the EC as a supply control and budget stabilising instrument. Insofar as land and fertiliser, particularly nitrogen, are close substitutes in the production of most agricultural commodities, the exploration of this option makes economic sense.

The impact of a fertiliser quota on production obviously depends on the form and parameters of the relevant production function. Given a fixed land input, the critical relationship is between fertiliser input and crop yield. Time-series regression analysis of the relationship between cereal yields and nitrogen usage in the UK, 1966–85, pointed to a strong positive correlation between these two variables: but when the influence of a time trend reflecting technological growth, particularly in the breeding and adoption by farmers of higher-yielding varieties, was removed, a different picture emerged. The 'static' yield response to the nitrogen curve turned out to be relatively 'flat' over a wide range of application rates below actual usage. It follows that if the instrument of a fertiliser tax were adopted to reduce N usage, a very large tax would be needed to have an appreciable effect on production (Rickard, 1986). This suggests that an on-farm N quota would be a more efficient instrument than a tax as an instrument for reducing the yields of cereals and other crops in structural surplus: given the same yield reduction, the quota would certainly be less costly to producers in terms of income loss.

The case for restricting the usage of N fertilisers, whether by means of a tax or a quota, also includes potential environmental and natural resource conservation benefits. Excess nitrates in water supplies is already a problem in some areas of the UK, for example, and reducing N fertiliser consumption would contribute to the conservation of fossil fuels. However, the implementation of quota restrictions on N fertiliser usage would present complex and costly administrative problems. But fertiliser rationing schemes have been operated in the past (as in Britain during the Second World War). The crux of any rationing scheme would be the basis of allocation to individual producers.[15]

Environmental and ecological issues

Most critiques of the CAP have concentrated on the hidden income transfers implicit in the import levy/intervention/export refund system of price support, and the impossibility of realising the multiple agricultural policy objectives, as set out in Article 39 of the Treaty of Rome, with the single instrument of price policy. But a few reform proposals have started from the premise that, for social and environmental reasons, the prevention of an over-rapid decline in farm numbers and the size of the agricultural population are objectives of the CAP, jointly with other production and income objectives. One study of possible solutions to the EC's agricultural surplus problem concluded that for structural and institutional reasons, it is unrealistic for the Community to strive to have an internationally competitive agricultural sector: a more realistic objective is Community self-sufficiency at least in temperate and sub-tropical products (Weinschenk, 1987). But even under a regime of agricultural autarky or self-sufficiency the need to reduce aggregate production can still arise, as the Community's own experience demonstrates only too well. Weinschenk argues that given the necessity of reducing production, a choice of policy instruments exists between either the 'economic way', or the 'ecological way'. Taking the economic way implies the elimination of production in marginal regions through rigorous price reductions sufficient to achieve equilibrium of supply and demand on domestic markets. In contrast, the ecological way implies a general decrease in the intensity of land use through changing the price ratio between products and yield-increasing inputs, such as fertiliser, to achieve market equilibrium. On the basis of his own value judgement, Weinschenk argues strongly in favour of taking the ecological way, for social and environmental reasons. But the ecological way itself presents a choice of policy options. One option is to combine a general reduction of product prices with direct income payments differentiated on a regional basis to guarantee a basic agricultural income in all regions. A second option is to tax the usage of yield-increasing inputs especially N fertiliser. Weinschenk claims that compared with the product price reducing option, the fertiliser tax option is preferable for several reasons. First, it is likely to result in smaller farm income losses. Second, the budget costs are likely to be lower, presumably due to lower expenditure on direct income payments. Thirdly, the fertiliser tax would tend to induce ecologically desirable changes in farming practices, such as greater reliance on organic manures and widening of crop rotations. The main disadvantages of the fertiliser tax option include higher administrative costs and higher consumer prices.

Costs of the CAP
Much has been written about the 'costs of the CAP' and attempts have been made, by different analysts at different times, to quantify them empirically. However, the results of such studies have rarely been strictly comparable for two reasons. First, different analysts have used different techniques of estimation, as well as different base periods. Second, and more importantly, they have estimated the costs of the CAP in its present form, relative to different alternative policy scenarios. Thus, some analysts have assumed that without the CAP national agricultural policies in all the countries now comprising the EC, would maintain agricultural prices at much the same level as at present, though common

financing and Community preference would, of course, disappear. But this assumption is quite arbitrary and open to serious question. It is at least equally plausible to suppose that, under renationalisation of agricultural policy, different countries would choose to support agricultural prices at different levels, reflecting differences in domestic policy priorities, attitudes to trade and so on. Other analysts have based their estimates of the cost of the CAP on the 'first-best' alternative of zero support and free-trade. Despite its underlying economic rationale, this assumption can also be criticised for being out of touch with reality. However, although all such arbitrary and extreme assumptions are easy to criticise, there is no obvious solution to the problem of finding better or 'more realistic' policy scenarios. A large element of subjective judgement is inevitably involved.

Most CAP cost estimates have been concerned with income transfers of one or both of two kinds. First, there are the transfers from consumers and taxpayers to agricultural producers, either within individual member states or within the Community as a whole. Second, there are transfers between member states, arising from both net contributions to the agricultural budget and intra-Community agricultural trade at common prices.

Unsurprisingly, the results of studies of the first type indicate that, depending upon how much the alternative policy scenario reduces producer prices, consumers and taxpayers gain at the expense of producers. But when consumer and taxpayer gains are offset against the producer loss, the net gain/loss is affected by the net trading position of the country concerned. Because, *ceteris paribus*, net exporting countries produce relatively more than net importing countries, the former stand to lose relatively more from any common price reduction. Similarly, consumers and taxpayers in net importing countries stand to gain relatively more from price liberalisation than those in net exporting countries. Thus, for example, the results of a comparative static estimate of the costs of the CAP in 1980, relative to a 'free market' alternative policy scenario with all price support removed, indicated substantial potential consumer and taxpayer gains from liberalisation, coupled with large producer losses in all the EC(9) member states. A net welfare gain was indicated for the EC(9) as a whole as well as separately for Germany, France, Italy, Belgium/Luxembourg and the UK. But for the Netherlands, Ireland and Denmark – all net agricultural exporters – net welfare losses were indicated (Buckwell et al., 1982, table 10.1).

In studies of the second type, where the objective is to quantify CAP-induced income transfers between member states, it is useful to distinguish between budget and trade effects. Budgetary transfers are the result of member states' net contributions to the budget, accounted for mainly by the difference between import levy and tariff revenues (budget obligations) and the costs of intervention and export restitution (claims on the budget). Trade transfers result from intra-Community trade at a common price higher than the world price (Buckwell et al., 1982, chapters 3 and 10). For obvious reasons, both types of transfer tend to favour net exporting member states at the expense of net importers. However, their relative magnitudes and even their signs can vary between countries. Thus, the results of estimates made by the British Ministry of Agriculture, Fisheries and Food, relative to 1979, indicated for the UK a total CAP-induced outward transfer to the rest of the EC(9) of some £1110 million. Some £882 million, or nearly 80 per cent of the total, consisted of a budgetary transfer leaving only about 20 per cent to be accounted for by the trade effect. In contrast, virtually the whole of Italy's outward transfer of £700 million was attributed to the trade effect. At the other end of the scale, France captured the largest total inward transfer of some £850 million, of which trade transfers accounted for about 70 per cent. But the next largest total inward transfers, accruing to Denmark and the Netherlands respectively, were almost equally divided between budgetary and trade effects in both cases (House of Lords, 1981, as cited by Harris et al., 1983, table 14).

Attempts have also been made to quantify the costs and benefits of marginal adjustments to the CAP, for individual commodities, as well as in the aggregate (for example Buckwell et al., 1982, ch. 10). In the absence of agreement or a consensus on what constitutes the most appropriate alternative policy scenario, this is probably the more useful approach to the use of cost–benefit analysis as an aid to CAP reform.

Political and Institutional Barriers to CAP Reform

We referred in the first chapter of this book to alternative theories of the reasons for government intervention in the affairs of particular industries. Two main theories were outlined. First, the public interest theory which posits that government intervention in any part of the economy is simply a response to public demand for the correction of imperfections in the operation of the free market and other market failures. Specifically in the case of agriculture, the adjustment problems resulting from the decline in the relative importance of agriculture with economic growth, associated with the relative immobility of certain agricultural resources, particularly labour, has often been regarded as a market failure justifying government intervention to ease the burden of adjustment. However, the public interest theory is challenged by the economic theory of regulation which posits that government intervention is the result of political pressure by self-interested economic agents or groups. Specifically in the case of agriculture, producer interest groups tend to be stronger and better organised than organisations representing food consumers or taxpayers. Whereas farmers believe that their incomes are directly and critically dependent on the degree of protection they can obtain from the government, consumers and taxpayers are only marginally affected by food prices and the budget costs of agricultural support. Thus, according to the economic theory of regulation, government intervention in agriculture is largely explained by the success of the rent-seeking activity of farmers and their political allies in the input supply and food processing industries. In this section we briefly examine political and institutional barriers to CAP reform from the standpoint of the economic theory of regulation or public choice theory.

The EC's institutional framework and its effect on CAP decision making

The three institutions principally concerned with Community decisions on agricultural policy are the Commission, the Council and the European Parliament. The formal position is that policy initiatives can be taken only by the Commission which then makes proposals to the Council for decision. Although the European Parliament enjoys the prerogative of being informed and consulted by the Council about policy initiatives, the final decision-making process remains solely with the Council.

In the past the vast majority of decisions on agricultural policy have been taken by the Council of Agricultural Ministers, consisting of the ministers of agriculture of the national governments of the member states. However, on a few occasions when the agricultural ministers have been unable to reach a decision, or when decisions on agricultural policy have become enmeshed with decisions on other issues, unresolved problems have been passed up to the European Council, consisting of heads of state, for the impasse to be resolved. This occurred, for example, in February 1988 when the European Council took the final decision on the introduction of 'stabilisers' to place an absolute ceiling on FEOGA expenditure and the related policy initiatives of set-aside, direct income aids for low-income farmers and a new pre-pension scheme for farmers opting for early retirement. The Council is very susceptible to political pressure by agricultural producers. The ministers of agriculture who compose the Council are exposed to such pressure in their own countries, quite apart from the fact that in most countries agricultural ministries are strongly producer-orientated. In addition, the Council President meets directly with COPA (Comité des Organisations Professionelles Agricoles) the most powerful agricultural pressure group in Brussels, during the course of annual farm price reviews (Tracy, 1985).

Unlike the Council, the European Parliament is a directly elected body and, as such, it can take a more objective view of agricultural policy. Indeed, some MEPs have shown themselves to be especially sensitive to the interests of EC taxpayers (Nello, 1985). But the composition of the European Parliament's Agriculture Committee is different from that of the assembly as a whole. The Committee's membership is dominated by farmers and other politicians committed to promoting the interests of the farm lobby. However, since, like the European Parliament itself, the Agriculture Committee possesses virtually no real power, its views scarcely affect actual policy (Tracy, 1985).

As regards exposure to agricultural lobbying pressure, the Commission appears to be less exposed than the Council, but more so than the Parliament. The Commission is the main Community institution to which COPA, and all other pressure groups with an interest in agricultural policy including trade organisations, firms and individuals, are officially expected to convey their views. Such representations may be made either directly in Brussels or indirectly through national organisations with permanent channels of communication to the Commission.

Although proposals for agricultural policy initiatives are primarily the responsibility of the Commissioner for Agriculture and his cabinet, all major proposals are approved by the Commission as a whole before being sent to the Council for a decision. The Commissioner for Agriculture and his senior advisers are obviously in a strong position to influence policy. Most agriculture commissioners have been appointed to the post from agricultural backgrounds. Indeed, several previously held office as Minister of Agriculture in their own country and this background may have inclined them toward continuing to be especially protective of the interests of farmers after they arrived in Brussels. However, the Commission's attitude on agricultural policy is bound to be somewhat ambivalent. On the one hand, its performance on agriculture is bound to be at least partially judged by the degree of its success in reforming the CAP to reduce the costs of support and improve agricultural efficiency. On the other hand, in order to accomplish this task, the Commission depends on information garnered from grassroots sources both in Brussels and in the member states. However, since farm pressure groups tend to be better organised than other interest groups, including consumer organisations, the information upon which the Commission bases its agricultural policy recommendations tends to be producer-biased (Nello, 1985). However, producer bias is less marked in the Commission than in the Council (composed of national ministers of agriculture), so that had the Commission been given more power to determine policy rather than merely proposing it, faster progress with CAP reform would probably have been made. But, in fact, the Commission has tended to lose power *vis-à-vis* the Council. The reasons advanced for this relative loss of power include the Commission's lack of political legitimacy and direct political contacts in member states (Nello, 1985). It is also argued that the Council's adoption of the 'unanimity rule' for reaching all major decisions weakened the power of the Commission. The probability of a Commission proposal receiving the unanimous assent of the Council without substantial amendment is thought to be much lower than the probability of commanding a qualified majority vote (Tracy, 1985).

We now proceed to a more detailed consideration of the Council's decision-making procedure, and the effect this has on the quality of Council decisions.

Consequences for the CAP of the Council's 'unanimity rule'

The Treaty of Rome intended most Council decisions to be taken by a qualified (or weighted) majority vote (Art. 43). However, the Luxembourg Compromise of 1966 effectively put an end to this. The 'unanimity rule' then adopted meant that any member state could object to a Council decision on the ground that its national interest was endangered. In other words, individual member states were given the power of veto. The effect of replacing qualified majority voting with the unanimity rule is that, in practice, very few Council decisions are put to the vote. Instead, the discussion of issues and the modification of policy proposals continues until unanimity is reached. Compared with reaching decisions on the basis of a vote, reaching unanimity is obviously much more time-consuming. And the more controversial the issue the longer the time needed to reach a unanimous decision. The history of the CAP is replete with marathon sessions of the Council when Ministers have not only 'burnt the midnight oil' but even 'stopped the clock' when it has been impossible to reach a decision by a pre-set deadline.

However, time being valuable, ministers attending Council meetings adopt strategies to economise its use. Since under the unanimity rule every member state has the power of veto, each can expect to extract a special concession from the others as the price of agreeing to the complete 'package' (Petit, 1985). The 'special concession' is normally particularly advantageous to the member state concerned. Thus, what has been termed the 'time-constrained unanimity rule' (TCUR) which governs most major CAP decisions, protects national interests. It also provides a safeguard against defection from the Community. But the costs of reaching decisions in this way are very high. The granting of concessions raises commodity support price levels higher than they would otherwise be, thus exacerbating overproduction and increasing the costs of disposal, as well as increasing the budget costs of ad hoc measures to compensate for divergencies in farm incomes and transfer effects (Runge and von Witzke, 1987). The costs of using the TCUR to reach Council decisions are raised even more by the effect of the CAP principle of financial solidarity whereby individual member states bear only a proportion of the marginal cost of increased protection, according to their budget shares. This effect, which enables member states to partially externalise the costs of higher protection and national aids has been termed the 'shared restaurant bill effect'.[16]

In the final analysis, despite a tendency to expand the budget to meet rising expenditure, the overall budget constraint has been the dominant influence on Council decisions. However, since the Council of Agricultural Ministers is not directly responsible for the Community budget, even this has been only an indirect constraint. The application of the TCUR subject to the overall budget constraint has left little room for the pursuit of other objectives such as reducing the resource costs of the CAP or improving the competitiveness of European agriculture. Due to the influence of exogenous factors such as the supplies and prices of competing agricultural products in the rest of the world, and exchange rate fluctuations, ex post budget expenditure has frequently deviated considerably from the ex ante budget estimate. Thus, the overall budget constraint dominating Council decisions, particularly on prices, has from time to time been relaxed by unanticipated but favourable changes in exogenous variables. By temporarily relaxing budget pressures, such events have tended to reduce outside economic and political pressures on the Council of Ministers to undertake fundamental CAP reform.

Decision-making reform proposals

Various options have been proposed for overcoming political and institutional barriers to CAP reform. Some of these concern the process of decision making in the Council of Ministers; others involve partially transferring the responsibility for reaching decisions to other bodies.

Dealing first with reforming decision making in the Council, an obvious option is to abandon the unanimity rule in favour of a reversion to qualified majority voting. By removing individual member states' ability to block decisions by veto, this might speed up the decision-making process, as well as removing the necessity to grant expensive concessions in order to achieve unanimity. Moreover, the adoption of this option might be made more acceptable by offering some form of compensation to the 'losers' from the consequences of taking decisions by majority voting. Such compensation might include EC-financed direct income payments or even partial renationalisation of agricultural policy (Runge and von Witzke, 1987). However, regardless of any change in its decision procedures, the Council's decisions would continue to be influenced by the principle of financial solidarity, even though the joint restaurant bill effect might be somewhat diluted by majority voting. Moreover, removal of the power of veto would increase the risk of defection from the CAP, or even from the Community itself.

Another option for compelling the Council to undertake CAP reforms directed to curbing agricultural budget expenditure is to make the Council of Agricultural Ministers directly responsible for the budgetary consequences of its price decisions. By imposing a definite ceiling on the growth of expenditure on agriculture, the agricultural budget capping provision included in the 'stabiliser package' agreed at the February 1988 European Council Meeting appears to have been a move in this direction. The stabiliser measures which were simul-taneously agreed could be interpreted as being 'CAP reforms', though perhaps not of a very fundamental nature. However, it is significant that the February 1988 package was imposed on the Council of Agricultural Ministers by a summit meeting of heads of state.

If the power to make decisions about the CAP is to be partially or even fully transferred from the Council to another institution, the obvious choice lies between the Commission and the European Parliament. The case for giving more power to the Commission could be based on the argument that it possesses good technical qualifications to undertake fundamental CAP reform. Moreover, although the Commission is more directly exposed to agricultural lobbying pressure than the Council, its record suggests that it is less inclined to succumb to such pressures. It has been observed that the Commission's price recommendations have generally been lower than the Council's price decisions (Runge and von Witzke, 1987).

A powerful argument against giving more power to the Commission is that it lacks political legitimacy. Commissioners are not elected: they are nominated by the national governments of member states. More-over, it is argued that although they are appointed to serve the Community, and so take a 'Community view', in practice they see their role partly as that of safeguarding the interests of their country of origin (Tracy, 1985). Thus, giving more power to the Commission would not necessarily reduce the tendency for Community decisions to be dominated by considerations of national self-interest. Another contrary argument, based on the theory of bureaucracy (Downs, 1967), is that the Commission would be unlikely to adopt reforms which reduced its own power and influence, even though reforms having this effect might be desirable in the wider social interests of citizens of the Community.

A major argument in favour of giving increased power to the European Parliament to determine the future of the CAP is that, being directly elected, its political legitimacy is beyond question. Thus, as a long-term objective, the case for transferring power from the Council to the Parliament is very strong. But, due to the Parliament's lack of real decision-making power under the Treaty of Rome this is not a feasible option for the short term. A fundamental constitutional reform to give the European Parliament real political power is a pre-condition of achieving CAP reform via this route.

In sum, shifting the balance of power in decision making away from the Council of Ministers in favour of the European Parliament would in principle probably be conducive to more rapid reform of the CAP in favour of the interests of taxpayers and consumers. But the conversion of this principle into practice depends upon prior constitutional reform to which the governments of some member states might be opposed on 'nationalistic' grounds. Giving more power to the Commission, and abandoning the Council's unanimity rule in favour of majority voting, would tend to have the same, but a weaker, effect (Nello, 1984).

US POLICY 1973–85: INSTABILITY IN AN INTERNATIONAL SETTING

Introduction

The early 1970s ushered in a new economic environment for US agriculture (Schuh, 1981). The agricultural transformation process was virtually over and coping with the secular adjustment problem was largely a policy problem of the past, the 1950s and 1960s. However, new problems largely associated with instability were surfacing and were to dominate agricultural policy over the next decade. Importantly, US agriculture was integrated into the world agricultural economy and became closely related to the domestic non-farm economy. Shocks emanating from these sources were to have large repercussions on both the agricultural sector and the out-turn of agricultural policy.

The 1950s and 1960s had been a period of relative stability for US agriculture, albeit that it faced a secular adjustment process over those years. Domestic demand was relatively stable and fluctuations in export demand and domestic supply were absorbed by CCC stock changes and land retired from production via government programmes. Price supports insulated farmers from shifts in market forces. Macroeconomic policy largely affected agriculture via the labour market in terms of the extent of excess labour removed from farming.

In the late 1960s and early 1970s there was a change in agricultural policy toward less reliance on price supports and more reliance on the use of direct payments (deficiency payments). US market prices became aligned with world prices particularly after 1973 with the shift to floating exchange rates. Reserve stocks of grain were disposed of in the early 1970s removing a 'cushion' to the market. A rising proportion of production was sold abroad making agricultural prosperity more dependent upon the export markets. Part-time farming by small scale producers increased so that farm household income became dependent upon off-farm earnings as well as farm earnings. A high and rising proportion of non-farm inputs was used in agricultural production; increased capitalisation meant that agriculture was increasingly influenced by changes in interest rates and costs of production in input supplying sectors. Macroeconomic policy had a bigger effect on the farm economy than in the past by its impacts on the exchange rate, the labour market, the cost of credit and the overall rate of inflation.

In short, comparing the 1970s and early 1980s with the previous decades, the interface between the farm economy and the general economy broadened and the interaction between agricultural policy and macroeconomic policy deepened. In addition, there was increasing interdependence between US agricultural policy and farm policies pursued in other countries because of the effects of the latter on US export demand. Simplified schematic representations of these linkages are given in Figures 5.1 and 5.2.

General Economic Background

Vice President Gerald Ford succeeded Richard Nixon as President in the aftermath of the 1974 Watergate scandal. He remained in office until 1976 when the Democrat Jimmy Carter was elected President. Political leadership returned to the Republicans in 1980 with the elec-

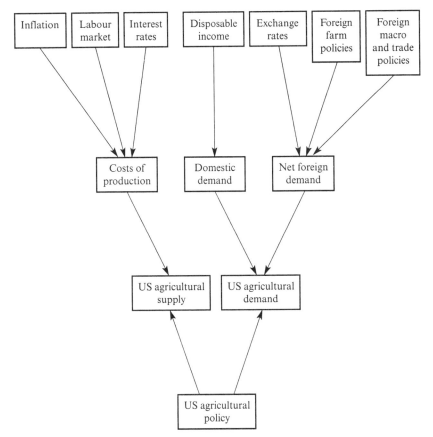

Figure 5.1   Linkages from the macroeconomy to agriculture

tion of Ronald Reagan who was subsequently re-elected for the period 1984–88.

Macroeconomic policy in the 1970s focused mainly on the problem of inflation. The economy boomed during 1971–73 under the encouragement of expansionary policies but inflation remained relatively low at around 4–5 per cent per annum until 1973. In that year food and raw material prices rose, and at the end of 1973 the first oil price shock disturbed the economy. Prices rose rapidly and inflation peaked at over 10 per cent during 1974–75. Monetary policy was restrictive post 1973 and inflation was less than 5 per cent per annum by 1976. However, after 1975 the economy grew rapidly and inflation reached 9 per cent per annum by 1978–79. A further stimulus to inflation was given by the second oil price shock in 1979. Inflation rose again in 1980–81 to over

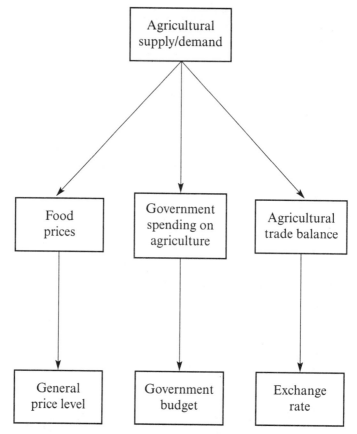

Figure 5.2   Linkages from agriculture to the macroeconomy

10 per cent. A new monetary policy was introduced in 1979 to combat inflation. The Federal Reserve Bank moved away from interest rate controls and set targets for the rate of money stock growth. Inflation fell dramatically between 1981 and 1983, and by 1983 the inflation rate was down to less than 5 per cent. Unemployment rose continuously between 1979 and 1982, peaking at over 10 per cent in 1982–83.

The Reagan administration altered the course of fiscal policy in 1981; its first year of office. There was a commitment to supply side economics with an emphasis on reducing taxes and the size of government. Fiscal policy in 1981, 1982 and 1983 embraced tax cuts particularly in personal income taxes. These tax cuts led to immediate rises in the Federal budget deficit. After 1969 the Federal budget was in deficit every year varying cyclically around a rising trend (low in a boom, high in a recession). The deficit as a percentage of GNP averaged 0.4 per cent in the 1950s, 0.8 per cent in the 1960s, 2.1 per cent in 1970–82, and over 6 per cent in 1983–4 (Dornbusch and Fischer, 1984, p. 500 and Stiglitz, 1986, p. 42). Nevertheless, the ratio of national debt (the result of current and past deficits) to GNP fell almost continuously over the period 1954–79 (from 58 per cent to 24 per cent). After 1979, the ratio was around 28 per cent (Dornbush and Fischer, 1984, p. 27) but rose in the early 1980s. Whilst President Reagan was successful in his objective of cutting taxes, he failed to secure a corresponding reduction in federal expenditure despite a stated commitment to balanced budgets. The Senate's concern over deficits and the administration's support for a balanced budget objective led Congress to pass the Gramm Rudman Act in 1985. The bill called for automatic reductions in expenditure when the deficit reaches a stated critical level with the goal of achieving a balanced budget by 1991. These automatic cuts were designed as disciplinary controls on the budget. If they fail the Gramm Rudman Act calls for across-the-board cuts in most areas of expenditures.

The 1970s and early 1980s saw sharp fluctuations in nominal and real interest rates. (Nominal interest rates tend to rise in periods of (expected) high inflation and fall in periods of (expected) low inflation.) However, comparisons of nominal interest rates and actual inflation rates indicate that real interest rates were frequently negative in the 1970s but were strongly positive in the early 1980s.

The real exchange rate of the dollar depreciated some 20 per cent over the period 1971–79 and then appreciated. It rose by some 60 per cent between 1980–85 but then depreciated by some 27 per cent in that year (from February). The US ran a trade deficit in the 1970s but generally had a surplus on the current balance, with earnings on US investments abroad being the main offsetting item. However, the trade deficit increased more than fivefold in the six years 1980–86, deteriorating from $25 billion to $148 billion. The current account moved from a surplus of $1.83 billion to a deficit of $141 billion over the same period. The deterioration in US trade occurred across a broad spectrum of commodities and with respect to most trading partners.

The appreciation of the dollar in the early 1980s was attributed to the rise in real US interest rates relative to rates abroad and induced capital inflows. The trade deficit was blamed on domestic demand growth after the recession of 1982 as well as the appreciation of the dollar. A further factor influencing the deficit was low growth in import demand in Western Europe, Japan and the LDCs. However, a root cause was the expansionary effect of the budget deficit on the non-tradeable sector. Demand for non-tradeables – in construction, services, defence and government – was increased relative to demand for tradeable goods and the burden of adjustment fell on exchange rate sensitive sectors. In addition, international financial markets were highly integrated in the 1980s, capital was mobile and dollar assets appeared secure and attractive. As interest rates rose in the US relative to foreign rates a massive capital inflow occurred pushing up the dollar. Macroeconomic policy characterised by tight monetary policy and lax fiscal policy tended also to raise interest rates and appreciate the dollar.

Trade Relations with the Soviet Union and China

Detente – the relaxation of political tensions – between the US and the USSR and China, and changing political priorities in the latter countries, led to an expansion of agricultural exports from the US. Prior to 1972, US agricultural trade with the Soviet Union was relatively unimportant (less than $10 million per annum). In the 1970s, Soviet leaders gave priority to increasing the quality of diets (especially increased meat consumption) enjoyed by their population. This, coupled with a succession of poor harvests, led to increases in agricultural imports. US agricultural exports to Russia, mainly of wheat and feed grains (mostly corn), expanded from $1 billion in 1973 to almost $2 billion in 1985.

US agricultural trade with China was subject to an embargo until 1971. The normalisation of relations between the US and China subsequently increased US exports. The major commodities exported were wheat and feed grains.

The US entered into grain agreements with Russia and China in 1975 and 1980 respectively. The objective of the agreements was to guarantee security of supply to the importer and to avoid market disruption for the exporter. The US–USSR agreement specified that the Soviet Union would purchase a minimum of 6 million tons of wheat and corn (in roughly equal proportions) each year between October 1976 and September 1981. Purchases in excess of 8 million tons could only be made after consultation with the US government. However, the agreement was disrupted by a US embargo placed on grain shipments to the USSR in January 1980 after Russia's invasion of Afghanistan in 1979. The embargo was in effect for fifteen months. Subsequently, a new US–USSR grain agreement was effected in July 1983. This agreement was intended to last for five years but the USSR reneged on contracts in 1984–85 and 1985–86. The US–China grain agreement was for a four year period from January 1981 providing for the export of 6–8 million tons of grain per annum to China. No subsequent agreement was negotiated.

Agricultural Legislation in the 1970s[17]

The Agriculture and Consumer Protection Act 1973 (duration 1974–77)

In the presidential election year of 1972, farm prices were rising as a result of strong export demand for grains and oilseeds (and products). The Nixon administration adopted the expansion of exports as 'the cornerstone of its farm policy' (Cochrane and Ryan, 1976, p. 64). The Republican platform pledged to intensify efforts to expand farm exports whilst controlling inflation, assisting farmers in bargaining for fair prices and exempting farm prices from price control. In order to achieve export expansion, the Flanigan Report of 1972 (see ibid., p. 65) recommended a move away from high price supports and the use of direct payment programmes, if required, to support farm incomes. Nixon was re-elected in 1972 and the export orientation of farm policy was confirmed in the shift to deficiency payments as the main instrument of farm income support with loan levels set at low levels in relation to the current market prices. Thus, the use of deficiency payments facilitated the integration of the US and world markets and US market prices would not be above world levels unless loan rates become operative via CCC support buying.

The Agriculture and Consumer Protection Act was passed in August 1973: it was an omnibus act to last for four years extending and amending the Agricultural Act of 1970 'for the purpose of assuring consumers of plentiful supplies of food and fibre at reasonable prices' (quoted in ibid., p. 172). The act was passed in a year of record farm commodity exports and sharply rising farm and food prices. Grain exports nearly doubled between 1972 and 1973 (for the year ending in September) and total agricultural exports were up by over 25 per cent. The main impetus had come from the expansion in foreign demand resulting from poor crops in Asia and the USSR and the change in Soviet food and trade policy. Government grain stocks were virtually liquidated and it appeared that demand would remain strong for a number of years. Strong export demand, rising farm prices and food price inflation made a shift in the orientation of farm policy inevitable.

The Secretary for Agriculture, Earl Butz, stated that the 1973 legislation represented 'an historic turning point in the philosophy of farm programs in the US' (USDA, 1984, p. 29). The act emphasised the expansion of production to respond to growing worldwide demand for food and fibre and to hold down price increases. This was in contrast to previous programmes used to curtail production of the major crops. It was argued that the increase in production would come about by market forces; agriculture would no longer be managed and directed by government. Nevertheless, it was to be provided with price and income safety nets in the form of minimum 'target' prices.

More specifically, the programmes for wheat, feed grains and cotton specified fixed target prices for 1974 and 1975. These prices were guaranteed to producers by deficiency payments provided by the government if market prices fell below targets. The deficiency payment was to be equal to the difference between the annual target price and the higher of the loan rate or the average market price received by farmers during the first five months of the marketing year (calendar year that the crop was planted for cotton). The payments would be on a farmer's allotment for the crop. As in the past, allotments were based on the acreage required to meet domestic and export demand and desired stock adjustments for each year (minimum allotments were established for cotton). Payment rates could not exceed the difference between target prices and non-recourse loans. Target prices for the 1976 and 1977 crop years were not linked to parity; rather they were to be the 1975 price adjusted for changes in production costs and growth in yield (on a three-year moving average basis). Loan rates for wheat and feed grains were to be varied between maximum and minimum limits at the Secretary's discretion but were in practice set at levels similar to previous years and well below 1973/4 market levels. Loan rates for cotton were based on 90 per cent of the average world price of US cotton for the previous three years.

Standby set-aside authority was retained for wheat, feed grains and cotton with provision from the 1970 Act. The Secretary was still directed to determine and apportion national acreage allotments for these crops. Compliance with cropland set-aside was a condition of eligibility for loans, purchases and payments.

In fact, between 1974 and 1977 (crop years), market prices were above target prices (except 1977 for wheat); no deficiency payments were made and neither were set-aside programmes required.

The 1973 Act further restricted the payment limitation for price support (defined simply as deficiency payments) for grain and cotton farmers to $20 000 (from $55 000) per individual farmer. It also introduced the concept of a disaster payment for grain and cotton farmers: a direct payment to cover losses due to natural causes which either prevented the crop being planted or resulted in abnormally low yields. The payment rate was a percentage of the target price. The disaster payments programme was to prove costly, partly because it encouraged production on marginal land. It was replaced by the all-risk crop insurance programme introduced in the Federal Crop Insurance Act of 1981.

Four other aspects of note of the 1973 Act were as follows. First, PL480 was extended for another four years despite the lack of CCC inventories. Secondly, as in previous acts since 1949, the milk support price was to be at a level between 75 and 90 per cent of parity except that until 1975 it was to be set at 80 per cent of parity. The instrument of support was support buying as in the past. Thirdly, soybean production was encouraged by providing farmers the option of planting soybeans on allotted acreages of basic crops to maintain their allotment history. Fourthly, the Food Stamp Act of 1964 was extended and eligibility for food stamps was expanded.

Immediate professional commentary on the 1973 Act was generally favourable. The major critique was that undue reliance was placed on market forces and private stockholding to stabilise prices.[18] For example, Tweeten and Plaxico (1974, p. 364) stated that 'the ... Act has much to recommend it ... we detect consensus even amongst economists by and large toward a program of low price supports, flexibility and market orientation not unlike the provisions of the act'. They further stated that 'a most notable feature of the Act is its flexibility, with management of set aside and other features largely at the direction of the Secretary of Agriculture'. The central point of the paper by Tweeten and Plaxico was that although US agriculture had the capacity to meet anticipated future demands, 'the balances are shaky and veil the problems of accommodating farm policy to the need for stability in an inherently unstable world' (ibid., p. 364). This was in contrast to the 1960–72 period when the agricultural economy had 5 per cent excess capacity. After 1973, there was a propensity for instability in the absence of excess capacity.

Cochrane (1974) commented that 'although I am of the opinion that the 1973 Act may be the best farm bill ever passed it fails the flexibility test with regard to loan rates and target prices since it projects them four years into the future at fixed levels' (ibid., p. 992). In addition, he criticised the Act for not including an explicit reserve stock programme. Zero reserve stocks were being coupled with an uncertain future as to shortage (rocketing prices) or glut (serious farm depression). Cochrane argued that if the US were to reap the advantages of being a major exporter it required a policy which would enable it to sustain and increase its export sales whilst protecting itself from adverse unpredictable worldwide market forces. 'The cornerstone of this policy must be an effective reserve stock program' (ibid., p. 993). This would guarantee a reasonably stable domestic farm price level (for example varying between the loan rate and the target price).

The Food and Agriculture Act 1977 (duration 1978–81)

Background   The mid-1970s were good years for American farmers. Export demand expanded rapidly, commodity prices boomed in 1973–75 and net farm income reached historically high levels in the years 1973 to 1976. Direct Federal payments to agriculture were at low levels; the 1974 direct budgetary outlays were the lowest in current dollars since 1955. However, prices were declining in 1975 from their peak levels. In that year, Congress introduced a bill to raise target and loan rates, but this was vetoed by President Ford in response to consumer concern about inflation. In 1976 and 1977, the outlook for US agriculture was uncertain with prices and net farm income dropping. The farm sector was viewed favourably by policy makers for its contribution to the balance of trade; for example, in 1976 an agricultural trade surplus outweighed a non-agricultural trade deficit. However, the greater dependence of the farm sector upon export demand implied increased price and income instability.

Thus, the policy background of 1976 and 1977 saw uncertainty about future farm prices and incomes, including some signs that farm incomes would be depressed relative to non-farm incomes and recognition of agriculture's contribution to the balance of trade. In addition, the policy agenda was being increasingly shaped by urban interests connected with the availability, cost and quality of food with particular attention being focused on, firstly ensuring adequate nutrition of low income households and, secondly, stability of food prices.

In 1976, an immediate task for the newly elected President Carter, his Secretary of Agriculture, Bergland, and the new Congress was to prepare the ground for an Agricultural Act to replace that passed in 1973. The 1973 Agriculture and Consumer Protection Act was due to expire on 31 December 1977 with reversion to the provisions of the 1949 Act if no new Act was forthcoming. Proposals in early 1977 were made by the Administration, the Senate and the House. The Carter administration proposed a farmer owned reserve (FOR) to control price fluctuations, price supports that could be adjusted downwards to world levels and replacement of acreage allotments by a concept of current plantings that reflected actual plantings in the 1970s. The Senate wished to set loan rates and target prices much higher than the administration in response to concerns about falling farm income. Urban spokesmen in the House 'wanted a reformed food program for the poor' (Spitze, 1978, p. 228). A compromise was achieved in a Senate–House Conference in August 1977 and was signed as the Food and Agriculture Act by President Carter on 29 September 1977 to be effective until December 1981.

Details The main features of the act are set out in the Appendix to this chapter. The act continued the dual system of target prices and loan rates for the major traded crops. Target prices for 1977 were raised above those specified by the 1973 Act (except for cotton). Target prices for wheat, feed grains and cotton were specified at higher levels for 1978 and for 1979–81 'were to be adjusted to reflect any change in the moving 2 year average of variable costs, machinery ownership and general farm overhead costs' (USDA, 1984, p. 32). Spitze (1978, p. 231) commented that the 'compromise' target prices were substantially higher than those of the 1973 Act but generally reflected cost increases since 1972. The act extended the mandatory loan and purchase provisions to include soybeans for the first time.

The farmer owned reserve (FOR) was the main innovation of the act and was intended to reduce instability in grain markets. The FOR was a long-term storage programme and left control of stocks in the hands of farmers and allowed them to gain from a rise in market price. This was in contrast to CCC loan operations whence farmers passing control of stocks to the CCC had no opportunity to realise any gain if the value of stocks rose. The FOR was also flexible since farmer redemption of loans was discouraged by penalty when prices were less than 1.4 per cent of the loan and forced when prices reached 1.75 per cent of the loan rate.

Commentary Spitze (1978, p. 225) commented that 'the Food and Agriculture Act of 1977 is not a new imaginative policy, nor is it an old rerun. Rather, the Act signals a continued evolution of public price and income policy within the US'. In particular, he saw it as a merger of agricultural and food policy concerns. He believed the act permitted considerable flexibility via production control and the FOR enhancing stability. However, because floor prices were edged upwards, this would set the lower bound to farm incomes at around 70–80 per cent of non-farm incomes. He thought the strengthened prices and production controls would marginally reduce trade. However, treasury transfers to producers and aid recipients (domestic and foreign) were likely to be substantial.

D. Gale Johnson (1978) commented on the cost of production formula for determining target prices. Grain target prices in the 1977 Act were 'set (approximately) equal to average national costs of production including a return on land of 4%. In terms of changes in the target prices for 1979 through 1981, the target price is supposed to be changed in accordance with an unduly complicated formula for changes in variable production costs per unit of output' (ibid., p. 790). He believed the return to land to be around 3.5 per cent, so that the 4 per cent figure would inflate future target prices as well as changes in variable costs. Relative prices were out of line: wheat was well above its market price whilst the target price for corn was close to its market price. Johnson also discussed the FOR. He argued that substantial quantities would be put into the FOR because storage payments were liberal and the real interest cost negative. Moreover, the loans being 3–5 years would mean that current loans would extend beyond the 1980 presidential election. However, his main point was that through the FOR the US was once again indicating willingness to accept the role of residual supplier and other exporters were likely to reduce stocks as a consequence.

Events 1978–80   Between 1978 and 1980 prices for the major, supported commodities recovered, and exports continued to expand. In January 1980, President Carter imposed a partial suspension of agricultural exports to the USSR in response to the invasion of Afghanistan. To prevent the action affecting farmers adversely, loan rates were raised for wheat and corn, release and call rates were raised for grain in the FOR and the FOR was opened to all farmers. Loan rates were raised again later in the year. Despite the embargo, agricultural exports actually rose during 1980. Farm income was adversely affected in 1980 by continuing high inflation in the price of inputs and a sharp rise in interest rates. Drought in the summer of 1980 severely reduced yields for feed grains, cotton and peanuts. Total net farm income dropped by one-third (compared to the previous year). The Federal Crop Insurance Act 1980 brought in an expanded Federal crop insurance programme with subsidised payments.

Commentary on the Period 1973–81

The US farm economy experienced almost unprecedented growth and prosperity in the 1970s. Aggregate output volume increased at an annual average rate of nearly 3 per cent between 1973–79 (Ball, 1985, p. 485) and gross farm income surged in the early 1970s (particularly 1973 and 1974) and remained high in most of the subsequent years in real terms (Table 5.13). A major contributing factor was the expansion of exports which more than doubled in real terms between 1970 and 1973 and then remained high for the rest of the decade (Table 5.10). The value of agricultural exports as a proportion of gross farm income increased from around 12 per cent in 1970 to over 25 per cent in 1980. Major US field crops constituted the major proportion of exports, particularly

Table 5.10   US agricultural exports and the exchange rate, 1970–85

Year	Real value of US agricultural exports $billion (1980 dollars)	Per cent change in trade weighted dollar		Per cent change in trade weighted (agricultural trade) dollar	
		Nominal	Real	Nominal	Real
1970	14.9	–	–	–	–
1971	14.8	–2.5	–3.6	–2.6	–3.1
1972	17.4	–7.2	–8.8	–6.0	–7.9
1973	30.5	–8.3	–10.4	–6.6	–9.3
1974	34.8	2.5	–1.0	1.9	–4.4
1975	31.7	–1.0	–3.6	1.5	–2.8
1976	31.5	5.2	1.6	6.9	1.4
1977	30.3	–0.5	–3.3	2.8	–3.9
1978	35.0	–8.6	–8.1	–3.5	–7.0
1979	33.7	–2.1	1.0	4.0	1.4
1980	41.2	0.2	2.5	10.6	2.2
1981	39.5	12.6	13.4	24.7	9.9
1982	31.4	11.7	9.5	36.5	9.1
1983	29.8	5.4	3.1	88.3	4.6
1984	30.0	–	–	–	–
1985	22.4	–	–	–	–

Sources: USDA, *Agricultural Statistics* (annual); IMF, *Financial Statistics* (annual); Paarlberg et al. (1984).

grains, oilseeds and oilseed products (in aggregate, around 66 per cent of total agricultural exports in 1980). Producers of these crops became more dependent upon export markets. For 1976–80, exports provided over half the cash receipts for wheat and rice, around 40 per cent of cash receipts for feed grains and nearly one half of cash receipts for soybeans.

The agricultural trade balance improved significantly in the 1970s whilst the overall trade balance deteriorated. By the end of the 1970s the agricultural trade balance was around $20 billion whilst the overall trade balance was in deficit at around minus $27 billion. Agricultural exports accounted for around 20 per cent of total US exports in the mid to late 1970s.

The growth in US exports was partly accounted for by the increase in world agricultural trade in the 1970s and partly by a rising share of world exports accounted for by the US. The most rapid expansion in US exports was in feed grains and soybeans but there was also a substantial increase in foreign wheat sales. By the late 1970s the US was the dominant exporter in the grains and soybeans markets. In the mid- to late 1970s, US market share of world exports was over 40 per cent for wheat, around 60 per cent for feed grains and around 80–90 per cent for soybeans.

The increase in the real value of US farm exports was facilitated by the depreciation of the dollar in the 1970s. As the value of the dollar fell, the volume and price (in dollars) of exports rose. Export expansion was also aided by detente, which opened up trade with the Eastern bloc and by the alignment of price supports for grains and oilseeds around world levels.

The increased dependence of the US farm economy on exports implied increased instability since external shocks had more influence on demand. This instability was enhanced by the nature of the world markets for grains and oilseeds. The import demand of the centrally-planned economies was determined mainly by political factors rather than market mechanisms. In addition, import demand in many developed countries was impeded by barriers to trade and was insulated from world price movements.

Policy changes had given some protection against demand instability. Thus, the target price/deficiency payment system gave some protection against low prices to crop producers but did not insulate consumers and livestock producers from fluctuating prices. The FOR was introduced in order to dampen volatility in grain prices and was by intention a national reserve programme. The FOR tended to raise prices in surplus periods and depress prices in shortage years. However, there were political pressures for the FOR to be used as an income support mechanism (with the release price above long-run market equilibrium) rather than a stabilisation mechanism.

The export boom led to a significant reduction in both the taxpayer costs of support and the use of set-aside (Table 5.11). In principle, grain crops were supported by the Target Price/Deficiency Payment System and soybeans by a loan and purchase programme. However, for most of the crop years 1974–75 to 1980–81, market prices were above target prices for grains[19] and in every year above loan rates for soybeans. But loan rates for wheat, corn and soybeans and the target price for wheat were all substantially increased in the late 1970s, in both nominal and real terms. Whilst loan rates for soybeans were still well below market prices, loan rates for grains approached market prices and encouraged

Table 5.11 Government intervention into US agriculture: Federal Government expenditure and land idled, 1970–85

Fiscal year[a]	Government $billion (current dollars)	Expenditure $billion (constant 1980 dollars)	Land idled[b] under government programmes (million acres)
1970	4.6	9.4	57
1971	3.7	7.1	37
1972	5.1	9.4	62
1973	4.1	7.1	19
1974	1.5	2.4	2
1975	0.8	1.2	–
1976	1.6	2.2	–
1977	4.5	5.8	–
1978	6.6	7.9	18
1979	4.9	5.3	13
1980	7.4	7.4	–
1981	9.8	8.9	–
1982	14.3	12.3	11
1983	21.3	17.6	78
1984	11.9	9.5	27
1985	23.8	18.4	34

Notes
a Ending in year shown. Fiscal year 1 July–30 June until 1976; 1 October–30 September after 1976.
b Acreage idled in calendar year in which fiscal year ends.

Sources: Statistical Abstract of the US (annual); IMF, *Financial Statistics* (annual).

storage. Higher target prices for wheat provided an incentive for the expansion of wheat area. There was a tendency toward the end of the period for grains output to be encouraged beyond the amount that markets would absorb.

Excess capacity built up in the dairy sector in the late 1970s under the stimulus of increased price supports. From 1973 to 1979 (except 1977) net removals of milk from the market by the USDA was a low proportion (around 1–2 per cent) of milk deliveries, but by 1980–81 the proportion was approaching 10 per cent with associated heavy budgetary expenditures.

In review, after 1972, market prices for crops were generally above loan rates and acreage set-aside for supply control was little used in the face of the export boom. No significant deficiency payments were made before 1977. The crop sector operated in a virtually free and strong market during the mid-70s. During the late 1970s, supports began to operate as price floors and deficiency and diversion payments were made as markets began to stabilise and support levels were increased. Government intervention into livestock product markets was confined to dairy where again effects were only significant in the late 1970s. However, the crop programmes affected livestock feed costs and the incomes of livestock producers. High grain prices had adverse effects on beef cattle returns whilst hog returns varied considerably but average returns were not high (Ray et al., 1982).

In general, American farmers prospered in the 1970s. The average income (excluding capital gains) of specialist farm operators' families was below the average non-farm family incomes from the 1930s to 1970 but was well above in the 1970s, particularly from 1973 to 1979 (Langley et al., 1985, p. 37). It then declined falling below the non-farm average in 1981. Some indication of the prosperity of the US farm sector is given in Table 5.13 by looking at data on real income from farm assets and capital gains on real estate. In the 1970s, capital gains were positive and at least as great as net farm income for the majority of years (Harrington and Manchester, 1985, p. 40). For the average farm, aggregate assets nearly quadrupled in nominal terms between 1970 and 1980 but real growth was about 67 per cent (ibid., p. 38). The debt-to-asset ratio declined and the farm sector entered the 1980s in robust financial condition. On 1 January 1980 the debt-to-asset ratio was 16 per cent for the farm sector (Tweeten, 1985, p. 83). Debt per dollar of assets was comparatively low over the 1970s (ibid., p. 87).

Most farm assets – around 70 per cent – are in the form of real estate. There was a farmland boom in the 1970s with land prices rising significantly (Table 5.12). This increase in farm wealth was not created by government but by the rapid growth in exports. Melichar (1984, p. 17) provides an apposite comment:

> Initially, enormous gains in earnings of crop producers resulted from market forces propelled by foreign drought and the US drought of 1974, a drop in the exchange value of the dollar and rising incomes around the world. Land prices responded both to ongoing gains in profitability and to strong expectations of continued future gains.

From 1977 onwards, price intervention supported a further rise in land prices. But, as will be seen later, continued growth in real land prices

Table 5.12   US real farm income and land prices, 1970–85

Year	Gross farm income $billion (1980 dollars)	Net farm income $billion (1980 dollars)	Capital gains on farm real estate $billion (1980 dollars	Income from assets $billion (1980 dollars)	Total return from assets* $billion (1980 dollars)	Real land price $per acre (1980 dollars)
1970	120	29	−1	10	7	400
1971	119	29	15	11	29	390
1972	132	36	33	21	67	405
1973	171	59	59	45	118	424
1974	156	43	25	30	29	479
1975	146	37	50	23	76	493
1976	141	28	74	13	88	544
1977	139	26	35	12	46	607
1978	153	33	57	22	97	632
1979	164	34	35	25	64	682
1980	150	20	−2	12	4	737
1981	151	27	−53	21	−52	747
1982	139	21	−64	12	−54	706
1983	124	12	−2	17	20	651
1984	138	27	n.a.	n.a.	n.a.	622
1985	n.a.	n.a.	n.a.	n.a.	n.a.	525

Note: * Total return from assets is not equal to the sum of capital gains on real estate plus income from assets largely because of variation in the asset value of livestock.

Sources: Just and Miranowski (1988); Melichar (1984); USDA *Agricultural Statistics* (annual).

was unsustainable once the export boom was over: there was a collapse in land prices in the 1980s.

The Agriculture and Food Act of 1981 (duration 1982–85)[20]

Background to the 1981 Act
Major influences on the shape of the 1981 Act included a desire by the government to contain and reduce spending on agriculture, a perception amongst many analysts that commodity markets in the 1980s would be tight (for example Schnittker, 1981) and an inflationary psychology

affecting business and the land market. The 'scarcity syndrome' (Paarlberg, 1982) had particular impact on policy making: there was considerable optimism as regards farm exports and an expectation of rising commodity prices.[21]

The Reagan administration was inaugurated in January 1981 with John R. Block as Secretary for Agriculture. Explicit economic policy objectives were '(a) reductions in federal spending and programs (b) a balanced budget (c) increased defence spending and (d) tax reform' (Infranger et al., 1983, p. 2). Associated objectives for farm policy were '(a) reduction of the role of government in agriculture (b) continued emphasis on agricultural exports and on productivity in the agricultural sector and (c) pursuit of the above objectives at the least possible cost to the government whilst maintaining maximum program flexibility' (ibid., p. 2). The budgetary implications of farm policy were paramount; farm policy was to be subject to budgetary constraints.

Changes in the legislature included a Republican controlled Senate with Republican chairmanship of the Agricultural and Budget Committees (Senators Helm and Dominici respectively). The Republican controlled Senate worked with a Republican administration to reduce government expenditures and legislate for massive three-year tax cuts. Budget reductions of $35.2 billion for the fiscal year 1982 were accepted by Congress before farm legislation came to the floor of the House or the Senate.

Lesher (1985, p. 45), (at that time Assistant Secretary for Economics, USDA) stated that:

> At the time the 1981 farm bill was formulated, the main concern was that world food needs would outpace production. Many believed – inside and outside of government – that the agricultural issue of the 1980s was going to be how to produce enough for a hungry world rather than how to deal with surpluses. Many believed that the US was the country that possessed the most potential for expanding food production in order to meet world needs. (ibid., p. 45)

However, whilst there was optimism about exports 'there was great concern over inflation and rising production costs. Inflation was running at double digit rates, the prime interest rate was around 20 per cent and inflationary psychology was influencing all business decisions' (ibid.).

Secretary Block brought out a farm bill in March 1981 in line with the objectives of reducing the role of and spending by government on agriculture and relying on exports for farm income. However, the enactment of the farm bill was a protracted affair and a compromise version was not signed by President Reagan until December 1981.

Whilst the agricultural committees were under severe pressure to reduce spending, they were also subject to lobbying from farm groups to provide greater income protection. 'The farm sector performed worse than expected in 1981 with prices of most supported crops dropping well below 1980 levels' (USDA, 1984, p. 37). Moreover, the grain embargo was not lifted until April, just before the Senate Agricultural Committee completed work on the farm bill.

The Block farm bill proposal endorsed the basic 1977 framework but eliminated target prices/deficiency payments, reduced dairy supports to 70 per cent of parity, suspended rice and peanut allotment acreages, cut back on the food stamp programme, replaced release and call prices in the FOR by a single trigger price and gave the Secretary more discretion to determine loan rate levels. The House and Senate agricultural committees 'reported out' farm bills in May. The House bill was a continuation of the 1977 Act: it included target prices/deficiency payments, continued authority for disaster payments and set-asides, a new sugar programme, revision of the trigger mechanism in the FOR, minimum dairy price supports at 75 per cent of parity and revision of a number of the food stamp items. The Senate bill was closer to the administration's proposals but refused to do away with target prices, disaster payments and peanut acreage allotments. Both bills were well over the budget limits. 'Floor action' in both House and Senate was taken to reduce the cost of the bills, but discussion was protracted and the Senate–House conference did not begin until 5 November 1981 (the 1977 Act expired on 30 September 1981). Final agreement was not reached until 8 December 1981. The major issues were the levels of crop loan rates, specific levels for dairy supports and the sugar title in the House bill.

The major difficulties in conference were Senate objections to the programme cost of House legislation and House objections to inadequate prices in the Senate legislation. Conference agreed to final target prices below the House proposals in order to minimise budget costs (it was estimated, for example, that each 1 per cent reduction in wheat prices resulted in budget cost reductions of $20m). The tie between target prices and cost of production was eliminated and target prices were set for 1982–85 with annual increases at 3–5 per cent on the assumption that high inflation would continue. It was believed that no deficiency payments would be necessary at the mandated target prices. Minimum dairy price supports were established without regard to parity. Acreage allotments for peanuts were suspended through 1985 and abolished for rice, allowing these crops to be grown by all farmers. The final conference bill was similar to the Senate version and was only passed in the House by two votes; 'it was perceived by many that it provided too little to farmers' (Lesher, op. cit., p. 45). However, in general it appeared a workable compromise between the administration's concern to keep down support costs and congressional concerns over farm income. According to USDA (1984) 'it was a less expensive version of the 1977 bill'.

The main provisions of the act are set out in the Appendix to this chapter. The main feature of the act was the establishment of a link between target prices and forecast inflation over the duration of the act. Specifically, minimum target prices were set to increase at 3–5 per cent per annum. In addition, loan rates were set at high levels compared to previous years.

The 1981 Act and subsequent events[22]

Events in 1982 were rather different to the expectations built into the framing of the 1981 Act. Production was high for grain and other crops as a result of good weather, but worldwide recession and a strong dollar caused exports to decline for the first time in eight years. Prices fell, grain carry-overs were at high levels and total net farm income in real terms fell to its lowest level since 1933. Farm income per farm was at its lowest level since the mid-1960s. Loan delinquencies grew; farm land prices levelled off after tripling over the past ten years. There was a sharp increase in government payments.

ARPs (that is short-term set-aside) of 10 per cent for feed grains and 15 per cent for wheat, cotton and rice were announced by Secretary Block for the 1981 crops, but record crops were harvested. Larger ARPs of 20 per cent for wheat and rice and 15 per cent for corn were announced for the 1983 crops. An export promotion programme was instituted with $175m for 1982 and reaching $190m in 1985. Loan rates were raised in 1983 for wheat and corn.

A payment in kind (PIK) programme was announced in January 1983 with the objectives of reducing production, cutting CCC stock levels and lowering government budgetary outlays. Farmers were to be paid not to produce with payments in the form of government held commodities. The PIK programme applied to wheat, feed grains, rice and upland cotton. Farmers had to set land aside to participate in price supports. They also had the option of diverting between 10–30 per cent more land from payment crops in return for PIK payments. In addition, farmers could bid to remove their whole base acreage from production. Payments were set at 80 per cent of normal yield for all crops except wheat (95 per cent). Participation was high. Eighty-two million acres were pledged to diversion under ARP and the PIK programmes; this represented over a third of land normally planted to the PIK crops. It was the largest amount of land ever taken out of production in one year.

1983 saw the worst drought since the 1930s. CCC stocks of wheat and cotton were not large enough to pay PIK farmers and grain was used from the FOR. Prices rose, participating farmers did well but those in drought areas who did not participate in PIK suffered heavy losses. The PIK programme was expensive: $9 billion in commodities was paid to farmers.

Dairy price supports were frozen for 1983 and 1984 at their 1982 levels to reduce surpluses and cut budget costs. Modest legislative changes were in the 1983 Dairy and Tobacco Adjustment Act which reduced support prices and provided for diversion payments for production control. Attempts to reduce the cost of price supports continued in 1984 with the Agricultural Programs Adjustment Act 1984 (signed in April). This prevented the automatic target price increases scheduled in the 1981 Act from being effected. ARPs continued through 1984 and 1985; there was a 20 per cent ARP with a 10 per cent paid diversion. There was a 10–20 per cent PIK programme for wheat in 1984 with payment at 85 per cent of normal yield.

Target prices for feed grains, upland cotton and rice were frozen at 1984 levels for 1985. For 1985, feed grains were subject to an ARP of 5–20 per cent if carryovers were expected to be over 1.1 billion bushels. Cotton and rice acreages were also to be reduced if carryover reached trigger levels.

Evaluation with hindsight

Lesher (1985) suggests that the 1981 Act appeared 'workable' at the time it was framed; in just over a year it had become unworkable. The rigid price supports impeded exports under competitive market conditions. The target price provisions were viewed as providing moderate income support but turned out to be very high. Export volume turned down from 1981 to 1984 with the world recession, LDC debt problems and the rise in the dollar. The record harvests of 1981 and 1982 coincided with slack demand and 'resulted in the largest surpluses in history' (ibid., p. 47). These surpluses overhung the market until 1983. The PIK programme was a temporary measure to deal with the record surpluses. 'In short, the administration struggled with farm legislation that was designed for an economic environment that never materialised' (ibid., p. 48).

The general economic environment for agriculture deteriorated considerably in the period 1981–85, mainly because of policies and events in the trade and macroeconomic areas. The rising value of the dollar, increasing world agricultural production, growing protection in developed country agriculture and declining demand by food deficit countries all contributed to a difficult export position and slack markets for farm products. The high interest rates created cash flow problems for farmers. The end of the agricultural boom had led to a collapse in farm asset values. The rising budget deficit limited the extent of additional government intervention. The economic conditions surrounding agriculture were '(a) declining agricultural exports and worsening relations with our trading partners; (b) declining commodity prices and farm incomes and continued high real interest rates to which the capital intensive farm sector is highly sensitive; (c) three years of declining farm asset values which, with the reduced cash flow, have seriously eroded the financial position of many farm firms; (d) extraordinarily high farm programme costs in a time of serious financial concern' (Penn, 1984, p. 572).

Table 5.13 indicates changes in the economic environment facing agriculture between 1979–80 when the 1981 Act was being framed and 1983–84. The decline in export performance was mirrored by a corresponding deterioration in the agricultural trade balance[23] and was of particular importance given the export dependence of the US farm sector. For example, in 1984 US farmers exported 55 per cent of wheat output, 25 per cent of corn output, 32 per cent of soybean output and 48 per cent of cotton output. 'About one of every three crop acres produced for the export market' (Drabenstott, 1985, p. 4). The fall in US agricultural exports was largely associated with a loss in market

Table 5.13   Changes in the economic environment facing US agriculture between 1979–80 and 1983–84

Year	Agricultural exports	Farm prices received	Total farm interest costs	Total net farm income	Farm price and income programme costs
	$billion (1982$)	(1982$, 1977 = 100)	$billion (1982$)	$billion (1982$)	$billion (1982$)
1979–80	44.2	161.8	17.8	31.5	3.9
1983–84	36.0	130.2	20.1	23.4	12.3
% change	−18.5	−19.5	+12.6	−26.0	+219.0

Source: Spitze (1987).

share in fairly static world markets between 1980 and 1984. Comparing 1984 with 1980, the US share of world exports fell from around 50 per cent to 40 per cent for all grains, 59 per cent to 50 per cent for coarse grains, 41 per cent to 34 per cent for wheat and 83 per cent to 77 per cent for soybeans. The major factors were the real appreciation of the dollar in the first half of the 1980s and the high and inflexible levels at which loan rates were set. The rise in the dollar had increased US export prices, choked off demand and made other exporters more competitive. Higher prices increased incentives for production expansion by other exporters. US surpluses went into stocks given inflexible price supports via loan rates and the FOR. These supports also provided a floor to the world market. The corollary of declining exports and inflexible supports was rising budgetary costs and considerable idling of land.

The ending of the export boom in 1981–82 also led to a decline in farm income and an incidence of financial stress (an inability to meet cash flow commitments) in the early 1980s for many farmers. A major factor was rising nominal and real interest rates. Interest payments increased as a proportion of production expenses which led to a rise in downside risk. Financial stress in 1981–83 began with lower farm incomes but was exacerbated by increased debt service requirement stemming from the higher interest rates and a decline in asset values which impaired borrowing (Boehlje and Eidman, 1983). As an indicator of the financial crisis, the number of farm operators discontinuing operations between June 1981 and June 1982 was 20 per cent higher than normal: these probably being new entrants and other farmers who expanded rapidly during the 1970s via extensive use of debt (ibid.).

Real net farm income bottomed out in 1983 (see Table 5.12): mid-1983 was a turning point in the financial situation for agriculture. Inflation had abated, interest rates had declined, price supports and deficiency payments had increased and the PIK programme had increased expectations about future farm income (Barry and Lee, 1983). Nevertheless, real farm income was lower in the early to mid-1980s than in the 1970s (see Table 5.12). Serious debt problems persisted into 1984 with about 20 per cent of commercial farmers having a negative cash flow and about 9 per cent having a serious debt problem (Drabenstott, 1985).

Farm asset values declined considerably in the early 1980s. Real (nominal) farmland values peaked in 1981 (1982) and declined by about 20 per cent in the period to 1984.

Overall, the US farm economy faced a difficult period in the early to mid-1980s, despite extensive government intervention in the main commodity markets. Both farmers and agricultural policy makers had made decisions at the start of the period on the basis of erroneous expectations. They had been too optimistic about future market conditions and had not foreseen the impacts of changing macroeconomic policy on the exchange rate and interest rates.

The effects of specific commodity programmes

Johnson (1985b) and Gardner (1985) evaluated grain policy under the 1981 Act. Johnson pointed out that although the 1981 Act cut the link between target prices and production costs, target prices and loan rates were set at levels which encouraged a level of grain output well beyond the level of demand at the market prices implied by the loan rate. Johnson also noted that the 1981 Act continued the high ratio of target price for wheat to that of corn.

Gardner described the operation of the grain support system. The target price was set high enough to induce a tendency toward excess supply (overconsumption plus exports). Market prices (world trading prices) were thereby reduced. Simultaneously, the loan rate put a floor to the market. Because deficiency payments and the threat of CCC stock accumulation increased budget outlays there was continuing pressure for ARP programmes (used in every year since 1981). Furthermore, whilst the FOR was conceived as a stabilisation device, the FOR entry price was used to support the market above the loan rate. This intensified stock build-up and pressure for production control. Gardner commented that 'the 1981 Act programs have made producers better off... the real gains (to farmers) are the deficiency payments and higher market prices that the programs have generated' (Gardner, 1985, p. 84). For corn, the market price was higher than the target price for 1981 to 1984 (except 1982). The main effect on returns was acreage diversion. Gardner suggested that the average 1981 to 1984 cutback of 7 per cent increased corn prices by about 14 per cent (using a demand elasticity of –0.5 per cent). For wheat, target prices were above market prices for 1981 through to 1984. The market price was supported by CCC and FOR programmes. At the same time there were significant production control programmes shifting the supply curve inwards. Gardner suggested that 1981–84 production control reduced output by 15 per cent. Producer prices were probably raised by 20–28 per cent as a result of the programme. (Gardner used a demand elasticity of –1 and a supply elasticity of 0.3.) Gardner suggested that for grains as a whole the programmes increased revenue by 15 per cent ($5.5 billion for a typical crop year). Thus, a 15 per cent reduction in prices would eliminate net benefits to producers. Gardner also estimated that the grain programmes cost consumers about $3 billion and taxpayers about $5 billion for a typical year.

The dairy programme was costly to both taxpayer and consumers with production expanding rapidly in the early 1980s whilst consumption rose slowly. Programme purchases and costs rose markedly in the 1981–84 period. Programme costs exceeded $1 billion in each year. In the 1982/3 marketing year, costs reached a record $2.6 billion or 13 per cent of total receipts from farm marketings (about $13 000 per commercial dairy farmer). In the calendar year 1983, the CCC purchased the equivalent of 12 per cent of total milk marketed (32 per cent of butter production, 70 per cent of non-fat dry milk production and 28 per cent of cheese production). Government stocks rose rapidly in the early 1980s and were very high at the beginning of 1984. Consumer costs were around $9 billion per annum in the period 1982–84.[24]

Programmes for certain other commodities were costly to consumers but not to taxpayers. In particular, sugar was protected by import quotas cum tariffs whilst beef was protected by VERs backed up by import quotas. Johnson (1985a) estimates that the cost to consumers of the sugar programme was around $2.5 billion and of the beef and veal programme around $1.4 billion in 1982/3. The OECD (1987) estimated consumer costs in 1984 of $2.6 billion for sugar and $7 billion for beef and veal.

The 1985 Food Security Act (duration 1986–90)

Background

Spitze (1987) has described the political conditions surrounding the making of the 1985 Act. The 1981 Act was due to be terminated on 30 September 1985. President Reagan was re-elected in a landslide in 1984 whilst the House remained under Democratic control and the Senate under Republican leadership. The administration wanted to remove government from agriculture as well as other sectors of the economy: that is, reduce the size and role of government intervention. The legislature was concerned about the fall in agricultural prosperity as well as stating a commitment to 'balance the budget'.

The Secretary of Agriculture, Block, commented that the New Deal programmes were not working for agriculture in the 1980s and put forward a new AAA which 'provides a transition from high and rigid price supports to flexible and market clearing price supports and gradually phases out acreage reduction programs (and associated target prices), quotas and allotments which keep low-cost American products from competing with those of less efficient foreign producers' (quoted in Spitze, 1987, p. 180). In essence, the administration proposed a 'safety net' consistent with minimal government intervention.

More specifically, the Administration proposed that:

1. Price supports for all commodities be limited to non-recourse loans at 75 per cent of the applicable three-year moving average of US market prices for each commodity. Target prices to be phased out over a five-year period.
2. Payments limitation to decline to $10 000 for the 1990 crop year.
3. Supply control (ARPs) to be phased out.
4. Access to foreign markets to be increased via trade negotiations and by use of special export assistance measures (credits on subsidies).

The House and Senate agricultural committees proposed less radical changes. There was discussion of supply control: the issue of mandatory supply control was voted on at least six times in the House and several times in the Senate but was soundly defeated. Spitze noted that 'all parties were trapped between the imperatives of their budget commitments and the irresistible demands arising from the farm crisis' (ibid., p. 182). Duncan (1985) noted in May 1985 that convergence in Congress had been reached on certain aspects of agricultural policy:

> First, there has been growing appreciation that national policies outside agriculture are unusually important to the sector's improved well being ... farm legislation cannot solve all of agriculture's problems. Second, in a more competitive world market place, market-clearing prices for farm commodities are not only critically important signals to foreign producers and buyers but also an indication to US producers of the challenge ahead. Finally, new agricultural legislation must spend resources more effectively – to make a contribution to reducing the federal budget deficit. (ibid., p. 506)

Duncan stressed that the debate was not over whether agricultural policy would become more market-oriented but when and how. The reality of financial stress in agriculture implied a need for a multi-year adjustment programme to assist farmer acceptance of market pricing. Duncan believed that proposals to set CCC loan rates as moving averages of recent years' market prices would be fundamental to shifting towards market pricing. However, target prices and acreage diversion payments would be required as part of the adjustment assistance, whilst US capacity for agricultural production exceeded market requirements. In this respect, retirement of fragile land also seemed prudent for reduced production capacity and enhanced conservation. Finally, export development was essential: development assistance to low- and middle-income countries could strengthen export demand.

Consensus was achieved in Congress over the following: 'a need to change the basis for setting loan and target prices; the continuation of existing domestic food distribution efforts, foreign aid programs; research and education policies; the urgent need for aggressive export initiatives and subsidisation; and the need for major new farmland conservation initiatives to jointly reduce soil loss, lower-stream sedimentation and slow down production' (Spitze, 1987, p. 182). However, negotiations continued well into December (the House Bill was completed on 8 October 1985 and the Senate Bill on 23 November 1985). Stumbling blocks were the setting of target prices, the dairy programme and whether or not there should be a food distribution bill separate from the Commodity Act. The conference committee negotiated for eight days until a compromise combining food and farm provisions was struck on 14 December 1985. The Act was signed by President Reagan on 25 December 1985 as the Food Security Act.

Main features of the Food Security Act
The main provisions of the Food Security Act are set out in the Appendix to this chapter. The act had five main goals:[25]

1. Provide cash income to farmers and relieve financial stress in agriculture.
2. Reduce the budgetary cost of agricultural support.
3. Reduce grain stocks.
4. Regain US export share in world grains and oilseeds markets.
5. Reduce the environmental costs associated with agriculture especially soil erosion.

The major mechanisms employed under the act were target prices, acreage control (ARP), loan rates, frozen payment yields, export promotion (EEP and TEAP) and the establishment of the Conservation Reserve (CRP). Target prices were to be reduced slowly so maintaining a flow of deficiency payments to producers whilst attempting to put a lid on budgetary costs. The ARP was to be tied to trigger stock levels, and by controlling production was to reduce crop surpluses, raise market prices and control budget costs. The frozen payment yield feature of the 1985 farm bill effectively fixed the notional yields used in calculating deficiency payments, at a historic base level, for an indefinite period. With the benefit of hindsight this later came to be perceived as a very important first step in 'decoupling' support payments from current levels of production (see chapter Appendix for more precise technical details of frozen payment yields). Loan rates for the major crops were to be lowered substantially by being tied to 75–85 per cent of the previous five year average market price (excluding the high and low year); in addition, there was discretionary authority for a reduction of up to 20 per cent to maintain export and domestic sales of wheat and corn. The reduction in loan rates was intended to limit CCC stock acquisitions, thereby reducing storage costs, and expand exports. Export promotion was introduced to counter 'unfair' (subsidised) foreign competition. The CRP was initiated to conserve and improve soil and water resources; namely, reduce soil erosion, improve water quality, protect wetlands and enhance wildlife habitat.

Trade-offs between objectives were likely through the use of these instruments. For example, the use of the ARP would tend to contain production and budget costs but limit export share; the CRP would meet an environmental goal but increase budget costs; deficiency payments channel taxpayer monies to producers so tending to put pressure on the budget; lowering loan rates tends to increase exports but increases the budget costs of deficiency payments in weak markets.

Initial impact of the Act

In 1986, agricultural exports continued at a much lower level than in the early 1980s and were slightly down on 1985. However, subsidised exports, provided for in the 1985 Act, were of significance accounting for around 15–20 per cent of total exports (Smith, 1987). Food aid accounted for about 5 per cent, CCC credit about 10 per cent and export enhancement (EEP) for about 5 per cent of overall agricultural exports. Crop production was high and crop prices dipped to a 15 year low in weak markets whilst stocks mounted. Corn stocks were their highest (90 per cent of annual crop size) for 30 years (Drabenstott, 1986). Net farm income declined moderately by about 10 per cent from 1985. Farm debt declined and farmland values began to stabilise. Low prices and the new initiatives meant that government payments reached around $18 billion, a new record. About 9 million acres were enrolled in the conservation reserve by the end of 1986 (Dicks and Reichelderfer, 1987).

The US farm economy turned round in 1987. 'Farm income hit record highs, farmland values bottomed and the farm financial crisis faded further from memory' (Drabenstott and Barkema, 1987, p. 28). The high stocks of 1986 triggered a sizeable acreage limitation programme: more than 20 per cent of cropland was idled. Despite good crop yields, production was lower in 1987 than in 1986 and exports edged up partly due to export enhancement. Crop prices started to recover from the low levels of 1986. Livestock growers saw product prices increase but feed cost remain low. Government support payments declined slightly, but crop producers remained heavily dependent upon government programmes for a substantial part of their earnings (ibid., p. 32).

The initial impact of the 1985 Act was favourable to the farm economy but saw record programme costs. The two major and inter-related policy concerns were containment of this spending and a desire for agricultural trade liberalisation. As discussed in the next chapter, the US administration adopted a tough stance on the agricultural trade negotiations held under the GATT and commencing in 1986. It was expected that liberalisation of agricultural trade would enlarge US agricultural exports and reduce US farm programme spending and commodity stocks.

Final Comment on the Period 1973–85[26]

US agriculture became heavily dependent upon exports with the move to flexible exchange rates and the growth in agricultural trade in the 1970s. By the late 1970s, US agricultural exports accounted for almost 40 per cent of agricultural output and 20 per cent of US total exports (Rausser, 1985, p. 211). Export dependence made for instability in US agriculture in the 1970s and 1980s. Sizeable movements in dollar exchange rates and fluctuations in import demand from countries such as the USSR led to abrupt changes in US agricultural export sales. Price movements and/or government stock accumulation (for grains) were magnified by the insulation of many foreign markets such as the EC from trade shocks causing adjustments to be borne by the US and other countries, predominantly exporters, that practised relatively free trade.

The US agricultural sector is highly capital intensive[27] and is sensitive to movements in real interest rates[28] and hence changes in monetary and fiscal policies. Changes in interest rates also affect the value of the dollar so influencing export demand. The agricultural sector has also become more reliant over time upon production items purchased from other sectors of the economy. In the early 1970s around 25–35 per cent of gross farm income was spent on purchases from other sectors; by the early to mid-80s this proportion had risen to 45–50 per cent. These linkages with other sectors of the economy further expose the agricultural sector to external shocks passing through the unit cost of purchased production inputs.

The 1970s were characterised by a significant expansion of world trade and a depreciating dollar – hence rising US agricultural exports

– low real interest rates and relatively high inflation. In contrast, in the early to mid-1980s, world agricultural trade was stagnant and the dollar appreciated significantly – hence falling US agricultural exports – and real interest rates were high and inflation relatively low. 'Since the early 1970s, then, the US agricultural sector has been subjected to a roller-coaster ride, the valleys and peaks of which have been defined in part by the external linkages to the US macroeconomy and the international economy' (ibid., p. 209). Fluctuations in the price of agricultural land – the resource in least elastic supply – reflected the fluctuating fortunes of the agricultural sector with a land price boom in the 1970s and a collapse in the early to mid-1980s. The linkages between fluctuations in agricultural prosperity and forces external to agriculture have increased the importance of timing, with respect to entry into and exit from agriculture, on wealth accumulation by and the viability of a farmer's business.

However, because government continued to intervene into agriculture, sector-specific commodity policies continued to have a significant bearing on the development of the farm sector. US policy intervention is concentrated on the major crops and the dairy sector; livestock sectors and perishable crops are relatively unprotected. Agricultural policy has tended to encourage overallocation of resources to protected commodities except as moderated by supply control. Fluctuations in external forces are then reflected in part by variations in government programme costs, government acquired stocks and short-run responses in the idling of land.

Rausser has argued that external shocks can give rise to macroexternalities for agriculture because commodity markets are 'flex-price' and prone to price overshooting in the presence of 'fix-price' markets in the manufacturing sector of the economy. In a commodity boom (slump), agriculture receives an implicit subsidy (is subject to an implicit tax) except as overshooting is moderated by commodity programmes. For example, in the period 1980–83, high interest rates and the strong dollar coupled with a contraction in export demand tended to drain resources out of agriculture. Farmers were in a sense faced with an adjustment tax because of agriculture's export dependence and its capital intensity. This took the form of higher interest payments, lower commodity prices and a fall in wealth. However, part of the burden of adjustment was borne by government in the form of increased budget cost of agricultural programmes which protected prices received by farmers (via the target price/deficiency payment system).

Whilst external forces gave rise to instability of the farm sector, secular changes continued to influence its long-term development. We briefly mention here continuing technological improvement, structural change and the shift to part-time farming. Ball (1985) reports that over the period 1973–79, aggregate farm output grew at around 2.75 per cent per annum, whilst aggregate input grew at around 0.7 per cent per annum. Within the aggregate input category, the fastest growing inputs were chemicals and durable equipment at around 3.5 per cent per annum, whilst operator labour (including family workers) declined at around 1.5 per cent per annum. Total factor productivity growth was measured at an annual rate of around 2 per cent per annum, somewhat higher than in the period 1960–73 (around 1.5 per cent per annum), but slightly lower than the rate for the period 1953–60 (around 2.7 per cent per annum). This strong productivity growth helped to maintain agriculture's international competitiveness: not only did the US remain a low-cost producer of farm commodities but its relative efficiency may have increased (Paarlberg et al., 1985). However, government intervention affected both the realisation of productivity gains and the distribution of benefits. Thus, with high loan rates, productivity gains show up as increased stock accumulation rather than increased exports (*ceteris paribus*) and the high target prices ensure that producers retain the benefits of technological advance at the expense of taxpayers.

The secular transformation process led to a continuing decline in labour in agriculture. However, the external circumstances surrounding agriculture meant that instability rather than agricultural adjustment was perceived as the major policy problem. Nevertheless, technological change and input substitution provided incentives for further structural change within agriculture and the organisation of agriculture began to receive attention as a policy issue. Generally speaking, technological change was associated with increasing capital intensity of production, increasing specialisation, a reduction in the number of farms and an increase in farm size. However, technical economies of size were being reaped by family size crop farms in the 1980s[29] (Harrington and Manchester, 1985, p. 32).

Structural change in the 1950s and 1960s was a case of 'get bigger' or 'get out'. In contrast, in the 1970s and 1980s, the farmer had an incentive to 'get bigger' or 'get smaller' (become part-time) (ibid., p. 32). A more diverse structure was the result. There was a small number of large-size commercial farms producing the bulk of output and a relatively large number of small farms, largely part-time, producing comparatively little. Farm families with low incomes were those who were unable to generate much off-farm income but were operating a farm unit that was not large enough to be viable. An analysis by Bullock (1984), showed that 28 per cent of farms (sales of > $40 000) accounted for 86 per cent of cash receipts and 95 per cent of net farm income. Large farms (sales of > $200 000) represented only 5 per cent of farms and accounted for around 50 per cent of total sales and 80 per cent of net farm income. However, small farms (sales of less than $10 000) accounting for 50 per cent of farms had an average combined on and off-farm income providing a reasonable standard of living (Tosterad, 1983).

The rise in part-time farming and the importance of off-farm income throughout the 1970s and early 1980s was a fairly steady phenomenon. In the early 1970s, off-farm income accounted for around 55 per cent of total income of all farm operators; by the early 1980s this proportion had risen to around 60–70 per cent. In the early 1980s, for the majority of farm operators, off-farm income accounted for most or all of net income (Johnson, 1985b).[30]

The following conclusions emerge. First, the economic wellbeing of the majority of farmers is tied more closely to the non-farm economy than the farm economy. Second, production is highly concentrated; a small minority of farmers receive a high proportion of net farm income. Third, the distribution of the benefits of commodity programmes are highly skewed to the large farms (and specific commodities) even with payments limitations.

During the 1970s and 1980s, the traditional rationale for agricultural policy intervention – coping with the agricultural adjustment problem – became largely irrelevant. In recognition of the characteristics and diverse nature of agriculture, new forms of transfer payments were proposed by economists to replace the 'vintage' commodity programmes. As discussed in the next chapter, decoupled and targeted income 'deficiency' transfers began to receive increasing attention. In essence, these would not link the size of payment benefits to production and would be targeted at mid-sized low-income family farms to preserve the rural fabric of the countryside.

COMMENTARY: AGRICULTURAL POLICY IN THE US AND THE EC[31]

By the 1980s, US agriculture had reached an advanced stage of the transformation process with only 3 per cent of the labour force remaining in agriculture. Production is dominated by large farms and off-farm earnings are greater than farm incomes for farm households as a whole. Basic policy issues were concerned less with agricultural adjustment than with adaptation to trade and macroeconomic forces.

The prosperity of US agriculture became increasingly dependent on exports from the 1970s into the 1980s. Changes in the value of the US dollar had significant impacts on US farm export volumes and unit prices. Agricultural policy was progressively altered in reaction to the changing external environment. However, the 1981 Agricultural and Food Act was conceived with a faulty preconception – the scarcity syndrome – of future prospects. The taxpayer cost of agricultural support increased sharply with the declining trend of world prices in US dollars and falling US exports.

In discussions leading up to the 1985 Food Security Act, it appeared timely for the US government to withdraw from blanket support for agriculture to more of a safety net role given that the secular agricultural problem no longer existed. In addition, budgetary pressures and the ideological convictions of the Reagan administration pointed toward a withdrawal of government from agriculture. Thus, the US administration proposed a progressive reduction in farm support prices, and phasing out of target prices and crop area control. However, the farm debt crisis and the growing US trade deficit constrained the action that was taken. Congress insisted on retaining deficiency payments and in seeking an expansion of agricultural trade. The 1985 Act introduced measures to engage in competitive export subsidisation to regain markets that were seen to be 'unfairly' captured by other exporters, particularly the EC.

In the EC, the agricultural transformation process is well advanced in northern regions of the Community but has still to run its course in many southern regions. There has been a shift to part-time farming which has given income supplements to those disadvantaged by structural change. However, many small-scale farmers remain whose livelihood depends principally upon agricultural production, particularly in southern and 'disadvantaged' regions. The Community has found it difficult to shift from blanket price support to targeted income payments because of the budgetary cost that would be incurred.

Technological change coupled with a high degree of price support and fairly static demand led the EC to shift from being a net importer of most agricultural products in the 1970s to a net exporter of several commodities in the 1980s. Under the basic mechanism of agricultural support in the EC, this transition was critical in budgetary terms: import levies fell whilst the costs of export subsidies increased. Rising budgetary cost led to pressures for CAP reform, but these pressures were partially alleviated in the early 1980s as the dollar fell against the ECU (see Table 5.14) and unit export subsidies diminished. However, despite its slow pace, budgetary driven reform occurred typically via indirect and direct supply control measures. Thus, reform may be traced from the introduction of co-responsibility levies for milk in the late 1970s and production thresholds for cereals in 1982, through the inception of production quotas for milk in 1985 and the bringing in of the stabiliser measures in 1988. However, the CAP remained expensive to taxpayers and consumers.

Policy reform in both the US and the EC was largely budget driven and displayed similarities in the emphasis placed on supply control. Voluntary land retirement has a long history in US policy; this was reintroduced and refined as a policy instrument in the 1980s. EC policy makers turned to this option for the first time in that decade. Mandatory production quotas were discussed as a policy reform option in the US in the run up to the 1985 Act but dismissed. In contrast, the EC moved down this road with the introduction of milk quotas in 1982. However, price policies were dissimilar: the US showed a willingness to lower market prices, although maintaining income support to producers via the deficiency payments system, whilst EC policy makers were reluctant to abandon traditional support mechanisms which maintained internal prices well above comparable world levels.

The policy agenda was widened in both the US and the EC to embrace environmental issues. Agricultural expansion in the 1970s heightened concerns over land and water degradation. Specific measures were introduced such as the CRP in the US and the range of environmental programmes accompanying the 1992 reform of the CAP in the EU (see Legg, 1997).

However, the interaction of US and EC policies in the weak world markets of the 1980s gave domestic policy reform an international dimension. Of particular concern was the trade distorting effects of the CAP mechanisms. World markets were viewed as a vent for internal surpluses and a source to meet internal deficits, and world prices had few direct effects on Community production and consumption. The dual pricing and insulation characteristics of the CAP tended to depress world market prices and increase world price instability for domestically-produced commodities. The trade distorting effects of the CAP gave rise to trade tensions between the EC and the US in the 1980s, particularly in the light of rising EC farm exports as against declining US exports (see Table 5.14).

Whilst the competitiveness of US exports was affected by the value of the dollar, various studies have indicated that US agricultural exports were damaged by subsidy practices in other countries in the 1980s. For example, Roningen and Dixit (1989) estimated that if agricultural supports had been withdrawn worldwide, the agricultural trade balance

Table 5.14 EC(10) and US export volumes of agricultural products and ECU/$, 1980–86

	1980	1981	1982	1983	1984	1985	1986
EC(10)	100	109	109	116	124	132	136
US	100	93	89	90	73	67	–
Other developed countries	100	110	108	106	111	113	119
ECU/dollar	0.72	0.90	1.02	1.12	1.27	1.31	1.02

Source: GATT International Trade 81–88, Vol. 1, App. Table III (annual).

of the US would have improved by some $3 billion and that of the EC would have deteriorated by some $9 billion.

The weakness of world commodity markets and the continuation of price support policies in the US and EC meant that the extent of government support for agriculture increased substantially in the 1980s. Thus the average rate of government assistance as measured by the net percentage PSE in respect of agricultural commodities increased from 21–34 per cent in the US and from 35–43 per cent in the EC between 1979–81 and 1984–86.[32]

During the 1980s there was increasing recognition that domestic agricultural support policies distorted agricultural trade and the interaction of these policies through world market linkages raised worldwide costs of protection. In the next chapter, we examine the attempts under the Uruguay Round of the GATT trade negotiations to liberalise agricultural trade via reforms of domestic support policies paying particular attention to the key roles of the US and the EC.

APPENDIX: US AGRICULTURE ACTS: 1977, 1981 AND 1985

Main Features of the 1977 Food and Agriculture Act

1. *Target prices, deficiency payments, and loan rates* for wheat, corn, feed grains, cotton, rice. Target prices linked to production costs for each crop. Current plantings used to determine deficiency payments.
2. *Payment limitations.* Payment limitations were revised upwards for wheat, feed grains and cotton and reduced for rice. For the 1980 and 1981 crops the annual payment limit for wheat, feed grains, cotton and rice combined was to be $50 000.
3. *Acreage bases and set-aside* for wheat, feed grains and cotton. Allot-

ments were replaced by current plantings. Under the 1977 Act, deficiency payments were based on normal production from current plantings adjusted by a programme allocation factor for each commodity. Authorisation for set-aside was given to the Secretary if he deemed that supplies were likely to be excessive. Compliance with set-aside was a condition for receipt of price and income supports.

4. *FOR for wheat and feed grains.* The FOR permitted farmers who complied with set aside to place grain into the reserve initially for three years but subsequently for three to five years. Farmers agreed to hold grain in storage until the contract matured or until a specified release price was reached in the market. In return, farmers received payment for storing their grain and interest was waived on the loan after the first year of the contract. The FOR loan rate was higher than the regular CCC loan rate. The FOR was mandatory for wheat and discretionary for feed grains.

5. *Soybeans.* A loan and purchase programme became mandatory for the first time. Previously soybeans were a non-basic crop eligible for discretionary intervention.

6. *Sugar.* A loan and purchase programme for sugar cane and sugar beet launched for the 1977 and 1978 crops to maintain a minimum price for raw sugar. For 1979–81, price support authority reverted to Title III of the 1949 AA which provided for price support at up to 90 per cent of parity.

7. *Dairy.* Minimum dairy support prices fixed at from 75–80 per cent of parity.

8. *Food stamps.* The programme continued but the rules amended to encourage participation.

Main Provisions of the 1981 Agriculture and Food Act

1. *Target prices, deficiency payments and loan rates* for cereals and cotton and loan rates for soybeans. Minimum target prices and loan rates specified rising over the period of the act. Crop-specific acreage bases established to make deficiency payments. Deficiency payments only payable to participants in area control programmes (if specified). The production eligible for payment was defined as the farmer's programme acreage times programme yield.

2. *Payment limitation* of $55 000 per person.

3. *Crop area control and set-aside authority*: provision made for crop-specific acreage reduction programmes (ARPs) in addition to set-aside. The ARP required diversion into an approved conservation use from a crop specific acreage base. It was mandatory for cotton

and rice and an alternative to set-aside for wheat and feed grains. Cross compliance eliminated under an ARP but retained for set-aside. Paid diversion retained as an option to set-aside.

4. *FOR* extended to include all feed grains and the cap on the reserve was raised.

5. *Sugar.* A non-recourse loan and purchase programme supplemented by provision for fees, duties and quotas to be imposed on imports to avoid stock accumulation by the CCC.

6. *Dairy.* Support levels partially separated from parity and set for 1982–85 (fiscal years). The minimum support level related to the size of CCC purchases.

7. *Export Promotion.* A revolving export credit fund set up for CCC use. The Secretary required to provide for standby export subsidies to match export subsidies used by foreign governments. The ceiling on PL480 donations abroad raised.

Main Provisions of the Food Security Act 1985[33]

1. *Target prices, deficiency payments and loan rates* for cereals and cotton and loan rates for soybeans. Target prices frozen for two years with subsequent maximum declines of 2, 3 and 5 per cent for the final three years of the Act. Basic loan rates for grains (soybeans) set at 75–85 per cent (75 per cent) of the 'middle three of the previous five years' moving average market price. The basic loan rate not permitted to fall more than 5 per cent per year but the actual loan rate (for wheat and feed grains) could be set as much as 20 per cent below the basic rate at the discretion of the Secretary for Agriculture.[34] Discretionary reductions in soybean loan rate permitted but a minimum floor specified. Eligibility for deficiency payments dependent upon participation in acreage control programmes (if specified). Deficiency payments calculated as the payment rate times a programme yield times permitted acreage. The payment rate is the difference between the target price and the higher of the market price and the loan rate. The permitted acreage is the crop acreage base (average of planted and idled acreage in crop years 1981–85) less idled land area. The programme yield is the average of farm programme yields for the 1981–85 crop years excluding the highest and lowest yields. Programme yields for 1986–90 crops frozen at the level prevailing in 1985.

2. *0–92 and 50–92 deficiency payment/ARP programmes.* Under the 0–92 programme (grains), a producer is permitted to devote to

conservation use from zero up to all of the maximum permitted acreage (base acres minus idled acres) under an ARP. The producer receives regular deficiency payments on planted acreage plus deficiency payments on 92 per cent of the remaining acreage (permitted acres minus planted acres). The 50–92 programme (cotton and rice) requires that the producer plant at least 50 per cent of the permitted acres to be eligible.

3. *Generic (commodity) certificates programme* payments made in the form of CCC commodities: certificates denominated in a cash amount and backed by commodities owned by the CCC. Facilitates PIK.

4. *Acreage control: paid land diversion, set-aside and acreage reduction programmes.* Discretionary authority to allow producers to increase a crop acreage base by up to 10 per cent providing there is a corresponding decrease in another crop acreage base. Acreage control tied to stock trigger levels.

5. *Marketing loans* mandatory for cotton and rice and discretionary for other major field crops. A marketing loan allows for loan repayment at the market price even if that price is below the loan rate.

6. *Payments limitation* $50 000 per person for deficiency payments and land diversion payments.

7. *FOR* continued but loan period reduced to three years.

8. *Land conservation.* A Conservation Reserve Programme (CRP) authorising up to 40–45 million acres (10 per cent of all cropland) created to reduce erosion. Under the CRP, the government would rent highly erodible cropland for ten years on the basis of farmer bids with a target of 5 million acres for the first year. The land to be placed under grass or trees; harvesting and grazing not allowed. Sod buster and swamp buster provisions aimed at preventing production on erodible land and wetlands also included. (Operators denied programme benefits if erodible land were ploughed.)

9. *Sugar.* Fixed loan rates for sugarcane and sugarbeet. Discretionary authority to raise loan rates if costs of production rise. Import quotas set to minimise loan forfeitures (market reference price above the loan rate) and enable the sugar programme to be run at zero budgetary cost.

10. *Dairy.* Price supports lowered over the five years with further reductions triggered if annual CCC purchases exceed a target figure. Production control via Dairy Termination Programme: whole herd buyout.

11. *Export Promotion* via Export Enhancement Programme (EEP)

and Targeted Export Assistance Programme (TEAP). The EEP gives a subsidy or bonus through the release of CCC stocks (generic certificates) to qualified US exporters. The TEAP provides generic certificates to enable US exporters to expand foreign sales in specific markets.

NOTES

1. In fact, growth rates were very variable in this period, being largely negative in 1974 and 1975 following the first oil price shock and quite strong in the late 1970s.
2. Data sources: Growth rates in national product – Eurostat, *European Economy*. Trade growth rates: GATT, *International Trade*.
3. Changes in the pattern of trade have been an important contributory factor. The western industrialised countries have been purchasing a growing share of manufactured imports from Japan and East Asian NICs since 1965; this trend accelerated in the 1980s. Both the US and the EU had massive trade deficits with Japan in the 1980s and were particularly concerned over the imports of motor vehicles, steel and certain high technology products. The willingness of governments to supply protection increased in the recession since governments are limited in other ways of providing adjustment assistance to affected industries. NTBs such as quotas or VERs were the preferred instrument – domestic producers got a guaranteed share of the domestic market and exporters got some compensation in the form of higher prices.
4. This section draws on Hathaway, 1987, ch. 2 and Hine et al., 1989b.
5. This section draws on Newman et al., 1987. As a backcloth to the secular changes described below, the following comparisons between the agricultures of the US and the EU are relevant. First, the US covers five times the physical area of the EC(10) and has four times the arable area. Secondly, farms in the US are larger and fewer than in the EU: 438 acres per farm and 2.3 million farms compared to 42 acres per farm and 6.8 million farms (1984 data). Thirdly, US crop farming is less land-intensive than EU agriculture (that is, crop yields are lower in the US), primarily because of higher chemical inputs in EU agriculture, whilst dairy yields are higher in the US than in the EU. Livestock, grains and oilseeds dominate US agricultural production whilst dairy, livestock products and grains account for the bulk of EU agricultural production.
6. The treatment of MCAs in the Community budget is peculiar. Although a proportion of MCA revenue payments are a revenue source (the 'tax' element) they are not shown as such in the Budget. Rather MCA revenues are shown only in the expenditure account as 'negative expenditures' (Harris et al., 1983, p. 310). Positive and negative MCA expenditures rarely, if ever, cancel out. Having regard to the forces which cause MCA percentages to differ amongst member states, both positively and negatively, there is no reason why they should. Aggregate expenditure has, in fact, tended to exceed aggregate revenue, so that MCAs have generally been a net drain on the Budget.
7. The choice of this period appears to have been arbitrary. The world market prices of some commodities such as sugar were relatively high then, and more recent estimates show that the general level of PSEs was rising in the early and mid-1980s, not only in the EU but in other DCs as well.
8. During the early days of the CAP, cereals regulation (Reg. 120/67 and Reg. 2727/75) made provision for the payment of a denaturing premium on common wheat as a means of diverting wheat of milling quality to the livestock feed market. Denaturing took the form of dyeing the grain or contaminating it with fish oil. However, the idea of rendering bread grain unfit for human consumption fell into political

disfavour during the short period of world grain scarcity and high prices in the mid-1970s, and the provision permitting denaturing was allowed to lapse in 1976 (Harris et al., 1983, p. 71).

9. The conversion of other surplus crops, such as cereals and sugar, into alcohol and related products, has also been much discussed. But there is the basic problem that by-products based on agricultural raw materials cannot compete with their conventional counterparts at normal price levels. So, for example, although it is technically feasible to produce ethanol for use as a motor fuel, from either sugar or cereals, the process is uneconomic except when oil prices are unusually high (or very low marginal returns for sugar or cereals are acceptable).

10. Based on financial data derived from CEC, *General Report on the Activities of the European Communities*, various years, and Agra Europe, *CAP Monitor*.

11. It is relevant to note that during the negotiations leading up to the accession of Spain and Portugal, Greece and France blocked their admission until an integrated Mediterranean programme of regional aid had been agreed at the Brussels Summit of 1985, including assistance with the expansion of crops not in surplus (Swann, 1988, p. 262).

12. The Commission's 'conversion' to proposing the adoption of set-aside as a CAP policy instrument appears to have been quite sudden. The 1985 Green Paper contained no hint of such a proposal. The initiative appears to have come from the UK which, in 1986, suggested the possibility of a voluntary scheme of retiring land from production. The initiative then passed to West Germany which, at the European Council Meeting held in December 1987, insisted on the inclusion of a set-aside scheme in the 'stabiliser' package finally agreed at the February 1988 Summit Meeting (Tracy, 1989, pp. 323–4).

13. This proposal was made before the creation of ECUs in 1979.

14. In his evidence to the House of Lords Select Committee, Marsh also stressed that agricultural price policy is an inefficient policy instrument save with respect to the goals of efficient resource allocation. Therefore, if other agricultural policy goals are to be met, such as protecting farm incomes, or retarding rural depopulation, or safeguarding the environment, specific policy instruments and actions to match these goals are needed. Due to the diversity of agricultural conditions and levels of economic development within the EC, Marsh was of the opinion that no single Community scheme is likely to produce acceptable policies for agricultural objectives beyond that of efficient resource allocation. Only nationally differentiated and financed policies could efficiently serve these supplementary goals.

15. Rickard suggests three basic options of (a) past total usage, (b) allocation by farm size (land area), (c) allocation per unit of crops and livestock, with differential allowances according to type. The feasibility of the first option would depend upon the availability of adequate records which might not exist in all EU countries. The second option would probably be easiest to administer but would afford no scope for discrimination amongst products or farming types. The third option would be most complex, but would afford scope for discrimination. As well as reducing farmers' incomes more, an N fertiliser tax would not permit discrimination between different farm products or farming types: but compared with a quota system, it would be easier and less costly to administer.

16. If a group of diners agrees to split its bill equally between the participating members, each participant has an incentive to order a more expensive meal for himself than he otherwise would, because he will bear only a proportion of the extra cost himself (Tangermann, 1985).

17. Commentary below is restricted to the Agricultural Acts passed in 1973 and 1977 respectively. Acts not covered include the Rice Production Act (1975), Emergency Assistance Act (1978), and the Meat Import Act (1979).

18. The administration's view (see Houck, 1974) was that intervention to stabilise prices and markets was largely unneeded or unworkable.

19. In 1977/78 and 1978/79 deficiency payments were made for wheat. In these years

payments averaged 21 per cent and 15 per cent of the farm prices (Johnson, 1986, p. 69).

20. This section draws on USDA (1984) and Infranger et al. (1983).
21. Paarlberg (1982), Johnson (1981) and Schuh (1981) were in a minority of US agricultural economists in arguing that the long-term trend was likely to represent a slow decline in the real prices of major US crops.
22. This draws on USDA (1984).
23. The agricultural trade balance fell from $26.6 billion in 1981 to $18.5 billion in 1984.
24. See for example Johnson (1985a, p. 77) and OECD (1990a, p. 181). This estimate takes the existing world prices as the opportunity cost of supplies to consumers.
25. USDA (1990).
26. This section draws in part on Rausser (1985).
27. 'If we take account only of physical capital, not land, the US agricultural sector is twice as capitalised as manufacturing on a per worker basis' (ibid., p. 248).
28. Interest rates affect private stockholding of durable crops, livestock investors and demand for capital equipment items and buildings.
29. Long-run average costs consistently decline as small farms expand, then taper off for medium-sized farms and fall very little for large farms.
30. 'Farms with sales of less than $40 000 represent two-thirds of farms, but contribute only 10 per cent of production and households associated with these farms earn more than three-quarters of off-farm income' (Ahearn et al., 1985, p. 1089).
31. This section draws on Hine, Ingersent and Rayner (1989b).
32. Source: OECD (1989).
33. This draws on Spitze (1987) and Stucker and Collins (1986).
34. The so-called reduced (Findley) loan rate. If the reduced loan rate is operative the deficiency payment is the original deficiency payment plus an emergency compensation payment (Findley deficiency payment: equal to the difference between the basic loan rate and the higher of the reduced loan rate and the market price).

6. International policy adjustment

INTRODUCTION

In this chapter we review:

1. the growth in agricultural protectionism and the rising budgetary costs of support in the 1980s;
2. attempts to reform agricultural policy and lessen trade conflict through the Uruguay Round negotiations in the GATT.

GROWTH IN PROTECTIONISM AND RISING BUDGETARY COSTS OF SUPPORT

Growth in Protectionism

As described in earlier chapters of this book, agricultural protectionism has been an institutional norm both in Western Europe and the United States for a very long period. Apart from a brief experiment with free trade around the middle of the nineteenth century, most West European countries have protected domestic agriculture by erecting barriers against competing imports since the Middle Ages. For a considerable period before the onset of the great depression of the inter-war years, the United Kingdom (a net agricultural importer), Denmark and the Netherlands (net agricultural exporters) were exceptions to this generalisation. But from about 1930 onwards they also succumbed to pressure to adopt the protectionist norm. In the immediate aftermath of the Second World War, when agricultural supplies were relatively 'tight' for a few years, there was some relaxation of protection. But by the mid-1950s, levels of protection were being raised again in response to falling prices in oversupplied markets.

Another important feature of the evolution of agricultural protectionism dating from the period of the inter-war depression was the growing resort to non-tariff barriers (NTBs) to restrict imports, and the adoption of domestic production subsidies to supplement import protection. So, for example, extensive and growing use was made of import quota restrictions on both sides of the Atlantic, starting during the 1930s and continuing after the Second World War. The introduction of domestic production subsidies followed a similar pattern. For example, in the UK, deficiency payments were first introduced (for wheat) in 1932 and in the US, under the Agricultural Adjustment Act of 1933, farmers became eligible to receive 'rental payments' in compensation for complying with supply control (termed 'acreage allotments'). Both schemes were continued and extended after the war.

Until quite recent times, actual empirical evidence on levels of agricultural protection has been sparse and fragmentary, even in relation to tariff protection. For many years, such data as was available pertained only to nominal tariff rates. Then, following development of the concept of effective tariff rates in the 1960s (Corden, 1971), some estimates were made of the difference between nominal and effective tariffs on imports of various agricultural commodities. An extension of this approach was to extend the measurement of direct import protection to include non-tariff barriers, such as variable import levies. So, for example, Sampson and Yeats (1977) estimated and compared nominal and effective protection of agricultural commodities in the US, on this somewhat broader basis, for selected years in the later 1950s and mid-1960s, as well as for the EC in 1974 (Table 6.1). Apart from showing the generally higher rates of effective compared with nominal protection (as expected) this work also underlined two further features of agricultural protection. First, the substantial inter-commodity variation within years, and second, the instability of levels of protection across commodities from year to year.

A major shortcoming of these more traditional methods of measuring agricultural protection is that they are confined to border protection and ignore the impact of non-border measures, such as deficiency payments, directly upon levels of domestic production and indirectly upon trade. This deficiency was met in the 1970s by the introduction of a new and more comprehensive measure of agricultural support and protection, the 'producer subsidy equivalent' or PSE. The PSE, defined as 'the payment which would be required to compensate farmers for the loss of all forms of government support and protection', includes all budgetary expenditure on agriculture as well as the value of border protection.[1] The PSE is clearly superior to measures of border protection as a measure of total support and protection to agriculture. However, since some forms of budgetary support such as publicly-funded agricultural

Table 6.1a   Nominal and effective protection in US agriculture, 1958, 1963 and 1968

| | 1958 | | 1963 | | 1968 | |
	TN	TE	TN	TE	TN	TE
Wheat	4.0	139.7	42.3	159.9	8.6	153.0
Soybeans	0.0	−5.1	0.0	−6.8	0.0	−6.7
Sugar	57.4	227.7	−6.3	72.6	195.8	662.2
Meat animals	8.6	10.8	9.2	14.6	7.5	13.8
Farm dairy products	17.6	41.3	13.6	31.9	16.8	48.2

Notes
TN = % nominal protection rate, including non-tariff measures.
TE = % effective protection rate, including non-tariff measures.

Table 6.1b   Nominal and effective protection in EC agriculture in 1974

| Product sector | Nominal rate (%) | | | Effective rate (%) | | |
	Tariffs	Levies	Total	Tariffs	Levies	Total
Farmgate products						
Oats	13.0	84.2	97.2	25.8	177.9	203.7
Rye	16.0	75.8	91.8	32.1	160.0	192.1
Wheat	20.0	73.0	93.0	40.6	154.1	194.7
Rice	16.0	34.5	50.5	32.1	72.8	104.9
Maize	6.0	34.1	40.1	10.7	72.0	82.7
Sheep	14.8	n.a.	14.8	33.7	−42.7	−9.0
Swine	15.8	26.4	42.2	37.7	34.4	72.1
Poultry	12.0	15.9	27.9	25.5	3.8	29.3
Bovine animals	15.2	16.0	31.2	34.9	5.0	38.9
Meat products						
Bovine meat	20.0	64.2	84.2	38.2	215.2	253.4
Pig meat	20.0	30.4	50.4	36.7	52.9	89.6
Mutton	20.0	20.0	40.0	39.3	80.0	119.3
Poultry meat	18.0	23.3	41.3	38.5	51.9	90.4
Dairy products						
Cheese	23.0	82.5	105.5	58.8	217.2	276.0
Butter	21.0	328.0	349.0	76.5	1244.2	1322.7
Cond./evap. milk	21.3	98.5	119.8	44.3	290.1	334.4

Source: Sampson and Yeats (1977).

R & D and extension are thought to be trade-neutral, the PSE is not an accurate measure of trade-distorting support and protection (it was not designed for that purpose). But, since particular forms of budgetary support which impact directly on production, such as deficiency payments, clearly can be trade distorting, the PSE will be generally superior to nominal and effective protection in measuring overall trade distortion. However, percentage PSEs are fundamentally different from nominal and effective rates of protection in another respect. Thus, whereas the latter are expressed relative to external or world prices, the percentage PSE is expressed relative to the internal or domestic price.[2] In effect, whereas nominal and effective rates of protection relate to a 'first-best' world, the percentage PSE relates to a 'second-best' world in which the higher domestic prices resulting from protection are the norm. Thus, measures of nominal and effective protection on the one hand, and percentage PSEs on the other, are strictly non-comparable for two reasons: (a) PSEs include the effect on farm incomes of direct agricultural subsidies which the other measures do not, and (b) unlike the other measures which are first-best, the PSE is a second-best measure of support and protection (see Hine, Ingersent and Rayner, 1989b, for a more detailed treatment of this point).

The earliest empirical estimates of commodity PSEs relating to EC and US agriculture go back only to the year 1968. Estimates for the EC(6), the United Kingdom, and the US for individual years over the period 1968–74 (Tables 6.2 to 6.4), indicate four important points. First, the general levels of protection for crops and dairy as between the EC(6) and the US were similar during this period, though with differences in detail. For example, feed grains (barley and maize) were less highly protected in the US than in the EC. Second, sugar stands out as being exceptionally highly protected in terms of the percentage PSE. But in terms of producer subsidy value, or total PSE, dairy was considerably more expensive to consumers and taxpayers than any other single commodity sector in all three regions. Third, the protection of crops fell dramatically in 1973 and 1974 due to the temporary shortfall of supplies worldwide and high prices in those two years. Fourth, protection in the UK was markedly lower than in the EC(6) at this time.[3]

The earliest PSE estimates derived from the FAO, but as one consequence of the mandate given to the OECD by its Ministerial Council in 1982, agricultural commodity PSEs have been regularly estimated and published by the OECD for its member countries, including the EC and the US, from 1979 onwards.[4]

Table 6.2 *EC(6) producer subsidy equivalents and values by commodity, 1968–74*

	1968	1969	1970	1971	1972	1973	1974
Producer subsidy equivalents (PSE)				per cent			
Wheat	34.3	41.2	39.0	41.6	24.3	-42.1	-29.3
Barley	39.2	53.3	32.4	50.4	26.1	-1.3	-11.8
Maize	52.0	43.1	32.3	48.7	35.4	5.2	0.7
Rice	30.5	30.5	51.7	60.0	61.8	14.2	-58.0
Sugar	167.3	157.6	153.8	145.9	112.6	98.1	-180.1
Dairy	67.2	70.1	59.0	28.7	26.2	33.0	33.0
Producer subsidy values (PSV)				US$m			
Wheat	989.4	1104.7	1021.8	1252.5	864.6	-1802.5	-1468.7
Barley	509.7	705.6	406.5	712.6	470.4	-29.7	-309.5
Maize	431.1	400.7	360.2	587.9	470.0	101.8	14.5
Rice	30.8	30.8	67.2	72.9	89.9	20.6	-119.6
Sugar	1510.7	1342.4	1265.7	1395.7	1230.5	1324.0	-2254.6
Dairy	4902.0	5122.0	4234.0	2209.7	2464.6	3579.0	3579.0

Source: FAO, Agricultural Protection and Stabilisation Policies, C75/LIM/2 (Rome, 1975).

Table 6.3 *UK producer subsidy equivalents and values by commodity, 1968–74*

	1968	1969	1970	1971	1972	1973	1974
Producer subsidy equivalents (PSE)				per cent			
Wheat	26.2	24.7	18.2	28.0	17.8	1.6	–16.7
Barley	22.3	24.2	14.0	14.0	10.9	3.2	1.3
Sugar	22.8	50.5	64.5	67.9	117.0	13.8	12.0
Dairy	52.3	52.9	52.4	41.7	28.2	23.4	20.1
Producer subsidy values (PSV)				US$m			
Wheat	58.8	56.9	56.9	107.3	73.3	11.8	143.5
Barley	110.2	129.1	70.8	85.0	74.6	38.0	15.7
Sugar	25.9	48.5	67.7	97.5	143.4	24.3	18.7
Dairy	554.4	564.0	602.4	563.5	430.3	456.1	425.7

Source: FAO, Agricultural Protection and Stabilisation Policies, C75/LIM/2 (Rome, 1975).

Table 6.5 compares total PSEs and percentage PSEs in the EC and the US, as estimated by the OECD for selected individual commodities and commodity groups, relative to the period 1979–88. The OECD estimates of PSEs are more comprehensive than those published earlier by FAO. Starting with the highest level of aggregation, the net total and percentage PSEs for all products (bottom line of Table 6.5) is the weighted sum of individual commodity PSEs, such as wheat and milk. The PSEs shown for all crops and all livestock products are similarly weighted aggregates. Starting with changes during this period in the net percentage PSEs for all products it is apparent that in the EC this figure dropped from 40 per cent in 1979 to not much above 30 per cent in the early 1980s. But after 1984 the rate of overall support rose again to reach a peak of 50 per cent in 1986, followed by a modest decline in 1987 and 1988. By comparison, the pattern of overall support in the US, as shown by movement in the all products net percentage PSE, was somewhat different. In 1979, the US figure of 21 per cent was only about half the corresponding level of 40 per cent in the EC. Thereafter, overall support in the US remained virtually unchanged until 1983–85 when the figure rose to around 30 per cent. In 1986 and 1987 overall support rose to a PSE of around 40 per cent before declining again to 35 per cent in 1988. By the end of the period, although the US all

Table 6.4 US producer subsidy equivalents and values by commodity, 1968–74

	1968	1969	1970	1971	1972	1973	1974
Producer subsidy equivalents (PSE)				per cent			
Wheat	29.2	41.0	43.8	35.9	45.0	6.8	0.1
Barley	0.8	12.4	12.0	1.4	18.8	7.7	0.0
Maize	20.7	21.4	19.1	13.2	17.6	6.2	0.6
Rice	1.0	4.5	6.2	10.7	5.3	5.3	5.3
Sugar	106.3	79.4	71.0	65.5	27.9	11.4	10.0
Dairy	53.0	59.8	59.9	45.0	27.9	42.8	54.4
Producer subsidy values (PSV)				US$m			
Wheat	789.1	1093.0	1187.2	1090.5	1478.4	494.6	9.2
Barley	3.1	52.0	53.1	8.2	114.0	77.7	0.0
Maize	1223.5	1418.7	1273.0	919.0	1527.8	975.3	76.5
Rice	5.0	20.2	26.4	48.9	30.3	30.3	30.3
Sugar	690.2	523.1	512.8	502.2	244.3	103.0	164.6
Dairy	3258.0	3818.9	4016.5	3132.7	2038.6	3599.7	5203.9

Source: FAO, Agricultural Protection and Stabilisation Policies, C75/LIM/2 (Rome, 1975).

products net percentage PSE index was still below its EC counterpart, the gap between them had narrowed considerably with the rate of overall agricultural support in the US moving up closer to the level of the EC.

Turning now to the net percentage PSEs for all crops and all livestock products, the pattern of change is similar but with variations. In the case of all crops in the EC, the percentage PSE started quite high at 45 in 1979 before dropping to 30 or under during 1980–84, apart from a 'high' aberration in 1982. But by 1986 and 1987 all crops support had risen again to a peak approaching a 70 per cent PSE before dropping again to about 40 per cent in 1988. In the US, by comparison, the all crops PSE started below 10 per cent in 1979 and 1980, far below the comparable EC figure, and remained below 30 per cent until 1986, apart from an aberrant 34 per cent in 1983. But in 1986 and 1987 the all crops PSE jumped to more than 40 per cent before subsiding to 35 per cent in 1988. Again, the PSE rate was consistently lower in the US than in the EC, but it tended to rise in both regions and the gap between them tended to narrow.

Comparing all crops with all livestock products, the net percentage PSE patterns are interestingly different. Two features of the comparison stand out. First, on both sides of the Atlantic, the figures pertaining to all livestock products changed much less during the period than figures for all crops. In other words, the upward trend in support and protection during the period was much less pronounced in relation to livestock products than to crops, even though support in both commodity groups did 'peak' during 1986 and 1987. The second interesting feature of the comparison between crop and livestock product percentage PSE aggregates is that the gap between levels of support and protection in the EC and the US was much less pronounced with respect to livestock products. The level of support tended to be somewhat lower in the US than in the EC, but only by a comparatively narrow margin.

Amongst individual commodities, sugar and milk again stand out as being the most highly protected in terms of percentage PSEs. There is little to choose between the EC and the US in this respect. However, due to the volatility of sugar prices on the world market the percentage PSE for sugar tends to fluctuate much more than the milk PSE. The empirical evidence on agricultural protectionism in Western Europe and the USA, as presented in this section, indicates that levels of protection are subject to substantial short-term variation. This is to be expected due to the influence of exogenous variables affecting market prices both from the supply side (for example variable harvests) and relating to demand (for example shifts in macroeconomic variables such

Table 6.5 Producer subsidy equivalents in the EC and the US, 1979–88

		1979		1980		1981		1982		1983	
		EC(10)	US	EC(10)	US	EC(10)	US	EC(10)	US	EC(10)	US
All crops	Total PSE (mECU/$)	9 139	3 815	5 553	4 675	7 332	5 810	11 761	6 948	7 173	17 426
	% PSE	45	8	25	9	30	12	42	14	26	34
Wheat	Total PSE (mECU/$)	2 848	696	2 579	1 364	3 045	2 106	4 216	1 705	2 609	4 381
	% PSE	34	8	27	14	30	18	35	16	21	37
Coarse grains	Total PSE (mECU/$)	4 242	1 796	2 614	2 190	2 610	2 435	4 481	3 032	2 133	10 363
	% PSE	49	8	29	10	27	11	40	12	20	45
Other oil seeds/ soybeans	Total PSE (mECU/$)	145	817	254	867	297	924	504	1 022	350	1 196
	% PSE	38	6	40	6	42	8	48	8	33	9
Sugar (refined equiv.)	Total PSE (mECU/$)	1 829	424	139	135	1 266	211	2 399	817	1 924	817
	% PSE	68	30	5	6	34	14	63	53	59	52

All livestock products	Net total PSE (mECU/$)	22 965	18 254	24 428	17 827	21 982	19 772	23 812	18 951	29 029	19 127
	Net % PSE	38	31	38	29	31	32	31	31	36	31
Milk	Net total PSE (mECU/$)	12 884	8 968	13 227	9 516	10 263	9 559	11 080	9 633	14 019	10 766
	Net % PSE	62	60	59	57	43	52	41	52	47	57
Pigmeat	Net total PSE (mECU/$)	936	498	1 094	450	980	514	1 014	578	950	620
	Net % PSE	7	5	8	5	6	5	6	6	6	6
All products	Net total PSE (mECU/$)	32 105	22 069	29 982	22 512	29 314	25 581	35 573	25 899	36 202	36 553
	Net % PSE	40	21	35	20	31	23	34	23	33	33

Table 6.5 (continued)

		1984 EC(10)	1984 US	1985 EC(12)	1985 US	1986 EC(12)	1986 US	1987 EC(12)	1987 US	1988 (est) EC(12)	1988 (est) US
All crops	Total PSE (mECU/$)	8 072	10 533	13 071	12 895	22 423	19 337	21 913	20 114	13 196	15 044
	% PSE	24	21	44	26	66	44	66	42	39	35
Wheat	Total PSE (mECU/$)	2 148	3 509	4 970	3 996	8 942	5 207	8 800	5 764	4 010	3 366
	% PSE	14	32	40	40	63	59	66	65	30	39
Coarse grains	Total PSE (mECU/$)	2 929	4 373	4 489	5 688	8 508	10 666	7 716	10 932	4 393	7 701
	% PSE	24	18	40	23	66	48	63	46	34	41
Other oil seeds/ soybeans	Total PSE (mECU/$)	146	919	484	1 124	1 039	1 226	1 322	1 229	1 012	1 812
	% PSE	10	9	30	10	66	13	61	11	53	15
Sugar (refined equiv.)	Total PSE (mECU/$)	2 588	1 199	2 711	1 216	3 222	1 204	3 063	1 393	2 838	110
	% PSE	70	79	76	80	76	74	80	71	71	61

All livestock products	Net total PSE (mECU/$)	29 959	20 907	35 911	21 876	41 026	25 348	37 352	25 510	39 652	24 264
	Net % PSE	36	34	43	36	44	41	42	39	44	35
Milk	Net total PSE (mECU/$)	14 484	11 390	19 944	14 383	23 669	14 589	20 712	12 679	19 045	10 401
	Net % PSE	49	64	66	78	73	81	68	71	60	56
Pigmeat	Net total PSE (mECU/$)	998	586	1 070	645	1 044	820	1 011	861	1 093	791
	Net % PSE	6	6	6	7	5	9	5	8	6	8
All products	Net total PSE (mECU/$)	38 031	31 440	48 982	34 771	63 449	44 684	59 265	45 625	52 847	49 308
	Net % PSE	33	28	43	32	50	42	48	40	43	35

Notes: Total PSEs are denominated in mECU *vis-à-vis* the EC and in m$ *vis-à-vis* the US$.

Sources: OECD, *Updating of PSE/CSE Analysis; Country notes in the EEC and the United States, Paris*, 1989; OECD (1990a).

as exchange rates, interest rates and unemployment). However, the evidence also points to an underlying upward trend in support and protection on both sides of the Atlantic, which appeared to accelerate during the 1980s. This trend, and the associated rise in the budgetary costs of agricultural support (the subject of the next section) was an important contributory factor to the decision by governments to launch the Uruguay Round of MTN negotiations, under the auspices of the GATT, in 1986.

Rising Budgetary Cost of Agricultural Support

In reviewing available information on the budgetary costs of agricultural support in the EC and the US, we confine attention, as far as possible, to the direct costs of supporting farm incomes. Thus, in the case of the EC, rather than looking at total EAGGF expenditure, including the Guidance Section, we consider only Guarantee Section expenditure. Similarly, in the US case, attention is confined to federal government expenditure on farm income stabilisation. Substantial federal government expenditure under other 'agricultural' headings, such as consumer food subsidies, agricultural R&D and agricultural extension, is ignored.

Official information on EAGGF guarantee expenditure is readily available only for 1973 and subsequent years. For the purpose of comparing budgetary expenditure in the EC and the US, we therefore confine attention to the period 1973–89 in both cases.

EC budgetary costs of support

The growth of the EC's EAGGF Guarantee Expenditure, net of expenditure on agri-monetary measures, between 1973 and 1989, is shown by column (5) of Table 6.6. The roughly tenfold increase in net expenditure which occurred between 1973 and 1989 can be partially explained by (a) Community-wide inflation and (b) Community enlargement, from EC(9) in 1973–79 to EC(12) in 1985–89. The influence of inflation can be crudely 'netted out' by comparing the growth of EAGGF guarantee expenditure with the growth of Community GDP. Thus, over the same period, Community GDP increased roughly five-fold (column (6)). Thus, net EAGGF guarantee expenditure increased by roughly double the amount of the increase in Community GDP, as shown by the approximate doubling, over the period, of net EAGGF guarantee expenditure's share of Community GDP (column (7)). Net guarantee expenditure's share of Community GDP displayed a highly significant linear trend with a slope parameter of 0.02 per cent per annum.[5]

Table 6.6 *Evolution of EAGGF guarantee expenditure excluding agri-monetary measures, 1973–89[a]*

(1) Year	(2) Units[b]	(3) Gross expenditure	(4) Receipts from import and sugar levies	(5) Net expenditure	(6) Community GDP at current market prices and exchange rates (1 000 million ECU)	(7) Net expenditure share of GDP[c] (%)
1973	m.ua	2 769.6	551	2 218.6	870.4	0.26
1974	m.ua	2 799.4	330	2 469.4	986.4	0.25
1975	m.ua	3 998.1	590	3 408.1	1 108.6	0.31
1976	m.ua	4 500.4	1 164	3 336.4	1 268.8	0.26
1977	m.ua	4 895.2	2 138	2 757.2	1 409.2	0.20
1978	m.EUA	7 485.0	2 279	5 206.0	1 562.1	0.33
1979	m.EUA	9 708.1	2 143	7 565.1	1 753.6	0.43
1980	m.ECU	10 984.6	2 002	8 982.6	2 026.3	0.44
1981	m.ECU	10 721.8	1 747	8 974.8	2 220.9	0.40
1982	m.ECU	12 056.4	2 228	9 828.4	2 421.3	0.41
1983	m.ECU	15 299.6	2 434	12 865.6	2 593.1	0.50
1984	m.ECU	17 952.1	2 950	15 002.1	2 776.2	0.54
1985	m.ECU	19 536.1	2 179	17 357.1	3 328.8	0.52
1986	m.ECU	21 638.3	2 287	19 351.3	3 525.3	0.55
1987	m.ECU	22 521.1	3 098	19 423.1	3 721.2	0.52
1988	m.ECU	25 745.3	2 895	22 850.3	4 020.2	0.57
1989	m.ECU	26 175.3	2 736	23 439.3	4 377.9	0.54

Notes

a Data relate to EC(9), 1973–79; EC(10), 1980–84; EC(12), 1985–89.
b Purchasing power of the EUA and ECU are identical: purchasing power of the old, pre-1978 u.a. may have been slightly higher than the EUA which replaced it, but no conversion coefficient appears to have been published by Eurostat.
c (7) = [(5)/(6)]100.

Sources: Eurostat Review, various issues; *European Economy*, No. 42, November 1989, Statistical annex; *The Agricultural Situation in the Community, 1988 and 1989 Reports*; Agra Europe, *CAP Monitor* (levy receipts).

The impact of Community enlargement on guarantee expenditure and its share of GDP is more difficult to estimate. However, estimates of the effect of enlargement on the Community's utilised agricultural area and volume of final agricultural output can be cited as crude indicators.

Whereas the enlargement from EC(9) to EC(12) appears to have increased the utilised agricultural area of the Community by nearly 40 per cent, the volume of final agricultural output apparently increased by less than 20 per cent. The discrepancy between those two figures may reflect differences between the EC(9) and the three newly acceding Mediterranean countries in patterns of land use, and the unequal distribution of Community agricultural guarantee expenditure amongst commodities. By and large, Mediterranean-type commodities, such as fruit and vegetables and wine, attract lower levels of budget support than North European commodities like cereals, sugar, dairy and beef. Thus, over the period 1980–89, the unweighted average annual shares of EAGGF guarantee expenditure were respectively 29 per cent for milk and milk products and 15 per cent for cereals. In contrast, the shares of fruit and vegetables and wine were respectively only 6 per cent and 5 per cent.

On the basis of these admittedly rather crude pieces of evidence, we are dubious as to whether Community enlargement can be blamed for EAGGF guarantee expenditure's rising share of Community GDP. Rather, the roots of this trend would appear to have been firmly planted in the northern states of the Community forming the EC(9) before enlargement. The trend is also consistent with the rising level of agricultural protection in the Community already quantified and discussed in this chapter.

US budgetary costs of support

The growth of farm income stabilisation expenditure at current prices by the US Federal Government between 1973 and 1988, is shown in column (1) of Table 6.7. As in the case of the EC, the increase in expenditure over this period was approximately tenfold, and can be partially explained by inflation. The growth of GNP at current prices in the US over the same period is indicated by the figures in column (2) of the table. The effect of correcting the rising level of stabilisation expenditure for inflation is given by the figures in column (3) showing stabilisation expenditure's share of GNP. Again, as in the case of the EC, a rising trend is indicated, though with more short-term variation about the trend. Comparing US stabilisation expenditure (column (1) in Table 6.7) with EC net EAGGF guarantee expenditure (column 5)

Table 6.7   US Federal Government expenditure on farm income stabilisation, 1973–88 ($ billion)

Year	F I stabilisation expenditure[a]	GNP at current prices	Stabilisation expenditure's share of GNP[b]
1973	4.1	1 326	0.31
1974	1.5	1 434	0.11
1975	2.2	1 598	0.14
1976	1.6	1 718	0.09
1977	4.5	1 918	0.24
1978	10.2	2 164	0.47
1979	9.9	2 418	0.41
1980	7.4	2 732	0.27
1981	9.8	3 053	0.32
1982	14.3	3 166	0.45
1983	21.3	3 406	0.63
1984	11.9	3 772	0.32
1985	23.8	4 015	0.59
1986	29.6	4 240	0.70
1987	25.5	4 527	0.56
1988	20.3 (est)	4 881	0.42

Notes
a   Figures for 1979–81 correspond roughly with those shown in OECD, 1987, United States, Table C, with categories 2, 3 and 5 excluded.
b   (3) = [(1)/(2)] 100.

Source: US Bureau of the Census, *Statistical Abstract of the United States*, various years.

of Table 6.6) suggests a higher degree of short-term variation about a rising trend in the US case. US expenditure was particularly low in the immediate aftermath of the commodity boom of the early 1970s, and again in the early 1980s when world prices of major agricultural commodities were again relatively high. Stabilisation expenditure's share of GNP over the period 1973–88 displayed a significant linear trend with a slope parameter of 0.03 per cent per annum.[6]

By and large, the evidence on agricultural budgetary expenditure trends in the EC and the US since the early 1970s suggests substantial similarities. In both cases the agricultural income support budget's share of national income approximately doubled from around 0.3 per cent at the beginning of the period to approaching 0.6 per cent at its end.

However, budgetary expenditure in the US was notably more unstable in the short term. In both cases the figures of budgetary expenditure on farm income support are incomplete. Whereas the EC data excludes national expenditure in the member states which supplements Community budget expenditure, the US data excludes state government expenditures which supplement Federal Government outlays. In both cases, the omissions are substantial, but not readily quantifiable.

Attempts to Reform Agricultural Policies and Lessen Trade Conflict through GATT Negotiations

Background to the Uruguay Round

The volume of world agricultural trade grew rapidly during the 1970s, but made little further headway after about 1980. The earlier rapid growth in trade was particularly marked for grains following the temporary decline in world output in 1972/73 (Hathaway, 1987). The major grain price increases which followed this temporary scarcity of supplies provided a major stimulus not only to production but also to trade as stocks were rebuilt. Production and trade also responded to a growing demand for current consumption, particularly by the Soviet Union and developing countries, including China. But by the early 1980s, the world market prices of most agricultural commodities were declining, at least in real terms, due to a combination of overabundant supplies and flagging demand due, in part, to the second 'oil shock' in 1979.

Thus, as far as agriculture was concerned, the next round of multilateral trade negotiations (MTNs) in GATT was launched against a background of 'excess production capacity relative to flagging demand [resulting] in the growth of exportable surpluses, the collapse of prices, a subsidised scramble for available markets and heightened political frictions over agricultural trade matters' (Warley, 1988). Technical preparations for a possible further round of MTNs concerning agriculture were initiated by the OECD Ministerial Council which authorised a study programme (the Trade Mandate Study) in 1982. The OECD Committees for Agriculture and Trade were instructed to undertake three tasks.

1. To prepare 'an analysis of the approaches and methods for a balanced and gradual reduction of protection for agriculture and the further integration of agriculture within the open multilateral trading system'.
2. To examine 'relevant national policies and measures which have a

significant impact on agricultural trade with the aim of assisting policy-makers in the preparation and implication of agricultural policies'.

3. To suggest 'the most appropriate methods for improving the functioning of the world agricultural market'.

The main fruit of this endeavour was the development of common measures of the total level of government assistance to agriculture – called producer subsidy equivalent (PSE) and consumer subsidy equivalent (CSE) – suitable for use in all OECD countries. The first Trade Mandate Study report, containing empirical estimates of PSEs and CSEs in all OECD countries, was published in 1987 (OECD, 1987). The GATT also formed a study group in 1982 (the Committee on Trade in Agriculture) which reported in 1984.

Part of the impetus for initiating a fresh round of MTNs in GATT came from the enactment of the US Food Security Act of 1985 which, by reducing the loan rate, effectively lowered the floor to world grain prices. The act also reintroduced the use of agricultural export subsidies by the US as a trade weapon.

As a prelude to the Uruguay Round negotiations on agriculture, simulation studies were conducted on both sides of the Atlantic in an attempt to model economic benefits and costs of agricultural policy reform (EC Commission, 1988; Roningen and Dixit, 1989). Although there were methodological similarities between the studies, their objectives differed, reflecting the different approaches of the EC and the US to agricultural policy reform. Whereas the study sponsored by the EC was designed to examine the implications of adopting staged reductions of support in different commodity sectors, but without removing support altogether, the study conducted by the US Department of Agriculture was designed to model the consequences of eliminating all agricultural support measures in the US, the EC and other developed countries.

Despite their differing objectives the results of these two studies pointed to a number of common conclusions at least regarding the identity of the main 'winners' and 'losers' from agricultural policy and trade reform and the scope for compensating the losers.

There were both similarities and differences between these two models. On the one hand, both were based on comparative static partial equilibrium analysis. But they were dissimilar respecting both the policy options considered and geographical scope. Whereas the EC model considered only specific policy options to lower but not eliminate agricultural support, the USDA model examined the implications of completely removing support across the board. Moreover, whereas the

EC model only dealt with bilateral reduction of support by the EC and the US, the USDA model examined the implications of multilateral liberalisation on a global scale.

Despite their dissimilarities, the two models were in broad agreement on certain conclusions. So, for example, both suggested that compared with the benefits of unilateral liberalisation of agricultural trade, the additional benefits of multilateral liberalisation were rather modest except that the producer income loss is significantly lower. Also, the EC tended to gain more in total welfare and lose more producer surplus from the adoption of liberalisation than the US. Because the USDA model did not consider any compromise options short of complete liberalisation, the EC model was less 'inelastic'.

Although the results of both models were subject to all the well-known limitations of comparative static partial-equilibrium analysis, they were nevertheless pertinent to the Uruguay Round negotiations on agriculture. Whereas the EC model simulated the welfare effects of lowering but not eliminating agricultural support on both sides of the Atlantic, the USDA model was concerned only with the root and branch elimination of support. Thus, the construction of the two models and their results were a direct reflection of the limited negotiating positions taken up by the EC and the US early in the Uruguay Round. Both studies pointed to major potential long-run benefits to be derived from reducing agricultural support and liberalising agricultural trade. Although the results of both studies suggested that consumer and tax-payer gains from reform would be sufficient to compensate agricultural producers for their loss of income and still leave a net welfare gain, the political problem of making compensation acceptable to producers remained. The studies also ignored possible adverse external effects of reducing agricultural production such as the loss of rural amenities and the consequences of rural depopulation.

Other simulation studies relevant to the agricultural objectives of the Uruguay Round included the OECD's MTM model (OECD, 1990b) and the Tyers and Anderson model (Tyers and Anderson, 1988).

Inauguration of the Uruguay Round
Thus, by the mid-1980s political pressures were building up for a fresh round of international negotiations in GATT to search for alternatives to the escalation of a major agricultural trade war which might well damage non-agricultural trade as well. Prompted mainly by the US, a special meeting of the GATT contracting parties was held in Punta del Este, Uruguay, in September 1986. At that meeting, a ministerial declaration launching a new round of MTNs, covering a total of 14

separate negotiating areas, was adopted. As far as agriculture was concerned, the crux of the Punta del Este Declaration was that:

> Negotiations shall aim to achieve greater liberalization of trade in agriculture and bring all measures affecting import access and export competition under strengthened and more operationally effective GATT rules and disciplines taking . . . [account of]
>
> 1. improving market access through inter-alia the reduction of import barriers.
> 2. improving the competitive environment by increasing discipline on the use of all direct and indirect subsidies and other measures affecting directly and indirectly agricultural trade, including the phased reduction of their negative effects and dealing with their causes.
> 3. minimising the adverse effects that sanitary and phytosanitary regulations and barriers can have on trade in agriculture . . . (GATT, 1986a).

It was determined that the negotiations would be concluded within four years and, later, that there would be a mid-term review of progress in December 1988.

The GATT initiative marked by the Punta del Este Declaration was complemented by similar moves within the OECD. In May 1987 the OECD issued a Ministerial Communiqué affirming that the governments of OECD countries would treat the Uruguay Round seriously as a means of reforming both the conduct of agricultural trade and domestic agricultural policies. Domestic policy reform was to be based on stated principles, namely that:

1. agricultural support levels should be lower;
2. lower guaranteed prices or production controls should be applied to commodities in excess supply;
3. agricultural supplies should be determined more by market signals and mechanisms and less by administrative decisions;
4. public support of farmers' incomes should be direct, rather than indirect through product price support or input subsidies (Warley, 1987).

These GATT and OECD initiatives were strongly supported by the declarations supporting the process of agricultural policy and trade reform included in the communiqués issued after the Tokyo Economic Summit and Venice Heads of Governments Summit Meeting in June 1986 and June 1987.

By the end of 1987 six countries or groups of countries had tabled initial negotiating positions in GATT on the reform of agricultural trade (GATT, 1988a).

US proposal   The US was the first in the field with the quite radical proposal that all agricultural production and trade subsidies, and all agricultural import barriers including the use of sanitary and phytosanitary regulations to hinder trade, should be phased out over 10 years. The US also proposed two stages of negotiations. In the first stage agreement would be sought on the choice of a comprehensive method of measuring agricultural protection, such as producer subsidy equivalent (PSE), and an overall schedule of reductions under which levels of protection would be brought to zero, in all countries subscribing to the GATT, during the period stipulated. The US recognised that some classes of farm income support, such as direct income subsidies not linked to production or marketing (that is, pure transfer payments), and bona fide 'food aid' programmes might be exempted from the phasing out process. But all instruments of agricultural support, other than 'decoupled' payments, would have to go. The US envisaged that in the second stage individual countries' plans and policy changes for achieving the necessary phasing out of government support would be identified and monitored.

EC proposal   The US proposal was shortly followed by a very different type of proposal by the EC. The EC's initial proposal for multilateral negotiations on agriculture recognised that structural imbalances between supply and demand are the 'root problem affecting world agricultural markets'. Moreover, concerted farm policy reforms to reduce uncertainty, disequilibria and instability prevailing on these markets would entail:

- better control of production by means including the phased reduction of support affecting agricultural trade;
- a greater sensitivity of agriculture to market signals;
- recourse to direct methods of supporting farmers' incomes which are not linked to output.

The EC proposal maintained that agricultural policy adjustments concerted along these lines in the GATT to reach reciprocal, equivalent undertakings would 'reduce the strains on international markets' which would consequently 'function better and resume greater importance in guiding production decisions'.

More concretely, the EC position paper distinguished between a series of short-term actions needed to stabilise agricultural commodity markets, and long-term reforms intended to achieve balances and significant reductions in levels of support. A very significant difference between the US and EC proposals was that whereas the US wanted the total abolition of trade-distorting agricultural support within 10 years, the EC was prepared to commit itself under certain conditions to no more than some reductions in support over an unspecified period.

The short-term actions proposed by the EC were of two types: first, action to reduce current instability in particular commodity markets and, second, action to reduce excess supply overhanging international markets through negotiation to reduce levels of producer support and protection. Under the first type of action the EC wanted agreement in GATT on the management of the markets for cereals (and cereal substitutes), sugar and dairy products in order to achieve greater market stability. Under the second type of action, it was proposed that any reductions in support should be concentrated on the most problematic commodities, namely, the three already identified under the first action type, plus rice, oilseeds and beef.

Under the heading of longer-term reforms, the EC position paper proposed a concerted move towards the reduction of domestic support over a wider range of agricultural commodities allied with a reduction of external protection. Moreover, the EC was prepared to contemplate countries binding reduced levels of maximum protection in GATT, using the PSE or a similar measuring device, suitably modified to give credit for domestic production restraints imposed by the government and to allow for the effects of world price and exchange rate fluctuations. However, it was clear that any offer by the EC to reduce agricultural protection would be subject to two important provisions. First, any agreement on the binding of maximum overall levels of protection must be flexible enough to permit the protection of some individual commodities to be *increased* (our italics), provided others are reduced sufficiently to enable the overall target of reduced protection to be honoured. So, for example, such a provision would enable the EC to escape from the low or zero-tariff bindings on oilseeds and cereal substitutes to which it committed itself in the Dillon Round. The second provision was that the EC was clearly not prepared to negotiate on changing the fundamental principles of the CAP, that is, the principle of Community Preference maintained by means of the instruments of the variable import levy and the variable export subsidy. Thus, negotiations on the possibility of binding maximum levels of agricultural support in GATT must, in the view of the EC, take account not only of world price and currency fluctuations, but also protection and export compensation 'where such measures [are] necessitated by the existence of a *double pricing system*' (our italics) (GATT, 1987).

Thus, despite some signs of greater readiness to consider concerted and reciprocal reductions in agriculture support levels, the EC's negotiating position on agriculture at the beginning of the Uruguay Round was little changed from the position taken up and defended in the Tokyo Round, that is, that radical changes in the most basic elements of the CAP, such as a pricing system which insulates EC producers from the effects of movements in world prices, cannot be the subject of negotiation in GATT. In a later proposal, tabled in Geneva in October 1988, the EC proposed that GATT contracting parties should agree to make progressive reductions in their levels of domestic agricultural support over five years from a 1984 baseline. The proposal also included the details of a new device put forward by the EC both for monitoring progress in reducing support and for binding support levels in any new GATT arrangement. The proposed 'support measurement unit' (SMU) was much more restricted in conception than the PSE. The SMU excluded direct payments for restricting production (such as set-aside payments) and allowed credit for the effects of quotas and similar restrictions on production. The SMU would be based not on the difference between domestic and current world commodity prices, but the difference between the domestic price and a fixed external reference price, with adjustments for both currency fluctuations and, where necessary, inflation (GATT, 1988b).

Cairns Group proposal   Intermediate between the extremes of the US and EC negotiating positions was a proposal tabled by a group of 14 countries, both developed and developing, all with a major interest in agricultural export expansion. The proposal of the 'Cairns Group'[7] resembled the US proposal in aiming at major liberalisation of agricultural trade in the long term, with tariffs bound at zero or near zero levels and new GATT rules and disciplines relating to the use of subsidies and other support measures. But for the shorter term, certain 'early relief' measures and an intermediate reform programme were proposed. The early relief measures included freezes on access levels and production and export subsidies, together with commitment to non-disruptive releases of stocks. The intermediate reform programme envisaged specific and easily monitored commitments regarding reduced levels of overall support (as measured by the PSE or similar measure) according to agreed targets, giving priority attention to the most trade distorting support measures. Like the US, the Cairns Group were prepared to concede that decoupled farm income subsidies, consumer food subsidies and other agricultural development aids might be excluded from the calculation of PSEs. Although it was hoped that the long-term reform programme would be initiated within ten years, the Cairns Group proposal was more flexible than the position taken by the US on the time needed to complete the process of agricultural trade reform.

Canadian, Nordic and Japanese proposals   Other negotiating positions were tabled by Canada, a group of Nordic countries and Japan. The Canadian position was very near to that of the Cairns Group (of which Canada was a member) except that it proposed that the tool used to establish initial levels of agricultural protection and subsequent reductions should be something called the trade distortion equivalent (quantifying all access barriers and distorting subsidies except for measures agreed to be trade-neutral) instead of the PSE.

The Nordic country position was relatively conservative in wishing to confine reform in both the short and long terms to those support measures which most seriously distort agricultural trade. It envisaged the binding of some levels of support and minimum targets for reducing them, using a Canadian-style TDE as the measurement and monitoring device.

The position paper tabled by Japan was the most conservative. It emphasised that national agricultural policies are concerned not only with narrow economic issues like productive efficiency and competitive markets, but also with social issues like food security, aggregate employment and environmental protection. However, Japan was prepared to support the freezing of export subsidies followed by their gradual elimination: also a strengthening of disciplines on the use of other trade-distorting subsidies. On improved market access, it was proposed that tariffs could be reduced using the traditional request-and-offer procedure. On quantitative import restrictions, although prepared to support the principle of their gradual elimination, the Japanese also wanted to retain rules permitting the use of waivers. The introduction and use of comprehensive measures of protection and support such as the PSE was considered by Japan to be unnecessary.

Montreal Mid-term Review, Geneva Accord and beyond

Very little movement in the initial position on agriculture occurred until after the stalled Montreal Mid-term Review in December 1988 and the Geneva Accord (GA) of April 1989. The text of the GA contained no reference to the elimination of trade-distorting support and protection but only its progressive reduction, with credit being allowed for measures already taken since 1986. A revised US position paper, tabled in

October 1989, did not reflect abandonment of the zero option. But, importantly, it proposed the conversion of all NTBs, including agricultural import quotas currently authorised by Article XI:2 (c) (i) of the GATT, to expanding tariff quotas in the short run and simple tariffs after ten years. The zero option implied eventual zero tariffs on all farm products.

The EC responded with a partial tariffication proposal subject to a number of provisions.[8] The two main qualifications were, first, an insistence on the rebalancing of protection and, second, retention of a reformulated Article XI to permit the use of import quotas in exceptional circumstances. The CG supported the US stance on tariffication except that Canada continued to insist on the retention of certain import quotas. Japan offered to reduce tariffs on most food products but rejected the notion of converting import restraints on rice to tariff equivalent form.

Despite reaching a substantial measure of accommodation with the EC on tariffication, the United States did not yield ground on the longer-term issue of the zero option until tabling its 'final' position paper on agriculture, shortly before the intended date of the conclusion of the Round at the end of 1990. The United States was now prepared to settle for a 90 per cent reduction in subsidised exports and a 75 per cent reduction in domestic support and border protection over 10 years. However, at this stage, the EC continued to decline to commit itself to any specific reduction in border protection, apart from offering to reduce internal support by 30 per cent over 10 years, expressed in terms of an AMS. The EC somewhat vaguely claimed that this would open the way for the fixed element of the EC's partial tariff to be reduced *pari passu*. Such an indefinite undertaking was unacceptable to the United States and the CG, and the EC's unwillingness to make a firmer commitment on this point, as well as upon the equally sensitive issue of export subsidies, resulted in the collapse and temporary suspension of the Uruguay Round in December 1990.

Resumption of negotiations

The GATT Secretary-General's efforts to restart the Uruguay Round negotiations were rewarded on 20 February 1991, when officials meeting in Geneva accepted a formula for reviving negotiations on agriculture. Under the formula, all the contracting parties, including the EC, undertook to negotiate towards reaching 'specific binding commitments to reduce farm supports in each of three areas: internal assistance, border protection and export assistance' (*Financial Times*, 22 February 1991). This agreement appeared to represent a concession by the EC to the

US/Cairns Group position. The GATT Secretary-General also made it clear that this agreement on the objectives of the agricultural negotiations also marked the resumption of negotiations in all 15 areas covered by the Uruguay Round.

At this juncture the fate of the agricultural negotiations appeared to hang particularly upon two eventualities: first, the outcome of the MacSharry Plan for reforming the CAP (as discussed more fully below) and, secondly, the result of the US President's bid to extend his fast-track negotiating authority. Although the EC continued to insist, officially, that efforts to reform the CAP were purely an internal concern, quite separate from the Uruguay Round negotiations, most independent observers thought that in reality they were connected and subsequent events tended to support this view. Although the prospects for reforming the CAP along the lines of the MacSharry Plan appeared quite good, mainly for budgetary reasons, the big unanswered question was whether internal Community agreement on the details of the reform could be reached in time to save the Uruguay Round. The effective time limit appeared to be imposed by the second eventuality. Even if the US Congress acceded to the President's application to have his fast-track trade negotiating authority extended for two years, until 1 June 1993, it was thought that early preparations for the November 1992 presidential election might crowd out from the US political agenda anything as controversial as trade liberalising legislation, from about the end of 1991 (Agra Europe, 15 March 1991). Thus, assuming that the eventual success of the Uruguay Round negotiations did hinge to a major degree on the nature and speed of CAP reform, and considering the strength of policy inertia (Moyer and Josling, 1990), meeting an end of 1991 deadline for both reforming the CAP and bringing the Uruguay Round to a successful conclusion appeared to be a formidable task.

Internal EC negotiations for the reform of the CAP, based upon Commission proposals spearheaded by the then Agriculture Commissioner Ray MacSharry, were initiated in the autumn of 1990 and brought to a successful conclusion in May 1992. The main thrust of MacSharry's reform proposals was to phase in substantial reductions in commodity support prices, nearer to world market levels, particularly for arable sector crops. However, the reform also afforded producers compensation for the cuts in support prices in the form of fixed acreage payments. These were to be based upon the product of the difference between the 'old' and 'new' support price levels and a historic regional average yield. Thus, in effect, compensation was to be partially decoupled from current production. Like the support price cuts, compensation payment levels were to be phased in over three years.

Thereafter they would continue at the fully phased in level for an indefinite period. Similar shifts away from price support towards fixed income payments, at least as an interim measure, were proposed and eventually adopted for ruminant livestock. But other sectors of EC agriculture, most notably dairy and sugar, were virtually excluded from the 1992 reform package, which is described and discussed at greater length in the next chapter. Because it provided for major reductions in some domestic support prices, the 1992 CAP reform was also conducive to breaking the log-jam in the Uruguay Round agriculture negotiations.

Resolution of negotiation problems

Dunkel draft agreement on agriculture   At the very end of 1991 the Secretary-General of GATT acted to break the UR stalemate by tabling a draft 'Final Act' covering all areas of the negotiations. The Dunkel draft agreement on agriculture (DDA) dealt specifically with the three contentious issues of improving market access, reducing domestic support and reducing export subsidies. Its key provisions were:

1. On improved market access: an average reduction of 36 per cent in specific tariffs, including those resulting from the tariffication of all NTBs, subject to a minimum reduction of 15 per cent in every tariff line. In addition, minimum access provisions were stipulated, applying to all national markets and set at 3 per cent of the importer's base period consumption in the first year of implementation and rising to 5 per cent in the final year. There were also special safeguard provisions to cushion the effects of unusually large import surges or falls in import prices, based upon the EC's partial tariffication proposal and the similar position ultimately adopted by the US.
2. On domestic support reduction: a uniform cut of 20 per cent, expressed in terms of an AMS and applied individually to all supported commodities, with credit allowed for cuts already made since 1986. 'Green box' policies, defined as 'having no or at most minimal trade distortion effects', to be exempt from reduction. A set of criteria also prescribed for use in determining whether particular schemes of direct payments to farmers could qualify for green box treatment by being effectively decoupled from current levels of production and prices.
3. On export subsidy reduction: twin requirements of a 36 per cent cut in budget outlays on export subsidies and a 24 per cent cut in

the subsidised export volume, both types of cuts to be commodity specific.

Dunkel proposed a common six-year implementation period of 1993–99 for all these reforms. However, two different base periods of 1986–88 and 1986–90 were suggested, applying respectively to (i) improved market access and reduced domestic support and (ii) reduction of export subsidies.

The US and most of the CG countries (but not Canada) were prepared to accept the DDA as the basis for concluding negotiations. But the EC held back for various reasons, including a continuing unwillingness to be tied to any specific commitment to reducing its subsidised exports.

Blair House Agreement   Following the internal EC agreement on CAP reform in May 1992, the prospects for bringing the UR agricultural negotiations to a successful conclusion appeared to be greatly improved. But bilateral negotiations between the EC and the US were still needed to resolve outstanding disagreements on agriculture. From the EC's standpoint any accord with the US would clearly have to be compatible with the recently concluded CAP reform. The US strategy was to minimise concessions to the EC involving departures from the terms of the Dunkel Draft Agreement (DDA).

The effect of the so-called Blair House Agreement (BHA), concluded between the EC and the US in December 1992, was to amend the DDA in certain respects.[9] On market access the EC agreed to conform with the DDA subject to the inclusion of a 10 per cent Community Preference margin in all its tariff equivalent calculations. This implied that, regardless of any GATT commitment to convert variable import levies into tariffs, the EC could always maintain a minimum ad valorem tariff of that amount. On domestic support reduction the recommendations of the DDA were confirmed with two exceptions. First, all direct payments under production limiting programmes might be exempt from reduction subject only to the provisos that either crop payments must be based upon a fixed area and yield, or restricted to 85 per cent of the base area of production, or that livestock payments be based upon a fixed number of animals.[10] Second, the BHA was responsible for weakening the commitment to bind and reduce AMS-denominated domestic support from a commodity-specific basis (as recommended by the DDA) to no more than a global reduction commitment embracing all supported commodities. On export subsidy reduction the EC again agreed to abide by DDA provisions, except that the quantitative export subsidy reduction commitment was relaxed from 24 per cent of base period exports to only 21 per cent. Thus, on what was probably the most critical aspect of the DDA, the BHA yielded a small but possibly quite significant concession to EC position, although the US stood to benefit too.

The BHA also included a 'Peace Clause' which stipulated that provided that domestic support measures conformed fully with commitments under the Agreement they would be exempt from the imposition of countervailing duties as long as they did not cause injury, as well as being exempt from other actions, provided total support did not exceed 'that decided in the 1992 marketing year'. Further, export subsidies conforming with the Agreement would not be subject to countervailing duties, unless they caused injury, and would be exempt from other actions. It is thought that the Peace Clause was added to the BHA at the insistence of the EU seeking protection from further challenges to the legitimacy of the CAP.

A noteworthy feature of the Dunkel Draft Agreement, as amended by the Blair House Accord (DDA–BHA) was the stipulation of proportionately greater reductions in barriers to market access and export competition than in domestic support. There are two possible reasons for this asymmetry. First, with the adoption of CAP reform in the EC and the passage of the 1990 Farm Bill in the US, both protagonists had recently undertaken domestic policy reforms for which they expected to get credit should the DDA–BHA form the basis of an actual UR agreement. Hence, at least as far as the two principal UR participants were concerned, pressure from other participants to concede still deeper cuts in domestic support may have been defused. Second, since farm incomes are affected most directly by reductions in domestic support, the political opposition of producers to larger reductions in this area might be expected to be intense. Thus, where domestic support would remain relatively high even after the modest 20 per cent cut stipulated by the DDA–BHA, governments may have been reluctant to buy off opposition to deeper cuts during the current GATT round.

Final adjustments   Apart from one or two minor adjustments the DDA–BHA effectively resolved outstanding UR disagreements on agriculture between the EC and the US. But two principal unresolved problems stood in the way of reaching a multilateral agreement on agriculture. First, the EC had to overcome internal opposition to the terms of the BHA, particularly from the French. Second, the terms of the DDA–BHA required the assent of other UR participants, including the CG countries and Japan.

Within the EC France took the lead in questioning the compatibility of the DDA–BHA with the reformed CAP, particularly with respect to the cereals sector and cereal exports. France adhered to this position in the face of a Commission document purporting to confirm and demonstrate their compatibility subject to certain assumptions (EC Commission, 1992). A number of independent assessments pointed to the same broad conclusion, that is, that the MacSharry reforms would allow the Community to meet the export constraints proposed by the Dunkel draft document, at least for cereals (for example Josling and Tangermann, 1992). As by far the largest exporter (particularly of wheat) in the Community, France was extremely reluctant to accept any curbs on cereal exports. Thus, on the GATT front, France pressed for a further relaxation of restrictions on subsidised exports beyond the terms of the BHA. But, apparently being realistic enough to realise that this GATT strategy might fail, France also adopted a fall back position of seeking further reforms of the CAP to compensate French and other EC farmers for the alleged adverse effects of the provisionally agreed curbs on subsidised exports.

In the event, France achieved a measure of success on both these fronts. In the UR negotiations a last minute adjustment in the draft agreement on subsidised exports resulted in the so-called front-loading arrangement whereby both the EC and the US would be able either to spend more on export subsidies, or subsidise a larger volume, than the original agreement would have permitted, especially during the early years of the implementation period.[11] Mutual agreement on this adjustment was reached because although the EC wanted it to facilitate the disposal of accumulated stocks, particularly of wheat, beef and some dairy products, the US too stood to benefit from it for similar reasons. In addition, the outcome of the French claim for further reform of the CAP to compensate EC farmers for the alleged adverse effects of the proposed GATT constraints on subsidised exports, was a minor concession at the 1993 farm price review where it was agreed that from 1994 onwards unit set-aside payments would be some 27 per cent higher than in May 1992 when CAP reform was finalised.

We move now to the question of the EC and the US gaining the multilateral assent of all UR participants to the terms of their bilateral agreement on agriculture. Japan had remained adamantly opposed to the liberalisation of its rice imports throughout the negotiations, for reasons of domestic politics and, in the final days of the UR negotiations, it became clear that in order to obtain Japan's assent to an overall settlement, the US and other participants would have to yield ground on this issue. Thus, a country-specific derogation from the terms of the market access agreement was finally conceded permitting Japan and South Korea to postpone the tariffication of their rice import regimes until the end of the implementation period, that is until after the year 2000.[12] As well as gaining the assent of Japan, the EC and the US also needed the backing of the CG countries to their deal on agriculture. Because these countries had hitched their star in the agricultural negotiations mainly to the stance of the US (though the CG position tended to be less extreme in the early stages) they might have felt disappointment at the rather modest gains in prospect for them from the final outcome. However, due to the previous closeness of the CG and US positions, any attempt by the CG to put a spanner in the works at the final stage might lack credibility. Thus the CG might well choose to accept the modest gains on offer under the DDA–BHA and hope for further gains in a subsequent GATT round.[13] In the event no adjustments appear to have been made to the UR Agreement on Agriculture (UR-AA) in order to get the CG countries on board.

The text of the Final Act of the Uruguay Round, signed by 111 countries in Marrakesh on 15 April 1994, included not only the text of the Agriculture Agreement but also the Country Schedules detailing the commitments relating to agriculture entered into by each signatory country. Specifically, these commitments related to the reduction of AMS denominated domestic support, to tariffication and increased market access and to the reduction of export subsidy expenditures and volumes.[14]

Terms of the Uruguay Round Agriculture Agreement: what was achieved

The successful conclusion of a Uruguay Round Agriculture Agreement (UR-AA) means that, for the first time, agriculture is unambiguously subject to GATT disciplines. Whereas before the protection of agriculture had either been treated as a special case (for example by permitting import quotas under Art. XI) or had not been explicitly covered by GATT provisions (for example variable import levies and domestic subsidies), the UR-AA appeared to close these loopholes. The agreed reductions in support and protection, concerned with domestic support, market access and export subsidies, are summarised in Table 6.8. There follows a brief discussion of salient points of the agreement under each of these headings.

Domestic support commitments   Four aspects of these commitments require emphasis. First, the stipulated 20 per cent reduction in support is not commodity-specific but global, that is, it relates to supported

Table 6.8   UR-AA reductions in agricultural support and protection, 1995–2000

Domestic support commitments

20 per cent reduction in total aggregate measurement of support (AMS) over six years from 1986–88 base (price support measured against fixed external reference prices (FERPs))

Credit for reductions since 1986

Green box instruments exempt (for example R&D)

Direct payments under production limitation programmes (blue box instruments) exempt (for example US deficiency payments, EU compensation payments)

Special provisions for developing countries

Market access commitments

All NTBs converted to tariffs

No new NTBs to be created

All base period tariffs including NTBs equivalents to be reduced by unweighted average of 36 per cent over six years from 1986–88 base (tariffs measured against FERPs)

Minimum 15 per cent reduction in each tariff line

All tariffs bound at end of implementation period

Minimum access provision of 3 per cent rising to 5 per cent of base period domestic consumption. Base period imports count towards access requirement. Minimum access provision cannot be cut below actual base period import level

Country-specific derogations (for example Japan and Korea to postpone tariffication of rice imports until 2000)

Special safeguards

EC 10 per cent Community Preference Margin

Special provisions for developing countries

Export subsidy commitments

Agriculture still receives exceptional treatment in that existing export subsidies permitted but capped at base period (1986–90) levels in expenditure and volume terms

Subsidised export expenditure to be reduced by 36 per cent and subsidised export volume by 21 per cent over six years, in each of 22 product categories

Prohibition of export subsidies on commodities not subsidised in base period

Food aid shipments exempt

---

commodities in the aggregate. Thus support of individual commodities may be cut by more or less than 20 per cent (including no reduction). Second, all the stipulated reductions in support are based upon the prices prevailing in 1986–88, that is they are fixed external reference price (FERP) based. Third, 'direct payments under production limiting programmes' are exempt from AMS measurement and reduction, subject to the provisos mentioned earlier in this chapter in discussing the BHA. This exemption was a fudge clearly designed to exempt from reduction EU producer compensation payments under CAP reform as well as US cereal deficiency payments. Fourth, the AA specifies numerous 'green box' policy instruments with 'no, or at most minimal trade distortion effects on production', which are also exempt from reduction. The list of qualifying policies includes public agricultural R&D expenditures, agricultural extension, land retirement (including set-aside) and structural policies like state-assisted early retirement for sub-marginal farmers.

Market access commitments   The conversion of all NTBs to tariffs (that is, tariffication) is an important achievement giving a 'transparency to trade' which was previously missing (Josling, 1993). Whereas previously NTBs such as import quotas and variable levies were the main instruments of border protection, agricultural products are now brought into line with industrial products in this respect by the proscription of all forms of border protection other than tariffs. No new NTBs may be created and all existing ones are required to be converted to tariff equivalent form. All base period tariffs, including those resulting from the conversion of NTBs, are required to be reduced over six years by an unweighted average of 36 per cent, subject to a minimum reduction of 15 per cent in every tariff line. At the end of the implementation period all tariffs are bound at their final level, The guidelines prescribed by the agreement for the determination of base period tariff equivalent levels of former NTBs are somewhat loose.[15] This may help to explain why in some cases the base period tariffs shown in national schedules of reduction commitments appear very high, at several hundred per cent. In these circumstances an average tariff reduction of only 36 per cent (or even lower at only 15 per cent in the case of some individual commodities) can have little impact on market access. Another important feature of the tariffication process is that 'current access opportunities' are required to be maintained at the level of actual import quantities in the base period 1986–88. The effect of this somewhat illiberal provision is that, despite tariffication, traditional importers who previously had preferential market access, through the allocation of import quotas for example, are guaranteed the continuance of their traditional market shares under the new regime.

The problem of import access continuing to be blocked by high tariffs, despite the agreement on tariffication, is met to some extent by the minimum access provisions. The modus operandi of these is a system of tariff quotas with within-quota tariffs set at a low level. But no numerical rule defining 'low level' is written either into the UR-AA itself, or the Modalities Document issued by the GATT to remind participant countries of their 'specific binding commitments under the reform programme'. The agreement does not oblige countries to ensure that their imports reach the minimum access level but only to permit them to do so by providing the requisite access opportunities. Moreover the terms of the agreement give no guidance on the sharing of access opportunities amongst competing importers.

One section of Annex 5, headed 'Special Treatment under Article 4.2', stipulates the conditions under which countries may be permitted to postpone the dismantling of NTBs to agricultural imports until the end of the implementation period. Special treatment can be invoked only where, during the base period, imports of the commodity in question accounted for less than 3 per cent of domestic consumption. Also, the commodity must be the subject of 'non-trade concerns' such as food security and environmental protection, and its domestic production must be constrained by effective supply control measures. Moreover, slightly more generous minimum access opportunities, of 4 per cent rising to 8 per cent of domestic consumption, must be accorded to imports. Although the text of the UR-AA refrains from naming countries for whom the special treatment arrangement may appear to have been designed, it is unremarkable that Japan and South Korea in fact chose to avail themselves of its provisions, specifically regarding the tariffication of rice imports.

A further important aspect of the agreement's market access provisions is the inclusion of special safeguards (SS) to cushion the effects of unusually large surges either in import volumes or import price reductions. In both cases normal tariffs are permitted to be supplemented by additional duties as and when actual import volumes rise above, or import prices (denominated in domestic currencies) fall below, trigger points based upon actual base period levels. Although the amount of the extra duty is proportional to the difference between the actual import volume or price and the level of the trigger, the application of the SS provision is not analogous to a variable import levy since, however large the difference is, the additional protection afforded by the extra duty is never complete. Nevertheless, the operation of this provision could in principle and perhaps also in practice interfere with the realisation of the main goal of the agreement's market access provisions, namely the systematic reduction of tariffs over the implementation period.

The major significance of tariffication, as achieved by the UR-AA, was not so much that major reductions in levels of protection would ensue but rather that internal/domestic prices would no longer be fully insulated from external/world prices. The nature and importance of this change derives from the distinction between 'stabilising' and 'constant margin' support (McClatchy and Warley, 1992, p. 140). Under stabilising support, the width of the price wedge between the domestic and world prices of a protected commodity is manipulated so as to completely stabilise the domestic price. This is the mechanism of the variable import levy (VIL) now outlawed by the UR-AA. Under constant margin support the width of the wedge remains constant so that although the domestic price remains higher it is not isolated from changes in the world price. The working of a flat-rate tariff, which has now partially replaced the VIL in the CAP, exemplifies constant margin support. However, the type of protection afforded by the form of tariffication agreed under the UR-AA does not in fact correspond with either of these models. It is rather, for two reasons, a hybrid form combining features of both. First, the SS provision cushions domestic prices from the full impact of world price fluctuations beyond certain limits. Second, the tariffication process is based upon the 'fixed external reference price' (FERP) principle. Thus the tariffs, or tariff equivalents, subject to systematic reduction over the implementation period are based not upon current world prices but upon average world prices in the base period, 1986–88. Whenever current world prices are below the FERP, the protective impact of the flat-rate tariff is enhanced, in ad valorem terms, and vice versa when current prices are above the FERP. The application of the FERP principle to all measures of reduced support and protection was a major plank in the EC's position on agriculture in the UR. Moreover, the final acceptance of this principle as the basis for tariffication under the UR-AA was a major concession by the US and the CG to the EC position.

Export subsidy reduction commitments   On the contentious issue of export subsidies, the exceptional treatment of agriculture under the GATT (now the World Trade Organisation (WTO)) remains intact, though somewhat modified in form. Although agricultural export subsidies are still 'legal' they are now capped at the base period level respecting both the amount of budgetary expenditure and the volume of exports subsidised. In addition, UR signatories are committed to making commodity-specific export subsidy reduction commitments, excluding food aid shipments. The export subsidy base period is 1986–90, extending two years beyond the base period applying to domestic support reduction and improved market access commitments. But, under the 'front-loading' agreement concluded between the EU and the US just before the end of the Round, if expenditure on subsidised exports in 1991–92 or their volume during the same period actually exceeded their base period levels, the required cuts could be made from that higher level, provided that by the final year of the implementation period the expenditure and volume were both down to the same reduced levels, that is, budgetary expenditure down 36 per cent and volume down 21 per cent from their base period levels. Apart from the front-loading agreement, the effect of the UR-AA's export subsidy provisions is to redefine the 'equitable market shares' referred to in Art.XVI:3 of the GATT as the actual market shares prevailing in 1986–90, the base period (Tangermann, 1994, p. 13). Although all exporters are committed to reducing their subsidised exports, their global market shares should remain unchanged.

The UR-AA does not specify any constraint on the use of one class of export subsidy, the granting of export credits. Regarding these the agreement merely commits GATT (now WTO) signatories to working to develop internationally agreed disciplines. Another notable feature of the agreement's export subsidy reduction provisions is that as long as aggregate expenditure and volume limits are respected there is no limit to the magnitude of unit export subsidies. This omission contrasts with the constraint imposed by the acceptance of the principle of tariffication on importers' freedom to raise unit tariffs in response to lower border prices (apart from the SS provisions). It may therefore be claimed that, due to this asymmetry in the agreement's market access and export subsidy provisions, the latter afford greater scope for domestic market insulation (Tangermann, 1994, p. 29).

Peace Clause   Article 13 of the UR-AA, based upon a section of the BHA concluded between the EU and the US in December 1992, stipulates that, notwithstanding the provisions of the UR Agreement on Subsidies and Countervailing Measures, domestic support measures and export subsidies will be immune from most actions under these provisions as long as the terms of the AA are strictly adhered to. The Peace Clause may be interpreted, particularly by the EU, as signalling for the first time the granting of outside recognition to, and conferring legitimacy on, the (reformed) CAP (Tangermann, 1994, p. 16).

Sanitary and phytosanitary provisions   The UR Agreement on the

Application of Sanitary and Phytosanitary Measures (SPS) is separate from the Agreement on Agriculture (AA). But because technical standards and regulations clearly have economic implications the two agreements are clearly linked.

The main concerns of the Agreement on SPS are food safety and animal and plant health regulations, and its intention is to make it more difficult for these to be used as disguised restrictions on trade. This Agreement calls for all regulations to uphold health and minimum safety standards to be based solely upon objective scientific evidence. The international harmonisation of standards based upon international scientific organisations, such as the Codex Alimentarius Commission, the International Office of Epizootics and the International Plant Protection Organisation, are encouraged (Sanderson, undated, p. 15). However, the autonomous raising of national standards in the light of scientific evidence is not precluded. The agreement also provides for the establishment of a WTO Committee on Sanitary and Phytosanitary Measures to provide a forum for consultation and to monitor the process of international harmonisation.

Although this agreement may succeed in improving the transparency of SPS standards it may not be strong enough to prevent such measures being used to restrict trade. It seems likely that with consumers becoming increasingly health conscious, especially in richer countries, national SPS standards, particularly those concerning food safety will be raised over time in response to public demand. Moreover, standards based solely upon scientific evidence may not be acceptable to either consumers or national governments. Governments may decide that it is politically expedient to base food safety standards upon some blend of scientific evidence and 'irrational' consumer preferences. Moreover, regardless of the basis upon which national SPS standards are raised in response to public demand, it is virtually inevitable that equivalent imports will be required to meet identical standards and that import suppliers who are unable or unwilling to comply will be 'discriminated against', possibly in the face of different and less exacting scientifically-based international standards. It is also easy to see how disparate national SPS standards may lead to 'green protectionism'. In countries with relatively stringent standards, producers may maintain that their marginal costs are higher than those of producers in countries with less exacting standards. Producers in countries with more exacting standards may therefore claim some form of protection against imports from countries with standards which are easier and less costly to meet. From the point of view of trade liberalisation, the harmonisation of SPS standards appears to be a *sine qua non* of success. Yet although the agreement identifies the international harmonisation of standards as a very desirable objective it appears to be weak on the means to achieve that goal. In other words, the agreement lacks the teeth needed to enforce adherence to international standards where these are in conflict with national preferences.

Ex-post evaluation of the Uruguay Round Agriculture Agreement
The actual achievement of the UR-AA fell considerably short of the much greater reductions in agricultural support and protection which the US and CG countries originally hoped for and set as their target. Indeed, the initial position taken up by the US was the zero option calling for the elimination of all trade-distorting support and protection within 10 years. The initial position of the CG was similar, though with a somewhat longer phase-out period. With the EC adamantly opposed to the zero option and the US continuing to cling to it until after the Geneva Accord in 1989, the negotiations became deadlocked for a long period.

With the benefit of hindsight it now appears that the stalemate was broken when, in response to a US proposal for the tariffication of all border measures, the EC offered to tariffy its VIL. It is at this stage of the negotiations that the US appears to have virtually abandoned getting rid of trade-distorting domestic support in favour of securing major reductions in tariffs and export subsidies (Sanderson, 1994, p. 5). Thus, the final outcome strongly reflected this shift in trade liberalising priorities away from achieving major reductions in domestic support in favour of improved market access and restraints upon export subsidies.[16] But even in these latter areas the actual achievements fell considerably short of the keenest liberalisers' original targets. For example, the final position paper on agriculture, tabled by the US as late as the autumn of 1990, still called for a 75 per cent reduction in tariffs and a 90 per cent reduction in subsidised exports over 10 years.

It was inevitable that the retreat on the original objective of cutting domestic support to a major degree should have been matched by rather modest achievements in the linked areas of market access and export subsidies. If domestic agricultural policies induce the production of excess supplies relative to international price levels, then, in order to clear domestic markets, relatively high tariffs are needed to limit imports and generous export subsidies may also be needed to dump abroad such domestic supplies as exceed domestic market requirements.[17] This analysis suggests that the fundamental reason why the actual achievement of the UR fell short of the hopes of countries committed to the cause of major agricultural policy and trade liberalisation was that the objective of seriously reducing domestic support proved to be beyond reach. Indeed, a cynic could argue that the fact that the UR-AA did not call for major changes in domestic policy was one of the main 'selling points' leading eventually to its acceptance (Josling, 1993).

The full explanation of why domestic agricultural support remains resistant to reduction is doubtless complex. But the political opposition of farmers, agribusiness firms and landowners expecting to lose from the withdrawal of support is an obvious contributing factor (DeRosa, 1992; Josling, 1993). Despite agriculture's relatively small contributions to GNP and employment in most developed countries, farmers are skilled lobbyists out of proportion to their numbers, for reasons at least partially explained by public choice theory. So most governments seek to minimise the opposition of farmers, as expressed through their representative organisations, to changes in agricultural policy. A possible means of buying off producer opposition to the reduction of domestic support is to compensate farmers for their consequent producer surplus loss. The economic feasibility of producer compensation appears to be proven provided that the producer surplus loss resulting from policy reform is more than offset by consumer and/or taxpayer gains large enough to leave a net welfare gain (for example, Anderson and Tyers, 1991). Producer compensation was a central feature of the 1992 reform of the CAP. But if producers are nearly fully compensated for the reduction of price support, as under CAP reform, the costs of support are merely transferred from consumers to taxpayers. It is pertinent here to refer to the results of a simulation study (Rayner et al., 1995) of the welfare implications of the 1992 CAP reform for the EC cereals sector, constrained to be consistent with UR-AA obligations, especially regarding the reduction of subsidised exports. These results suggested that, compared with a rather improbable counterfactual of no reform/no price cuts, the reform would yield quite substantial gains to consumers substantially outweighing losses borne by producers and taxpayers. The magnitude of the cut in market prices implicit in the reform was large enough to leave room for a large net welfare gain even if farmers were to be fully compensated for their loss of producer surplus. However, the estimated net gains from CAP reform compared with the more probable counterfactual of continuously falling support prices, at a rate of around 3 per cent per annum, are considerably lower. Under this second scenario consumers gain less from CAP reform due both to the steady erosion of market prices in the counterfactual case and, for the same reason, the budgetary costs of reform (mainly for producer compensation) are higher. In contrast to consumers and the budget, who do less well from CAP reform compared with the declining support price scenario, producers do better. In fact, except in the first year of the projection period (1994), producers actually gain from CAP reform compared with this second counterfactual case.

The foregoing analysis points to the conclusion that substantial further improvements in market access and reductions in subsidised exports are unlikely to be realised without achieving major reductions in domestic support on the scale originally sought by the US and CG countries in the UR, but later abandoned for reasons of political expediency. It is true that under agricultural price support regimes, a disproportionate share of the benefits of support accrue to large-scale farmers who do not 'need' income support. But where past government policies have encouraged farmers to expand production and invest long term, an implied moral obligation not to change the terms of the social contract at short notice may be seen to exist. However, the form of compensation is crucial in order to achieve simultaneously the linked goals of reduced domestic production, better import access and fewer subsidised exports.

To avoid the distortion of trade, compensation for the reduction or withdrawal of government support linked to production should take the form of decoupled payments, as defined in the DDA and later in Annex 2 of the UR-AA. In order to count as being 'decoupled', compensation payments must satisfy three criteria. First, they must be limited to producers with a historic or base period production record; second, the amount of compensation producers are eligible to receive must be fixed and tied to base period (and not current) production and prices; third, producers entitled to receive compensation (based upon their base period production record) are not obliged to produce anything in the current period (in which they receive compensation). A possible weakness of this set of criteria is that the question of whether base period levels of production and prices, to which the amount of compensation is tied, can ever be revised appears to be ambiguous (Sanderson, undated, p. 9). If upward revision were to be permitted, and producers anticipated this taking place, then clearly the payments would not be production neutral.

Few, if any, existing schemes of direct payments to farmers meet all the decoupled payment criteria specified in Annex 2 of the UR-AA. So, for example, CAP compensation payments are not decoupled from current production since producers have to at least plant the crop in order to qualify for payment. Taking US deficiency payments as a second example, until they were abolished by the 1996 Farm Bill, these were tied to current rather than base period prices. On the other hand, in waiving any current production requirement, US deficiency payments were superior to CAP compensatory payments in meeting decoupled payment criteria.[18] However, if genuinely decoupled payments are viewed by public opinion as being largesse granted to producers for 'doing nothing' they may not be acceptable to farmers, particularly if other non-decoupled forms of support are still available. By the same token, the public at large, as taxpayers, may find it difficult to accept the notion of pensioning off farmers on terms which are noticeably more favourable than those available to the victims of other declining industries. Thus, a programme of public re-education may be required to reconcile both agricultural producers and taxpayers to the implied 'revolution' of policy instruments, as a prelude to the universal replacement of all production and trade-distorting agricultural support with genuinely decoupled compensation payments.

NOTES

1. The conceptualisation of the PSE as a comprehensive measure of all forms of protection from foreign competition is usually credited to Corden (1971) and its development specifically in relation to agriculture to Josling (see FAO, 1973 and 1975).
2. That is, nominal tariff equivalent (NTE) = $(Pd - Pw)/Pw$ and effective protection rate (EPR) = $(VAd - VAw)/VAw$ and $\%PSE = \{(Pd - Pw) + \text{direct subsidies}\}/Pd$ where: Pd = domestic price, Pw = world price, Vad = value added at domestic price, Vaw = value added at world price.
3. The UK did not join the European Community and adopt the CAP until 1973.
4. OECD (1987) *National Policies and Agricultural Trade* is the pioneering study giving definitions and methodological details, as well as PSE estimates for 1979–85 inclusive. Some of the original estimates for this period have since been revised (see sources quoted at foot of Table 6.5). Estimates for the years 1986–88 are given by OECD (1990a), *Agricultural Policies, Markets and Trade: Monitoring and Outlook, 1990*.
5. A simple linear time series regression of net expenditure's share of GDP yielded a t-statistic of 9.35 on the slope parameter, with $R^2 = 0.84$, F-Ratio = 87.39 and DW = 1.41. The somewhat low DW statistic suggests a cyclical tendency in the dependent variable, but at only 16 per cent the proportion of random variance is quite low.
6. The value of the t-statistic on the slope parameter was 4.16 (significant at the 1 per cent level), with $R^2 = 0.52$ and DW = 2.03. Though the DW statistic indicates the absence of serial correlation the relatively low value of R^2 indicates a substantial white noise with the model able to 'explain' only about 50 per cent of the variation in the growth of expenditure.
7. A group of 14 countries, both developed and developing, with a common interest in the improvement of trading conditions for agricultural exports. The members were: Argentina, Australia, Brazil, Canada, Chile, Colombia, Fiji, Hungary, Indonesia, Malaysia, New Zealand, Philippines, Thailand and Uruguay. Despite being a CG member, Canada tabled a separate proposal (see below in text).
8. A technical analysis of both the US tariff quota proposal and the EC partial tariff is given by Rayner et al. (1990). The EC proposal and a revised US proposal also contained references to corrective factors for world price and exchange rate changes (see O'Connor et al., 1991).

9. The BHA negotiations were concerned not only with the resolution of outstanding disagreements in the UR, but also with ending a longstanding dispute between the EC and the US concerning the legality in the GATT of the EC's oilseeds support regime. In effect the US made resolving the oilseeds dispute a precondition for reaching accord in the UR.

10. This creation of a 'blue box' category of domestic support measures was clearly designed to exempt from reduction EU producer compensation payments under 1992 CAP reform as well as the cereal deficiency payments which were then an established feature of US agricultural policy.

11. Specifically, under the front-loading arrangement it was agreed that where either subsidised export expenditure or the volume of subsidised exports in 1991–92 (defined as the 'current period') exceeded the 1986–90 base level, reduction commitments could be honoured by starting from the higher 1991–92 level provided that by the end of the implementation period subsidised exports were down to the level already agreed (expressed as a proportion of base period level).

12. South Korea benefited too from this concession because of its close trading links with Japan and the similarity of their agricultural trade policies.

13. The results of a simulation study reported by Tyers (1994) suggest that worthwhile gains for the CG countries are likely to be garnered from the UR–AA. These results point to an estimated 33 per cent increase in the net food export earnings of the CG as a whole due to the combined effects of the UR–AA, CAP reform and the incorporation of the EFTA countries in an enlarged EU. Tyers claims that it is virtually impossible to separate CG gains from the UR–AA *per se* from the gains from CAP reform.

14. The Agriculture Schedule of the EC(12) also included a 'Memorandum of Understanding on Oilseeds' deriving from the section of the BHA of November 1992 resolving the longstanding dispute between the US and the EC in GATT concerning the trade effects of the latter's oilseeds regulation. Thus, effectively, the whole of the bilateral BHA between the US and the EC was finally written into the UR Final Act.

15. These guidelines, which appear in Annex 5 of the UR–AA, clearly leave scope for considerable flexibility in their interpretation and application. The calculation of base period tariff equivalents and final bound tariffs, as presented in national schedules of market access commitments, appears to have been left entirely to national governments, with no provision for monitoring of adherence to the guidelines.

16. The magnitude of this change in priorities is underlined by the fact that although tariffication had been discussed in the GATT before the launch of the UR, it was not a feature of any of the main contenders' opening positions (Tangermann, 1994, p. 18).

17. Under a deficiency payment system, due to the absence of border intervention, domestic market prices should equate with border prices so that export subsidies are unnecessary. A drawback of this system is that the taxpayer cost of support may be very high, particularly under an open-ended system without supply control. Under such a system taxpayer support inevitably extends to subsidising exports once the domestic market becomes saturated.

18. Resulting from the so-called 0/92 provision of the 1985 Food Security Act, a US producer with the requisite base period acreage qualification was entitled to receive 92 per cent of the total deficiency payment to which he would have been entitled had he planted the whole of his permitted acreage even when, by deliberate planning, he had actually planted nothing.

7. Policy reforms in the 1990s and the prospects for further adjustments

INTRODUCTION

In this chapter we review the most recent reforms of agricultural policy on both sides of the Atlantic, within the context of the Uruguay Round agricultural negotiations. We deal first with the EU's 1992 reform of the CAP (the so-called MacSharry Plan) and then turn to proposals put forward subsequently by the EU Commission for 'extending and deepening the 1992 reform'. Particular attention is given to the 'Agenda 2000' proposals formally presented to the EU Council of Farm Ministers in March 1998. Next follows descriptions and analyses of the two most recent US farm bills, the Food, Agriculture, Conservation and Trade Act (FACTA) of 1990 and the Federal Agricultural Improvement and Reform Act (FAIRA) of 1996. In discussing domestic policy reform in the EU and the US, we draw attention to the influence of the relevant provisions of the Uruguay Round Agricultural Act (UR-AA.) Finally, we speculate on the prospects for further progress with agricultural trade reform in the context of the 'Mini-Round' of agricultural trade negotiations due to commence in December 1999.

POLICY REFORM IN THE EU

The 1992 (MacSharry) CAP Reform and the UR-AA

Rationale for the 1992 CAP reform

The central issue in the Uruguay Round agricultural negotiations was the trade distorting effects of national farm support programmes. The US and the Cairns Group countries in particular were adamant that there must be a substantial degree of agricultural trade liberalisation. Compared with this the dismantling of domestic subsidies turned out to have a lower priority for the EC's trading partners. Thus, as far as they were concerned, the CAP had to be reformed in such a way that it became more trade neutral, although this did not necessarily require a reduction in transfers to the farm sector. The CAP reform actually achieved in 1992, involving a pronounced shift away from price support towards direct income or compensation payments (CPs), coupled with supply control, like set-aside in the cereals sector, enabled these objectives to be met. However, as the Uruguay Round (UR) progressed, strong domestic pressures for CAP reform were developing within the EC, concerned particularly with the containment of stocks and the control of the agricultural budget. Thus, quite apart from the external pressures represented by the UR negotiations, the early adoption by the EC of measures to reform the CAP was virtually inevitable by the beginning of the 1990s.

The forging of the 1992 CAP reform within the inner councils of the EC and the critical final stages of the Uruguay Round certainly coincided in time. However, the question of precisely how, if at all, these two parallel political processes impinged upon each other is controversial. Two polar answers to this question have been postulated. On the one hand, CAP reform may be viewed as an outcome of the Round, with the corollary that had it not been for strong international pressure the reform would not have taken place. On the other hand, it may be held that CAP reform would have occurred when it did regardless of the UR (Josling et al., 1996, p. 173). The most accurate answer to this question probably lies somewhere between these polar extremes.

From an institutional standpoint, it is important to recognise that, in consultation with the Commission President (Jacques Delors), Agriculture Commissioner MacSharry was jointly responsible for CAP reform and the agricultural component of the UR negotiations.[1] Nominally at least, the commencement of the UR negotiations, in 1986, predated the start of the internal debate on the 1992 CAP reform by several years. However, there is evidence that the Commission commenced plans for reforming the CAP soon after Ray MacSharry was appointed Agriculture Commissioner in January 1989 (Kay, 1998, p. 187), nearly two years before really substantive UR negotiations on agricultural policy reform started shortly after the collapse of what had been intended to be the 'final' meeting of the Round in Brussels in December 1990.

There is plenty of evidence that, even before the inauguration of the UR, internal pressures for CAP reform would eventually have to be addressed by action. The Commission published a number of documents detailing the reasons for the necessity of reform, including the inexorable growth of intervention stocks and unsustainable agricultural budget costs (see Chapter 5, 'Commission proposals for the reform of the Common Agricultural Policy'). By the end of the 1980s, attempts at piecemeal reform, such as the introduction of milk quotas in 1984 and cereals 'stabilisers', imposing retrospective price penalties on producers for exceeding aggregate production thresholds, had clearly failed to solve the twin problems of ever rising stocks and excessive budget costs. Up to this time all attempts at reforming the CAP had involved tinkering with the until then basic mechanism of producer price support. The new Commission appointed early in 1989, guided by Agriculture Commissioner MacSharry, deserves credit for apparently perceiving that a fundamentally different approach to supporting Community agriculture was needed. Instead of attempting to support farm incomes by underpinning agricultural prices, price intervention should be abandoned in favour of direct income support (DIS). Price support could be replaced by fixed annual payments based upon a qualifying arable land area in the case of crops and a defined herd/flock size in the case of livestock.

During the run-up to the 1992 CAP reform, the Commission repeatedly drew attention to the inequity of the distribution of the benefits of the CAP amongst farmers with different resource endowments. The Commission claimed (though without explicit evidence) that 80 per cent of the benefits went to a minority of relatively large-scale farms accounting for a mere 20 per cent of the overall farm population. This line of thinking may explain why the MacSharry Plan, as originally formulated by the Commission, envisaged some modulation of DIS. Specifically, whereas small-scale farmers would qualify for compensation over the whole of their tillage crop area, including the area required to be set aside, large-scale farmers would be subject to a relatively low set-aside compensation ceiling. The Commission may have seen modulation as one means of reducing the budget cost of substituting DIS for price support. Otherwise it was difficult to see how the proposed reform could be expected to reduce the budget cost of the CAP, compared with maintaining the status quo, though it might improve the controllability and predictability of the budget.

1992 CAP reform and the Uruguay Round negotiations

Returning to the question of the impact of the UR negotiations on the 1992 CAP reform, it is true that the Commission's February 1991 green paper, spelling out the reasons for the necessity of CAP reform (EC Commission, 1991a), referred inter alia to 'tension between the Community and its trading partners' caused by the consequences of the production and price distortions inherent in the unreformed CAP. This strongly suggests that in paving the way for fundamental CAP reform, the Commission *was* mindful of international pressure for reform exerted through the ongoing UR negotiations. However, acknowledging that the UR was one of several reasons for CAP reform advanced by the Commission, is not tantamount to contending that international pressure was the sole, or even the dominant reason why the reform occurred when it did.

The EC clearly perceived advantages for itself outside agriculture, and particularly in the area of trade in services, from cooperating to bring the Uruguay Round to a successful conclusion. Thus, the EC's UR negotiators, including Agriculture Commissioner MacSharry, could not ignore the possibility of potential losses from making concessions on agriculture being more than offset by gains in other areas. So why did MacSharry and other EC negotiators allow the Round to collapse in December 1990 by refusing to negotiate further on agriculture? Tangermann maintains that the EC stalled the Round at that time because MacSharry did not believe that the Community could honour its latest 'offer' on agriculture (tabled in November 1990) without reforming the CAP first (Tangermann, 1998).[2] But the EC's final position paper on agriculture could hardly have been tabled against the Agriculture Commissioner's advice. So, in agreeing to it, either he anticipated the breakdown of the negotiations in Brussels or he was prepared to accept an agricultural agreement close to the EC's 'final' offer. Treating the second of these alternatives as being more plausible than the first, it may be argued that had the Round been concluded 'on time' in December 1990, with the CAP still unreformed, drastic reductions in support prices would have been inevitable to enable the EC to meet its UR commitments on agriculture (as held by Tangermann). Faced with this dilemma, Commissioner MacSharry appears to have risked torpedoing the negotiations in order to buy more time to pilot through the Commission's plans for a fundamental reform of the CAP, substituting DIS for price support to a major degree. In the event the outcome of MacSharry's gamble was successful. The UR negotiations collapsed, but only temporarily, and the Commission's original plan for CAP reform was accepted by the Council of Agriculture Ministers, with a few mostly minor changes some 18 months later in June 1992. This event paved the way for the UR to be brought to a successful conclusion in 1994.

Commissioner MacSharry might be criticised for failing to push through a reformed CAP, compatible with the parameters of a likely UR agreement on agriculture, in time to meet the original UR deadline at the end of 1990. By allowing the internal debate on reform to drift, so that the CAP remained unreformed at that time, he was faced with choosing between (a) an 'unacceptable' UR agreement (at least to EC agriculture) had the Round ended in 1990, or (b) risking an irrecoverable breakdown of the Round in order to buy time to bring the internal process of CAP reform to a successful conclusion. In the event opting for choice (b) paid off for MacSharry, though it might not have done. In response to the criticism that MacSharry should have acted faster in reforming the CAP, it might be argued that, in view of the inherent political and other difficulties of the task, he did well in achieving it in only about three and a half years from the date of his appointment early in 1989.

Reverting to the question posed at the beginning of this section concerning how, if at all, the UR negotiations impacted on the 1992 CAP reform, we are inclined to the view that internal pressures for reform would have brought the reform process to fruition in the early 1990s in any case. But the fact that the reform process happened to coincide with the Uruguay Round added to the prospective benefits of reform should the Round come to a successful conclusion. Thus, the perception that CAP reform was needed to bring the UR to a successful conclusion, with favourable consequences for the EC and other Round participants, may well have accelerated the final stages of the CAP reform process.

Another reason advanced for the timing of the 1992 CAP reform is that, in considering the implications of prospective EU enlargement to include East European countries with much lower farm prices, it was recognised that the budget cost of raising the new entrants' prices to current EU levels would be unacceptably high (Josling, 1993). It is difficult to avoid the conclusion that CAP reform was inevitable for principally domestic reasons. The most that can be said of the effect of external pressure as represented by the Uruguay Round negotiations is that this may have somewhat hastened the reform.

Rationale of the 1992 CAP reform

In February 1991 the Commission published a green paper which emphasised the fundamental imbalance inherent in the CAP system of farm income support (EC Commission, 1991a). This imbalance was attributed by the Commission to guaranteeing market prices rather than incomes *per se*, and to maintaining support prices above market clearing levels, with the result that agricultural output had grown at a rate 'increasingly beyond the market's absorption capacity'. The growing costs of holding rising stocks and subsidising a growing volume of subsidised exports had both borne heavily on the budget.

Although the green paper argued that price support encourages the intensification of agricultural production, it did not specifically refer to the impact of autonomous technical progress on aggregate output either on individual farms or at the aggregate Community level. Price support certainly encourages producers to raise output by intensifying the use of variable inputs like fertiliser. But autonomous technical progress in agriculture occurs virtually regardless of product price levels. The empirically validated theory of the agricultural treadmill postulates that farmers are obliged to adopt unit-cost reducing and generally output-increasing technologies, such as higher-yielding crop varieties, in order to survive the pressures of competition. The effect of price support upon the rate of technological progress in agriculture has not been adequately researched. It might be argued, a priori, both that price support encourages investment in technological innovations (by reducing price uncertainty) and also that the rate of innovation is retarded through the protection price support gives to technological laggards. But despite this ambiguity it is at least clear that because, *ceteris paribus*, aggregate agricultural output inevitably rises in the long run due to technical progress and to low income elasticity, the growth in the demand for food and most other agricultural products lags behind the growth of supply, at least in developed countries, a secular decline in real agricultural prices is essential to achieve market-clearing equilibrium between aggregate supply and aggregate demand. Although there is evidence supporting the Community's claim that, in recent years, EC producer prices for farm products have declined in real terms, real world prices have fallen even faster. Hence the gap between EC prices and world prices to be bridged by export subsidies falling on the CAP budget has widened.

Related to production expanding faster than consumption is the Community's transition from being a net agricultural importer in the aftermath of the first expansion from EC(6) to EC(9) in the early 1970s, to its more recent status as a net exporter. The ratio of total import levy revenues to total export subsidy costs has changed radically for the worse over the last 20 years. Because EC export subsidy expenditures dominate EAGGF guarantee expenditures, comparing the latter expenditures with import levy revenues over time illuminates this problem. The relevant statistics relating to the EC(9) and covering the years 1976 to 1991 are shown in Table 7.1, together with the ratio of import levy receipts to total guarantee expenditure in the furthest right-hand column. It is clear that, even at the beginning of this period, import levy receipts covered only about one fifth of export subsidy and other guarantee expenditure. But by the late 1980s and early 1990s the proportion covered was down to only about one twentieth and apparently still declining.

Having presented the budgetary case for CAP reform, the Commission's

Table 7.1   Agricultural budget expenditure and import levy receipts in the EC(9), 1976–91

Year	Guarantee expenditure (million ECU)	Import levy receipts (million ECU)	ILR/GE (%)
1976	5 721	1 040	18.0
1977	6 830	1 868	27.0
1978	8 673	1 873	22.0
1979	10 314	1 679	16.0
1980	11 315	1 535	14.0
1981	11 141	1 265	11.0
1982	12 406	1 522	12.0
1983	15 956	1 347	8.4
1984	20 464	1 122	5.5
1986	22 911	1 176	5.1
1987	23 876	1 626	6.8
1988	28 830	1 505	5.2
1989	27 225	1 419	5.2
1990	29 742	1 152	3.9
1991	33 306	1 218	3.7

Source: Agra-Europe, *CAP Monitor*, Table 6.5.

green paper went on to argue that the only way to remove the incentive to ever-higher production (and budget cost) inherent in the existing system of support was to lower market prices. But since, other things being equal, lowering market prices would reduce farm incomes, farmers would have to be compensated with direct income aids to make the price reform politically viable.

So here lay a dilemma. Substantial price cuts were needed to improve the efficiency of the CAP (and rescue the budget). Yet considerations of equity and political realism pointed to the adoption and financing of a new budgetary instrument to compensate farmers for the price cuts. Thus the net budgetary saving of price reform, after allowing for the costs of compensation, would certainly be considerably less than the gross saving. Indeed, although the Commission did not admit as much in the green paper, if the scheme of compensation was 'too generous' its budgetary cost might equal or exceed the saving from price reform. However, it may be argued that the budgetary cost of any scheme of discretionary direct income support payments is more 'controllable' than the cost of subsidising a given volume of exports where, due to the instability of world prices and exchange rates, the subsidy per unit of exports is similarly unstable.

In sum, although containing the agricultural budget was the main reason for CAP reform given by the Commission in its 1991 green paper, careful examination of the actual reform proposal points to the conclusion that the major motivation may have been to make the budget less subject to external shocks by switching to a quite major degree from market price support to direct income support.

The fact that a number of important sectors of agriculture were excluded from the 1992 reform of the CAP must inevitably have limited its budgetary impact. However, due to differences in the choice of support instruments, substantial shares of the costs of supporting some excluded sectors, notably dairy and sugar, have been borne by EC consumers rather than the budget.

Summary details of the 1992 CAP reform
Although the Commission's CAP reform proposals had a broader commodity coverage, our discussion of the details of reform is confined to the arable sector (cereals, oilseeds and protein crops) and ruminant livestock (sheep and beef).

The February 1991 green paper did not include any quantitative proposals for support price reductions, but a revised version, published in July 1991, proposed a phased 35 per cent reduction in the price of cereals over the three years 1994–96 (EC Commission, 1991b). Similar proposals were made applying to oilseeds and protein crops. Compensation for the cut in price support would take the form of a fixed area payment based upon the product of the difference between the 'old' and the 'new' support price levels and a 'historic' regional average yield. Thus, in this way, compensation was partially decoupled from current production. The decision to base producer compensation upon regional average yields, rather than upon the historic average yields of individual producers, has important distributional implications. Those with yields above the regional average are penalised whereas those with below average yields gain. The interests of greater equity in the distribution of support are served at the expense of rewarding technical efficiency (Josling and Mariani, 1993).

Except for 'small' producers, defined as those with an annual production of not more than 92 tonnes of cereals (or approximately 20 hectares at the Community average cereal yield), eligibility to receive compensation was to be conditional upon participation in a scheme of 'voluntary' land set aside. The Commission proposed that, initially, scheme participants should be required to set aside 15 per cent of their arable land. In order to avoid production spillovers to other agricultural sectors, farmers would not be permitted to produce any food crop, even for consumption by farm animals, on set aside land. Scheme participants would be eligible to receive the compensatory area payment, not only upon the area planted with cereals, oilseeds or protein crops, but also upon some of the area set aside as well. The Commission originally proposed limiting set-aside compensation to 7.5 hectares of set-aside land per farm regardless of the farmer's total set-aside requirement. Thus, under this 'modulated' set-aside compensation proposal, larger-scale producers would have been penalised directly in proportion to the magnitude of their 'excess' set-aside area.

The proposal to withhold full compensation for set-aside from larger-scale producers proved to be particularly controversial when the Commission's proposals for CAP reform came to be considered by the Council. Countries with a predominance of relatively large farms, like the Netherlands and the UK, were particularly opposed to this aspect. Moreover, the opponents of modulated set-aside succeeded in getting this provision excluded from the modified version of CAP reform finally agreed by the Council, after a prolonged debate of many months, in May 1992. All producers, regardless of their scale of operations, would receive compensation for the whole of their set-aside area. The effect of abandoning the modulation of set-aside payments is, of course, to greatly weaken the distributional bias against large-scale 'professional' farms, and in favour of small farms, which was a distinctive feature of the Commission green papers (Josling and Mariani, 1993). A second important modification of the Commission's original proposal for reforming arable crops support was that the cereal support price reduction (over three years) was eased from 35 per cent to only 29 per cent. Then, at the 1993/94 farm price review early in 1993, set-aside payment rates were raised by some 27 per cent from 1994. This action resulted from a claim by France that the November 1992 Blair House bilateral agreement (BHA) between the EC and the US, on the terms of a Uruguay Round agreement on agriculture, was incompatible with the terms of the CAP reform which preceded it.

The Commission's CAP reform green papers did not define clearly the extent of the crop area which would be eligible to attract compensation payments. Specifically, it was not clear whether the qualifying area was to be limited to a historic level (comparable to the historic constraint imposed upon regional average yields). However, Art. 2 of Council Regulation (EEC) No. 1765/92 of 30 June 1992 makes it clear that, at the regional level, arable crop compensatory payments are restricted to the 'regional base area' defined as 'the average number of hectares ... down to arable crops ... during 1989, 1990 and 1991.' If the area actually planted exceeds the regional base area, producers in the region suffer the collective penalty of having the amount of compensation cut back pari passu in the current marketing year, as well as having an uncompensated 'special set-aside' imposed in the following year. Thus, although the reformed CAP arable regime does not entail the application of crop area quotas at the farm level, the penalty for over-planting at the regional level is likely to deter individual producers from expanding their planting (above their individual base period level) in order to qualify for additional compensation. It should be noted that this implicit constraint upon crop area expansion on individual farms is concerned only with the totality of 'combinable crops' (cereals, oilseeds and protein crops). Thus producers can substitute individual crops (such as oilseeds and wheat), within their overall planting of arable crops, without fear of penalty.

Like the tying of compensation to base period regional average yields, the historic base area constraint partially decouples compensation from current production decisions. However, since under the reformed CAP arable producers are obliged to at least plant crops (except upon land set aside) in order to qualify for compensation, it is not a fully decoupled support regime.

We turn now to a brief summary of how CAP reform affected the milk, beef and sheep sectors. Milk quotas, introduced in 1984, preceded the 1992 CAP reform which, apart from a small producer price reduction, left the milk regime of quotas combined with administered prices of milk and milk products virtually unchanged. The budgetary cost of the milk regime arises from the costs of storing and disposing of excess production at the administered price.

In contrast to the negligible impact on milk, CAP reform has had significant effects upon the sheep and beef support regimes. In the case of sheep, open-ended ewe headage payments were replaced by total payments to individual flockmasters limited by the size of flock for which they had claimed a headage payment in the pre-reform base period (termed the 'reference flock'). The number of ewes comprising the base period flock is termed a 'sheep quota'. The penalty for exceeding the quota is forfeiture of the headage payment (the only remaining form of support for flockowners) on all 'surplus ewes'. Quota rights are transferable amongst flockowners in a region, except that 15 per cent of all transfers must be surrendered without payment to a national reserve (for the benefit of new entrants and other cases of hardship). Regardless of reference flock size, there is a ceiling upon the maximum number of ewes in a single flock eligible to receive the full headage payment – 1000 and 500 respectively for flocks in less-favoured (mainly upland) and other (mainly lowland) regions. Above these ceilings flockowners qualify only for headage payments on the surplus ewes at half the normal rate. Thus, having rejected the modulation of DIS payments for producers of arable crops (apart from the exemption of small-scale producers from set-aside) the Council nevertheless agreed to an element of modulation in payments to sheep flockowners.

The reform of the CAP beef regime is similar to that of sheep, though differing in detail. A first difference is that the reformed beef regime retains an element of market intervention. Intervention buying remains, though for a shorter period each year. Two categories of cattle qualify for beef headage payments: suckler cows and 'male bovine animals' (that is, bulls and steers). In both cases the number of animals qualifying for the full headage payment is subject to restrictions. First, total regional payments are restricted to the number of animals in the region for which claims were made in the pre-reform base period (the 'regional reference herd'). Second, payments on adult male cattle are restricted to 90 per claimant. Third, all payments are subject to a maximum stocking rate ceiling or 'density factor'. The density factor is denominated in terms of 'livestock units' embracing sheep as well as cattle. Exceeding the stocking rate ceiling disqualifies herdowners from receiving any headage payments. However, herdowners with a 'low' stocking rate falling below a pre-determined level qualify for an additional headage payment (or 'extensification premium'). 'Beef quota' rights appear to be transferable amongst holders within a region on a similar basis to sheep quota transfers.

Bearing in mind that EC sugar producers are subject to supply control in the form of production quotas (though the 1992 CAP reform did not alter the sugar regime), it is apparent that virtually all the major temperate agricultural sectors, except wine, are now subject to ceilings, either on the amount of production (milk and sugar), or the crop area (combinable crops), or the number of livestock (sheep and beef cattle), eligible for support financed either from the budget or by consumers. The only significant exceptions to this generalisation are pigs, poultry and horticultural products, all of which receive only minimal support under the CAP.

Implications of UR-AA Ratification for the EU

Introduction
Implementation of the UR-AA commitments began in July 1995 and extends over the six marketing years 1995/6 to 2000/1. The enlargement

of the EU(12) to the EU(15) in January 1995 has required some adjustment of the EU's UR-AA commitments. The new members – Austria, Finland and Sweden – replaced their individual agricultural support systems by CAP mechanisms on joining the EU and aligned their prices with EU levels. The minimum access and export subsidy commitments are adjusted by amalgamating the separate obligations of the new member states with those of the EU(12) netting out base-period trade between the twelve and the three. Adjustment of the tariffication provisions has been more complicated and has involved negotiations between the EU and its trading partners over compensation to the trading partners for the impact of the three adopting the EU's import regime. The outcome of these negotiations is that some third country suppliers were granted improved access to the EU market under the tariff quota arrangements; for example, Canada was granted an increase in the import duty rebate for quality cereals and additional tariff-free quotas for durum wheat and processed oats.

In examining the implications of the UR-AA for the EU, it is relevant to note that the choice of 1986–88 as the base year (or 1986–90 in the case of export subsidies) relates all commitments back to a period of low world prices. Protection levels were high under the 'old' CAP since variable levies and export refunds were increased in this period to offset low external prices. Consequently reduction commitments as regards domestic support, tariffs and export subsidies all commenced from a high base.

Domestic support commitments

The domestic subsidy provisions require a reduction in total trade-distorting domestic support, aggregated across all commodities, of 20 per cent in the six-year implementation period from a 1986–88 base. The domestic support commitments are binding on a calendar year basis. The AMS is calculated for each product and product AMSs are aggregated to derive total domestic support. The AMS includes market price support, non-exempt direct payments and input subsidies. It excludes buying-in or storage subsidies. Market price support dominates the measure; this is equal to the gap between the 'applied administered price' (commercial ECU intervention price) and external world reference price (1986–88 ECU price) multiplied by the quantity of production. A credit is allowed for reductions in support occurring after 1986. Table 7.2 presents AMS data for the EU.

The OECD (1995, p. 41) estimates that the actual total AMS for the EU(12) in 1993, the first year of implementation of CAP reform, was around 62 billion ECU, a fall of some 11 billion ECU from the base

Table 7.2   EU AMS commitments, 1995–2000 (billion ECUs)

	(1) base AMS average 1986/7–88/9	(2) Credit for reduction in support since 1986	1995	1996	1997	1998	1999	0.8*(1)+(2) 2000 AMS allowance
EU(12) Total AMS	73.5	2.4	71.5	69.4	67.4	65.3	63.3	61.2
EU(15) Total AMS	81.0	–	78.7	76.4	74.1	71.8	69.5	67.2

EU(12) Base AMS (billion ECUs): division between product groups

EU(12) crops AMS[a]	EU(12) livestock AMS[b]	EU(12) Other products AMS[c]	EU(12) Total AMS
31.6 (cereals: 20.1)	27.5 (beef: 18.5)	14.4	73.5

Notes
a   Includes cereals, oilseeds and protein crops.
b   Includes livestock and milk products. Includes fruit and vegetables.
c   Includes fruit and vegetables.

Sources: HGCA (1996); MAFF (1994); OECD (1995).

period. This estimated 1993 AMS is close to the final bound level and the EU 'should not experience any difficulty in meeting its AMS commitment, given the current and planned policy configuration' (OECD, 1995, p. 40). There are a number of reasons why the AMS commitment does not constrain the reformed CAP. First, base period support was at a high level when ECU-denominated world prices were historically low. Second, support prices for cereals, oilseeds and protein crops were cut by around one-third and the intervention price for beef by 15 per cent under the 1992 (MacSharry) reform and associated arrangements. Third, compensatory payments introduced as part of the reform and now accounting for some two-thirds of the EU guarantee agricultural budget (FEOGA), are excluded from the AMS calculations. Fourth, the aggregate nature of the AMS allowed the larger cuts in the AMS of some products (for example cereals) to be offset by the smaller cuts in other sectors (for example sugar). The price cut for cereals (note that cereals account for nearly 30 per cent of base-period total AMS) and the exclusion of compensation payments are sufficient for the EU to deliver on its commitment.

Since the AMS excludes budgetary payments made in respect of buying-in or storage costs, intervention stockholding can be used under the CAP to avoid policy adjustments without transgressing its domestic support commitments.

However, the 'due restraint' section of the peace clause constrains the scope for increases in support. This provision is commodity specific, is actionable over 1995–2004, and effectively constrains support expenditure (including that provided by production-limiting programmes as well as that included in the AMS) to the level decided in the 1992/3 marketing year (this covers decisions taken in that year, even if they relate to future years). Thus, as far as the peace clause is concerned existing compensation payments are not in the 'blue box' and can be increased only if, for example, intervention prices are reduced on a proportional basis.

Market access

Tariffication and tariff reductions All NTBs are converted into equivalent tariffs and all base period tariffs, including those resulting from the conversion of NTBs, must be reduced over the six-year implementation period by an unweighted average of 36 per cent subject to a minimum reduction of 15 per cent in every tariff line. The EU calculated base period (average of 1986–88) tariff equivalents by reference to the difference between the internal support price (typically the intervention price plus a 10 per cent 'Community preference' margin) and export prices charged by major suppliers.

Rates of protection were high for many products in the EU in the base period so that initial tariffs were large; for example, 50 per cent for many fruit and vegetables, over 150 per cent for cereals, over 200 per cent for SMP, beef and sugar and over 300 per cent for butter (IATRC, 1994, p. 41). The EU is using three reduction rates: 20, 36 and 100 per cent. The 20 per cent rate has been applied to 'sensitive' products such as sugar, SMP, olive oil and wine, whilst the 36 per cent rate applies to most other products (ibid.). For cereals (excluding oats), the duty paid c.i.f. import price is limited to the intervention price increased by 55 per cent. This is a special commitment made by the EU during its last minute negotiations with the US in December 1993 (Blair House II). The import duties paid under this commitment are typically well below those the EU would have levied on the basis of tariff equivalents. In order to implement this commitment, the EU has established an import reference price system for six categories of cereals (high, medium and low quality wheat, durum wheat, maize and other feed grains). The tariff for each category is fixed as to the difference between the EU intervention price increased by 55 per cent and the c.i.f. Rotterdam ECU import price for the reference cereal calculated as the sum of an appropriate US reference price (f.o.b. Gulf) and freight charges to Rotterdam. In essence, the EU has reintroduced an arrangement akin to the 'old' threshold price/variable levy system. However, protection has been reduced on imports of high quality milling wheats since the new 'threshold' price is lower than the threshold price under the CAP pre-1992.

The process of tariffication and tariff reductions is unlikely to bind the CAP during the implementation period. As already noted the initial tariffs are set so high that even after the reduction commitments have been honoured, the reduced tariffs will still be high enough to keep out imports of most commodities. (Tangermann, 1996).

Minimum access   Under the minimum access commitments, import opportunities are granted for a share of domestic consumption rising from 3–5 per cent to apply to products where NTBs have been tariffied. Importation of these quantities is not guaranteed, rather a reduced duty (32 per cent of the applicable tariff) is charged on these imports. Moreover where exporters had market access in the past, their access opportunities remain protected under a 'current access' provision (for example sheepmeat trade with New Zealand).

The EU is not much affected by these commitments. Due to the special import quota arrangements for certain agricultural products which the EC(12) already had with third countries during the base period (for example sugar imports from ACP countries under the Lome agreement), there are many cases where current access exceeds both the initial and final access commitments. Moreover, the preferential trade arrangements with the countries of Central and Eastern Europe under the Europe Agreements also count against minimum access quantities. However, EU imports of a few commodities are affected to some extent: for example, wheat, pigs and poultry (and products) and dairy products.

Oilseeds

The UR-AA contains a special provision for EU oilseeds stemming from Blair House I. In particular, the Agreement specified a maximum oilseeds area (equal to the average planted area in 1989–91) and that the area would be reduced each year by the rate of set-aside on arable land subject to a minimum rate of 10 per cent. However, the base area relates only to producers benefiting from the crop-specific oilseeds payments system; it does not apply to 'small' producers who do not have a set-aside obligation and who receive compensation at the rate applicable to cereals for all areas sown to arable crops.

In order to comply with this provision, the EU established a 'maximum guaranteed area' for oilseeds (specifically for each category of oilseeds – rapeseed, soybeans, sunflowers) and if the area is exceeded, the crop-specific payments are reduced by 1 per cent for each 1 per cent overshoot in both the current and subsequent marketing year. If the area is exceeded in subsequent years, the reductions are cumulative.

Imports of oilseeds are free of tariffs and no refunds are granted on exports; the internal price is essentially a 'world' price.

Export subsidies
The export subsidy provisions require budgetary expenditures on export subsidies to be reduced by 36 per cent and the volume of subsidised exports to be reduced by 21 per cent over the six-year implementation period from a 1986–90 base in each of 22 product categories. Under Blair House II, 'front-loading' of the reduction schedule is permitted using a higher base (average 1991–92). The volumes and expenditures constrained by the export subsidy commitments are quite large for a number of products and give rise to significant absolute reductions over the six-year period. For example, the total base volume for cereals for the EU(15) is around 36 million tonnes (around 22 million tonnes wheat and 14 million tonnes coarse grains) and this is reduced to around 25 million tonnes by 2000 (14 million tonnes wheat and 11 million tonnes coarse grains). For sugar, beef and dairy products there are also large absolute volume reductions. The total reduction in export subsidies is around ECU 4 billion comparing the 2000 commitment with the base level outlay.

Several analysts (for example, Tangermann, 1998; Thomson, 1998 and Tracy, 1997) and the EU Commission itself (EU Commission, 1997a) have pointed out that the constraints on subsidised export volumes may eventually require adjustments to the CAP for products such as cereals, beef, dairy products, sugar and possibly poultry and pork. However, it appears unlikely that such adjustments will be required before 2000. This is partly because of the short-run impact of the 1992 reform, partly because of the surge in world commodity prices in 1995–96 and partly because of flexibility built into the commitment schedule until 2000, such that a shortfall in one year can build up a credit in succeeding years. In addition, food aid is excluded from the reduction commitments and intervention storage and, for the crops sector, set aside can be used to avoid temporary problems.

Much attention has been paid to the constraints on subsidised cereal exports, cereals being at the centre-stage of both the Uruguay Round negotiations and the 1992 reform package. The MacSharry reform has allowed the EU to meet its constraint on export subsidy outlay quite comfortably because of the large cut in the intervention price and the consequent reduction in unit export refund. EU support prices were reduced by some 30 per cent over 1992–95 and world prices have risen since the base period so that the unit export refund declined considerably between 1992 and 1996. Indeed, the EU imposed a cereals export tax in 1996 and only reintroduced export subsidies in 1997. The 1992 reform also led to a reduction in cereals production and an increase in domestic cereals usage so that EU cereals exports declined significantly and by 1995/6 were well below the ceiling on subsidised exports, and intervention stocks had been run down. However, over the course of the implementation period, the limit on subsidised export volume declines whilst the EU's export potential rises because of the likely growth in production (from yield gains) which outstrips the likely growth in domestic cereals use. Hence export potential might exceed the UR-AA constraint at some stage in the future. Whilst analysts have disagreed about the quantities involved, there is some agreement that the EU will have difficulty in meeting its commitments on subsidised export volume by 2000 and thereafter without making adjustments to the CAP. For example, in the Agricultural Strategy Paper published in 1995, the EU Commission predicted that by 2000, the EU export availability for cereals would be some 12 million tonnes above the GATT constraint.[3]

The 1997 EU Commission assessment of prospects for agricultural markets in the light of the UR-AA commitments

In April 1997, the EU Commission published market balance forecasts for certain key agricultural products over the period 1997–2005 assuming an unchanged CAP and that the GATT commitments made under the UR-AA would remain unchanged for the 2001–2005 period (EU Commission, 1997a). It was assumed that subsidised exports would be equal to the annual GATT limits and that imports would be equal to minimum access quantities, or above these quantities where relevant. The principal conclusions by sector are as follows:

1. Cereals: with an assumed set-aside rate of 17.5 per cent, cereals area is expected to stabilise at around 36 million hectares with the area under wheat increasing at the expense of that under coarse grains. Cereal yields are expected to grow so that production increases from 202 million tonnes in 1996/7 to 214 million tonnes in 2005/6. Consumption is expected to increase at a slower rate

rising from 170 million tonnes to 178 million tonnes over the same period. From 2001/2, the GATT constraints on subsidised exports for both wheat and coarse grains are expected to bind limiting exports to 14 million tonnes per annum for wheat and 11 million tonnes per annum for coarse grains whilst cereals imports are at 5 million tonnes per annum. Intervention stocks are forecast to increase rapidly to some 58 million tonnes (46 million tonnes of wheat and 12 million tonnes of coarse grains) by 2005/6.

2. Beef and veal: Beef production is expected to exceed consumption over the forecast period with production predicted at 7.7 million tonnes and consumption at 7.2 million tonnes in 2005. Exports are constrained by the GATT commitment to 0.7 million tonnes per annum after 2000 and imports are 0.5 million tonnes per annum. Intervention stocks are expected to rise to over 1 million tonnes by 2005.

3. Pigmeat and poultrymeat: the GATT constraints on subsidised exports are expected to bind throughout the forecast period.

4. Milk and dairy products: the excess of production over domestic consumption – the 'milk surplus' – is expected to be between around 9 million tonnes (whole milk equivalent) per annum over the forecast period, some 8 per cent of consumption. GATT ceilings limit exports of cheese and skimmed milk powder but not butter. However, the Commission is sceptical that a market exists for potential butter exports and intervention stocks are expected to increase. Intervention stocks for skimmed milk powder are also expected to rise.

The Agenda 2000 Proposals for Further CAP Reform

Policy background to the Agenda 2000 proposals[4]
The reform process initiated by Ray MacSharry has been continued since his term of office as Agricultural Commissioner ended in 1992. In 1993, René Steichen was appointed the Agricultural Commissioner in the new Commission headed by Jacques Delors as President. Steichen saw through the implementation of the MacSharry reforms in the arable and livestock sectors and launched reform proposals for the wine and fruit and vegetable regimes. A new Commission was appointed in January 1995 headed by a new President – Jacques Santer – and with Franz Fischler as the new Agricultural Commissioner. Fischler has emerged as a major figure in this new Commission and has imprinted his stamp on proposals for the evolution of agricultural policy. During his period of office he has consistently articulated and refined his views

on the desirable shape of European agriculture in the twenty-first century. In 1998, he set out his 'vision for European agriculture' as (Fischler, 1998, p. 2):

> What Europe continues to need is an agricultural sector that is geared towards market requirements, operates in a competitive and sustainable manner, produces top-quality products, ensures stewardship of the farming countryside throughout Europe and maintains the quality of life in rural areas.

Commissioner Fischler's first important paper detailing new long-term directions for the CAP was issued in November 1995 as the 'Agricultural Strategy Paper' (EU Commission, 1995). This paper was prepared for the Madrid summit of the EU Heads of State in December 1995; this meeting being convened to discuss eastward enlargement of the Union. The EU has had Association Agreements with ten countries of Central and Eastern Europe (the CEECs) since 1991. These agreements were viewed on both sides as holding arrangements pending eventual membership of the Union, possibly in the early years of the twenty-first century. The strategy paper discussed the major implications for the future of the CAP in the light of the challenge of enlargement and other issues regarded as critical, such as increasing market imbalances, UR-AA commitments and the next round of WTO negotiations. The paper also discussed the prospects for the agricultural relations between the EU and the CEECs during the pre-accession period. It was made clear that the accession of the CEECs 'will change the economic and political environment for the CAP decisively' (Marsh and Tangermann, 1996, p. 2), not least because the size of agriculture in the Union will be enlarged significantly, and much more so than the EU's GDP. The message of the Strategy Paper was that the CAP required adjustment because of the implications of eastward enlargement for the following reasons:[5]

1. Agriculture in the CEECs has the potential to produce large surpluses at the current CAP support prices noting that (a) CEEC farm prices are below CAP prices and (b) that the completion of structural reform in the agriculture of the CEECs would increase production potential.
2. Higher food prices would impose burdens on consumers in the CEECs where per capita incomes are below those in the EU.
3. Extension of the CAP to the CEECs would impose a large burden on the EU's budget.
4. The UR-AA commitments of the CEECs are tighter than those of

the EU; extension of the CAP to the CEECs would make it more difficult for the (enlarged EU) to meet its commitments.

The Strategy Paper examined three options for the future of the CAP:

Option 1: Maintain the post 1992 CAP reform status quo
Option 2: Radical reform beyond the parameters set in 1992.
Option 3: Developing the 1992 approach.

Option 1 was rejected by the Commission on the ground that, because of technical progress, yields are bound to go on increasing, leading to growing surpluses and market imbalances due to stagnant internal demand and export market constraints imposed by the UR-AA. In addition, enlargement to the East would make major CAP reform inevitable under the status quo giving rise to high budgetary costs in the form of large compensation payments to CEEC farmers.

Option 2 would involve the phasing out of both price support and compensatory payments, with DIS being limited to payments for environmental services. The Commission took the view that adopting this option would entail exposure to unacceptably high social and environmental risks. The repair of possible consequent social and environmental damage could impose heavy stress on the Community budget. Moreover, to the extent that the damaging effects of radical reform were unequally distributed amongst member states, the Community's economic and social cohesion would be undermined, particularly if the costs of compensation were to be transferred back from Brussels to national exchequers (as advocated by some radical reformers).

Option 3, or 'Developing the 1992 approach' was the strategy favoured by the Commission. The adoption of this option would entail further reforms on three fronts:

1. Reduced reliance on price support (but not necessarily its abolition).
2. The continuance of direct income payments to compensate producers for possible loss of income due to price cuts.
3. Increased emphasis on linking direct income payments with social needs and the provision of environmental services.

Under Option 3, the Commission's paper also stresses the need for additional reforms such as:

1. Measures to make Community agriculture more competitive in order to participate more fully in world trade.

2. To consolidate existing parallel strands of the CAP – agricultural price and marketing policy, structural policy and the as yet limited agri-environmental programme – into an 'integrated rural policy'.
3. To simplify the CAP, particularly at the EU level, and to give member state governments greater latitude in implementing centrally determined decisions.

A major omission from the Commission's discussion of Option 3 was the future of the EU's sugar and milk quota regimes. Would these be phased out in the interests of domestic production efficiency and competition amongst member states? Or would such a drastic measure be beyond the bounds of political feasibility?

By rejecting Option 1, the Commission appeared to agree that further CAP reform was inevitable, if only for budgetary reasons and possibly also to foster improved international trade relations. The Commission also rejected what it chose to call 'radical reform' (Option 2). However, the difference between this and Option 3 (developing the 1992 approach) appears to be largely a question of degree. By endorsing inter alia reduced reliance on price support and improved competitiveness of EU agriculture, the Commission was being considerably more radical than its predecessors. The Commission also made a quite radical proposal under the heading of simplification in that it proposed five-year (rather than annual) negotiations over CAP price support and related instruments.

In a number of speeches in 1995 and 1996, Commissioner Fischler reiterated and amplified the key points in the Strategy Paper. Importantly, he articulated the challenges to be faced by the CAP in the future and his vision for European agriculture. These views were consolidated in the agricultural policy chapter of a major document widely known as Agenda 2000, issued by the Commission in 1997 and formally presented (after some modification) to the Council of Farm Ministers (as Council Regulations) in March 1998. However, before turning to the Agenda 2000 documents we first summarise the pressures that have set the parameters for CAP reform in the next century.

Pressures for further CAP reform
The 1992 'MacSharry' reform of the CAP was thought to be quite radical at the time. However, the switch from price support to quasi-decoupled payments is representative of the general tendency in agricultural policy reform that is occurring in most developed countries in the 1990s. This commonality is no accident; countries are locked into a path of reform that is dictated by the UR-AA which requires a reduction in the trade distorting impacts of farm policy.

In retrospect, the 1992 reform was a 'holding' operation which enabled the EU to simultaneously conclude the UR-AA and stave off immediate pressures from rising surpluses. In essence, as Tangermann (1998) points out, the 1992 package was the beginning rather than the end of fundamental reform of the CAP. Indeed, a number of factors are creating pressures for further reform of the CAP.[6]

1. *Rising market imbalances and UR-AA constraints on subsidised exports* As noted earlier, the Commission projects rising 'structural' surpluses for a number of commodities, especially for cereals, beef and dairy products, after the year 2000. The UR-AA constraints on subsidised export volumes would limit the disposal of these surpluses onto world markets; consequently, rapidly rising intervention stocks are projected without policy change.
2. *The 'mini-round' of WTO agricultural negotiations beginning in 1999* The negotiations under the auspices of the WTO on the 'continuation of the reform process' in agriculture portend additional pressures on the CAP. The US and the Cairns Group are likely to press for further curbs on, and possibly the elimination of, subsidised exports and also improved import access and tariff cuts. In addition, domestic subsidies will come under further scrutiny, with pressures to have all income transfers fall into the 'green-box'. Derogation of the 'blue-box' is likely to be a major issue so that the EU may be under pressure to convert its compensation payments into fully decoupled payments or to substitute 'green-box' compatible environmental payments for compensation payments.
3. *EU enlargement* Enlargement of the EU to the East will give rise to major problems for the CAP if it is applied in unmodified form to the CEECs, after accession. These problems include a marked rise in budget cost and increased difficulties for the enlarged Union in meeting its UR-AA commitments. Compensation payments pose a particular problem since farm prices are likely to rise within the CEECs after accession but it would be difficult to withhold such payments from the new member states whilst they continue to be paid in the old member states.
4. *The budgetary constraint* Agricultural support expenditure is limited by the overall ceiling on the EU budget and the agricultural guideline which constrains FEOGA spending within the budget ceiling. In view of the drive toward European Monetary Union, there is pressure for budgetary restraint; in particular, EU governments are refusing to commit themselves to higher contributions to the EU budget when they have to practise domestic budgetary

restraint to meet the criteria for joining economic and monetary union due for launch in January 1999. In short, there is no prospect of the Union's own resources exceeding its ceiling of 1.27 per cent of EU GDP or of the agricultural guideline being increased.

5. *Environment*   Environmental issues have emerged as important agricultural policy concerns in the last decade. Examples are the preservation of countryside amenity, preservation of biodiversity and curbing pollution spillovers from the use of farm inputs. Thus as the major user of land, agriculture makes a distinctive contribution to the appearance of landscapes throughout the EU. In addition, insofar as farming promotes the cultivation of economically valuable species it may result in the loss of other species which nevertheless have 'external' value. Finally, pollution side effects from the use of fertilisers and pesticides and the irreversible impacts of non-sustainable farming practices are issues of public concern. Moreover, environmental practices are likely to become increasingly important in international trade negotiations.

6. *Food quality and safety*   There are growing consumer concerns over the safety and quality of food, especially since the BSE crisis. In general, there are public health concerns over the transmission of disease from animals to humans in the food chain; the impact of chemicals in foods and the genetic modification of food raw materials. In addition, there is an increasing focus on links between diet and health. Overall, agricultural policy is seen to have a role in ensuring a supply of 'wholesome' food.

7. *Food industry interests*   Farmers are increasingly suppliers of raw materials to a highly concentrated food industry on conditions stipulated by the demands of the later stages of the food chain in a situation of European-wide competition. Agricultural policy reform which lowers price support and liberalises trade would give direct benefits to the food industry and allow it to realise its export potential.

8. *Rural development*   A consequence of market liberalisation is that major structural adjustment is likely in much of EU agriculture. Whilst the situation differs between regions, it is possible that there could be substantial reductions in the number of farmers and workers employed in agriculture and ancillary industries, as well as a continuing shift to part-time farming. In addition, capital would move to more profitable rural industries. It has been argued, by for example Buckwell (1997), that an integrated rural policy could play an important role in assisting this transformation.

Agenda 2000 Proposals for the CAP

Introduction
In response to these pressures, the Commission proposed adjustments to the 1992 reform to come into force by the turn of the century. In particular, in July 1997, the EU Commission published 'Agenda 2000: For a stronger and wider Union'. This document outlines the broad perspectives for the development of the Union and its policies beyond the turn of the century, discusses issues related to enlargement to the East and sets out a proposed financial framework for EU-wide policies beyond 2000. It also includes proposals for further CAP reform building on the discussion in the 'Agricultural Strategy Paper'. The modified proposals for CAP reform that were subsequently formally presented to the Council of Farm Ministers were published as a Commission document in March, 1998 (EU Commission, 1998).

The agricultural policy strategy expressed in Agenda 2000 consists of 'deepening and extending the 1992 reform through further shifts from price support to direct payments and developing a coherent rural strategy to accompany this process' (EU Commission, 1997a, p. 29). This strategy is set within the context of updated policy objectives for the CAP. These objectives may be summarised as follows:[7]

1. Improve the competitiveness of EU agriculture on both internal and external markets.
2. Ensure food safety and food quality.
3. Ensure a fair standard of living for the agricultural community and contribute to the stability of farm incomes.
4. Integrate environmental goals into the CAP and develop the 'stewardship' role of farmers in managing the countryside.
5. Assist the creation of alternative job opportunities for farmers and their families.
6. Contribute to economic cohesion within the EU.
7. Simplify EU legislation.

In its 1998 Paper, the Commission explains that the CAP needs further reform in the light of internal and external 'challenges'. In the Commission's view 'the challenges facing the CAP are first and foremost internal in nature' (EU Commission, 1998, p. 1). It lists three of these:

1. Without a reduction in support prices, surpluses would reappear, stocks would rise and the budget costs of support would become intolerable. Furthermore, there would be declines in the EU's inter-

national market shares in raw and processed agricultural commodities.
2. The CAP gives rise to negative impacts: (a) support is distributed unequally and is not concentrated on regions and producers who are the most disadvantaged and (b) farming practices were often excessively intensive and had a serious impact on the environment and animal health.
3. The operation of the CAP is complex and bureaucratic.

The Commission also notes that these challenges 'are reinforced by two external factors':

1. Enlargement of the Union.
2. The new round of agricultural negotiations under the WTO.

Guidelines and proposals
Below, we list the Commission guidelines forming the basis of the reform proposals and a summary of the proposals themselves. Details of the proposals are listed in the Appendix to this chapter. It should be noted that the guidelines as listed below are an interpretation of those published and not an exact copy.

Guideline 1   Cut support prices and take related measures to increase the competitiveness of EU agriculture on domestic and world markets and increase direct (compensation) payments to safeguard farmers' incomes.[8] The proposals include:

- A 20 per cent cut in the intervention price for cereals; a 30 per cent cut in the intervention price and a conversion of intervention into private storage for beef and a 15 per cent cut in the intervention price for basic milk components (butter and SMP).
- A rise in the compensation payment for cereals (by 50 per cent of the cut in the intervention price); an increase in headage payments (premia) for beef animals and the introduction of direct payments to dairy producers in the form of a dairy cow premium (notionally split between a dairy component and a beef component).
- A reduction in the area payment for oilseeds so that it is equal to the area payment per hectare (compensation payment multiplied by historic yield) for cereals. However, supplementary payments for protein crops and durum wheat are retained.
- The effective abandonment of 'compulsory' set-aside in the arable

sector (by 'compulsory' we mean the requirement to set-aside land in order to qualify for compensation payments). The authority to require compulsory set-aside is retained but the reference rate is set at 0 per cent rather than at the current 17.5 per cent. As currently, the actual set-aside rate is discretionary but the expectation is that 0 per cent will be the norm.

- The retention of voluntary set-aside at a minimum 10 per cent rate. The payment rate for both voluntary and compulsory set-aside (when in force) to be equal to the area payment on cereals.
- The retention of the essential elements of the 1992 reform in relation to compensation payments for arable crops in that they would be linked to both historic base areas and to historic yields. In addition, if base areas are exceeded financial penalties would still apply but 'extraordinary set-aside' is to be abolished. So partial decoupling is to be retained in that compensation payments are tied to base period average yields and historic base areas both at a regional level.
- An increase in the global milk quota of 2 per cent.
- The retention of ceilings on the number of animals that premia payments can be claimed for in the beef sector.

Guideline 2   Expand the role of environmental policies and lay the foundations for an integrated rural development policy. The proposals include:

- Increased payments for the provision of environmental services and extensive farming methods.
- Consolidation of structural adjustment assistance, support for farming in less favoured areas (LFAs), agri-environmental aid, support for forestry, rural assistance (farming related) and support for processing and marketing into a new Rural Development Regulation. The transfer of expenditure on these measures from the Guidance to the Guarantee section of the CAP budget.
- Cross-compliance: environmental conditions to be attached to all direct payment schemes with individual member states deciding what form the conditions take.

Guideline 3   Transfer some functions to member states from the Commission. The proposals include:

- A minority portion of the compensation premia to beef and dairy producers to take the form of 'national envelopes' financed by the

CAP budget but distributed according to member state priorities as to the balance between intensive and extensive production.
* Member states to have the opportunity to define their own priorities within the Rural Development Regulation.

Guideline 4   Reduce the inequality in the allocation of direct aid. The proposal is to introduce a ceiling on the total amount of direct aid a farm can receive on sums over ECU 100 000 by tapering the payments in excess of this figure by 20–25 per cent.

Expected impacts of the proposals
The Commission document includes forecasts of the impacts of implementing the reforms through 2000 to 2006 for the EU(15) compared to continuing with the CAP status quo. A brief summary of these expected impacts is given below.

Arable sector   The production of both wheat and coarse grains increases substantially. The EU export price for wheat is above the intervention price so that wheat can be exported without resort to export subsidies and wheat exports rise. However, coarse grain exports are constrained by the UR-AA ceiling since a refund is still required, although the unit refund is much lower than under the CAP status quo. Intervention stocks for cereals are expected to be around 25 million tonnes by 2005 (lower overall stocks but higher stocks of coarse grains than under the status quo). The budgetary costs of export refunds and intervention decline whilst the costs of direct payments increase. Overall, there is expected to be a marginal saving in budget costs of ECU 0.03 billion by 2006. Finally, the reduction in the cereals intervention price leads to the elimination of export refunds for pigmeat, eggs and poultry meat and cereal products leading to budgetary savings of around ECU 0.3 billion.

Beef sector   The consumption of beef rises, the unit export refund falls and intervention stocks are eliminated. The budgetary savings on export subsidies and intervention are outweighed by the increase in direct aid so that there is a net increase in budgetary costs of ECU 1.99 billion.

Dairy sector   The price reduction leads to increased cheese exports without subsidy, higher internal consumption of butter, a substantial reduction in the export refund for SMP and the elimination of intervention stocks for butter and SMP. Budgetary savings on export refunds, intervention and aid for internal disposal are outweighed by the cost of the introduction of direct aids so that net budget costs increase by ECU 1.9 billion.

Overall financial impact By 2006 the outlays under the guarantee section of the CAP budget for the commodity regimes rise by ECU 3.145 billion. In addition, the rural development measures add ECU 2.19 billion to the guarantee section but with some savings in the guidance section. Overall, the cost of the CAP budget (guarantee and guidance) increases by some ECU 6 billion.

Initial reaction by the Council of Farm Ministers[9]
The Council of Farm Ministers generally denounced the Agenda 2000 blueprint when it was presented on 18 March 1998. A majority of ministers complained about the perceived inadequacy of the proposed increases in direct payments to be given as compensation for the cuts in support prices for cereals, beef and milk. Germany, Ireland and Spain led the attack on the proposals supported by France; however, the UK and Denmark were generally supportive of the principles of reform although critical of some of the details. After the meeting, aides to Commissioner Fischler stated that they still expected the broad thrust of the proposals, including the cuts in support prices, to be adopted but conceded that some modifications would have to be made.

Comment on the Agenda 2000 proposals for CAP reform[10]
The central message of the Commission's recommendations is that income support should be increasingly decoupled from market policy, with price levels for a number of key products being aligned much closer to world market prices than in the past. The Commission believes that this increased market orientation would enable EU agriculture to participate in the expected expansion of world trade in farm commodities, facilitate the integration of the CEECs into the Union and minimise pressures on the CAP in the next (1999) round of multilateral trade negotiations. It is also clear that the quid pro quo for a reduced reliance on price support is a continuation of the system of compensation payments but with the effective abandonment of supply control (set-aside) in the crops sector. The Agenda 2000 paper shirks the issue of phasing out compensation payments which essentially date back to the 1992 reform package. However, after 2006, when further reform proposals will be required (for example to facilitate EU expansion), there will be pressures for reductions in and possibly the elimination of these payments. In addition, the Commission places emphasis in Agenda 2000 on the rising importance of rural and agri-environmental policies; it may

be preparing the ground for the eventual replacement of compensation payments by payments for social and environmental purposes in the context of an integrated rural policy. It is noteworthy that it states that 'rural development will become the second pillar of the CAP' (EU Commission, 1998, p. 6). Parenthetically it might be noted that market price support has been the traditional pillar of the CAP.

The market orientation of the reform proposals vary greatly between sectors. For cereals, the intervention price would be reduced by 20 per cent; the new price being below the Commission's expectation of world prices for wheat for most 'states of nature' so that the EU would routinely export without the aid of subsidies. The UR-AA constraint on the volume of subsidised wheat exports would then be irrelevant in most years and the prospective rapid build up of intervention stocks would be avoided. However, for coarse grains, the new intervention price is still expected to be above the world price and some build up of intervention stocks is likely to occur given the ceiling on subsidised exports.[11] The Commission's proposal for the suspension of 'compulsory' set-aside (that is zero rate) is consistent with its expectation that the EU would be able to export without resort to subsidies and thereby participate in the forecast growth in world cereals trade. Compensation for 50 per cent of the price cut is proposed, presumably reflecting the Commission's expectation that world prices would not normally drop down to the EU support level.

For oilseeds, the most notable proposal is the elimination of the higher oilseeds specific area payment so that the oilseeds payment becomes identical to the cereals (and voluntary set-aside) payment. This proposal implies a large cut in the oilseeds payment but by eliminating any special payment for oilseeds it removes the Blair-House constraint on EU oilseeds area.

The area payments proposals for the crop sector (cereals, oilseeds, protein crops and voluntary set-aside) represent a further step toward decoupling payments from production. However, decoupling is incomplete because of the retention of supplementary aids for protein crops and durum wheat and the retention of the power to reintroduce 'compulsory' set-aside to meet unforeseen contingencies.

The Commission proposes a significant cut of 30 per cent in the support price for beef and partial compensation through increases in premiums (headage payments). The Commission expects the internal price to be above this lower intervention price obviating the need for public intervention and storage; in addition, it expects a substantial reduction in the unit export refund and even the possibility of exporting without subsidies. The premium payments are unchanged in form and remain coupled to the scale of production.

The Commission's proposal of a 15 per cent cut in the support price for milk spread over four years represents a very limited move in the direction of market orientation, given the underlying problems in this sector – namely, a continuing structural surplus and UR-AA constraints on subsidised exports. In addition, the price cut would be compensated by the new dairy cow premium and quotas would not be removed. Tracy (1997, p. 103) is of the opinion that the Commission did not propose the replacement of the high-price quota system by substantial price cuts and compensation payments because the increase in budget costs that would be incurred could not be afforded within the agricultural guideline.

No proposals are made by the Commission for the sugar sector and the high-price quota system would be maintained. Tracy (ibid.) states that 'as with milk, the cost of compensation for price cuts could not be met within the budget; moreover the interests of producers and processors vested in the current system are a serious obstacle to reform'.

Beyond the CAP: a Scenario for EU Agricultural Policy early in the Twenty-first Century

What might the CAP, or a successor policy for EU agriculture, look like early in the next century, assuming that (1) the Commission's 'Agenda 2000' proposals are implemented without major revision; (2) EU enlargement is ongoing; and (3) further agricultural trade liberalisation is agreed in the WTO agricultural mini-round due to start in 1999? The thorny question of how the CAP might evolve after most of its traditional functions and instruments have been phased out is the subject of a Commission report entitled 'Towards a Common Agricultural and Rural Policy for Europe' published in April 1997 (dubbed the 'Buckwell Report' after Professor Allan Buckwell, chairman of the panel of independent experts who compiled it) (EU Commission, 1997b).

The Buckwell Report proposes that sometime early in the next century, possibly soon after the first phase EU enlargement to admit CEEC countries, the CAP should be replaced by a new policy termed a 'Common Agricultural and Rural Policy for Europe' with the acronym CARPE. The objective of the CARPE would be 'to ensure an economically efficient and environmentally sustainable agriculture and to stimulate the integrated development of the Union's rural areas'. The report argues that the process of transition from the present CAP to a

CARPE with this general objective, implies the adoption of a new policy consisting of four major elements, as follows:

1. Market stabilisation (MS).
2. Environmental and landscape payments (ECP).
3. Rural development incentives (RDI).
4. Transitional adjustment assistance (TAA).

The report argues that the first element, MS, is needed to provide a 'safety net' for producers of commodities which, due to the nature of agricultural production, are subject to large and uncontrollable market fluctuations. It seems fair to comment that the element MS really derives from the 'old CAP' where it was the central and virtually the sole objective of policy, and its inclusion can be interpreted as reflecting the 'political realism' of CARPE. However, whereas under the old CAP price stabilisation at a relatively high level was the central and virtually the sole objective of policy, under the CARPE a measure of relatively low level price stabilisation is only one of four complementary elements of policy.

The second element, ECLP, is needed to reward the provision of services to protect resources utilised by agriculture against damage and depletion, as well as protecting rural landscapes, where these are regarded as 'public goods', against irreversible damage. To guard against abuse, it is clearly important that such payments are provided for services that provide little commercial benefit to farmers but are judged to provide external benefits. Examples might include the maintenance of public footpaths and the repair of stone walls. Thus, it would be inappropriate for payments to be made from the public purse for the performance of tasks which are privately profitable or are required to be performed by the terms of a farm tenant's contract with his landlord. In AMS terms, ECLP payments would not count as PSEs, or even as 'transfers' to farmers, but payments for public services supplied by farmers. They would be similar to existing environmental payments to EU farmers, such as payments in environmentally sensitive areas (ESAs).

The third CARPE element, RDI, is thought to be needed, particularly to provide alternative gainful and socially productive employment for redundant agricultural resources, especially labour. In other words, this policy instrument is intended to hasten the exodus from farming and to promote the economic diversification of the countryside, including rural industrialisation, subject to environmental constraints. RDI payments would be similar to, for example, rural diversification grants already available to farmers in some areas of the EU, under FEOGA Guidance Section schemes.

The fourth element, TAA, which is clearly derived from the old CAP's inadequately financed structural adjustment programmes, is needed to compensate farmers (especially older ones) for hardship resulting from drastic change in the EU's 'social contract with agriculture': farmers were formerly publicly encouraged to plan and invest as if the protective umbrella afforded by the old CAP would continue indefinitely. The report argues that they are now morally entitled to indemnification for the adverse effects of recent changes in the terms of their contract with the government. Unlike the remaining three elements of the CARPE, which could be of indefinite duration, TAAs would be strictly transitional. New generations of farmers who were not parties to the old social contract, would not be eligible for the benefits of schemes of early retirement or retraining for jobs outside agriculture.

The Buckwell Report contains detailed discussion of each of the four elements of the CARPE, including the choice of policy instruments for giving effect to each of them. So, for example, would the objectives of MS best be met by continued holding of public stocks? Or by border controls? Or by some combination of both these instruments? Also of interest, under ECLP, a system of rising tiers of environmental standards attracting rising levels of payments is proposed. Whereas, at one extreme, safeguards are clearly needed to prevent polluters from claiming public payment for safely disposing of pollutants as required by law, at the other extreme, producers prepared to meet the extra costs of adhering to environmental standards above minimum legal requirements deserve to be paid accordingly (provided that the high standards concerned are public goods). Regrettably, available space will not permit an adequate summary or discussion of this and related parts of the Buckwell Report.

The final part of the report includes a section on the financing of the CARPE. The new policy should, in the short run, respect the financial guidelines already in place for the existing CAP. In the longer run, CARPE should cost less than the CAP, as TAA payments are phased out. But, in practice, the budget costs of the remaining 'permanent' elements may be hard to predict or even control. However, even if the switch from the CAP to CARPE failed to have much impact on the size of the EU budget, *ceteris paribus* a substantial proportion of the CARPE budget would consist of payments for public services by farmers and investment in rural development – unlike existing FEOGA Guarantee Section expenditure consisting of farm price and income support payments.

The proposals advanced by the Buckwell Report for transforming EU agricultural policy early in the next century are not so 'revolutionary' as may appear at first sight. None of the four elements composing the CARPE is entirely new. MS derives from price and income components of the existing CAP, and ECLP, RDI and TAA all have their counterparts in existing structural policy instruments under the FEOGA Guidance Section. The difference between the CAP and the CARPE is really only one of emphasis. Before the CAP reform of 1992, FEOGA Guidance Section expenditures were capped at a low level and the vast majority of the EU agricultural budget expenditure was accounted for by market price support. Following the 1992 reform, part of the price support was replaced by compensation payments, but expenditures on structural reform and the environment remained at relatively trivial levels. If CARPE were to go through, the composition of the budget would change dramatically, with ECLP and RDI expenditures accounting for the lion's share. TAA expenditures should be relatively small and diminishing over time. MS expenditures also should account for only a small proportion of the budget in most years, though subject to variation over time due to market fluctuations. Thus, rather than seeing CARPE as a revolutionary break from the CAP, it is probably more accurate to visualise the new policy as evolving from the old one in response to changing policy priorities. Persuading potential opponents to view the CARPE in this light may help it to gain political acceptance.

POLICY REFORM IN THE US

The 1990 US Farm Bill (duration 1990–95)

Setting and background

The Food, Agriculture, Conservation and Trade Act of 1990 was passed on 26 October 1990 shortly before the Congressional elections. In this section we discuss the setting and background to the passage of the 1990 Farm Bill.

As far as the Administration was concerned two issues were dominant in shaping proposals for the new bill. First, the US was committed to furthering the cause of agricultural trade liberalisation in the Uruguay Round of GATT negotiations. Second, it was imperative that the bill be compatible with the overriding macroeconomic objectives of reducing US budget and trade deficits. However, the Administration was confronted with the task of persuading the Congress to pass the kind of bill which it wanted and it was inevitable that there should be compromise on some issues before a bill acceptable to both sides could be passed into law.

Under its Uruguay Round proposals for liberalising agricultural trade, the US was committed to the virtual elimination of all trade barriers and export subsidies over ten years. Only 'decoupled' support policies, deemed not to affect production, would be allowed. However, it was implied that US commitment to the complete liberalisation of agricultural trade was conditional upon multilateral agreement and reciprocal action by all GATT contracting parties. Frequent use of the 'level playing field' metaphor implied that the US was not prepared to contemplate unilateral trade liberalisation.

Federal budget expenditure on agriculture reached a peak of nearly 3 per cent of total federal budget expenditure in 1986, but then dropped sharply in the following two years to only about 1 per cent in 1988 (USDA, Farmline, March 1990). However, the 1990 Farm Bill would inevitably be subject to a tight federal budget constraint due to the Gramm–Rudman–Hollings Deficit Reduction Act of 1985, as amended in 1987 (PL100–119). This law required annual reductions in the federal budget deficit to eliminate it by 1993. Although around 60 per cent of federal spending fell in categories exempted from this compulsory reduction due to either legal obligations or political necessity, agricultural price support expenditure was not protected and was, in fact, the second largest non-exempt expenditure category (after Medicare) (Conley, 1990). However, the federal budget constraint was not bound to affect all agricultural support programmes. So, for example, since the dairy and sugar programmes were largely paid for by consumers rather than taxpayers, they might be little affected.

In the four years following the passage of the 1985 Food Security Act, the US shares of world exports of wheat and corn (that is, maize) improved considerably. During the same period the US share of cereal stocks, particularly of wheat, also declined (Table 7.3). Changing US monetary policy, resulting in a weakening of the dollar exchange rate from the high level of the early 1980s appears to have contributed to these trends. But drought undoubtedly contributed to the reduction in stocks in 1988. In contrast to the market share improvement for wheat and corn, the US share of soybean exports declined, particularly in 1988, possibly due to the drought. But soybean stocks resembled stocks of wheat and corn over this period by also declining.

The ex post evaluation of the 1985 Food Security Act, particularly in Congress and amongst US producers, was that it had worked reasonably well. Between 1985 and 1989 net farm income increased from $31.2–$47.0 billion in nominal terms and from $28.1–$37.0 billion in real terms (relative to the purchasing power of the 1982 dollar) (USDA, *Agricultural Outlook*, December 1990, Table 32). A main criticism of

Table 7.3   US shares of world exports and ending stocks: wheat, corn and soybeans, 1985–88

Crop	Exports (million bushels)			Ending stocks (million bushels)		
	World	US	US share %	World	US	US share %
Wheat						
1985	3333	915	27	6169	1905	31
1986	3289	1004	31	6472	1821	28
1987	3899	1592	41	5374	1261	23
1988*	3465	1440	42	4149	616	15
Corn						
1985	2448	1241	51	5673	4040	71
1986	2471	1504	61	6364	4882	77
1987	2512	1732	69	5520	4113	75
1988*	2590	2008	78	2929	1660	57
Soybeans						
1985/86	959	741	77	666	536	80
1986/87	1047	757	72	566	436	77
1987/88	1116	802	72	455	302	66
1988/89*	846	530	63	293	155	53

Note: *preliminary

Sources: Harwood and Young (1989); Mercier (1989); Crowder and Davison (1989).

the 1985 Act was that by requiring deficiency payment programme participants to maintain their planting of programme crops in order to preserve their crop acreage bases, the support system afforded too little scope for planting flexibility. In particular, a major consequence of farmers' efforts to maintain their crop acreage bases for 'programme commodities' (corn, wheat and cotton) was perceived to be a relative decline in the planting, production and exports of soybeans, despite a higher market price for the latter crop (Crowder and Davison, 1989, p. 30). From the Administration's point of view, a major weakness of the 1985 Act was its high budget cost, particularly during 1986 and 1987 when target prices were frozen at 1985 levels. But the 1988 drought afforded some temporary relief.

In February 1990, the Secretary for Agriculture, Clayton Yeutter, presented Congress with the Administration's proposals for the 1990 Farm Bill. The proposals took the form not of a complete draft bill, but rather a detailed list of farm policy issues and problems together with specific recommendations for dealing with these (USDA, 1990). Under the heading of 'Price and Income Supports', the Administration proposed to retain the existing system of deficiency payment support for programme crops, with optional producer participation, but with enhanced planting flexibility to allow producers more scope to adjust cropping in response to market prices.

Specifically, it was proposed that, in any particular crop year, the (deficiency) payment acres for each programme crop be equal to its historic base acres, less acres required to be idled under the ARP. But, any programme crop or soybeans might be planted and harvested on a crop's payment acres with no loss of deficiency payments or base history. Moreover, conserving crops might be planted but not harvested. Crop bases would continue to be based on a five-year moving average of planted plus considered planted acres and programme yields would be frozen at the 1990 level. The Administration claimed that (USDA, 1990, p. 8):

> this flexibility program would make production decisions more responsive to market conditions, leading to higher production of crops in scarce supply and lower production of crops in surplus ... Farmers would have greater ability to alter their crop choices and to increase their income from the market. Farm program outlays would be reduced.

The Administration also proposed modifying the farmer-owned reserve (FOR) grain storage programme in various ways. Most importantly, 3–5 year storage contracts would be replaced with shorter 9–12 month contracts with government storage payments being halted when market prices exceeded trigger levels. Maximum FOR levels would be set and enforced and minimum levels eliminated. The Administration claimed that the revised programme would provide producers with protection from very low prices, assure commercial availability of stocks and reduce market uncertainties under existing legislation when market prices or quantities approached trigger levels or storage loans approached maturity dates. Also under the heading 'Price and Income Supports' the Administration proposed minor changes in existing dairy and peanut support arrangements to make them more sensitive to changes in surplus stocks (dairy) and less sensitive to changes in costs of production (peanuts). A significant omission from the document was any mention of the sugar programme let alone a proposal for changing it.

Under the heading of 'International Programs', the Administration proposed continuing the existing Export Enhancement (EEP) and Targeted Export Assistance (TEA) export subsidy programmes at least until the conclusion of the Uruguay Round of GATT negotiations. After that the programmes could be 'reassessed'.

The Administration's 'bill' contained no proposals concerning target price levels in 1990 and subsequent years or, indeed, any financial proposals whatever. But the Secretary for Agriculture indicated to Congress that the Administration was looking for a substantial cut in the budgetary cost of farm price and income support amounting to some $1.5 billion less than the estimated cost of extending the 1985 Act for a further four years. However, he thought Congress should decide the details of target price adjustments needed to bring the cost of the new farm bill within the Administration's budgetary guidelines (*Feedstuffs*, 26 February 1990).

In the event, the debate between Congress and the Administration on the cost of the new farm bill was overtaken by macroeconomic imperatives which caused the President to insist on agriculture submitting to an even larger cut in support and protection in contributing to the required reduction in the overall federal budget deficit from 1990 onwards. In effect, the Omnibus Budget Reconciliation Act of 1990 amended the farm bill even before it became law. Whereas the budget cost of the farm bill originally agreed by the Congress was estimated at around $54 billion over five years from 1991 to 1996 the overriding budget reduction legislation cut this amount by more than $13 billion to around $41 billion (*Agricultural Outlook*, December 1990, p. 33). By comparison, the 1985 Farm Bill was estimated to have cost approximately $80 billion over its five-year life (US Senate, Press Release, 16 October 1990). Thus, at least on paper, the 1990 Farm Bill appeared to offer a substantial federal budget saving with major implications for farm income support and, possibly, for the income actually received by farmers.

Main features of 1990 Food, Agriculture, Conservation and Trade Act[12]
Within the context of the deficiency payment system of farm income support, the most novel feature of the 1990 Act was its so-called 'triple base' provisions designed to combine some reduction in the extent of deficiency payment support with increased planting flexibility for producers. The triple base provision effectively divides a deficiency payment support programme participant's crop acreage base into three component parts:

1.   The proportion required to be diverted to conserving uses under the Acreage Reduction Program (ARP), as determined each year by the Secretary for Agriculture: the 1990 farm bill stipulates

maximum ARP proportions, 20 per cent each for wheat and feed grains, for example. ARP acres are ineligible to receive deficiency payments or other farm income support.

2. The proportion which may be planted to any crop, except fruit and vegetables, termed the 'flexible acreage': the 1990 farm bill sets the flexible acreage proportion at 25 per cent of the crop acreage base. Three-fifths of the flexed acres, or 15 per cent of the crop acreage base, are excluded from deficiency payment support, regardless of how they are cropped, under the last minute revision of the 1990 farm bill to reduce its budget cost. The remaining two-fifths, or 10 per cent of the crop acreage base, may be planted with 'alternative crops' without impairing the farmer's 'base history' *vis-à-vis* the relevant programme crop. But alternative crops do not attract deficiency payments, but only non-recourse and marketing loan support.

3. The proportion of the crop acreage base which may be planted only with the relevant programme crop, termed the 'permitted acreage', is the residual acreage left after the ARP and flexible acreage proportions have been deducted from the total acreage base. The permitted acreage attracts full deficiency payment support as well as non-recourse and marketing loans.

A hypothetical numerical example will serve to illustrate the application of the triple base provision. Suppose the ARP is 10 per cent of the crop acreage base; then on a hypothetical 100 acre farm, 90 acres are available for non-conserving crops. Of these 90 acres, 15 acres can be planted to alternative crops but are in any case ineligible for deficiency payment support under the budget saving provision. Of the remaining 75 acres, up to 10 acres may be planted with alternative crops at the cost of foregoing deficiency payment support. This leaves a maximum of 75 acres and a minimum of 65 to be planted either with the relevant programme crop or to be diverted to a conserving use, in order to qualify for deficiency payment support.[13]

Crop acreage bases for wheat and feed grains continue to be derived from the rolling average of acres planted and considered planted during the previous five years, as under the 1985 legislation. Programme payment yields were frozen for five years at the 1990 level.

Other notable features of the 1990 Farm Bill were:

1. Target prices frozen at 1990 levels for five years
2. Loan rates to be based on 85 per cent of the five-year moving average market price, but excluding the highest and lowest years (compared with 75–85 per cent under the 1985 Act).

3. Continued provision for export assistance through renewed funding
    for the Export Enhancement Program (EEP) as well as for a Market
    Promotion Program (MP) similar to the Targeted Export Assistance
    Program (TEA) legislated in 1985. Priority to be given to countering
    'unfair trade practices' under both programmes.
4. 'GATT Trigger': if an agreement on agricultural trade reform under
    the Uruguay Round of GATT negotiations was not reached before
    1 June 1992, the Agriculture Secretary must offer $1 billion in
    additional export subsidies, as well as advancing a marketing loan
    for wheat and feed grains permitting producers to repay their loans
    at world market prices (a further export subsidy). The GATT trigger
    provision also stipulated that if agricultural trade reform had not
    been implemented under the GATT by 30 June 1993, the Agri-
    culture Secretary could waive all or part of the budget constraints
    imposed on him by the 1990 Omnibus Budget Reconciliation Act.
5. The Conservation Reserve Program (CRP) continued and broad-
    ened to include wider environmental objectives including water
    quality.
6. A number of new programmes including the improvement of grain
    quality by raising grade standards, the establishment of organic food
    standards and the promotion of rural development.
7. Under 'Research' (Title XVI), increased funding for existing pro-
    grammes plus a number of new programmes including sustainable
    agriculture, water quality, environmental quality, food safety and
    global warming.
8. The 1990 legislation was also notable for leaving dairy and sugar
    price support arrangements virtually unchanged, apart from
    freezing the minimum support price for milk, subject to subsequent
    annual adjustments based on projected CCC purchases.

Comment on 1990 Farm Bill
The character of the 1990 Farm Bill was shaped by three major influences. First, producers, Congress and the Administration appeared to
share a desire for greater planting flexibility under the deficiency
payment programme. Second, the bill was gestated and eventually
passed under what came to be widely accepted as an unavoidable
necessity to reduce the federal budget deficit, with inevitable consequences for the budget cost of agricultural support. Third, the bill was
widely perceived to be a 'holding operation' pending the outcome
of efforts to liberalise agricultural trade under the Uruguay Round
negotiations.

Compared with the budget cost of the 1985 Farm Bill, the budget cut 'imposed' by the new bill (and the simultaneous budget reconciliation bill) was substantial – from approximately $80 billion over five years to only about $41 billion over an equal period. How this budget cut affected farm incomes would, of course, depend on how market prices changed. The Administration's strategy was to raise market prices, at least for export commodities, through multilateral agricultural trade reform successfully negotiated in the Uruguay Round. But the 1990 Farm Bill incorporated a fall-back provision in case the Uruguay Round failed. The GATT trigger gave authority to the Agriculture Secretary to restore agricultural budget expenditure nearer to its former level, including substantially increased expenditure on agricultural export subsidies, to meet that eventuality. But the possibility remained that, regardless of the outcome of the Uruguay Round negotiations, adherence to the objective of reducing the federal budget deficit might effectively prevent much, if any, increase in agricultural budget expenditure.

The Administration was less than fully successful in getting its policy change proposals written into the new bill. On the issue of planting flexibility, the Administration had proposed 100 per cent flexibility on non-ARP acres. But the bill as passed permitted flexibility only to a maximum of 25 per cent (corresponding with a zero per cent ARP).

On the reform of the FOR grain reserve, the Administration had proposed the curtailment of storage contracts from 3–5 years to only 9–12 months, as well as the suspension of storage payments above market price trigger levels and the limitation of FOR stocks to maximum levels. The bill as passed gave the Secretary for Agriculture increased powers of control on entry to the FOR based on the wheat ending stocks/use ratio and the wheat/corn ratio of market price to the loan rate: it also determined that storage subsidies would be suspended when market prices reached 95 per cent of target.

On the reform of dairy and peanut support, the Administration had proposed making dairy support more sensitive to changes in CCC stock levels and peanut support less sensitive to production cost changes. The bill as passed was broadly consistent with the Administration's (modest) proposal for reforming dairy support but less than fully successful in divorcing changes in peanut prices from production cost movements, though annual price increases were limited to 5 per cent regardless of cost changes.

In summary, the Food, Agriculture, Conservation and Trade Act of 1990 was in direct lineal descent from the Food Security Act of 1985 but with important differences (Erdman and Runge, 1991). Although the bill was not drafted and passed in anticipation of any particular outcome from the Uruguay Round agricultural negotiations, some of its provisions, such as the triple-base provision, were consistent with the US aim of progressively 'de-coupling' farm income support from production. However, the 1990 bill anticipated the possibility of failure in the Uruguay Round with its 'snap-back' provisions relating particularly to export subsidy expenditure. On the other hand, should the Uruguay Round succeed in achieving US objectives for agricultural trade liberalisation to a substantial degree, it might become necessary for Congress to draft and legislate a new and more liberal bill following the conclusion of the GATT negotiations.

The 1996 US Farm Bill (duration 1996–2001)

Background to the new bill
The new farm bill, originally due to be passed in 1995 to replace the FACTA of 1990, was debated and drafted against a background of several recent developments. First, on the international front, the US government had ratified the 1992 Uruguay Round Agreement including the Agreement on Agriculture. Compliance with the terms of this agreement would clearly have important implications for US agricultural and trade policy. But, at the same time, the conclusion of this agreement was expected to improve world market prospects for the export prices of grains and other commodities of major interest to the US. Second, apart from the effects of the UR-AA, which were likely to take time to be fully reflected in the market, there were other shorter term export market developments tending to push up prices. Third, on the domestic economic front, US fiscal and monetary policy continued to be dominated by the objective of either eliminating the federal budget deficit, or at least sharply reducing its size. Thus it was unrealistic to expect that agriculture could be exempted from budget cuts in 1995 any more than it had been in 1990.

Effects of UR-AA Ratification

The major implications of the UR-AA for the US concern market access and export subsidy commitments.

On market access the US is committed to converting its Section 22 import quotas, mainly for dairy products, peanuts, cotton and sugar into bound tariffs, these to be progressively reduced over the agreement implementation period. Also, the agreed switch to a tariff-quota system ensures specified minimum access levels for commodities previously subject to import embargoes, like peanuts and cotton, as well as increased access for dairy products regarding which smaller import quotas already existed. A notable feature of US market access commitments is the number of commodities where the base tariff is being cut only by the required minimum of 15 per cent. Included in this category are vegetable oils, unshelled peanuts and peanut butter, sugar, cotton, tobacco, beef, and most dairy products (Sanderson, undated, p. 40, App. C). Thus increased import penetration of the US market for these commodities, which the US presumably regards as being especially import sensitive, must largely depend upon the limited minimum access opportunities, in the form of reduced-tariff quotas, specified by the AA. In contrast to these commodities with minimum tariff reductions, the US is committed to reducing its tariff on wheat (except durum) by 55 per cent, and on corn by 75 per cent. These are product lines in which the US considers it possesses a comparative advantage so that the domestic market requires little or no protection except, possibly, in a few speciality lines.

Regarding export subsidies, the US is committed, like other UR-AA signatories, to the reduction of subsidy expenditure by 36 per cent from the baseline level, and of the volume of such exports by 21 per cent, between 1995 and 2000. The major quantitative reduction commitments appear to concern exports of wheat, rice, vegetable oil and eggs. The US also has a major interest in 'green box' categories of export assistance which are not considered to be trade distorting, such as market development and trade promotion expenditure, export credit programmes and bona fide food aid. When the US ratified the UR agreement the federal government in fact committed itself to minimum funding of green box programmes to compensate for the cutback of direct export subsidies required by the GATT (National Center for Food and Agricultural Policy, 1995).

The level of domestic support will scarcely be affected by the UR-AA since, like the EU, the US benefits from the decision to place all direct payments to producers under production limiting programmes in the 'blue box', that is, to exempt such payments from AMS measurement and reduction. For some years, such direct payments have been the dominant instrument of domestic support in the US. However, for the reasons already given they are not strictly decoupled. One of the alternative criteria laid down by the AA for the exemption from reduction of programmes of direct payments – that payments are restricted to 85 per cent of the base level of production – is clearly derived from the provision of the US 1990 Farm Bill under which farmers are eligible to receive deficiency payments on only 85 per cent of their 'permitted' acreage (base acreage less set-aside).

A baseline projection of the regional impact on the US of the UR-AA, up to the year 2000 and beyond, indicates higher US exports, particularly of wheat, feed grains and some animal products, higher farm income and lower budgetary costs of farm supports (USDA, 1994). Whereas grains, oilseeds and other competitive export-oriented sectors gain substantially, highly protected ones like sugar and dairy are little affected, reflecting continuing restrictions on imports despite tariffication and the minimum access provisions of the UR-AA. The exporting sector gains result from the product of the expected increments in world prices and increased export volumes expected to result from the reduced volume of subsidised exports, particularly from the EU. US agriculture is projected to benefit also from the dynamic gains in world income expected to result from the overall UR agreement, including its non-agricultural provisions. These dynamic benefits are expected to accrue particularly in the longer term. Agriculture is expected to benefit from the projected increase in world income despite its image as the producer of 'necessities' for which the income elasticity of demand is low and still falling in high income countries. The main dynamic income gains for US agriculture are expected to occur in sectors where income elasticities are still relatively high, such as meat, fruit, vegetables and other speciality products, particularly those with value added by processing.

Export market developments
During the period immediately preceding the passage of the 1995 Farm Bill, the short-term prospects for US farm exports were generally good. So, for example, during 1990–94 US export prices of wheat, excluding EEP bonus payments, were on a rising trend. Although in 1995 the buoyancy of prices continued, the volume of exports was somewhat down owing to lower yields. Between 1990–94 and 1994, the US share of world wheat exports went up from 32.4–35.6 per cent (Hoffman et al., 1995). The prices of corn and other feed grains, which also figure prominently amongst US farm exports, were also increasingly buoyant towards the end of the 1990–95 period and export prospects in this segment of the market were thought to be favourable with the US being expected to gain from an expansion in world import demand as well as from an increased market share (Lin et al., 1995). Also at the end of 1995, US agricultural export prospects appeared to be good not only for bulk commodities like wheat and corn, but also for livestock and high value products like processed foods, partly in response to greater trade liberalisation in many markets (USDA, *Agricultural Outlook*, 24 November 1995).

US domestic scene
It seemed clear from an early stage that, like the 1985 and 1990 bills, the 1995 Farm Bill would be subject to tight budgetary constraints. Continued reductions in the planned federal expenditure on agriculture seemed inevitable, particularly in the area of commodity support payments. With a large continuing federal budget deficit, the Clinton Administration was under severe Republican pressure to eliminate this deficit within seven years. In the event a Republican congressional budget resolution of June 1995 determined that, over the seven years from 1996 to 2002 Commodity Credit Corporation (CCC) expenditures would be cut by $13.4 billion relative to projected expenditure of $56.6 billion under the continuation of existing legislation, as estimated by the Congressional Budget Office (CBO) using a February 1995 baseline (Orden et al., 1996). Thus, the effect of this budget resolution was to cut CCC expenditure under a new farm bill by nearly a quarter compared with leaving legislation in place. However, in the event, the impact of this budget constraint on the negotiating process was offset by favourable short-term market developments in agricultural markets. By December 1995, relatively high grain prices, growing export volumes and other favourable market trends pointed to considerably reduced deficiency payment and other projected CCC expenditures than those written into the earlier February baseline. In fact, by this date, the CBO baseline expenditure projection for 1996–2002, under the continuation of existing legislation, was down to $48.8 billion, $7.8 billion lower than the February projection. Thus, due to changed market conditions, the required reduction in CCC expenditure relative to the new farm bill was implicitly reduced from $13.4 billion to only $5.6 billion.

A conference of Senate and House members reached agreement on a proposed Agricultural Reconciliation Act (ARA) on 16 November 1995. This would have reduced CCC expenditure by some $12.5 billion. However, the ARA was vetoed by the President because he considered the budget reduction too large and wanted it reduced to $5 billion (USDA, *Agricultural Outlook*, 27 December 1995).

Main issues for decision and policy alternatives
In drafting the 1995 Farm Bill US legislators were confronted by a small number of major issues requiring decision to determine the form of the bill. Although domestic agricultural policy and agricultural trade policy are in reality bound together by a seamless web, it is convenient to consider them separately for the purpose of policy analysis.

1. On domestic policy, two contrasting options appeared to present

themselves. Either (a) continue with the old style of price or direct income support, possibly with minor modifications; or (b) switch to a radically different style with fewer constraints upon producer freedom to vary the product mix, and the virtual abandonment of product price support in favour of decoupled payments.

2. On trade policy, the main issues appeared to be concerned with: (a) food aid; (b) foreign market development and export promotion; (c) export credits; (d) export subsidies (subject to UR-AA constraints).

3. Federal budget constraints.

4. Other issues impacting on the bill included conservation and the environment, consumer issues and R&D.

Evolution of 1995 Farm Bill: draft bills and political process

In May 1995 the USDA published a document containing the Administration's guidelines for the 1995 Farm Bill (USDA, 1995). As well as outlining changes the Administration hoped to see in commodity and marketing programmes, these guidelines also covered rural development; conservation and environment programmes; international programmes; research, education and economics; food safety. On the core issue of commodity and marketing programmes, the Administration pressed for increased planting flexibility in order to widen the scope for market forces to influence farm production decisions. It was suggested that the benefits of this policy adjustment would include not only better producer returns but also greater competitiveness of US farm exports, fewer adverse effects of production agriculture on the environment and an overall simplification of farm programmes, including less reliance on acreage reduction progammes. More specifically, the Administration wanted to increase planting flexibility by combining all crop bases into a (fixed) total acreage base (TAB). The proportion of the TAB allowed to be planted with permitted alternative crops would be gradually increased from the current 15 per cent to 100 per cent. Programme participants would continue to receive deficiency payments as under current support programmes, though the percentage of non-payment acres might be increased (from the current 15 per cent) in order to comply with overall budget restrictions. The Administation also proposed to target farm programme payments more closely on individuals primarily involved in farming by excluding those receiving $100 000 or more per year in off-farm income.

The Administration's guidelines for the 1995 Farm Bill were cautious. Although their underlying tone was to recommend the adjustment of farm programmes so as to allow farmers greater freedom to respond to market forces, the machinery of price support based upon deficiency payments would remain intact and in use. The proposed marginal adjustments in the direction of market liberalisation would be phased in only very gradually. It was therefore unremarkable that more radical proposals for reforming agricultural policy came from Congress, particularly in view of the fact that majority control in both houses had recently passed from the Democrats to the Republicans. Several draft bills were in fact tabled in both houses of Congress during the latter half of 1995, ranging in character from radical reform replacing existing price support for most crops with limited and largely decoupled payments for existing producers, to mere tinkering at the edges of existing support programs, However, in the end most interest focused upon a draft bill tabled by Congressman Pat Roberts in the House of Representatives.

Representative Roberts was chairman of the House agriculture committee. Title I of his bill, introduced on 4 August 1995, became known as the Freedom to Farm Act (FFA). The central thrust of the FFA was the replacement of existing price support programmes for feedgrains, wheat, rice and cotton with pre-determined annual payments tapering off somewhat over a seven-year period. Individual producer entitlement to such payments would be based upon their participation in the support programmes being replaced. Acreage set-asides were to be abolished and producers were to be given virtually complete freedom of cropping. The Congressional budget resolution of June 1995 limiting CCC expenditure over the seven-year period 1996–2002 to $43.2 billion (the CBO's February 1995 baseline projection of $56.6 billion, less a cut of $13.4 billion) was accepted as determining the overall cost of the decoupled payments programme. Annual payments were to be reduced by one-third, from $6 billion to $4 billion, between 1996 and 2002 and payments to individual producers strictly limited to $50 000 per annum. Non-recourse loans set at 70 per cent of a moving average of past prices would continue to provide producers with a low-level safety net (clearly more attractive to producers following periods of relatively high than low prices). A national commission would be set up to make recommendations on the role of government in agriculture after 2002. With some fairly minor modifications in response to political bargaining, the FFA, as originally tabled by Pat Roberts, did in fact form the basis of the new farm bill actually signed by the President on 4 April 1996. However, due to the inevitable compromises between interest group coalitions lobbying both houses of Congress, the FFA's apparently radical reforms of the feedgrains, wheat, rice and cotton support programmes were not matched by comparably radical reforms of other commodity support programmes such as dairy, sugar, peanuts and tobacco.

1996 Farm Bill: main provisions
The Federal Agricultural Improvement and Reform (FAIR) Act of 1996 replaced the Food, Agriculture, Conservation and Trade Act (FACTA) of 1990. The FAIR Act consists of a total of nine titles, as follows:

Title I   Agricultural Market Transition Program
Title II   Agricultural Trade
Title III   Conservation
Title IV   Nutrition Assistance
Title V   Agricultural Promotion
Title VI   Credit
Title VII   Rural Development
Title VIII   Research, Extension and Education
Title IX   Miscellaneous

Below, in concentrating on the most revolutionary features of the FAIR Act, we highlight the provisions of Titles I and II.

Agricultural market transition program (Title I)   Comparing the FAIR Act of 1996 with the FACTA of 1990, the most 'revolutionary' change occurs in Title I of the new farm bill. Although a broad range of commodities is covered by Title I, including peanuts, sugar and dairy, radical reform is confined to the seven 'contract commodities', wheat, corn, grain sorghum, barley, oats, upland cotton and rice. Producers who participated in the previous support programmes of these commodities anytime during the currency of FACTA, that is, between 1990 and 1995, are eligible to sign up for seven-year market transition contracts starting in 1996.

For contract crops the new 'decoupled' income support programme consists of two major elements:

1. *Contract payments*   Participants in the new production flexibility contracts (PFCs) are entitled to receive fixed annual payments based on the product of: (a) the contract acreage (fixed by participation in past support programmes); (b) the farm programme payment yield (based on historic yields, frozen since 1985); (c) the payment rate (per bushel) arbitrarily determined by the architects of the bill so that the actual cost of the income support falls below the budgetary ceiling imposed by the Budget Reconciliation Bill of November 1995. Total annual contract payments are scheduled to taper off from $5.6 billion in 1996 to $4.0 billion in 2002, that is, a

fall of some 40 per cent, adding up to a total expenditure of nearly $36 billion over seven years. Despite the termination of target prices and deficiency payments, the FAIR Act does provide producers with a price 'safety net' in the form of non-recourse marketing assistance loans. Producers who take out marketing assistance loans contract to repay at the lower of either the loan rate or the current market price. In the case of wheat, for example, the loan rate may not exceed the rate set in 1995 ($2.58 per bushel) and, apart from this restriction, the actual rate will be calculated as 85 per cent of the simple average farm price in the five preceding seasons, excluding the highest and lowest prices. The Secretary of Agriculture may also make loan rate reductions of up to 10 per cent based on stocks-to-use ratios. Contract payments appear to be genuinely decoupled in the sense that programme participants are not obliged to continue producing anything in return for the payments. Payments are subject to limitations: under production flexibility contracts the FAIR Act imposes a ceiling of $40 000 per person per year.

2. *Planting flexibility*   In contrast to the provisions of earlier recent US crop support programmes, the FAIR Act permits complete freedom of cropping on a participating producer's contract acreage, including grass and other forage crops except fruits and vegetables, and subject to cross-compliance provisions of certain conservation programmes, like the CRP. The FAIR Act eliminates the acreage reduction programme (ARP) under which producers could be required to set aside a proportion of their contract acreage, on a year-to-year basis. The 0/85-92 programme, permitting suitably qualified producers with no current production to nevertheless continue receiving deficiency payments, is also discontinued.

The provisions for dairy and sugar are as follows:

1. Regarding dairy products (butter, cheese, and so on), the FAIR Act marginally reduces the support price over four years until the end of 1999. Thereafter, price support is eliminated until 2002, but a recourse loan programme for dairy product manufacturers comes into force at the 1999 support price level ($9.90 per cwt.). New legislation will be needed to deal with dairy product support after 2002; otherwise the permanent parity price provisions of the 1949 Farm Bill would again be effective. Past arrangements for supporting producer prices of liquid milk, through the authorisation of milk marketing orders to restrict regional milk supplies, continue

with minimal change. However, the FAIR Act instructs the Secretary of Agriculture to consolidate milk marketing orders so as to reduce their total number from 33 to 10–14 within three years.
2. Domestic sugar processors continue to be eligible for CCC loans on terms depending upon the level of (preferential) imports. If imports are below 1.5 million tons, loans are 'with recourse', that is they are repayable with interest within nine months. But if imports exceed this level loans are 'without recourse', that is, not repayable. Loan rates for raw cane and refined beet sugar remain at their 1995 levels. Supply restriction by means of sugar marketing allotments is suspended by the FAIR Act.

Agricultural trade (Title II)   Under the FAIR Act, provisions for agricultural export subsidies under the Export Enhancement Program (EEP), inherited from earlier farm bills, remain in place. However, EEP expenditure limits are set, on an annual basis for the life of the legislation, to be consistent with Uruguay Round (UR) commitments to limit subsidised exports. The new farm legislation also requires the Secretary of Agriculture to monitor other countries' implementation of their UR commitments. If the Secretary obtains evidence that, by ignoring their UR commitments, other countries are constraining US agricultural exports, he must furnish his evidence to the US Trade Representative as well as informing Congress. The FAIR Act also commits the Secretary to monitoring the implementation of World Trade Organisation (WTO) member countries' commitments to observe UR requirements on sanitary and phytosanitary measures as these affect trade, again with an obligation to inform Congress if he suspects violations.

Evaluation of the 1996 Farm Bill
The FAIR Act has been described both as 'marking the end of an agricultural era' dating back to the 1930s, and as a further victory for traditional agriculturists intent upon maximising their short-term financial gains (Penn, 1996). From the market liberalising point of view, the former of these assessments could be termed 'optimistic', whereas the latter one looks 'pessimistic'. The grounds for optimism include the following 'facts' about the FAIR Act:

1. It abolishes price support, that is deficiency payments, in favour of decoupled income payments, at least for 'contract commodities'.
2. It allows producers complete planting flexibility, apart from fruit and vegetables.

3. By ending the former ARP, it eliminates the factor distortion inherent in that programme.
4. By being scheduled over seven years, it appears to afford an opportunity of breaking a 50-year-old tradition of legislating a new farm bill to coincide with every new presidential term of office.
5. It mandates the setting up of a national commission to study the options for the future of agricultural policy in the US and to make recommendations to the federal government.

The grounds for 'pessimism' include the following facts about the FAIR Act:

1. The termination of price support in favour of decoupled payments applies only to contract commodities: other major commodities, such as dairy, sugar, peanuts and tobacco are either not affected at all, or only to a minor degree.[14]
2. It may be argued that the acreage payments to be received by producers of contract crops are not fully decoupled because the marketing loan safety net, permitting producers to repay loans at less than the loan rate if the latter is above the current world price of the commodity, remains intact.
3. Because the FAIR Act does not actually repeal the Agricultural Act of 1949, with its permanent provisions for parity-based support of agricultural prices, price support of contract commodities can be revived at any time at the will of Congress.
4. Despite the constraints imposed by UR commitments, agricultural export subsidies, mainly under the aegis of EEP, continue as a major element of US agricultural policy.

These contrasting optimistic and pessimistic assessments of the FAIR Act possibly reflect political compromises that had to be made between opposing interest groups to get a new farm bill through both houses of Congress. It was more than could reasonably be expected to radically reform all commodity sectors simultaneously. The contrasting assessments may also point to a more balanced view somewhere between their extremes.

An optimistic assessment might be that the FAIR Act marks an irreversible ideological shift away from the protection of some major sectors of US agriculture, which had prevailed since the early 1930s, towards exposing farmers to the full rigours of the market place. This shift might be explained by any one or some combination of a number of plausible factors such as: (a) the declining relative importance of agriculture in the US economy to a very low level allied to a decline in the political influence of farmers relative to that of food consumers; (b) the perceived disappearance of an earlier persistent disparity between farm and non-farm incomes; (c) farmers themselves coming round to the view that on balance they would be better off without government regulation of their incomes in order to win complete freedom to respond to market forces; (d) a belief that world agricultural markets are gaining in stability due, for example, to the implementation of Uruguay Round decisions to increase trade.

However, for several reasons, the evidence given by the FAIR Act of a genuine ideological shift away from protection towards the willingness of US farmers to be fully exposed to market forces is not entirely convincing. First, as already noted, the abandonment of price support in favour of tapering decoupled payments applies only to contract commodities: other major sectors of US agriculture, such as dairy, sugar and peanuts remain largely unreformed. Second, despite being phased over seven years, the apparently radical reforms of contract commodity support are not necessarily permanent: the 1949 Agricultural Act entitling farmers to permanent parity-based price support in the absence of other legislation taking precedence over it remains unrepealed, and might be resurrected with changes in the economic and/or political climates.

It has been suggested that in agreeing to accept the substitution of tapering decoupled payments for deficiency payment support of contract commodities, Congressmen representing traditional agriculturists were playing a skilful political game (Orden et al., 1996).[23] Traditional defenders of agricultural protection may have perceived that if the movement of market prices was sufficiently favourable to farmers, they might be better off under the new regime of decoupled payments plus returns from the market than with a continuation of the old direct payments regime. Whereas, under the new regime, acreage payments continue regardless of the level of market prices, had deficiency payments continued they would have ceased as market prices rose above target prices. Thus it appears possible that in agreeing to the new income support regime for contract commodities, traditional agriculturists gambled upon market prices remaining sufficiently buoyant to make this the most profitable option for farmers. When the new farm bill was being debated in the Congress, late in 1995 and early in 1996, world grain prices were in fact buoyant and appeared likely to remain high for the forseeable future. So, for example, the implementation of the Uruguay Round Agriculture Agreement of 1994, particularly regarding the commitment to limit agricultural export subsidies, was generally perceived as helping to keep prices relatively high, *ceteris paribus*. However, should prices fall to unexpectedly low levels, emergency legislation might be enacted at short notice to save farmers from financial ruin.

A middle-of-the-road assessment of the FAIR Act

The FAIR Act appears to be a compromise measure giving something to both the advocates of radical agricultural policy reform and the defenders of status quo. With a presidential election in the offing, the Republicans and the Democrats both needed a prompt settlement on agriculture to encourage their rural constituents. The most radical elements of the FAIR Act, effectively eliminating deficiency payment support of contract commodities in favour of tapering fixed acreage payments, appeared to come mainly from the Republican side. These elements were clearly inspired by the FFA, introduced to the House of Representatives by Pat Roberts, the Republican chairman of its agriculture committee. Thus Republicans in favour of a radical break from the traditions of agricultural policy over the last 60 years could claim a victory perhaps appealing particularly to non-rural constituents. Yet more conservative Republicans with rural supporters to safeguard, as well as Democrats with a long tradition in favour of agricultural protection stretching back to the 1930s, could also claim victory in largely preserving the status quo for producers of non-contract commodities, as well as preserving a long-term safety net for all US farmers. They have the assurance of a substantial measure of continuing government support at least until the FAIR Act expires in 2002. After that, because permanent agricultural legislation remains in place in the form of the unrepealed 1949 Agriculture Act, it appears rather unlikely that US agriculture will be left entirely at the mercy of market forces.

A balanced assessment of the FAIR Act is that it represents a halfway house towards the liberalisation of US agriculture. At the next stage, after 2002, further measures of liberalisation affecting commodities scarcely affected by the FAIR Act may or may not be enacted. Market prices of grains and other commodities are virtually certain to fall from their recent high levels and much will depend upon the political reaction to such an eventuality. If the federal government intervenes to protect farm incomes from the effects of falling prices, the FAIR Act of 1996 may prove to have been a temporary experiment with market deregulation. But provided market prices remain reasonably stable, the FAIR Act might prove to be the first step in a longer-term transition to even greater liberalisation of US domestic agricultural markets and trade, involving sectors scarcely affected by the legislation of 1996. Much will also depend upon the results of future negotiations on the reform of agricultural trade. The next agricultural 'mini-round' under the WTO is due to start in 1999. Issues likely to be discussed there include: (a) whether deficiency payments should continue to be immune from AMS measurement and reduction by being classified as being in the 'blue box' rather than being reclassified as 'red' and therefore subject to progressive reduction over time; (b) whether there are to be further reductions in permitted levels of subsidised exports beyond the reductions agreed in the URAA. To the extent that negotiation of these issues at the international level results in agreement to further liberalise domestic agricultural policy and trade beyond what was achieved in 1994, so US agricultural policy after 2002 might be expected to follow suit. On the other hand, in view of the importance of its exports, particularly of grains and oilseeds, it seems unlikely that the US would be prepared to completely deregulate its agriculture unilaterally. As during the UR negotiations, the US seems likely to continue insisting upon its agricultural trading partners agreeing to compete on a 'level playing field'. Now that the US has partially deregulated its own agriculture it seems likely to pressure its trading partners, particularly the EU, to go down the same road.

Prospects for further reform of US policy

The Commission on Twenty-first Century Production Agriculture, mandated by the FAIR Act, has been appointed by the agriculture committees in Congress. Its eleven-person membership comprises seven farmers, three cooperative executives and a professor of agricultural economics (in the chair). Its brief is: (1) to conduct a mid-term review of the success of the 1996 FAIR Act; (2) review the future of production agriculture and the appropriate role of the federal government in its support after 2002, including specific recommendations for legislation to that end. US Agriculture Secretary Glickman is on record as stating that the Commission will answer the question 'Should we have a safety-net under farm income and, if so, what should be the size of the holes in that net?' (Flinchbaugh, 1998). The strong producer interest orientation of the Commission suggests a conservative rather than a radical answer being given to that question.

THE NEXT ROUND OF WTO NEGOTIATIONS

Maintaining the Momentum of Policy Reform

In the 1980s and 1990s, 'a new paradigm in agricultural policy emerged which recognised that the social and environmental objectives of supporting agriculture could be usefully separated from the manipulation of commodity markets' (Josling et al., 1996, p. 221). This strategic shift 'in the philosophy and practice of agricultural policy' (ibid.) was critical in securing an agreement in the long drawn out agricultural negotiations in the Uruguay Round.

A major achievement of the UR-AA was to secure international recognition that domestic agricultural policy decisions may be legitimately questioned by a country's trading partners in the process of international negotiations. More specifically, Article 20 of the agreement stipulates not only an implementation review of its provisions, but also a resumption of negotiations to realise the long-term objective of 'substantial progressive reductions in support and protection resulting in fundamental reform'. Moreover, it is stipulated that such negotiations shall commence one year before the end of the implementation period, that is in 1999.

The fact that the 1992 reform of the CAP broke the logjam in the UR negotiations suggests that further progress with agricultural trade reform is more likely to follow than to precede further reforms of domestic policy. More specifically, further progress with (a) improving market access and (b) reducing export subsidies, may be contingent upon a prior commitment to making much larger reductions in trade-distorting domestic support than was achieved in the UR. Success here is likely to depend upon governments deciding to further reform the instrumentation of domestic agricultural support so as to (a) further emphasise direct income support (DIS) at the expense of price support, and (b) effectively decouple DIS from current production.

With the passage of the 1996 Farm Bill the US has already made a first move in the direction of achieving these objectives (for some sectors of US agriculture) as discussed earlier in this chapter. Consequently, the US is positioned to take the lead in the 'Mini-Round' of agricultural trade negotiations commencing in December 1999. It can be expected to push for a further rollback of export subsidies and domestic supports, including the abolition of the 'blue box'. Furthermore the 'US negotiators will have the full backing of US producers' (Hathaway, 1996) – since US producers of grains, vegetable oils, meats and dairy products are now better positioned to take advantage of growth in world markets.

The Cairns Group led by Australia (but with the exception of Canada) will also press strongly for agricultural trade liberalisation as in the Uruguay Round. Their objectives are likely to include: (a) the total elimination of export subsidies; (b) a substantial reduction in tariffs; (c) a substantial rise in minimum access opportunities; (d) a limited 'green box' that no longer includes the 'blue box' (that is completely decoupled income support); and (d) no more exceptions for developed countries (for example Japan, Korea) (de Zeeuw, 1997). Canada is likely to support the Cairns Group objectives for cereals and oilseeds but will probably want to retain its dairy quota system with its allied import restrictions. The Cairns Group may also press for domestic support commitments to be amended from the current aggregate basis to a commodity specific basis.

The EU position will depend on the progress made with reaching agreement within the EU on the Agenda 2000 proposals for CAP reform. If these proposals are not adopted or are substantially watered down, then the EU will enter the negotiations in a defensive position. In particular, its ability to limit imports and subsidise exports is constrained by the continuing implementation of the UR-AA; in addition, the peace clause will expire in 2003 and allow the EU's domestic support measures and export subsidies to come under challenge in the WTO. However, a successful reform of the CAP along the lines of the Agenda 2000 proposals would give the EU some scope for negotiation. For example, the EU could offer to agree on further reductions in export subsidies and import protection in return for a continuation of the direct income support permitted in the 'blue box', with agreement that compensation aid (compensation payments for arable crops and livestock premia including the proposed dairy cow premium) was permitted for some further period of time.

Possible Agenda for the Next Round

There is an in-built agenda stemming from Article 20 of the UR-AA: there are to be further negotiations in the three areas of import access, export subsidies and domestic support. There will be pressures for tariff reductions and an increase in minimum access quantities. There will also be pressures for the elimination of export subsidies, especially as the EU was alone in the Uruguay Round in wanting to continue with export subsidies (de Zeeuw, 1997, p. 478). In addition, it is likely that the EU's standby provision for the imposition of export taxes will come under attack by the US and the Cairns Group who regarded the use of this instrument by the EU in 1995 and 1996 as disruptive to the world grain market. Finally, there will be pressure to have income support fully decoupled from production. As noted above the 'blue box' concept will be under attack. It is also likely that there will be more general discussion concerning the aid permitted under the 'green box'. In de Zeeuw's view, in the long term, decoupled income support will only be permitted permanently for social and environmental reasons and temporarily for restructuring agriculture in certain regions (p. 478).

In addition to issues deriving from the UR-AA of 1994, the agenda of the next round of agricultural MTNs is likely to include environmental regulation and 'green protectionism' (see Josling, 1993). The effectiveness of the 1994 SPS agreement in preventing national food safety and animal and plant health standards being used as a covert form of protectionism may come under close scrutiny. Other issues pinpointed for examination may include agricultural input subsidies and effective protection, labour standards and the regulation of wages, and competition policy. Furthermore, the composition of the agenda must change with the passing of time, as priorities alter and new issues emerge. But, due to the large number, the interrelatedness and the complexity of the issues at stake, considerable optimism is needed to suppose that the next round of international negotiations to advance the liberalisation of agricultural trade will be notably easier than the seven-year marathon leading up to the UR agreement.

APPENDIX: THE AGENDA 2000 PROPOSALS

Specific Reform Proposals for the Period 2000–2006[15]

Crop sector: cereals, oilseeds and protein crops

The objectives of the proposals for the crop sector are to (a) avoid the routine use of export subsidies; (b) reinforce the competitiveness of cereals as feedingstuffs on the internal market; (c) overcome GATT constraints for cereals and oilseeds and (d) simplify administration. The specific proposals are:

1. Set the cereals intervention price at a safety-net level of ECU 95.35/t in 2000; that is a 20 per cent cut in the intervention price from its current (1996/7) value of ECU 119/t. The intervention price to remain unaltered throughout the intervention season.
2. Set a non-crop-specific area payment (AP) for all crops equal to a compensation payment (CP) of ECU 66/t multiplied by the cereals reference yield; this payment is to be reduced if market prices are

sustained at higher levels than currently foreseen. The CP for cereals is increased from its current (1996/7) value of ECU 54/t by 50 per cent of the cut of ECU 24/t in the intervention price.

3. Set the reference rate for compulsory set-aside at 0 per cent; voluntary set-aside to be allowed and to be guaranteed for up to five years; set-aside land to receive the non-crop-specific area payment.
4. Pay a special aid for protein crops of ECU 6.5/t; continue with the present supplement for durum wheat of 359 ECU/ha.
5. The payment per hectare and the rate of set-aside may be modified according to market developments.
6. Silage maize continues to be eligible for aid.

Table 7.4 compares the proposed CPS and APs for the year 2000 and beyond with those existing for the CAP from 1995/6 to 1999/2000.

Table 7.4   EU compensation payments (CPs) and area payments (APs) for arable crops: Agenda 2000 proposals compared with 1997/8 payments

Crop	Proposed (existing) CP ECU/tonne		Proposed (existing) AP ECU/hectare	
Cereals[1]	66.0	(54)	321	(262)
Oilseeds[2]	66.0	(186)	321	(438)
Protein crops[3]	72.5	(78)	352	(358)

Notes
1   Wheat, coarse grains.
2   Rapeseed, soybean, sunflower.
3   Peas, beans, lupins.
APs for cereals based on a yield of 4.86 t/ha (EU Commission, 1998).

Beef regime
The objectives are to (a) avoid a build-up of intervention stocks, (b) reduce export refunds; (c) rebalance the internal meat market to the benefit of beef. The proposals are:

1. Reduce the intervention price from ECU 2780/t to ECU 1950/t over 2000–2002 (30 per cent cut) with private storage replacing public storage. The basic price for private storage is to be the effective market support level. Private storage aid may be granted when the average EU price is less than 103 per cent of the basic price.

2. Increase direct payments to beef producers: the proposed payments are set out in Table 7.5.

Table 7.5   EU beef premium payments: Agenda 2000 proposals compared with 1997/8 payments

Beef animal	Payment frequency	proposed payment: ECU	Current payment: ECU
Suckler cow	Yearly	215	145
Bull	One payment	310	135
Steer	Two payments	232	109
Dairy cow*	Yearly	70	nil

Note: *In beef context

However, the proposed payment regime is complicated by a division of the individual headage payment into a Community-wide basic payment (basic premium) – 70 per cent of direct payment – and an additional payment to be distributed by member states (national envelope) – 30 per cent of direct payment. Consequently, the level of premia to be received by any producer will depend on member states' decisions regarding the distribution of the financial envelopes.

Regional ceilings on premium rights for male animals remain and national ceilings for suckler cow premium rights are to be introduced. In addition, premium rights are limited by stocking density limits; additional payments are to be granted for extensive production methods.

Dairy regime
The objectives are to (a) avoid a build up of intervention stocks for skim milk powder, (b) overcome GATT constraints on cheese exports, (c) reduce the surplus of butter. The proposals are:

1. Extend the quota regime to 2006 but with the total quota increased by 2 per cent (1 per cent to young farmers and 1 per cent to mountain and arctic regions).
2. Reduce the butter and skim milk powder support prices by 15 per cent in four steps over 2000–2004.
3. Introduce a new yearly payment for dairy cows of ECU 145 (total dairy cow premium = 145 + 70 = ECU 215 equal to suckler cow premium). In effect, beef and dairy cows would obtain an identical

premium under the proposal. The dairy cow premium is complicated by being based on a premium unit (virtual cow): a producer's premium units are equal to his individual milk quota divided by the average Community milk yield (that is, if the average yield of the producer's herd is below the Community average, then he is deemed to have more virtual cows than actual cows).

Rural development

All rural and environmental measures are to be brought together under a new initiative on rural development. These measures include support for structural adjustment (investment in farm holdings, support for young farmers, training, early retirement) support for farmers in less-favoured areas (LFAs), support for agri-environmental activities, support for investment in processing and marketing facilities, for forestry and measures promoting the adaptation of rural areas. Greater emphasis is to be placed on environmental goals in rural policy measures including the maintenance of low-input farming systems. Member states will be able to make direct payments conditional on the respect of environmental provisions. The Commission signalled two areas deserving of further support: (a) the promotion of low-input farming in areas of high landscape and nature value (often in LFAs) and (b) targeted measures to encourage farmers to provide services such as organic farming, the maintenance of semi-natural habitats, the preservation of traditional orchards and hedgerows, the continuation of alpine farming and the upkeep of wetlands.

Individual ceiling for direct payments

There is a limit proposed on the total payments to an individual farmer in that there would be a 20 per cent reduction in payments between ECU 100 000 and 200 000 and a 25 per cent reduction on payments over ECU 200 000.

Modulation

Member states permitted to redistribute aid from larger to smaller farmers where there are national envelopes. Member states also permitted to cut payments where they consider that farmers are using less than an appropriate amount of labour on their farms.

Budgetary Implications

The proposed financial framework as set out in Agenda 2000 fixes the ceiling on the EU (total) budget at 1.27 per cent of Community GNP for 2000–2006; this percentage limit is identical to the limit which will apply in 1999. Consequently, overall resource availability (budget inflow) would rise pro rata with the EU growth rate.[16] Agricultural spending (FEOGA guarantee plus accompanying measures) is limited by the agricultural guideline which rises at 74 per cent of the EU's GNP. For the EU(15) (the existing member states), the proposed changes to CAP regimes give savings on export refunds and market intervention which are outweighed by increases in compensation payments. In particular, compared to the continuation of current CAP there is expected to be an increase in spending of some ECU 3 billion on CAP support by 2006. The expected increases in spending fall entirely on the beef and dairy regimes (around ECU 2 billion each). For the arable sector (cereals, oilseeds and protein crops), expected savings on market support and intervention (some ECU 1.6 billion) are offset by increases in compensation payments of the same order of magnitude. In addition, savings are expected in export refunds on pigmeat and poultry products, food aid and cereal products.

Table 7.6 Estimated CAP expenditure under the Agenda 2000 proposals, 2000–2006 (billion ECU in current prices, assuming 2% inflation per year)

	1999	2000	2001	2002	2003	2004	2005	2006
EU(15)								
Reformed CAP	41.7	40.1	43.1	44.5	46.3	46.5	46.4	46.5
New rural development accompanying measures		1.9	2.0	2.0	2.1	2.1	2.2	2.2
Pre-accession aid		0.5	0.5	0.6	0.6	0.6	0.6	0.6
Expenditure EU(15)		42.7	45.7	47.5	49.1	49.3	49.3	49.4
Guideline EU(15)	45.0	46.9	48.8	50.6	52.6	54.7	56.8	59.0
Enlargement								
CAP market measures		0.0	0.0	1.1	1.2	1.2	1.3	1.4
Rural development accompanying measures		0.0	0.0	0.6	1.0	1.5	2.0	2.5
Expenditure EU(21)				49.2	51.3	52.0	52.6	53.3
Guideline EU(21)				50.9	53.0	55.1	57.4	59.7

Source: EU Commission (1998), *Evaluation of the Financial Impact of the Commission Proposals concerning the Reform of the CAP*

The new rural development accompanying measures add about ECU 2 billion per annum to EU(15) CAP spending from 2000 onwards. Overall spending is expected to rise until 2004 and then stabilise. The estimated expenditure falls well within the budget guideline giving an estimated margin of some ECU 9.7 billion for the EU(15).

As far as agricultural budgetary expenditure in the new member states is concerned, Agenda 2000 assumes that five CEECs (Estonia, the Czech Republic, Hungary, Poland and Slovenia) plus Cyprus would join the EU in 2002. It is assumed that 'pre-accession' aid of about ECU 0.5 billion is given from 2000. This is initially distributed amongst all candidate countries. CAP market measures are assumed to cost just over ECU 1 billion per annum; this figure assumes that farmers in the new member states would not receive direct payments. Finally, post-accession rural development accompanying measures are assumed to be ECU 0.5 billion per annum in 2002 rising to ECU 2.5 billion in 2006. Table 7.6 sets out the details of the estimates for the development of agricultural expenditure.

NOTES

1. Strictly speaking, Trade Commissioner Andriessen was in overall charge of the UR negotiations whilst leaving the technical details of agriculture to MacSharry.
2. At the UR meeting in question, which preceded the Blair House Agreement of November 1992, the EU offered a 30 per cent reduction of product-specific AMS denominated support. Tangermann maintains that honouring this commitment would have compelled the EU to undertake major reductions in commodity support prices.
3. Similar conclusions concerning the incompatibility between the UR-AA constraint on the volume of subsidised cereal exports and the forecast exports were reached by, for example, Guyomard et al. (1992), Helmar et al. (1993), OECD (1995) and Rayner et al. (1995).
4. It is of some importance to note that CAP policy making in 1995 and 1996 was affected by two major shocks. First, the tight world grains market in 1995/6 led to international grain prices being above corresponding EU prices until September 1996. EU export subsidies were suspended and export taxes levied during this period with corresponding benefits to the EU budget and EU commitments on subsidised exports under the UR-AA, and enabling a drawdown on EU cereals stocks. In response the set-aside rate in the EU arable sector was reduced to 10 per cent in 1996 and 5 per cent in 1997. Second, a crisis in the EU beef sector unfolded in 1996 following an admission by the British government of a possible link between 'mad cow' disease (bovine spongiform encephalopathy or BSE) and the fatal Creutzfeld–Jacob disease in the human population. There was a collapse in EU beef consumption (a fall of around 10 per cent across the EU and some 30 per cent in some member states) and a ban was introduced on the export of British beef. Chaos ensued in the decision making of the Agricultural Council as the UK threatened to disrupt EU decision making across the whole range of EU business. In the face of the slump in EU beef consumption, and reduced export prospects for EU beef, special measures were introduced in the beef sector reversing previous reforms and adding to budgetary costs. The urgency of the problems in the beef sector dominated CAP

policy making in 1996 and diverted attention away from fundamental reform of the CAP. In addition, the overhang of the BSE crisis has affected subsequent policy making – in respect of both the special problems of the beef sector and enhanced attention to food safety in general.

5. This list is based on Marsh and Tangermann (1996).
6. The list of factors is based on Ingersent et al. (1998) and Tracy (1997).
7. The list below (p. 375) is the authors' interpretation based on page 29 of the 'Agenda 2000' document.
8. 'Continued competitiveness must be ensured by sufficiently large price cuts that will guarantee growth of home market outlets and increased participation by Community agriculture in the world market. These price reductions should be offset by an increase in direct aid payments in order to safeguard producers' incomes' (EU Commission, 1998, p. 5).
9. This section is based on the report by *The Financial Times* 19-3-98.
10. For a fuller assessment see Tangermann (1997) and Tracy (1997).
11. Tangermann (1997, p. 2) states that 'the proposed 20% cut in the cereals intervention price will go a long way toward relegating intervention buying to the role it should have had in the first place, i.e. serving as a safety net rather than as permanent price support'. However, although he expects the EU to be able to export wheat without the routine use of subsidies, he expresses concern that the price cut may not be large enough to make barley competitive on world markets. Consequently, he expects that at a future date, the intervention price for barley will need to be further reduced.
12. USDA, *Agricultural Outlook*, ERS, December 1990, pp. 32–45.
13. Like the 1985 Act, the 1990 farm bill contained a 0/92 provision. Under the 1990 legislation programme participants might divert up to 92 percent of their permitted acreage minus normal flex acres (i.e. 15 per cent of crop acreage base) to conserving uses and still qualify for deficiency payment support.
14. So for example, milk product price support is due to end in 1999, though milk processors will have the backing of a CCC recourse loan programme after that date and the market for fluid milk will continue to be distorted by marketing orders.
15. Based on EU Commission (1997a) and EU Commission (1998).
16. Agenda 2000 forecasts economic growth at 2.5 per cent per annum for the existing 15 member states and at 4.0 per cent per annum for the applicant CEEC countries for the period 2000–2006.

Bibliography

Agra Europe (annual with updates), *CAP Monitor*, Tunbridge Wells: Agra Europe.

Agricultural Policy (1926), Cmd 2581, London: HMSO.

Ahearn, M., J. Johnson and R. Strickland (1985), 'The distribution of income and wealth of farm operators', *American Journal of Agricultural Economics*, **67**, 1010–16.

Anderson, K. (1987), 'On why agriculture declines with economic growth', *Agricultural Economics*, **1**, 195–207.

Anderson, K. and R. Tyers (1991), *Global Effects of Liberalising Trade in Farm Products*, Brighton: Harvester Wheatsheaf.

Anderson, T.L. and P.J. Hill (1976), 'The role of private property in the history of American agriculture 1776–1976', *American Journal of Agricultural Economics*, **58**, 937–45.

Antle, J.M. (1988), *World Agricultural Development and the Future of US Agriculture*, Washington, DC: American Enterprise Institute.

Ball, V.E. (1985), 'Output, input and productivity measurement in US agriculture 1948–79', *American Journal of Agricultural Economics*, **67**, 475–86.

Barnett, M.L. (1985), *British Food Policy During the First World War*, Boston: Mifflin.

Barry, P.J. and W.F. Lee (1983), 'Financial stress in agriculture: implications for agricultural lenders', *American Journal of Agricultural Economics*, **65**, 945–52.

Beard, N.F. (1986), *Against the Grain: The EC Cereals Policy*, Reading: Centre for Agricultural Strategy; London: Knight, Frank and Rutley.

Benedict, M.R. (1953), *Farm Policies of the US, 1790–1950*, New York: The Twentieth Century Fund.

Benedict, M.R. (1955), *Can We Solve the Farm Problem?*, New York: The Twentieth Century Fund.

Benedict, M.R. and O.C. Stine (1956), *The Agricultural Commodity Programs*. New York: The Twentieth Century Fund.

Bergsten, C.F. (1973), 'Future directions for US trade', *American Journal of Agricultural Economics*, **55**, 280–88.

Bieri, J., A. de Janvry and A. Schmitz (1972), 'Agricultural technology and the distribution of welfare gains', *American Journal of Agricultural Economics*, **54**, 801–8.

Binswanger, Hans P. and Vernon W. Ruttan (1978), *Induced Innovation: Technology, Institutions and Development*, Baltimore and London: Johns Hopkins University Press.

Blunden, J. and N. Curry (1988), *A Future for our Countryside*, Oxford: Blackwell.

Boehlje, M. and V. Eidman (1983), 'Financial stress in agriculture: implications for producers', *American Journal of Agricultural Economics*, **65**, 932–44.

Bonnen, J.T. (1973), 'Implications for agricultural policy', *American Journal of Agricultural Economics*, **55**, 297–9.

Brandow, G.E. (1955), 'A modified compensatory price program for agriculture', *Journal of Farm Economics*, **37**, 716–30.

Brandow, G.E. (1960), 'Supply control: ideas, implications and measures', *Journal of Farm Economics*, **42**, 1167–80.

Brandow, G.E. (1961), 'Reshaping farm policy in 1961', *Journal of Farm Economics*, **43**, 1019–31.

Brandow, G.E. (1962), 'In search of principles of farm policy', *Journal of Farm Economics*, **44**, 1145–55.

Brandow, G.E. (1973), 'The food price problem', *American Journal of Agricultural Economics*, **55**, 385–90.

Brandow, G.E. (1977), 'Policy for commercial agriculture, 1945–71', in L.R. Martin (ed.), *A Survey of Agricultural Economics Literature*, Vol. 1, Minneapolis: University of Minnesota Press, pp. 209–94.

Brown, J. (1987), *Agriculture in England: A Survey of Farming*, Manchester: Manchester University Press.

Browne, C.V. and P.M. Jackson (1982), *Public Sector Economics*, 2nd edn, Oxford: Oxford University Press.

Buckwell, A.E., D.R. Harvey, K.J. Thomson and K.A. Parton (1982), *The Costs of the Common Agricultural Policy*, London: Croom Helm.

Buckwell, A.E. (1997), 'If . . . agricultural economics in a brave liberal world', *European Review of Agricultural Economics*, **24**, 339–58.

Bullock, J.B. (1984), 'Future directions for agricultural policy', *American Journal of Agricultural Economics*, **66**, 234–9.

Cannan, E. (ed.) (1937), *Adam Smith: The Wealth of Nations*, New York: Random House.

Carson, R. (1963), *Silent Spring*, London: Hamish Hamilton.

CEC (1973), *Memorandum Agriculture 1973–1978*, COM(73) 1850.

CEC (1975), *Stocktaking of the Common Agricultural Policy*, COM(75) 100.

CEC (1980), *Reflections on the Common Agricultural Policy*, COM(80) 800.

CEC (1981a), *Report on the Mandate*, COM(81) 300.

CEC (1981b), *Guidelines for European Agriculture*, COM(81) 608.

CEC (1983), *Common Agricultural Policy: Proposals of the Commission*, COM(83) 500.

CEC (1985a), *Perspectives for the Common Agricultural Policy*, COM(85) 333.

CEC (1985b), *A Future for Community Agriculture*, COM(85) 750.

CEC (1986), *The Agricultural Situation in the Community, 1986 Report*, Brussels/Luxembourg.

CEC (1987a), *Review of Action Taken to Control the Agricultural Markets and Outlook for the CAP*, COM(87) 410.

CEC (1987b), *21st General Report on the Activities of the European Communities*, Brussels/Luxembourg.

CEC (1987c), *Proposals Concerning Income Aids in the Agricultural Sector and Incentives to Cease Farming*, COM(87) 166.

CEC (1988), *Setting-Aside of Farmland*, Proposal for a Council Regulation (EEC) amending Regulations (EEC) No. 797/85 and No. 1768/87 as regards setting-aside of agricultural land and extensification and concentration of production. COM(88) 1.

Cecil, R. (1979), *The Development of Agriculture in Germany and the UK, 1. German Agriculture 1870–1970*, Ashford: Centre for European Agricultural Studies, Wye College.

Clapham, J.H. (1968), *The Economic Development of France and Germany*, 4th edn, Cambridge: Cambridge University Press.

Clark, C. (1960), *The Conditions of Economic Progress*, London: Macmillan.

Clawson, M. (1958), 'Agricultural adjustment reconsidered: changes needed in the next 25 years', *Journal of Farm Economics*, **40**, 265–77.

Cochrane, W.W. (1958), *Farm Prices: Myth and Reality*, Minneapolis: University of Minnesota Press.

Cochrane, W.W. (1959), 'Some further reflections on supply control', *Journal of Farm Economics*, **41**, 697–717.

Cochrane, W.W. (1970), 'American farm policy in a tumultuous world', *American Journal of Agricultural Economics*, **52**, 645–55.

Cochrane, W.W. (1974), 'Food, agriculture and rural welfare: domestic policies in an uncertain world', *American Journal of Agricultural Economics*, **56**, 489–97.

Cochrane, W.W. (1979), *The Development of American Agriculture*, Minneapolis: University of Minnesota Press.

Cochrane, W.W. and M. Ryan (1976), *American Farm Policy, 1948–73*, Minneapolis: University of Minnesota Press.

Commission of the European Community (1968), *Memorandum on the Reform of Agriculture in the EEC, (Mansholt Plan)*, COM(68) 100

Commodity Credit Corporation (1964), *Summary of 30 Years of CCC Operations*, Washington, DC: USDA.

Conley, H. (1990), 'Federal budget implications for 1990 agricultural and food policy', in USDA, ERS, *Policy Research Notes* No. 28, Washington, DC.

Cooke, G.W. (ed.) (1981), *Agricultural Research, 1931–81*, London: Agricultural Research Council.

Corden, W.M. (1971), *The Theory of Protection*, London: Oxford University Press.

Corden, W.M. (1974), *Trade Policy and Economic Welfare*, Oxford: Oxford University Press,

Crowder B. and C. Davison (1989), *Soybeans: Background for 1990 Farm Legislation*, USDA, ERS, Staff Report, AGES 89–41, Washington, DC.

Currie, J.M. and A.J. Rayner (1979), 'The British Experience', in S. Hoos (ed.), *Agricultural Marketing Boards: An International Perspective*, Cambridge, Mass: Ballinger.

Dardis, R. and J. Dennison (1969), 'The welfare costs of alternative methods of protecting raw wool in the US', *American Journal of Agricultural Economics*, **51**, 303–19.

DeRosa, D.A. (1992), 'Concluding the Uruguay Round: the Dunkel Draft Agreement on Agriculture', *World Economy*, 755–60.

De Zeeuw, A. (1997), 'International agricultural trade negotiations under GATT/WTO: experiences, future challenges and possible outcomes', *European Review of Agricultural Economics*, **24** (3–4), 470–79.

Dicks, M.R. and K. Reichelderfer (1987), *Choices for Implementing the Conservation Reserve*, USDA-ERS, Information Bulletin No. 507, Washington, DC.

Dornbusch, R. and S. Fischer (1984), *Macroeconomics*, 3rd edn, McGraw-Hill.

Dovring, F. (1956), *Land and Labour in Europe 1900–1950*, The Hague: Martinus Nijhoff.

Downs, A. (1967), *Inside Bureaucracy*, Boston: Little.

Drabenstott, M. (1985), 'US agriculture: the international dimension', *Economic Review*, Kansas: Federal Reserve Bank of Kansas City

Drabenstott, M. (1986), 'The long road back for US agriculture', *Economic Review*, Kansas: Federal Reserve Bank of Kansas City.

Drabenstott, M. and A. Barkema (1987), 'US agriculture on the mend', *Economic Review*, Kansas: Federal Reserve Bank of Kansas City.

Duncan, M. (1985), Statement to Congress: Senate Agricultural Committee 1 May 1985, *Federal Reserve Bulletin*, July, The Federal Reserve.

EC Commission (1988), *Disharmonies in EC and US Agricultural Policy Measures*, Brussels.

EC Commission (1991a), *The Development and Future of the CAP: Reflections Paper of the Commission*, COM(91) 100 final, Brussels.

EC Commission (1991b), *The Development and Future of the Common Agricultural Policy. Follow-up to the Reflections Paper – Proposals of the Commission*, COM(91) 258 final, Brussels.

EC Commission (1992), *Agriculture in the GATT Negotiations and the Reform of the CAP*, SEC(92) 2267 final, Brussels.

EU Commission (1995), *Study on Alternative Strategies for the Development of Relations in the Field of Agriculture between the EU and the Associated Countries with a View to Future Accession of these Countries*, CSE(95) 607, Brussels.

EU Commission (1997a), 'Agenda 2000: For a stronger and wider Union', Document drawn up on the basis of COM(97) 2000 final, *Bulletin of the European Union*, Supplement 5/97, Brussels.

EU Commission (1997b), 'Towards a common agricultural and rural policy for Europe' (Buckwell Report), *European Economy, Reports and Studies*, No. 5.

EU Commission (1998), *Evaluation of the Financial Impact of the Commission Proposals Concerning the Reform of the CAP*, COM(98) 158 final, Brussels.

Erdman, L. and C. Ford Runge (1991), *American Agricultural Policy and the 1990 Farm Bill*, Minneapolis: University of Minnesota, Department of Agricultural and Applied Economics, Staff Paper P91–2.

Eurostat (1975), *The Basic Statistics of the Community*, 12th edn.

Eurostat (1985), *Basic Statistics of the Community*, 22nd edn.

Eurostat (1986), *Demographic Statistics*.

Evenson, R. (1967), 'The contribution of agricultural research to production', *Journal of Farm Economics*, **49**, 1415–25.

FAO (1973), *Agricultural Protection: Domestic Policy and International Trade*, (C/73/LIM/9), Rome.

FAO (1975), *Agricultural Protection and Stabilisation Policies: a Framework of Measurement in the Context of Agricultural Support*, (C/75/LIM/2), Rome.

Faulkner, H.U. (1960), *American Economic History*, 84th edn, New York: Harper and Row.

Feedstuffs, **62** (9), Minneapolis, Minnesota, 26 February 1990.

Fennell, R. (1987), *The Common Agricultural Policy of the European Community*, 2nd edn, Oxford: Blackwell Scientific.

Fischler, F. (1998), *A Vision of European Agricultural Policy*, International Green Week, Berlin, 15 January.

Flinchbaugh, Barry L. (1998), 'Commission on twenty-first century production agriculture begins work', *Choices*, First Quarter.

Floyd, J.E. (1965), 'The effects of price supports on the returns to land and labor in agriculture', *Journal of Political Economy*, **73**, 148–58.

Freeman, O. (1962), 'Agriculture at the Crossroads', *Journal of Farm Economics*, **44**, 1158–67.

French Ministry of Agriculture (1969), *Vedel Commission Report*, Paris.

Friedmann, K.J. (1974), 'Danish agricultural policy, 1870–1970: the flowering and decline of a liberal policy', *Food Research Institute Studies*, **XII**, 225–38.

Fuller, V. and E.L. Menzie (1964), 'Trade liberalisation versus import restriction', *Journal of Farm Economics*, **46**, 20–38.

Fulton, A.C. (1988), *The Agri-Monetary System of the European Community: Principles and Practice*, Belfast: Department of Agriculture.

Gardner, B.L. (1985), 'Policy options for grains', in G.C. Rausser and K.R. Farrell (eds), *Alternative Agricultural and Food Policies and the 1985 Farm Bill*, University of California at Berkeley: Giannini Foundation, pp. 81–100.

GATT (1986a), 'Ministerial declaration on the Uruguay Round', Geneva: *GATT Focus*, **41**.

GATT (1986b), *The Texts of the Tokyo Round Agreement*, Geneva.

GATT (1987), *European Communities Proposal for Multilateral Trade Negotiations on Agriculture*, MTN.GNG/NG5/W/20, Geneva.

GATT (1988a), *GATT Activities, 1987*, Geneva.

GATT (1988b), *Agricultural negotiations: short-term measures (other than immediate measures) in the framework of the measures proposed by the European Communities*, MTN.GNG/NG5/W/62, Geneva.

Gordon, H.S. (1980), *Welfare, Justice and Freedom*, New York: Columbia University Press.

Gordon-Ashworth, F. (1984), *International Commodity Control*, London: Croom Helm.

Griffiths, R.T. and A.S. Mildward (1986), *The European Agricultural Community 1948–1954*, Florence: European University Institute.

Grigg, D. (1989), *English Agriculture*, Oxford: Basil Blackwell.

Guyomard, H., L.P. Mahé, C. Tavera and T. Trocket (1991), 'Technical change and EC-US trade liberalisation', *Journal of Agricultural Economics*, **42**(2), 119–37.

Guyomard, H., L.P. Mahé and T. Roe (1992), *The EC and US Agricultural Conflict and the GATT Round: Petty Multilateralism?*, European Association of Agricultural Economists, 31st European Seminar: Frankfurt.

Harrington, D.H. and A.C. Manchester (1985), 'Profile of the U.S. farm sector,' in USDA, *Agricultural-Food Policy Review: Commodity Program Perspectives*, USDA, ERS, Agricultural Economic Report No. 530, pp. 25–53.

Harris, S., A. Swinbank and G. Wilkinson (1983), *The Food and Farm Policies of the European Community*, Chichester: John Wiley and Sons.

Harvey, D.R. (1984), 'Saleable quotas, compensation policy and reform of the CAP,' in K.J. Thomson and R.M. Warren (eds), *Price and Market Policies in European Agriculture*, University of Newcastle upon Tyne, Department of Agricultural Economics.

Harwood, J.L. and C.E. Young (1989), *Wheat: Background for 1990 Farm Legislation*, USDA, ERS, Staff Report AGES 89–56, Washington, DC.

Hathaway, D.E. (1960), 'Potentialities and limitations of comprehensive supply control: an independent viewpoint', *Journal of Farm Economics*, **42**, 1190–95.

Hathaway, D.E. (1963), *Government and Agriculture*, London: Collier-Macmillan.

Hathaway, Dale E. (1987), *Agriculture and the GATT: Rewriting the Rules*, Washington, DC: Institute for International Economics.

Hathaway, D.E. (1996), *The US Farm Bill: Reform or Illusion?*, mimeo, Washington, DC: National Center for Food and Agricultural Policy.

Hayami, Y. and V.W. Ruttan (1971), *Agricultural Development: An International Perspective*, 1st edn, Baltimore: Johns Hopkins University Press.

Hayami, Y. and V.W. Ruttan (1985), *Agricultural Development: An International Perspective*, revised edn, Baltimore: Johns Hopkins University Press.

Heady, E.O. (1966), *Agricultural Problems and Policies of Developed Countries*, Oslo: Johansen and Nielsen.

Heady, E.O. and L.G. Tweeten (1963), *Resource Demand and Structure of the Agricultural Industry*, Ames: Iowa State University Press.

Heidhues, T. (1979), 'The gains from trade: an applied political analysis', in J.S. Hillman and A. Schmitz (eds), *International Trade and Agricultural Policy: Theory and Practice*, Boulder: Westview Press.

Helmar, M.D., W.H. Meyers and D.D. Hayes (1993), *GATT and CAP Reform: Different, Similar or Redundant?*, Center for Agricultural and Rural Development (CARD), Ames: Iowa State University Press.

HGCA (1996), *GATT Provisions for the EU Cereal Market*, Market Information Supplement, 21 November 1996, vol. 31, issue 22(4), Home Grown Cereals Authority: London

Hicks, J.R. (1969), *A Theory of Economic History*, London: Oxford University Press.

Hill, B.E. (1984), *The Common Agricultural Policy: Past, Present and Future*, London: Methuen.

Hillman, J. (1967), 'Food and agricultural policies for a changing agriculture', *Journal of Farm Economics*, **49**, 1057–70.

Hillman, J.S. (1978), *Nontariff Agricultural Trade Barriers*, Lincoln: University of Nebraska Press.

Hine, R.C., K.A. Ingersent and A.J. Rayner (1989a), 'Agriculture in the Uruguay Round', *Journal of Agricultural Economics*, **50**, 385–96.

Hine, R.C., K.A. Ingersent and A.J. Rayner (1989b), *The Agricultural Negotiations in the Uruguay Round*, Nottingham: CREDIT Research Paper, No. 89/3, University of Nottingham.

Hoffman, L.A., S. Schwartz and G.V. Chomo (1995), *Wheat: Background for the 1995 Farm Legislation*, USDA, ERS, Washington, DC.

Houck, J.P. (1974), 'Some economic aspects of agricultural regulation and stabilisation', *American Journal of Agricultural Economics*, **56**, 1113–24.

House of Lords, Select Committee on Agriculture (1968–69), *Report*, HL 137, pp. 443–5.

House of Lords, Select Committee on the European Communities (1981), *The Common Agricultural Policy – Directions of Future Development and Proposals for Process Related Measures*, vol. 2, HL 156, London: HMSO.

Huff, H. Bruce and C. Moreddu (1990), 'The ministerial trade mandate model', *OECD Economic Studies*, **13/Winter**, 1989–90.

Huizinger, W. and D. Strijker (1986), *Two Lectures on the Historical Development of Dutch Agriculture, 1600–1985*, The Hague: Landbouw-Econonisch Institut.

Hushak, L.J. (1971), 'A welfare analysis of the voluntary corn diversion program', *American Journal of Agricultural Economics*, **53**, 173–81.

Infranger, C.L., W.C. Bailey and D. Dyer (1983), 'Agricultural policy in austerity: the making of the 1981 Farm Bill', *American Journal of Agricultural Economics*, **65**, 1–9.

Ingersent, K.A. and A.J. Rayner (1993), *Rationale of 1992 CAP Reform*,

Nottingham: University of Nottingham, CREDIT Research Paper No. 93/12

Ingersent, K.A., A.J. Rayner and R.C. Hine (eds) (1998), *The Reform of the Common Agricultural Policy*, Basingstoke: Macmillan.

International Agricultural Trade Research Consortium (IATRC) (1988), *Bringing Agriculture into the GATT: (2) Designing Acceptable Agricultural Policies*, Ithaca: Cornell University Press.

International Agricultural Trade Research Consortium (IATRC) (1994), *The Uruguay Round Agreement on Agriculture: An Evaluation*, Stanford: Stanford University Commissioned Paper No. 9.

IWC (annual), *World Grain Statistics*, London International Wheat Council.

Jesness, O.B. (1958), 'Agricultural adjustment in the past 25 years', *Journal of Farm Economics*, **xi**(2), 255–64.

Johnson, D. Gale (1947), *Forward Prices for Agriculture*, Chicago: University of Chicago Press.

Johnson, D. Gale (1958), 'Labour mobility and agricultural adjustment', Ch. 12 in E.O. Heady, H.G. Diesslin, H.R. Jensen and G.L. Johnson (eds), *Agricultural Adjustment Problems in a Growing Economy*, Ames: Iowa State University Press.

Johnson, D. Gale (1963), 'Efficiency and welfare implications of US agricultural policy', *Journal of Farm Economics*, **45**, 331–42.

Johnson, D. Gale (1970), 'Current economic problems', *American Journal of Agricultural Economics*, **52**, 295–7.

Johnson, D. Gale (1973a), 'Government and agricultural adjustment', *American Journal of Agricultural Economics*, **55**, 860–67.

Johnson, D. Gale (1973b), *World Agriculture in Disarray*, London: Macmillan.

Johnson, D. Gale (1977), 'Postwar policies relating to trade in agricultural Products', in L.R. Martin (ed.), *A Survey of Agricultural Economics Literature*, Vol. 1, Minneapolis: University of Minnesota Press, pp. 295–328.

Johnson, D. Gale (1978), 'National agricultural policies and market relations', *American Journal of Agricultural Economics*, **60**, 789–92.

Johnson, D. Gale (1981), 'Agricultural policy alternatives for the 1980s', in D. Gale Johnson (ed.), *Food and Agricultural Policies for the 1980s*, Washington, DC: American Enterprise Institute.

Johnson, D. Gale (1985a), 'US agriculture and policy', in D. Gale Johnson, K. Hemmi and P. Lardinois (eds), *Agricultural Policy and Trade*, New York and London: The Trilateral Commission, New York University Press.

Johnson, D. Gale (1985b), 'The performance of past policies: a critique', in G.C. Rausser and K.R. Farrell (eds), *Alternative Agricultural and Food Policies and the 1985 Farm Bill*, University of California.

Johnson, D. Gale (1991), *World Agriculture in Disarray*, 2nd edn, London: Macmillan.

Johnson, D. Gale, K. Hemmi and P. Lardinois (eds) (1985), *Agricultural Policy and Trade*, New York and London: The Trilateral Commission, New York University Press.

Johnson, G.L. (1960) 'The labor utilisation problem in European and American agriculture', *Journal of Agricultural Economics*, **XIV**(1), 73–81.

Johnson, J. and N. Clayton (1983), 'Organisation and well-being of the farming industry: reflections on the Agriculture and Food Act of 1981', *American Journal of Agricultural Economics*, **64**, 947–56.

Johnson, P.R. (1965), 'The social cost of the tobacco program', *Journal of Farm Economics*, **47**, 242–55.

Josling, T.E. (1969), 'A formal approach to agricultural policy', *Journal of Agricultural Economics*, **XX**(2), 175–95.

Josling, T.E. (1970), *Agriculture and Britain's Trade Policy Dilemma*, London: Trade Policy Research Centre Essay No. 2.

Josling, T.E. (1973), 'The reform of the CAP', in D. Evans (ed.), *Britain in the EEC*, London: Gollancz.

Josling, Tim (1993), 'Agricultural trade issues in transatlantic trade relations', *World Economy*, **16**(5), 553–73.

Josling, T.E. and D. Hamway (1972), 'Distribution of costs and benefits of farm policy', in T.E. Josling et al. (eds), *Burdens and Benefits of Farm Support Policies*, London: Trade Policy Research Centre.

Josling, T.E. and A.C. Mariani (1993), 'The distributional and efficiency implications of the MacSharry proposals for reform of the CAP', *Journal of Regional Policy*, **13**, 27–49.

Josling, T.E. and S. Tangermann (1992), *MacSharry or Dunkel: Which Plan Reforms the CAP?* IATRC Working Paper No. 92–10, Food Research Institute, Stanford University.

Josling, T.E., S. Tangermann and T.K. Warley (1996), *Agriculture in the GATT*, Basingstoke: Macmillan.

Just, R.E. and J.A. Miranowski (1988), 'US land prices: trends and determinants', Paper prepared for the Plenary Session VII on *Land Markets, Agricultural Development and Agricultural Adjustment*, Buenos Aires: XXth International Conference of Agricultural Economists.

Kay, A. (1998), *The Reform of the Common Agricultural Policy*, Wallingford: CABI Publishing.

Kendrick, J.W. (1965), 'The gains and losses from technological change', *Journal of Farm Economics*, **46**, 1065–72.

Kindleberger, C.P. (1964), *Economic Growth in France and Britain*, Boston: Harvard University Press.

Kirk, J.H. (1958) 'Some objectives of agricultural support policy', *Journal of Agricultural Economics*, **XII**(2), 134–51.

Kirk, J.H. (1979), *The Development of Agriculture in Germany and the UK: 2. UK Agricultural Policy 1870–1970*, Wye: Centre for European Agricultural Studies.

Kock, K. (1969), *International Trade Policy and the GATT 1947–1960*, Stockholm: Almquist and Wiksell.

Koester, U. and S. Tangermann (1977), 'Supplementing farm price policy by direct income payments, *European Review of Agricultural Economics*, **4**(1), 7–31.

Koliris, Panos D. (1984), 'Global Mediterranean policy implications in view of the new EEC enlargement', *Journal of Agricultural Economics*, **XXXV**(3)

Kuznets, S. (1966) *Modern Economic Growth: Rate, Structure, Spread*, New Haven: Yale University Press.

Kuznets, S. (1971), *Economic Growth of Nations*, Cambridge, Mass.: Harvard University Press.

Kuznets, S. (1980), 'Driving forces of economic growth: what can we learn from history', *Weltwirtschaftlichen Archiv*, 409–32.

Lacy, M.G. (1923), 'Food control during forty-six centuries', *The Scientific Monthly*, **16**, 623–37.

Langham, M.R. and W.F. Edwards (1969), 'Externalities in pesticide use', *American Journal of Agricultural Economics*, **51**, 1195–201.

Langley, J.A. et al. (1985), 'Commodity price and income support policies in perspective', in USDA, *Agricultural–Food Policy Review: Commodity Program Perspectives*, USDA–ERS Agricultural Economics Report No. 530.

Lardinois, P. (1985), 'The common agricultural policy of the EC', in D. Gale Johnson, K. Hemmi and P. Lardinois (eds), *Agricultural Policy and Trade*, New York and London: The Trilateral Commission, New York University Press, pp. 99–111.

Learn, E.W. (1963), 'The impact of European integration on American agriculture', *Journal of Farm Economics*, **45**, 952–60.

Lee, J.E. (1981), 'Food and agricultural policy: a suggested approach', *Agricultural Food Policy Review: Perspectives for the 1980s*, USDA AFPR-4.

Legg, W. (1997), *Have OECD Agricultural Policy Reforms Benefited the Environment*? Paper delivered at the Agricultural Economics Society Annual Conference, Edinburgh, March 1997.

Lesher, W.G. (1985), 'Future agricultural policy', Ch. 3 in G.R. Rausser and K.R. Farrell (eds), *Alternative Agricultural and Food Policies and the 1985 Farm Bill*, University of California, Giannini Foundation.

Liepmann, H. (1938), *Tariff Levels*, London: Allen & Unwin.

Lin, W., P. Riley and S. Evans (1995), *Feed Grains: Background of the 1995 Legislation*, USDA, ERS, Washington, DC.

Mackie, A.B. (1966), 'Discussion – trade policies and agriculture', *Journal of Farm Economics*, **48**, 350–53.

MAFF (1983), *Household Food Consumption and Expenditure: 1981*, London: HMSO.

MAFF (1994), *The Implications for CAP Reform and the GATT Uruguay Round Agreement for Agriculture*, London: Ministry of Agriculture, Fisheries and Food.

Mansholt, S. (1979), *An Interview on the CAP*, Stowmarket: The Soil Association.

Marsh, John (1977), 'European agricultural policy: a Federalist solution', *New Europe*, **5**.

Marsh, John and Stefan Tangermann (1996), *Preparing Europe's Rural Economy for the 21st Century*, Land Use and Food Policy Group of the European Parliament (LUFPIG).

McClatchy, D. and T.K. Warley (1992), 'Agricultural and trade policy reform: implications for agricultural trade', in G.H. Peters, B.F. Stanton and G.J. Tyler (eds), *Sustainable Agricultural Development: the Role of International Cooperation*, Aldershot: Dartmouth Publishing.

McCrone, G. (1962), *The Economics of Subsidising Agriculture*, London: Allen & Unwin.

Mehren, G.L. (1963), 'Commercial export markets for farm products', *Journal of Farm Economics*, **45**, 952–60.

Melichar, E. (1984), *Farm Wealth: Origins, Impacts and Implications of Public Policy*, Ithaca: Cornell University Press.

Menzie, E.L. (1963), 'Special US restrictions on imports of agricultural products', *Journal of Farm Economics*, **45**, 1002–6.

Mercier, S. (1989), *Corn: Background for 1990 Farm Legislation*, USDA, ERs, Staff Report No 89–47, Washington, DC.

Meyer, W.H. and M.E. Ryan (1981), 'The farmer owned reserve: how is the experiment working?', *American Journal of Agricultural Economics*, **63**, 119–28.

Ministry of Agriculture and Fisheries (1946), *National Farm Survey of England and Wales*, London: HMSO.

Moore, L. and G.H. Peters (1965), 'Agriculture's balance of payments contribution', *Westminster Bank Review*, August.

Moser, P. (1990), *The Political Economy of the GATT*, Band 22, Schweizerisches Institut fur Aubenwirtschafts, Verlag Ruegger.

Moyer, H.W. and T.E. Josling (1990), *Agricultural Policy Reform: Politics and Process in the EC and the USA*, Hemel Hempstead: Harvester Wheatsheaf.

Nash, E.F. (1955), 'The competitive position of British agriculture', *Journal of Agricultural Economics*, **XI**(3), 222–41.

Nash, E.F. (1956), 'Some reflections on agricultural policy', *Lloyds Bank Review*, July.

Nash, E.F. and E.A. Attwood (1961), *The Agricultural Policies of Britain and Denmark: A Study in Reciprocal Trade*, London: Land Books.

National Center for Food and Agricultural Policy (1995), *Report of the Working Group on International Trade and Marketing, 1995 Farm Bill*, Washington, DC: Working Group Paper Series NCFAP-95WG-03.

Nello, S.S. (1984), 'An Application of public choice theory to the question of CAP reform', *European Review of Agricultural Economics*, **11**, 261–83.

Nello, S.S. (1985), 'An application of public choice theory to the question of CAP reform', in J. Pelkmans (ed.), *Can the CAP be Reformed?*, Maastricht: European Institute of Public Administration.

Newbery, D.M.G. and J.E. Stiglitz (1981), *The Theory of Commodity Price Stabilisation*, Oxford: Clarendon Press.

Newman, Mark, Tom Fulton and Lewrene Glaser (1987), *A Comparison of Agriculture in the United States and the European Community*, Washington DC: USDA–ERS Foreign Agricultural Economic report No. 233.

Nourse, E.G. (1927), 'The outlook for agriculture', *Journal of Farm Economics* **9**, 21–32.

O'Connor, H.E., A.J. Rayner, K.A. Ingersent and R.C. Hine (1991), *The Agricultural Negotiations in the Uruguay Round: Developments since the Geneva Accord*, Nottingham: University of Nottingham, CREDIT Research Paper No. 91/8.

OECD (1987), *National Policies and Agricultural Trade*, Paris: OECD.

OECD (1989), *Agricultural Policies, Markets and Trade: Monitoring and Outlook*, Paris, OECD.

OECD (1990a), *Agricultural Policies, Markets and Trade: Monitoring and Outlook*, Paris: OECD.

OECD (1990b), 'The ministerial trade mandate model', *OECD Economic Studies*, **13**, 45–67.

OECD (1995), *The Uruguay Round: A Preliminary Evaluation of the Impacts of the Agreement on Agricultural in the OECD Countries*, Paris: OECD.

Orden, D., R. Paarlberg and T. Roe (1996), 'Can farm policy be reformed?' and 'A farm bill for booming commodity markets', *Choices*, First and Second Quarters.

Organisation of European Economic Cooperation (1956), *Agricultural Policies in Europe and North America*, Paris: OECD.

Orwin, C.S. (1949), *A History of English Farming*, London: Nelson.

Paarlberg, D. (1962), 'Discussion: contributions of the new frontier to agricultural reform in the US', *Journal of Farm Economics*, **44**, 1179–87.

Paarlberg, D. (1980), *Farm and Food Policy: Issues of the 1980s*, Lincoln: University of Nebraska Press.

Paarlberg, D. (1984), 'Tarnished gold: US farm commodity programs after 50 years', *Food Policy*, **19**, 6–10.

Paarlberg, Philip L. et al. (1985), 'The US competitive position in world commodity trade', in *Agricultural–Food Policy Review: Commodity Program Perspectives*, Washington, DC: USDA–ERS Agricultural Economic Report No. 530, pp. 93–121.

Penn, J.B. (1981), 'The changing farm sector and future public policy: an economic perspective', in USDA, *Agricultural–Food Policy Review: Perspectives for the 1980s*, AFPR-4, Washington, DC.

Penn, J.B. (1984), 'Agricultural structural issues and policy alternatives for the late 1980s', *American Journal of Agricultural Economics*, **66**, 572–6.

Penn, J.B. (1996), 'End of the agricultural era', *Choices*, First Quarter.

Peterson, W.L. and J.C. Fitzharris (1977), 'Organisation and productivity of the Federal–State research system in the US', Ch. 2 in T. Arndt et al. (eds), *Resource Allocation and Productivity in National and International Agricultural Research*, Minneapolis: University of Minnesota Press.

Petit, M. (1985), *Determinants of Agricultural Policies in the United States and the European Community*, Washington, DC: Research Institute.

Phillips, T. and C. Ritson (1969), 'Reciprocity in international trade', *Journal of Agricultural Economics*, **XX**(3), 303–16.

Pollard, S. (1981), *Integration of the European Economy since 1915*, London: Allen & Unwin.

Posner, R.A. (1974), 'Theories of economic regulation', *Bell Journal of Economics and Motivational Science*, **5**,

Rausser, G.C. (1982), 'Political economic markets: PERTS and PESTS food and agriculture', *American Journal of Agricultural Economics*, **64**, 821–33.

Rausser, Gordon C. (1985), 'Macroeconomics and US agricultural policy', in Bruce L Gardner (ed.), *US Agricultural Policy: The 1985 Farm Legislation*, Washington, DC: American Enterprise Institute, pp. 205–52.

Ray, D. E., J. W. Richardson and E. Li (1982), 'The 1981 Agriculture and Food Act: implications for farm prices, incomes and government outlays to farmers', *American Journal of Agricultural Economics*, **64**, 957–69.

Rayner, A.J. (1982), *The Common Agricultural Policy: Budget Costs, Farm Income Support and Technical Change*, Nottingham: Department of Economics, Discussion Paper No. 32, University of Nottingham.

Rayner, A.J., J. Whittaker and K.A. Ingersent (1986), 'Productivity growth in agriculture revisited: a measurement framework and some empirical results', *Journal of Agricultural Economics*, **XXXVII**(2), 127–50.

Rayner, A.J. and C.T. Ennew (1987), 'Agricultural co-operation in the UK: a historical review', *Agricultural Administration and Extension*, **27**, 93–108.

Rayner, A.J., K.A. Ingersent and R.C. Hine (1990), 'Agriculture in the Uruguay Round: prospects for longer term trade reform', *Oxford Agrarian Studies*, **18**, 3–21.

Rayner, A.J., K.A. Ingersent, R.C. Hine and R.W. Ackrill (1995), 'Does the CAP fit the GATT?: Cereals and the Uruguay Round', *Oxford Agrarian Studies*, **23**, 117–32.

Reynolds, C.G. (1986), *Economic Growth in the Third World: An Introduction*, New Haven and London: Yale University Press.

Rickard, S. (1986), *Nitrogen Limitation: A Way Forward?*, unpublished paper delivered at the One-Day Agricultural Economics Society Conference, Reading University, 1 October 1986.

Robertson, R.M. (1973), *History of the American Economy*, 3rd edn, New York: Harcourt Brace and Jovanavich

Robinson, A.D. (1961), *Dutch Organised Agriculture in International Politics*, The Hague: Martinus Nijhoff.

Robinson, E.A.G. (1958), 'The cost of agricultural import saving', *Three Banks Review*, December

Roningen, Vernon O. and P.M. Dixit (1989), *Economic Implications of Agricultural Policy Reforms in Industrial Market Economies*, USDA, ERS, Staff Report No. AGES 89–36.

Runge, C.F. and H. von Witzke (1987), 'Institutional change in the

Common Agricultural Policy of the European Community', *American Journal of Agricultural Economics*, **69**, 213–22.

Ruttan, V.W. (1971), 'Technology and the environment', *American Journal of Agricultural Economics*, **53**, 707–17.

Ruttan, V.W. (1982), *Agricultural Research Policy*, Minneapolis: University of Minnesota Press.

Ruttan V.W. (1984), 'Social science knowledge and institutional change', *American Journal of Agricultural Economics*, **66**, 549–59.

Ruttan V.W. et al. (1978), 'Factor productivity and growth: a historical interpretation', Ch. 3 in H.P. Binswanger et al. (eds), *Induced Innovation: Technology, Institutions and Development*, Baltimore: Johns Hopkins Press.

Saloutos, T. (1982), *The American Farmer and the New Deal*, Amherst: Iowa State University Press.

Sampson, G.P. and A.J. Yeats (1977), 'An evaluation of the common agricultural policy as a barrier facing agricultural exports to the European Economic Community, *American Journal of Agricultural Economics*, **59**, 99–106.

Sanderson, F. (1994), *The GATT Agreement on Agriculture*, Washington, DC: National Center for Food and Agricultural Policy.

Sargent, M. (1982), *Agricultural Co-operation*, Aldershot: Gower.

Schmid, A.A. (1972), 'Analytical institutional economics', *American Journal of Agricultural Economics*, **54**, 893–900.

Schmidt, S.C., H.D. Guither and A.B. Mackie (1978), 'Quantitative dimensions of agricultural trade', Ch. 5 in *Speaking of Trade: Its Effect on Agriculture*, Minneapolis, University of Minnesota, Agricultural Extension Service Special Report No. 72.

Schnittker, J.A. (1963), 'Principles of economic policy-discussion', *Journal of Farm Economics*, **45**, 351–4.

Schnittker, J.A. (1973), 'Prospects for freer agricultural trade', *American Journal of Agricultural Economics*, **55**, 289–93.

Schnittker, J.A. (1981), 'A framework for food and agricultural policy for the 1980s', *American Journal of Agricultural Economics*, **63**, 324–7.

Schuh, G.E. (1974), 'The exchange rate and US agriculture', *American Journal of Agricultural Economics*, **56**, 1–13.

Schuh, G.E. (1981), 'US agriculture in an interdependent world economy: policy alternatives for the 1980s', in D. Gale Johnson (ed.), *Food and Agricultural Policy for the 1980s*, Washington, DC: American Enterprise Institute.

Schultz, T.W. (1945), *Agriculture in an Unstable Economy*, New York: McGraw-Hill.

Schultz, T.W. (1961), 'A policy to redistribute losses from economic progress', *Journal of Farm Economics*, **63**, 554–65.

Sharpe, G. and C.W. Capstick (1966), 'The place of agriculture in the national economy', *Journal of Agricultural Economics*, **XVII**(1), 2–21.

Shepherd, G.S. (1963), *Agricultural Price Analysis*, 5th edn, Ames: Iowa University Press.

Skrubbeltrang, F. (1953), *Agricultural Development and Rural Reform in Denmark*, Rome: Food and Agriculture Organisation of the United Nations.

Smith, M. (1987), *Increased Role for US Farm Export Programs*, Washington DC: USDA–ERS, Agricultural Information Bulletin No. 515.

Spitze, R.G.F. (1987), 'The evolution and implications of the US Food Security Act of 1985', *Agricultural Economics*, **1**, 175–90.

Spitze, R.G.F. (1978), 'Food and Agricultural Act of 1977', *American Journal of Agricultural Economics*, **60**, 225–35.

Statistical Office of the European Community (1968), *Selected Figures: the Common Market Ten Years On*, Luxembourg.

Stern, N. (1989), 'The economics of development: a survey', *Economic Journal*, **99**, 597–685.

Stigler, G.J. (1975), *The Citizen and the State*, University of Chicago Press.

Stiglitz, J.E. (1986), *Economics of the Public Sector*, London and New York: W.W. Norton & Co.

Stucker, B.C. and K.J. Collins (1986), *The Food Security Act of 1985: Major Provisions Affecting Commodities*, Washington, DC: USDA–ERS Agricultural Information Bulletin No. 497.

Swann, D. (1988), *The Economics of the Common Market*, 6th edn, Harmondsworth: Penguin.

Tangermann, S. (1982), *Agricultural and Food Policy in Germany*, University of Gottingen, Institute of Agricultural Economics.

Tangermann, S. (1985), 'Special features and ongoing reforms of the CAP', in The Curry Foundation, *Confrontation or Negotiation: United States Policy and European Agriculture*, Millwood, New York: Associated Faculty Press.

Tangermann, S. (1994), *An Assessment of the Uruguay Round Agreement on Agriculture*, Paper prepared for the Directorate for Food, Agriculture and Fisheries of the Trade Directorate of the OECD, Stanford University, June 1994.

Tangermann, S. (1996), 'Implementation of the Uruguay Round agreement on agriculture: issues and prospects', *Journal of Agricultural Economics*, **47**, 315–37.

Tangermann, S. (1997), *An Assessment of the Agenda 2000 Proposals for the Future of the Common Agricultural Policy*, Paper prepared for the Land Use and Food Policy Intergroup of the European Parliament (LUFPIG).

Tangermann, S. (1998), 'An ex-post review of the 1992 MacSharry Reform', Chapter 2 in K.A. Ingersent, R.C. Hine and A.J. Rayner (eds), *The Reform of the Common Agricultural Policy*, Basingstoke: Macmillan Press Ltd.

Taylor, G.C. (1969), 'Economic issues in controlling agricultural pollution', *American Journal of Agricultural Economics*, **51**, 1182–8.

Thirtle, C. and P. Bottomley (1992), 'Total factor productivity in UK agriculture, 1967–90', *Journal of Agricultural Economics*, **43**, 381–400.

Thompson, F.M.L. (1968), 'The second Agricultural Revolution, 1815–1880', *Economic History Review*, **XXI**, 69–70.

Thomson, K. (1998), 'The CAP and the WTO after the Uruguay Round Agriculture Agreement', Chapter 9 in K.A. Ingersent, A.J. Rayner and R.C. Hine (eds), *The Reform of the Common Agricultural Policy*, Basingstoke: Macmillan.

Tosterad, R.J. (1983), 'Commodity programs: discussion', *American Journal of Agricultural Economics*, **65**, 932–3.

Tracy, M. (1982), *Agriculture in Western Europe: Challenge and Response, 1880–1980*, London: Granada Publishing.

Tracy, M. (1985), 'The decision-making practice of the EC with reference to the CAP', in J. Pelkmans (ed.), *Can the CAP be Reformed?*, Maastricht: European Institute of Public Administration.

Tracy, M. (1989), *Government and Agriculture in Western Europe, 1880–1988*, Harvester Wheatsheaf.

Tracy, M. (1997), *Agricultural Policy in the EU and other Market Economies*, 2nd edn, Belgium: Agricultural Policy Studies.

Tweeten, L.G. and F.H. Tyner (1965), 'Toward an optimum rate of technological change', *Journal of Farm Economics*, **47**, 1075–83.

Tweeten, L.G. (1970), *Foundations of Farm Policy*, Lincoln: University of Nebraska Press.

Tweeten, Luther (1985), 'Farm financial stress, structure of agriculture and public policy', in Bruce L. Gardner (ed.), *US Agricultural Policy: The 1985 Farm Legislation*, Washington, DC: American Enterprise Institute, pp. 83–112.

Tweeten, L.G. and J.S. Plaxico (1964), 'Long run outlook for agricultural adjustments based on national growth', *Journal of Farm Economics*, **46**, 39–55.

Tweeten, L. and J. Plaxico (1974) 'US policies for food and agriculture in an unstable world', *American Journal of Agricultural Economics*, **56**, 364–71.

Tyers, R. (1994), 'The Cairns Group perspective', in K.A. Ingersent, A.J. Rayner and R.C. Hine (eds), *Agriculture in the Uruguay Round*, London: Macmillan.

Tyers, R. and K. Anderson (1988), 'Liberalising OECD agricultural policies in the Uruguay Round: effects on trade and welfare', *Journal of Agricultural Economics*, **39**, 197–216.

US Senate Press Release (1990), *Conference Committee Approves Five-Year Farm Bill*, Washington, DC, 16 October.

USDA (1984), *History of Price-Support and Agricultural Adjustment Programs, 1933–84*, ERS, AIB No. 485, Washington, DC.

USDA (1990), *1990 Farm Bill Proposal*, Washington, DC.

USDA (1994), *Effects of the Uruguay Round Agreement on US Agricultural Commodities*, USDA, ERS, Washington, DC.

USDA (1995), *1995 Farm Bill: Guidance of the Administration*, Washington, DC.

USDA, *Agricultural Outlook*, December 1990 and various later issues, Washington, DC: USDA, ERS.

van der Meer, C.L.J. and S. Yamada (1986), *Agricultural Development in the Netherlands and Japan*, Groningen: Research Memo. No. 182, Institute of Economic Research, University of Groningen,

van Zanden, J.L. (1988), *The Growth of Production and Productivity in European Agriculture 1870–1914*, Amsterdam: Vrije University, Faculty of Economics and Econometrics.

Wade, W.W. (1973), *Institutional Determinants of Technical Change and Agricultural Productivity Growth Denmark, France and GB, 1870–1965*, unpublished PhD Thesis, University of Minnesota.

Wagner, A. (1902), *AgrarundIndustriestaat*, Jena: Auflage.

Wallace, T.D. (1962), 'Measures of social costs of agricultural programs', *Journal of Farm Economics*, **44**, 581–94.

Warley, T.K. (1976), 'Western trade in agricultural products', in A. Shonfield (ed.), *International Relations in the Western World 1959–1971*, Vol. 1, Royal Institute of International Affairs, OUP.

Warley, T.K. (1988), 'Issues facing agriculture in the GATT negotiations', *Canadian Journal of Agricultural Economics*, **35**, 515–34.

Warley, T.K. (1990), 'Agriculture in the GATT: past and future', in A. Maunder and A. Valdes (eds), *Agriculture and Government in an Interdependent World*, Proceedings of the 20th Conference of Agricultural Economists, Aldershot.

Weinschenck, G. (1987), 'The Economic or the ecological way? Basic alternatives for the EC's agricultural policy', *European Review of Agricultural Economics*, **14**, 49–60.

West, G.M. (1972), 'World trade prospects for US agriculture', *American Journal of Agricultural Economics*, **54**, 827–33.

Whetham, E.H. (1978), *The Agrarian History of England and Wales, Vol. VIII, 1914–39*, Cambridge: Cambridge University Press.

Wilcox, W.W. and W.W. Cochrane (1960), *Economics of American Agriculture*, 2nd edn, Englewood Cliffs: Prentice Hall.

Williams, H.T. (ed.) (1960), *Principles for British Agricultural Policy*, OUP (for the Nuffield Foundation).

Wipf, L.J. (1970), 'Tariffs, non-tariff distortions and effective protection in agriculture', *American Journal of Agricultural Economics*, **53**, 423–30.

Wright, G. (1964), *Rural Revolution in France*, Stanford and Oxford: Stanford Press and Oxford University Press.

Yates, P.L. (1959), *Forty Years of Agricultural Trade*, London: George Allen and Unwin.

Author index

Subject index